D1232128

Lamentations of Youth

Lamentations of Youth

THE DIARIES OF GERSHOM SCHOLEM, 1913–1919

Edited and translated by Anthony David Skinner

THE BELKNAP PRESS OF
HARVARD UNIVERSITY PRESS

Cambridge, Massachusetts, and London, England / 2007

This work is a translation of selections from *Gershom Scholem Tagebücher, 1913–1923,*
© Jüdischer Verlag im Suhrkamp Verlag, Frankfurt am Main, 1995 and 2000.

Library of Congress Cataloging-in-Publication Data

Scholem, Gershom Gerhard, 1897–1982.
[Diaries. English. Selections]
Lamentations of youth : the diaries of Gershom Scholem,
1913–1919 / edited and translated by Anthony David Skinner.
p.   cm.
This work is a translation of selections from *Gershom Scholem Tagebucher,*
1913–1923 (Frankfurt am Main : Judischer Verlag im Suhrkamp Verlag, 1995–2000).
Includes bibliographical references and index.
ISBN-13: 978-0-674-02669-8 (alk. paper)
ISBN-10: 0-674-02669-1 (alk. paper)
1. Scholem, Gershom Gerhard, 1897–1982—Diaries.
2. Jewish scholars—Germany—Diaries.   3. Jewish scholars—Israel—Diaries.
4. Jews—Civilization.   5. Judaism.   I. David, Anthony, 1962–   II. Title.
BM755.S295A3 2007
296.092—dc22
[B]   2007019828

ACKNOWLEDGMENTS

Of the many people who had an important hand in making this volume possible, I first want to mention Lindsay Waters, executive editor for the humanities at Harvard University Press. In 1989 Lindsay visited Gershom Scholem's widow, Fanya. From that point on, Lindsay has been committed to bringing out an English edition of Scholem's letters, and now of his diaries. I also want to thank my agent and close friend, Dorothy Harman. Dorothy was with Lindsay the day he visited Fanya Scholem, and she has also been dedicated to seeing Scholem's letters and diaries published in English. As always, Paul Mendes-Flohr at the University of Chicago has been an indispensable source of advice, help, and friendship. I have also spent many valuable hours discussing—and attempting to unravel—the puzzles within Scholem's diaries with Steven Ascheim of the Hebrew University.

I am immensely grateful to Amanda Heller, whose superb eye and sense for language helped craft my draft of the diaries into this book. I finally thank Rachel Lev for all her support and love.

Anthony David Skinner

CONTENTS

A man never discloses his own character so clearly as when he describes another's.

—Jean Paul Richter

INTRODUCTION

GERSHOM SCHOLEM established his reputation as one of the world's foremost historians of religion directly after the end of the Second World War. From his apartment on a quiet street in Jerusalem, he had spent the war years publishing the results of twenty years of research into Jewish mysticism. His wartime essays ranged from a piece on the Jewish heretic Jacob Frank, a follower of the seventeenth-century false messiah, Sabbatai Sevi, to an essay he published in a Hebrew newspaper, "Sabbatai Sevi and Nathan of Gaza." His most significant accomplishment of all, and the first to be translated into English, was the book *Major Trends in Jewish Mysticism,* which he completed in 1941. And as the critics were lavishing their praise on *Major Trends,* he was busy working on what was to be his magnum opus, *Sabbatai Sevi: The Mystical Messiah.*

With the war over, and the European Jewry Scholem had spent his life writing about destroyed, he emerged as a thinker with near canonical authority, joining the ranks of other thinkers such as Reinhold Niebuhr, Martin Buber, Paul Tillich, Mircea Eliade, and Joseph Campbell in determining postwar religious discourse. In 1947 Gustav Jung extended an invitation to Scholem to participate in his ERANOS conference. He would soon be a yearly guest at the gathering, and it was there that over the years Scholem presented many of the key philosophical ideas that underlay his work on the history of Jewish mysticism.

Scholem's growing reputation was well deserved. When he began his formal studies into the Kabbalah in Munich in 1920, Jewish mysticism was dismissed by many scholars, Jewish and non-Jewish alike, as little better than voodoo. Over the ensuing years, Scholem applied what his friend Walter Benjamin called a "detective and inquisitional" approach to this ignored body of writings.[1] The indefatigable scholar, with his ruthless discipline and exacting standards, became one of the greatest philologists and historians of religion of the twentieth century, creating an entire discipline, its terminology and direction, while unlocking the meaning of forgotten books. He turned over every piece of evidence, sniffed out every clue. The bulk of his labors resembled the patient work of an archaeologist who locates a sunken city and spends a lifetime shoveling away the debris of millennia and carrying up scraps, pieces, fragments, and shards, each one to be carefully labeled, numbered, and archived. Or like a paleontologist reconstructing a vanquished prehistoric species from a tooth or a jawbone, he rediscovered a world of thought and life from scraps and shreds eaten away by age and neglect.

In the 1940s, as articles and books began to pour out, his research had a particularly poignant if melancholy resonance. His articles on Jakob Frank and Sabbatai Sevi, along with *Major Trends in Jewish Mysticism,* revealed the enormous creativity that had been at work within now annihilated eastern European Jewry. Scholem showed how over the centuries Jews had invariably responded to disaster by forging powerful mythopoetic works. In eastern and central Europe, surrounded by hostile neighbors, obscure and hitherto unknown figures had infused their ancient texts with great power and hope.

Ironically, Scholem's growing reputation as one of the world's premier Jewish intellectuals had a way of focusing people's attention on him just as much as on the figures populating his book. Why would a secular professor born and bred in Berlin devote a lifetime to a field long dismissed, as he put it, as an "impotent hallucination" and "degeneracy"?[2] Why would a spindly and priggish Prussian-style professor famous for his love of fine chocolate marzipan, a man who invariably wore a tie in rough-and-tumble Palestine, spend long years of his life researching false messiahs, mountebanks, and half-demented revolutionaries? The punctilious researcher's fascination with nihilism, madness, magic, death, and destruction intrigued and troubled friends and foes alike.

In the winter of 1943, during the darkest episode in Jewish history, Abraham Sonne, a Talmud scholar and Kantian living in Palestine, lashed out at Scholem in a Hebrew essay for his interest in Jakob Frank, a "Jewish Hitler" and "incomparable nihilist" who had won Scholem over through his "strong, despotic soul." Sonne warned against the "fascination with the 'destructive powers in the service of a new order' which has paved the way for the Hitlers of all times and places, and which has brought humanity to the edge of a precipice."[3]

There were friendlier voices. The Hebrew novelist and later Nobel laureate S. Y. Agnon likened his friend to a professor sifting through stacks of crumbling manuscripts in search of his own *Faust III*. Others were convinced that Scholem was a closet Kabbalist. To these and other attempts at understanding his deeper motivations, Scholem responded with a coy smile. Enigmatically, the final sentence in *Major Trends* characteristically raised more questions than it answered: "To speak of the mystical course which, in the great cataclysm now stirring the Jewish people more deeply perhaps than the entire history of exile, destiny may still have in store for us—and I for one believe that there is such a course—is the task of prophets, not of professors."[4] Did Scholem regard himself as a prophet, or just a professor, or both? No one knew, nor was Scholem about to tell them. To George Lichtheim, the man who had translated *Major Trends* into English, he wrote that "precisely the ability to deceive the world" was one of his "chief characteristics."[5]

The one exception to his general rule of stony silence regarding the deeper motivations behind his work took place just after his fiftieth birthday, in December 1947. To commemorate his teacher's birthday, Josef Weiss, Scholem's star pupil, published an article in a Tel Aviv daily in which he took a hard look at his teacher's work and at his paradoxical personality.

It was an odd article. The Holocaust had ended just two years earlier, and the Israeli War of Independence was about to begin. The daily sniping, bombings, and killings on the streets of Jerusalem spread a sense of dread that the mass annihilation which had just ended in Europe could happen again. Scholem feared that Jews faced "liquidation."[6] With war in the air, Weiss offered up a remarkable theory.

He started out with a pointed question. There is an incongruence, said Weiss, between his teacher's "lively personality and his seemingly dead scholarship." How could he write from such a dispassionate distance so soon after measureless horror had consumed European Jewry? Where was the fiery, romantic Scholem in his work? What about his love, his rage, his hope, and his deep humanism that went far beyond the confines of his discipline to address universal human concerns? Where were the "clearly articulated hopes and utopian motivations" that Weiss knew from sitting at the master's feet were unmistakable features of his inner life? How could a man who railed against the old guild of Jewish historians whose monographs were to him little more than a burial ceremony for Judaism—how could such a man approach Jewish mysticism with what seemed to Weiss an unemotionally detached scholarly objectivity?[7]

Weiss believed he had found the answer in his teacher's "consciously propagated private esotericism."

> Scholem does not want to let you in on either his dialectical negations or his paradoxical affirmations. But you can't undertake the task of sketching his intellectual portrait without coming to grips with the pronounced features of his esotericism. So what does this esoteric method of his consist of? It bears a resemblance to the way some medieval masters once liked to smuggle in their image into the features of one of the thousands of figures crowding a painting of masses of men. This is Scholem's esoteric ruse. His esotericism isn't absolute silence but rather a kind of camouflage. With his thick tomes and his philological research, he has apparently turned the figure of the metaphysician into that of a scholar. But his metaphysics reveals itself through concealment; it is camouflaged utterly to the point of imperceptibility within sentences and half-sentences tucked away within "pure" scholarly analyses, or in the form of a strange adjective that says nothing to the outsider and everything to those privy to the knowledge. And so in this way the secret metaphysician poses as an exact scientist. *His scholarship is Scholem incognito.* No one can therefore really know with certainty what Scholem wanted to find in the Kabbalah when he devoted himself to its study thirty years ago, and this ignorance of his ultimate spiritual desiderata puts his students into the Talmudic category of those pupils "whose apprenticeship has not yet been completed." It seems that for these students the best thing they can wish for their teacher on his fiftieth birthday is to find in Jewish mysticism what he was seeking to discover in it when he began his search.[8]

Weiss had stumbled across what Scholem's friend and fellow German Jewish scholar Leo Strauss would later call "esoteric writing."[9] As a sign that Weiss was following the spoor of the great philologist and historian, in a letter to his first wife, Escha, and her new husband, Shmuel Hugo

Bergman, Scholem complimented his student Weiss for having made such an "exquisite and audacious suggestion." His student was finally learning something from him, he remarked. In a letter Scholem wrote to Weiss months after the publication of Scholem's monumental biography of Sabbatai Sevi, he even borrowed from his student by likening himself to a "figure" painted into a masterpiece. "Even if differently than you once suggested, I have made myself into one of the figures who hides himself in famous paintings."[10]

In the hundreds of scholarly books and articles Scholem produced over the coming decades, he never went beyond dropping such hints. There is no mention of his esoteric self-concealment in his scholarship or his more personal autobiographical works. The people who intuited this esoteric dimension tended to be fiction writers, literary critics, and essayists rather than scholars. Alluding to the masterpiece *Paradise Lost,* Harold Bloom called him a "Miltonic figure in modern scholarship." Jorge Luis Borges, Scholem's friend and admirer, smuggled him into a poem on the Kabbalah by pairing the word "Golem" with "Scholem."[11] Cynthia Ozick, after meeting Scholem and reading his work, touched on this when she wrote about him: "Is the hidden cauldron not an entice-ment and a seduction to its investigator? Or, to say it even more terribly: it may be that the quarry is all the time in the pursuer."[12]

Weiss was so excited by his discovery, and even more so by his teacher's approving nod, that he planned to write Scholem's biography. Weiss keenly intuited that the "ultimate spiritual desiderata" that made his teacher tick were to be found in the years during World War I, when Scholem decided to devote his life to the study of the Kabbalah. Unfor-tunately, Weiss committed suicide shortly after embarking on his biogra-phy, and his sketches were lost.

Unraveling these initial impulses behind his work became much easier after Scholem's death in 1982. It was then that researchers were given ac-cess to the diaries Scholem began in 1913 and more or less concluded when he moved to Palestine in 1923.

For decades Scholem kept these notebooks locked away in his home in Jerusalem. His Jerusalem friends knew they existed, but they were strictly off limits to everyone, including his second wife, Fanya. This only increased the mystery surrounding them. (Some rumors hinted that they recorded his alleged experiments in black magic, which they do not.) Scholem often returned to them to refresh his memory of past events. Long passages of *Walter Benjamin: A Story of a Friendship* are little more than extracts culled from the diaries. Over the years, he occasionally jotted down notes in the margins. "Nonsense," he incredulously scrawled next to an entry recounting Benjamin's plan to study Hebrew.[13]

Scholem's diaries were eventually published in a two-volume edition, superbly edited and annotated by the German scholars Karlfried Gründer and Friedrich Niewöhner, with the help of Herbert Kopp-Oberstebrink. Over 1,200 pages in length, the two volumes combine diary entries with numerous unpublished essays and other short texts Scholem composed before his emigration to Palestine. The German researchers put years of work into deciphering Scholem's barely legible handwriting and provided the hundreds of references to obscure books, tracts, and people that populate Scholem's diaries.

While the published volumes are not entirely complete—Scholem's widow, Fanya, made them edit out many of the more personal and erotic passages—they do faithfully convey the genesis of what Weiss called Scholem's "singularly sculpted personality." They reveal the development of a great mind as he absorbed influences and accepted and rejected ideas, and disclose how he matured emotionally and intellectually during a time of enormous upheaval.

Most of all, they show that behind his later studies in Kabbalah were ecumenical concerns that place him far more squarely in the company of Carl Jung than what normally passes for "objective" academic scholarship. Behind the welter of religious terms in Scholem's diaries lurks an interest in the historical process of consciousness: how culture and tradition are formed and enriched; how they remain vibrant by adapting to new circumstances; and how the individual draws from and then feeds a tradition through creative spontaneity. In his diary Scholem reflects on the way people, responding to their circumstances, give life to an inherited canon. The task of the creative individual, now called a "mystic," now a "prophet," now a "critic," is to "uncover new messianic dimensions in [each] respective generation."[14]

These were the deeper interests Scholem brought to his scholarship. Just as Josef Weiss had discovered, his teacher was like the rabbis and heretics he spent a lifetime studying and describing, for like them he exhibited an extraordinary spontaneity and creativity by transforming old traditions in the face of horror.

�֍

This volume of Scholem's diaries is a selection taken from the two-volume German edition. In putting together this single-volume English edition, I have relied on the prodigious work of the German scholars, including much of their scholarly apparatus. This edition has a different aim from theirs, however. In reducing the two original volumes to one, I have had to cut and pare away hundreds of pages of material, much of which is of great interest. I have given preference to Scholem's personal diary entries over his unpublished essays, none of which are included here. Important issues in his early life, such as his ambivalent relationship to the Zionist youth movement in Germany, or his various reflections on the philosophy of mathematics, I have likewise omitted.

My main criterion in culling material has been to reconstruct the main lines of Scholem's personal and intellectual journey that make his youthful diaries a kind of *Bildungsroman* written during a fateful period that launched much of humanity into what Eric Hobsbawm has termed an "Age of Catastrophe." Scholem's friendship with Walter Benjamin is a major theme running through much of this volume, as is the development of Scholem's theory of allegorical literary interpretation—he calls it the "Teaching" Benjamin passed down to him—that turns the critic-interpreter-mystic into a sort of canonical time traveler.

In organizing the diaries, I generally followed Scholem's chronology and titles. I have hence separated the journal into four major parts, covering respectively Winter 1913 to January 1916; March to December 1916; January 1917 to April 1918; and May 1918 to August 1919. Each section begins with a historical survey that places the diaries in context and explains puzzling terms and ideas that often verge on the incomprehensible.

The titles of the various sections and individual chapters within the sections are often those provided by Scholem, who frequently gave titles to his notebooks. To avoid confusion, Scholem's original titles are in italics.

When Hebrew appears in the original, I have chosen to translate it into English.

A word should be said about content. Scholem's diary rarely captures quotidian happenings, and he is mostly silent about a war that consumed millions of lives and led to profound social and political upheavals. He writes nothing, for instance, on the day the war ended in November 1918. Permeating these pages are instead oracle-like pronouncements. The cryptic language he employs mirrors the ethereal content. Sentences with gnarled syntax can be half a page long and loaded down with a dozen clauses that lead nowhere, like stairways in a haunted castle. More effective than any lock, these grammatical challenges seem intended to trip up the uninitiated and keep out intruders. In the perpetual standoff between literality and readability, I opted for the latter. While I tried to remain faithful to Scholem's language and intentions, I am also aware of one of his deepest convictions: that translation is interpretation.

PART I

A ZARATHUSTRA FOR THE JEWS:
WINTER 1913–JANUARY 1916

Death, this most faithful of friends, was the constant companion of our generation.

—MARTIN GUMPERT on the death of Fritz Heinle

SCHOLEM'S GENERATION came into the world at the most auspicious of times. They were young and idealistic, raised in an age that knew nothing of war and civic unrest, public cynicism and revolutionary nihilism, which would later poison European culture after the First World War. Their dreams also tended to be ecumenical; for all the undercurrents of anti-Semitism in Germany, Jewish and German youth shared the same ideals.

Young people, especially in a metropolis such as Berlin, were reared in a cultural atmosphere that pulled at them from opposing directions. Germany was a rigidly hierarchical society based officially on the Prussian nobility, but in truth on the country's more middle-class industrial and scientific accomplishments such as its public transportation, universities, museums, publishing houses, and sewage treatment plants. While the nobility was increasingly anachronistic, the middle class continued to regard titles, degrees, and pedigree with almost supreme reverence. Nearly to a man they paid lip service to liberal principles, while they also viewed socialism with terror, and broadly supported whatever repressive measures were needed to keep the masses in their place. For middle-class youth, education was rational and rigorous. Those we call teenagers were considered young adults and were expected to behave as such. Suits and ties for young men were the norm.

The contradictions of a society that was at once superlatively dynamic and as cemented into place as the country's greatest monument to immobility, the Reichstag, bred deep discontent among the more privileged youth. Outwardly they conformed, but inwardly they chafed at society's endless rules.

One central complaint heard over and over among the most talented youth was that their parents' rational and commercial values stripped the world of all meaning, reducing the person to a mere private citizen and leaving him open to manipulation by systems of state, industry, and society. In a word, the "bourgeois" lifestyle crippled the imagination.

Things were not nearly so dire as youthful radicals thought. Compared to what was about to come—the "Age of Catastrophe"—Germany was enjoying an astonishing moment of tolerance and freedom. The old Prussian straitjacket was loosening, and a spirit of rebellion was in the air. In Berlin, the drive for increased personal freedom found an articulate—if at times bombastic and feverish—voice in the expressionist poets who held forth at Café des Westens, otherwise known as Café Megalomania. These poets were programmatically anti-bourgeois and anti-aristocratic. Freed from inherited social or literary forms, from the weight of the past and tradition, they proclaimed a new era of individualism.

At the opposite extreme was Stefan George, a visionary poet and homosexual who forged a circle of neoclassical revival. George considered himself the latest link in a chain stretching back to the Greeks and leading through Goethe and the poet Friedrich Hölderlin. Disciples looked on him as a high priest in a new religion of beauty. His neophytes formed a tight association, often known as the "Secret German Reich." It was an elite club thickly populated by Jewish intellectuals, who—according to Walter Benjamin—flocked to follow George's "teaching of the priestly calling of the poet and his references to Nietzsche, Hölderlin, and Jean Paul."[1]

The German middle class spawned secret societies by the score, all having their own cryptic initiation rules and generally following the words of a prophet or guru or "genius." Among the young, none rivaled the Wandervögel. Bored with their life in the cities and repelled by their parents' passionless mediocrity, bands of youth headed out into the wilds of the surrounding woods. They—both sexes together—drifted for days, sometimes weeks, living off the land and singing songs around bonfires. There was no adult supervision, no one to enforce the prudery that prevailed in the larger German society. No wonder that in 1912 Hans Blüher, one of its founders, titled his bible of the movement *The German Wandervögel Movement as an Erotic Phenomenon.*

Just as scandalous to Prussian authoritarianism was the education reform movement spearheaded by Gustav Wyneken, who set out to enlighten the children of shopkeepers and factory owners through the Greek ideal of pedagogic Eros.[2] Wyneken established the "Free School Community," located on the top of an isolated plateau in the Thüringian Forest. There he gathered his disciples and declared the coming of a new age. Wyneken's ideas combined the Gnostic pathos of a free life unconstrained by society's artificial shackles with the ideals set out in Plato's *Symposium.* His 1913 credo states that a young man can be initiated into a "higher world" of art and philosophy only through intimate companionship with his teacher.[3] This youth looks for a man "who understands his longings, someone he can love because he feels love radiating from him. He seeks a man who opens his heart to him and who shares his life with him, becoming for him the symbol of a higher, godly life."[4]

Wyneken was no pedophile, even if he was eventually put on trial for that crime.[5] The Eros he preached was intended to lead the young to authenticity through rigorous literary and philosophical training. In his mountaintop school, pupils were taught to love tradition but also to break free from its grip and to deny it its unquestioned sway over the present. The youth, instructed by charismatic teachers, were told to decide which aspects of the past would experience resurrection, which graves would be opened, which voices heard.

While middle-class Jewish youth joined German youth clubs, Jews from less assimilated families typically joined exclusively Jewish clubs, which, like the German clubs, focused largely on anti-bourgeois histrionics, drinking parties, and long forest outings with the opposite sex. The Zionists were no exception. The playful, pagan element in the movement was spelled out by Max Nordau, Theodor Herzl's right-hand man, when he called for a new "muscular Jew" to overcome the inbred debilitation of book-loving Jews. (Nordau was also the author of a best-selling work about the ills of modern society, *Degeneration,* or *Entartung.*) Zionism was a Wandervögel of the imagination, whose young members

roamed the German woods while dreaming of escape from their parents
through a return to their ancient homeland. The Germans at least paid
homage to the dark Germanic forests studded with ruins and mists, while
the Zionists longed for a land that no one had any realistic plan of visiting, much less colonizing.

In 1913 Gerhard Scholem began his journal while sitting in a Berlin
streetcar, pondering the looming crisis within himself. The sixteen-year-
old was already betraying traits that he would display for a lifetime, such
as the predisposition to harsh judgments and splendid intellectual talents.
His first diary entries create the impression of an astoundingly precocious teenager with nothing solid under his feet. He swore allegiance
now to Jewish orthodoxy, now to anarchism. Groping for a messiah, he
looked first to Martin Buber, then to Nietzsche. As he became increasingly unhinged, he took on the role himself.

Unlike most of his Jewish friends, Gerhard was not from the educated,
assimilated bourgeoisie. His parents were unmistakably parvenu. There
was a related handicap he had to contend with: the most dominant figure
in his early life, his father, Arthur, was in his eyes a hypocritical boor. Despite having moved his family to the right neighborhood and having
adopted the customary patriotism of middle-class Germany, Arthur was
uncomfortable in gentile society and had only Jewish friends. Yet the attempts he made to remain a part of the Jewish community were but half-
hearted. Arthur happily called himself an "atheist and freethinker" and
sneered at Jewish tradition. In truth, he never gave religion a second
thought. "Papa worked on Yom Kippur and didn't go to synagogue,"
writes Scholem. On the Sabbath Arthur would light his cigar from the
Sabbath candle and utter the mock blessing ". . . borei pri tabacco"
(Blessed be He who createst the fruit of tobacco).[6] This sent his youngest
son into a white heat.

It was with his mother, Betty, that Gerhard had a close relationship, particularly after Werner, the second youngest of the four Scholem
brothers, moved out of the house in 1913. Gerhard and his mother took
trips together, and it was to her that he poured out his heart. His being
the only child left at home also exacerbated Betty's solicitude for his
health and well-being, which in due course only seemed to make him
more prone to illness.

But Gerhard also owed much to Arthur, even if he never knew it. He inherited from his father a lack of confidence in gentile society, where he manifestly did not fit in: "For someone like myself who has never really had anything to do with them socially, the goyim are absolute strangers to me."[7] Gerhard's appearance didn't help matters. He writes in his autobiography that he "suffered far less in school from anti-Semitic harassment than from the teasing about my jug-handle ears, an inherited trait that almost all Scholems, going back three or four generations, had in common."[8] Not surprisingly, in his diaries the jug-eared Gerhard lashes out at the cult of the beautiful youth.[9] This sealed his reputation as an "eccentric sectarian and an asocial type."[10]

Another difficulty he had in both Jewish and non-Jewish society was a lack of easy elegance. His was a generation of striving bards with stupendous literary talent, but when Gerhard looked for a muse, he normally came up empty-handed. In his attempts to express his inner longings, the words got caught in his throat or came out with the sharp edges of his Berlin dialect.

Socially awkward and with a sulking, melancholy personality, Gerhard did not enjoy drinking or carousing and hence steered clear of the Wandervögel. Even if he had been a drinker, he was under no illusion of fully belonging to German society, at a time when most Jews eagerly declared the opposite and made every effort to prove it. He joined the small splinter group Agudah Yisrael, an Orthodox youth group. His main loyalty, however, was to Young Judah (Jung Judah), a youth group he joined in 1912, which met in a small café at the Tiergarten railway station. (Lectures were held in the back room of the Golden Goose Hotel.) It was in Young Judah that he met the friends who appear in his diary: Aharon Heller, Karl Türkischer, Erich Brauer, and his best friends Edgar Blum and Harry Heymann. Neither Blum nor Heymann would survive the World War.

Scholem's interest in Judaism began in 1911, when he read through three volumes of Heinrich Graetz's monumental eleven-volume *History of the Jews* (1853–1875.) Graetz set some people's teeth on edge with his defiant defense of Judaism. Scholem was thrilled. Along with his schoolmate Edgar Blum, he soon began learning Hebrew. The existence of a sizable colony of Hebrew-speakers in Palestine, mostly Russian Jewish emigrants inspired by Tolstoy's agrarian utopianism, greatly amplified the prestige of the language for young Zionists, and Gerhard took to the ancient language avidly. By the time the diaries open in 1913, he had mastered enough of the language to read it.

What he called his first "living experience" with Judaism occurred two years later, when the bookish young Scholem read a passage from the Talmud in the original under the tutelage of an Orthodox rabbi, Isaak Bleichrode. Henceforth, the Bible and the Talmud competed with his other teenage reading. It was an eclectic list. He discovered Søren Kierkegaard, the Danish philosopher often regarded as the father of existentialism, and Friedrich Nietzsche, perhaps the greatest of all enemies of rationalism. Another of his early favorites was Gustav Frenssen, a religious, quasi-mystical *Heimat* writer. The best-selling novelist would later become an enthusiastic Nazi.[11] Scholem, of course, did not know this at the time, though he was far more aware than most German Jews of the existence of anti-Semitic hacks infesting Germany with the seeds of racial hatred.

Martin Buber, his greatest single influence as the diary begins, was a bearded sage whose doctrine of ecstatic Experience taught Scholem about a Zionist journey that was less geographical than emotional. The redemption that Buber proclaimed—and Gerhard desperately wanted to be redeemed—required radical resolution. In his exploration of the more irrational elements of the Jewish tradition, Buber and those who followed him found such redemption in the folktales of eastern Europe, the Kabbalah, and the Midrash.[12]

❈

A century ago in central Europe it was common to see youths scribbling away in diaries to express their longings and loves and heartbreaks, and Gerhard Scholem was in certain respects no exception. Through the years from 1914 to 1919, a period covering the bulk of his diaries, we see him jotting down his notes late into the night, often interrupted by bouts of tears, suicidal fears, or exaltation and sublime insight.

What made Scholem an exception was the way in which he shook off much of neo-Romanticism after the outbreak of war in August 1914. In the months preceding the war, Gerhard's social problems were already mounting after he quit his youth group, the Agudah Yisrael, because the other members had a love of drinking parties that he, a born puritan, did not share.

With the outbreak of war, as others eagerly ran off to join, Scholem lost whatever faith he still had in the existing social order, beginning with God, then the state, all the way to the youth movement. Buberian homage to "Experience" would also soon fall by the wayside, while other notions—of history, philosophy, messianism, and religion—would take on new life, albeit in a very new context.

Scholem's razor-sharp intuition showed him just how theatrical the youthful anti-bourgeois "revolution" had been. With Prussian generals calling the shots, eighteen-year-olds volunteered with neo-Romantic poetry on their lips, eager to march along with everyone else in defense of the Fatherland. No longer were the country's youthful elite dancing nude in the wilds; students now donned uniforms and took up arms, with Wyneken and leaders of the Wandervögel cheering them on.

August 1914 also showed him just how German the Zionists were. That "assimilationists" such as Hermann Cohen, Walter Rathenau, and the then famous scientist Fritz Haber supported the war did not surprise Scholem in the least. (Rathenau took over Germany's department of economic war management, while Fritz Haber developed the poison gas for Germany's chemical warfare program.) What outraged him was the sight of Zionists rushing off to join the fighting just like their Christian peers. Martin Buber, who had been preaching his doctrine of primordial and collective "Experience" for well over a decade, now decided that the war's "magic powers" were a "fearful grace, the grace of a new birth." The diminutive philosopher, himself too old for the draft, predicted that the war would teach "Western Jews" the ethos of *Gemeinschaft*.[13] Buber's words struck such a deep chord that Hugo Bergmann, one of his neophytes at the time, eagerly climbed into the trenches with visions of "powerful and heroic deeds."[14]

Gerhard loathed the war from the start, though at first his hope in the youth of Germany persisted. Weeks after the German army began its rape of Belgium, on a stormy autumn evening Scholem's diary records a meeting he had with members of the German youth movement, whom he lauded for their "immeasurable youthful longing for Romanticism and the enormous lust for destruction."[15] He hopes for a "new generation" of Jewish youth embarked on a similar search "for its youth and for its homeland."[16] Scholem vowed to help direct the messianic search.

He was a good deal more grounded when discussing the war. His older brother Werner belonged to the radical left wing of the Social Democratic Party—spearheaded by Rosa Luxemburg and Karl Liebknecht—that was virtually alone in denouncing the war. Werner took his younger brother on trips to a restaurant in the working-class neighborhood to hear fiery denunciations of the war.

In February 1915 Gerhard got kicked out of school after writing a protest letter to Germany's main Zionist newspaper, the *Jüdische Rundschau*. The letter was in response to an article titled "We and the War," which culminated in a statement that sent him into a rage: "And so we went to war—not despite our being Jews, but because of our being Zionists."[17] He wanted Edgar Blum to sign a protest letter he planned on sending to the *Jüdische Rundschau,* but one of his schoolmates ferreted it out of his briefcase and denounced him.

After Scholem's expulsion from the *Gymnasium,* his father threatened to send him out to be an apprentice to a "herring tamer," Berlin slang for a grocer. Gerhard escaped this fate by taking advantage of an obscure rule enabling the children of Prussian Junkers to enter the University of Berlin, where he took courses in mathematics, Near Eastern languages, and history. Meanwhile, Gerhard's animus against Prussian militarism only increased after his closest friend, Edgar Blum, was drafted. Together with his friend Erich Brauer, who got out of the military for health reasons (Scholem called him "deformed and extremely sensitive"),[18] Gerhard set up a clandestine publishing operation in his father's printing house to bring out the homespun antiwar tract *Blue-White Spectacles.* The three issues that appeared all blasted away at his fellow Zionists who had betrayed the cause by supporting the war.

His first doubts about Buber surfaced due to the latter's pro-war stance, only to retreat because of Gerhard's newfound love of mysticism. Eight months into the war, Scholem still found himself in a "deep Buber spirit."[19] His extremely precocious mind, still afire with neo-Romantic anti-intellectualism, lashed out against "culture" and education because they deaden the spirit. Experience, not logic, was what he needed; or, in Jesus'—and Kierkegaard's—uncompromising assertion, "Only one thing is needful." Like other aspiring young intellectuals, he lived in the shadow of the Romantic poet Friedrich Hölderlin, the young genius who went mad. Another shadow that fell over Gerhard was cast from across the street: his family's apartment faced the printing house that published Stefan George's writings, which he voraciously read—volumes such as *The Year of the Soul, The Tapestry of Life, The Seventh Ring,* and *The*

Star of the Covenant. "Stefan George's *Star of the Covenant* is extremely tough going but sumptuous," he declared.[20]

Supplementing his religious and avant-garde reading were works of philosophy. It did not take him long to realize that modern scholarship had demolished God and True Faith and undermined the historical veracity of much of what had passed for divine history. His mind barreling ahead, he soon discovered that the culprit, "scientific" history, was itself in critical condition. Modernity, having uprooted all the old certainties, also put into question Reason itself. Gerhard was at the end of his tether.

It was in this context of shattered beliefs, severed loyalties, and an increasingly precarious handle on his life that Gerhard began to consider a new and concealed brand of messianism. As the war dragged on, many of his German peers started to long for a great military or political leader to save the nation from disaster; people at both ends of the political spectrum, left and right, hoped for a charismatic hero. It was shortly after the outbreak of war that Gerhard met the older and culturally more mature and urbane Walter Benjamin. Scholem found his redeemer in this man of towering intelligence.

Benjamin, the son of a man with business interests in art auctions and ice skating rinks, was reared among books, ideas, and artifacts of culture. He never had any of Gerhard's doubts about his place in German culture: Germany was his spiritual home. He was a firm believer in the religious calling of the literati, and he even told the poet Ludwig Strauss, who vainly tried to enlist him in the Zionist ranks, that he felt no stronger kinship with Jews than with non-Jews. His cultural values forbade him from "restricting the concept of culture to one part of humanity."[21] The distinguishing mark of the true Jewish mind was for him cosmopolitanism, and hence being genuinely Jewish required one to relinquish a specifically Jewish national identity. Benjamin could hardly bring himself to open one of Buber's books. Lining his bookshelves were works by Goethe, Friedrich Schelling, Stefan George, Plato, Meister Eckhart, a collection of detective novels, and lots of Friedrich Hölderlin.

Like most well-to-do young Jews, Benjamin was deeply involved in the German youth movement, more specifically in Gustav Wyneken's educational reform movement.[22] He spent nearly two years at Wyneken's forest school. After he returned to Berlin in 1906, he rented a room and established a group to study Wyneken's ideas. "My thinking still arises out of my first teacher, Wyneken, and goes back to him," he wrote on the eve of the war.[23]

What Benjamin absorbed from Wyneken and transformed into his own thinking was the need for an autonomous, anarchistic youth movement. A "new program [for renewal] must arise out of the essence of youth themselves and not be imposed on them from the outside," he said in 1913. Benjamin also took from Wyneken the ideal of a spiritual-erotic bond between student and teacher. "I'd like to read to you Plato's talk on love," Benjamin wrote to a female friend.[24]

> There are such beautiful and deep thoughts found nowhere else. This afternoon I had an additional thought that to be young means not so much to serve the spirit as to expect it, to look for spirit in everyone and in the farthest thoughts. I'd like to call youth the constantly vibrating feeling for the abstractness of thought. For when we keep our sights free to see the spirit wherever it is, we will become the ones who fulfill it. . . . Nearly everyone forgets that his person is the place where spirit actualizes itself.[25]

None of this had much in common with the individual's ecstatic experience as proclaimed by so many at the time but rather pertained to the complex interaction between inherited culture and the spontaneity of youth. The duty of the school was to be the "transmitter of all of the grand cultural materials that had been created by earlier generations and given over to the coming generation, who shall take on the heritage of their ancestors. . . . This takes place through the comradeship between pupils and teachers."[26]

The most important "teacher" who led Benjamin to his self-declared "spiritual existence" was the young poet Fritz Heinle.[27] The two became friends after Benjamin began studying neo-Kantian philosophy at the University of Freiburg.[28] Together they would take long walks through the hills surrounding the town or midnight strolls through the forest. Despite differences in age and background (Heinle, several years his junior, was a Protestant), Benjamin described his love for Heinle in lofty, Platonic terms. He composed a series of sonnets to him. "Each of us," he wrote, "could stand in the place of the other."[29]

Benjamin saw in Heinle a new Hölderlin, and not only because of his poetic talents or the fact that Heinle consciously regarded his work as a continuation of Hölderlin's later poetry.[30] Like the half-mad Hölderlin holed up in his Tübingen tower, Heinle spoke oracle-like in riddles, parables, and esoteric revelatory hints, never in slogans and programs.[31] In this he distanced himself from activist poets, with their constant call for social change and outward rebellion. True youth seeks no political "movement," Heinle believed. Youth knows nothing of the "confusion of gestures and the silhouette of programmatic personalities. It steers clear of all polemic."[32] Instead of bombast and rousing speeches, he looked to "silence" as the "clearest means of communication."[33]

The outbreak of war changed Benjamin forever. He was vaguely opposed to the war, though not enough to refuse serving in the military. Shortly after it began, he and his literary friends in Berlin gathered at the Café des Westens to discuss which unit to volunteer for. "Then occurred something that changed my attitude toward Berlin and this war forever," Benjamin later recalled in his autobiographical *Berlin Childhood*. He got word that Heinle and his girlfriend had opened the gas valve to kill themselves in the apartment Benjamin had rented to discuss Wyneken's teachings. He learned about his friend's suicide in a telegram. "You will find [me] lying in the apartment," read the note. Opposition to the war had led them to commit suicide. Heinle signed no protest letter, issued no public statement, and wrote no article in the newspaper. His protest was one he made with his life. And the fact that he chose to do so in the center of Benjamin's world, and had the telegram hand-delivered to his café, only added more weight to his silent protest. Here was a man whose voice had touched Benjamin like no other, someone he compared to the incomparable Hölderlin, and yet who died an obscure poet. But Heinle's voice came from a core of meaning none had ever touched, and in this way for Benjamin he had achieved immortality. Benjamin discovered that the purity of the spirit rests not in the practical life but in "language formed by the poet."[34]

Benjamin never fully recovered from Heinle's death. He not only refused to volunteer to fight; he also now devised elaborate means to stay out of the army. He entered into a period of silence in which he broke from Wyneken, from the youth movement and the sort of clamorous activism it promoted, and from most of his old friends. "They don't exist for me any longer," he announced.[35]

Far from his old café haunts, he began to work out of his family's villa in a leafy district of Berlin, where he followed the self-declared calling of the young intellectual to "protect the thoughts of culture and to rescue culture from a time of chaos."[36] Through his friend's death he discovered a realm of meaning and a range of voices otherwise completely forgotten or at least ignored by society. It was as if an esoteric tradition, very different from anything ever sounded out at "Café Megalomania," was now speaking to him through the memory of Heinle.

Out of his isolation, Benjamin launched into a period of stupendous productivity, writing poems and essays that he would describe to Scholem decades later as the "magnificent foundation" for his career.[37] The most important of these essays were one on Hölderlin's "Poet's Courage and Timidity" and another on Dostoyevsky's novel *The Idiot*.

Having lost Heinle and broken from Wyneken and his fellow neophytes, Benjamin gathered around him an ad hoc circle of followers for whom he was now the teacher. The group resembled Stefan George's poetic Reich, as it lacked all structure, was carried on mostly through letters, had no clear credo, and advanced no social agenda. The circle was composed of a smattering of friends who received Benjamin's cryptic writings in the mail. His correspondence was now replete with references to German mystics. His essays never mentioned politics, warfare, hopes of victory, or fear of violent death. They were esoteric notes that were part of an ongoing conversation carried on in private. They circulated among Benjamin's small coterie of friends like revelatory scriptures.[38]

The central message of the essays carried out a theme that Benjamin had developed during his days in Wyneken's reform movement: tradition as a product of the past filtered through the experiences of youth. But now it was anarchistic and secretive, available to only a select group, the deeper messages transmitted silently, through a profound sympathy and intuition. Only for the initiated whose intuition was sharp enough to break the code were they written and comprehensible.

✼

Scholem was already pulling out of his prewar neo-Romantic haze when he met Benjamin. In the weeks before their first meeting, his diaries reflect a zigzag course between messianism and atheism, scientific determinism and faint remnants of his earlier religious fantasies.

Scholem's first encounter with Benjamin took place in 1915 during a meeting organized by a student group to debate whether or not history had any importance. The speaker was the expressionist poet Kurt Hiller, a principal founder of the Neo-pathetic Cabaret. Hiller, along with nearly everyone else in the room, had no time for the dead weight of history. In a variation on Marx, Hiller believed in changing the present, not pining for the past.

Benjamin was one of History's only defenders in the room. He and Hiller had had a falling out due to Benjamin's new orientation. According to Hiller, Benjamin had dismissed "humanistic activism" and its efforts at changing the world as "banal and wrong-headed," preferring "analytic contemplation."[39] When Benjamin stood up to defend History, Gerhard was dazzled by the "ingenious sparks" flying out from his dark thoughts.[40]

Scholem was soon to receive a formal invitation from Benjamin: "Dear Sir, I should like to ask you to visit me this Thursday around 5:30 P.M."[41] During this and subsequent meetings Benjamin discussed Stefan George, Hölderlin's translation of Pindar, and Heinrich von Gerstenstein's drama *Ugolino*. The empty-handed Scholem countered with a bit of Buber. Benjamin, with his superior philosophical talents, was clearly the more dominant of the two. He quickly weaned his new friend of his attachment to Buber, whom he mocked as living in a "permanent trance" and whose followers he derided as being in a state of "Buberty."[42] Scholem now found more of an affinity with the thinking of Asher Ginzberg, who wrote under the name Ahad Haam, "One of the People." Ahad Haam did not trust political nationalism, seeing instead the future of Jewish culture in the revival of Hebrew learning.

Over the coming months Scholem's taste in non-Jewish literature vastly improved from hack writers such as Frenssen to Jean Paul, Paul Scheerbart, Friedrich Theodor von Vischer, and Josef von Eichendorff. He also picked up a love for detective novels—not cheap murder mysteries with characters in overcoats and dark glasses, but probing intellectual journeys such as Edwin Balmer's novel *A Wild-Goose Chase*.

What made Benjamin such a compelling figure for the young Gerhard went far beyond his erudition. Scholem later wrote about Benjamin's "secretiveness bordering on eccentricity, a mystery-mongering, though it sometimes was breached unexpectedly by personal and confidential revelations."[43] Scholem felt himself inducted into Benjamin's secret society. The imagery he uses in his diary is that of individuals in society as islands linked by rocks beneath the surface of the water.

NOTEBOOK 1

Winter 1913–August 17, 1914

undated

I descend from Jews originally from Glogauer. I don't know of any famous rabbis among my forebears. At best I could point to a cantor named Isaac from Koeben.[1] My great-grandfather was Marcus Scholem. He married a woman from Holland (the daughter of Mordechai Hollander, a middleman from The Hague), moved to Berlin at the beginning of the nineteenth century, and opened up a kosher eatery on Klosterstrasse 91. Back then it was quite renowned. He died in 1845 and is buried in the Schönhauser Allee.[2] His son, my grandfather, built the printing business. It seems that he wasn't very clever, as he and my father often quarreled. In the end my father started his own printing house. Grandfather died in 1901 as a result of a broken leg. My mother's father was, among other things, an elder of a synagogue. He was a giant of a man who loved big-breasted women. His wife was a sweet and pious housewife. My parents married on November 2, 1890.

I was born on the fifth of December 1897 at Friedrichsgracht 28. My earliest childhood memory is my fifth birthday. I wore dresses till the age of six.[3] On Easter of 1904 I began to attend school in Janke. After that point I didn't change schools, but neither did I sit still.

My Bar Mitzvah took place on December 2, 1911. Since that day I have been an Orthodox Jew (I hate the Lindenstrasse, where my Bar Mitzvah took place).[4]

February 17, 1913

[. . .] On Friday at the Heidereutergasse[5] I greeted my Zionist friend with the informal "Du." (I too am a Zionist.) I still don't know his name. [. . .] Right now I am reading materials from the general assembly of the Farmers' Association from the region of Busch.[6] The speeches are preposterous, full of attacks against us Jews, whose "degenerative influence" these racially pure "Teutons" wish to combat. Zionism is the only response to such humbug. [. . .]

[. . .] If I were Werner I would have run away from home ten times by now, run and tried to manage without the "family." There's obviously nothing left of the Jewish family with us.[7] This after 75 years!![8] I can only hope it'll be different with me. [. . .]

In the library I read one of Zunz's necrologies on Krochmal (blessed be his memory).[9] This man really must have been a first-rate genius. The Jews from Galicia are, after all, more than dumb cows. I also read some clever remarks on ecclesiastical issues. Really most interesting. Afterwards, and with a great deal of curiosity, I read what Graetz and Samson Raphael Hirsch had to say about poetry in their editions of the Psalms (the others I haven't yet got around to translating).[10]

You can learn a tremendous amount about these two gentlemen by reading their commentaries. Hirsch simply translates the text sitting in front of him, without any emendations or the like. He explains things in a highly reasonable fashion. With Graetz you notice in each line the presence of a hypercritic. And his translation (just like his commentary!) is arbitrary. [. . .]

[. . .] At six in the morning I went to the Workers' Welfare Museum in the Fraunhoferstrasse. It wasn't a pretty sight, as the advanced students simply gaped at the most interesting things, and we didn't get very far. I then went to hear a lecture by Rabbi Dr. Hoffmann from Emden, who wrote a book both pro and contra Sombart.[11] The lecture, on the "economic life of German Jews during the Middle Ages," succeeded quite well in exploding the widely held prejudices against our forefathers, in particular regarding the money trade. I went together with Horowitz.[12] Kallmann wasn't there.[13] He, like Werner, went to hear Herr Werner at the Marienhaus in order to practice getting booted out.[14] The lecture was on the "solution to the Jewish problem." Next time I'm going with them to hear about the "scientific basis for anti-Semitism." I'm still reading Chamberlain.[15]

[. . .] I'm supposed to go to Uncle George's for dinner, but I'd like to get out of it! The way we conduct these Friday evenings is nothing short of purest blasphemy![16] [. . .]

This evening I went to Adass Israel.[17] I would go there regularly if it didn't mean a half-hour walk. For this reason I go to the Old Synagogue, which is only twenty minutes away. [. . .] Today I picked up Frenssen's *Klaus Hinrich Baas.* I'm excited to read it. The day before yesterday I read *Käthchen:* it's a marvelous book![18] I didn't manage to get to Chamberlain today.

February 22, 1913

[. . .] I'm enthralled with *Klaus Hinrich Baas.* It's purest Gustav Frenssen—in the description of the milieu, in the eroticism, in the theological side-springs, but equally in the occasional meaningless portrayals. It's far above the level of *Anna Hollmann's Demise,* which I'm not even close to finishing.[19] [. . .]

In the Prussian state parliament today there was another incident. As Cassel[20] left the podium, after having delivered a speech on what's happening at the Berlin Senate (where the Social Democrats declared, "The people of Berlin have no reason to celebrate the year 1813"), Hoffmann called out, "If it weren't for Napoleon you'd still be in a ghetto."[21] Cassel used the occasion to make a patriotic remark: namely, that by 1813 the Prussian princes would have seen to it that the Jews would no longer be in ghettos, as if even without Napoleon emancipation would have taken place in 1812. One sees here how these liberal gentlemen of ours have a shallow understanding of history. [. . .]

February 24, 1913

[. . .] This afternoon I went to the library to return my books. I then checked out Hirsch's *Chorev,* Nordau's *Doctor Kohn,*[22] Hirsch's *Beziehung des Talmuds,* and Alexander Berg's *Social Democracy and the Jew*[23] (which is the one I read first). Few books are so stupidly eager to be scientific. Every sentence in this book is a lie, and a hackneyed one at that. Basically, there's nothing new in it, just the same old gibberish about the secret government of the Jews (Alliance Israelite Universelle!),[24] and so on and so forth. Drumont's *Judification of France*[25] says it all so much better.

Hirsch's (blessed be his memory) writings on the Talmud are just like those by Wünsche and Deutsch.[26] In particular, the reader fails to get a picture of the Talmud. On the basis of the passages he cites, one would think that the Talmud is composed of exclusively moral proverbs and the like, which isn't the case. It's always the same old story: On the one hand, the Talmud is put on a pedestal as the fountainhead of all wisdom, and on the other, it's slandered as the paragon of vulgarity. I would of course prefer to align myself with the former view. I began browsing through *Chover*[27]—a wonderfully written book. If Judaism were as Samson Raphael Hirsch thinks it should be, there wouldn't be any such thing as anti-Semitism. [. . .]

February 26, 1913

I took a walk for an hour this evening. I went down Linden Street, where all the cars drove in the direction of the Kaiser. Finally, he showed up with the Danish king. I didn't take off my hat; I had no reason to do so. On my walk I daydreamed once again the entire time. It wouldn't surprise me if I turned out to be a total failure. I dream away in visions of worlds and epochs that either don't exist or are already long past. I wonder what I'll say in twenty years when I read these lines.

February 28, 1913

On March 10, after the ceremony, there's going to be a church service. It's obligatory for the Protestant pupils to attend. Those who are not (Jews, in other words, as the Catholics have their own ceremony) can take part with their parents' permission. This is because it's not a religious ceremony; it's a patriotic one. At first I considered attending, but then quickly changed my mind. [. . .]

March 5, 1913

[. . .] I was horribly bored. I'm really incapable of enjoying such events (Father's birthday). I relate everything in my field of vision to Judaism. Someone could perhaps call me one-sided, but that's just the way I am. [. . .]

March 12

[. . .] This afternoon I begged from Mother enough money to go to Süssenguths and buy myself 4.50 marks' worth of books.[28] I picked up Marr's *Judaism's Victory over Germany*[29] and read it at once. The book's got it all wrong, even if the people at the *Berliner Tageblatt* would be glad if things were the way Marr portrays them.[30] Next I bought von Langen's *The Jewish Secret Law and the Representatives of the German States*.[31] This is a

run-of-the-mill, unabashed anti-Semitic fabrication! The best lie of all is
the one about the *Choschen ha-mishpat.*[32] Supposedly, the worst thing
imaginable is written there: that one shall not obey the laws of the
land. [. . .]

September 3, 1913

On Saturday July 5 I left with Mother. We first traveled to Strassburg and
got a good look at it. The cathedral is really quite pretty. From there we
continued on to Bern, one of the most beautiful cities I know. On the
sixth we were in Giessbach. There I did a seven-and-a-half-week cure,
whose cure ordinances I've saved for posterity's sake. There was a very
large number of Jews there. On the way back I stopped in Frankfurt and
went to Kauffmann's, then to Seligmann's synagogue.[33] I nearly died of
laughter.

Over the course of the trip I acquired thirty books in all. After my return I picked up *Old-New Land*[34] at Lamm's bookstore [. . .]

Undated 1914

In January 1914 a youth group of the Agudah was founded, and I was
elected to the executive committee.[35] My career in the Agudah ended in
May 1914 as a result of my and my friends' resignation. This took place
after a meeting of the executive in which Herr Dr. Segall[36] and Dr.
Hofmann raised a storm by accusing me of not being true to the Law.
Heymann read the declaration of resignation at the general assembly.[37]
An unbelievable row broke out, and I incited all sorts of boycotts against
me. A month later I left Orthodoxy. It wasn't an easy decision and it
caused quite a stir, but I'm now sailing full speed ahead in the direction
of Martin Buber. I've also become a socialist.

Later I resigned from the leadership of Young Judah and have withdrawn from the entire business. I'm fed up with organizations. People
laugh at me. [. . .]

June 14, 1914

In the evening I spent three hours with Jakob Jahr,[38] who was once again
immensely enthusiastic about Buber's *Rabbi Nachman.*[39] We agreed that
next Sunday afternoon we'll go to some isolated spot to discuss both of
Buber's books.

August 17, 1914

Travel Notes and Observations

The thoughts recorded here are not conjured up at a writing desk. I did not produce them line by line, to be placed into some meaningful context. I don't relate them to a coordinated system of where and how, and then violently press them into the jackboots of a disposition, that is, into an inadequate causal relationship. Only in retrospect can all of our experience be placed into categories. It has been said that later generations regard every revolution as an evolution. But what my lines here seek to seize hold of are thoughts that occasionally stream toward us, unprovoked and inexorable, and then slip our heads into their yokes. From high in the mountains, they come rushing down out of pure lust and sink into the crevasses of glaciers at your feet. But the fact that they come and go is not essential to them. They come out of the eternal sea of an unknown necessity and go into the nothingness of forgetfulness, out of which they first emerged. The only thing essential to these thoughts is the short span of time between them, which is an eternal moment of sacred experience.

This is necessity. Beyond the massive stream of foreigners who rush into Switzerland every year is a high Alpine valley of the Gotthard. I spent four weeks in the shadow of its magnificence. [. . .] Four weeks are not an eternity for a young man from the big city playing hooky from school. Fleeing from instrumental thinking and phony harmony, he stands before the wilderness and the magnificence of the high mountains. The only marching order, issued in a doctor's office in Berlin, is loneliness. My lonely wanderings through the snow and ice deserts of Windgälle and Düssistockes gave me sufficient leisure to chase after my own thoughts. Some call these thoughts childish, others say they're eccentric. I did so until war cries stirred a hideous echo even in Maderanertal. [. . .] And through constant avalanches my walking stick clearly announced its irritation at the disunity of the world. This stick is a companion to be reckoned with.

One sees why someone like me, for whom this journey is one not of pleasure but of discovery (not unlike Prometheus, who supposedly took fire from the heavens and brought it to men), has such unexpected thoughts. One sees that in this loneliness I have pondered the very same things that I otherwise carry within myself. Up there

I searched for a God who, according to David Strauss,[40] wanders about homeless down below. Only thus will someone understand my thoughts.

The path that leads from far in the distance up into the Maderanertal ends with a stone ledge in a glorious region. Rising up before the eyes of tourists is a glacier, a powerful and crevassed mountain of ice. Like stone giants, these mountains shoot into the skies. The blinding white of new snow covers the mountain peaks. Though visible only to those who know the area, the mountains are home to Alpine goats and marmots. And humans? They stay far from these crevasses and walls. Nature here takes in an eternal breath. This is God's nature. Everywhere it's quiet, only here on this valley path do people come and go. Aren't the cultivated people and their culture rather like a goddess striking visitors to this place with holy silence in order to protect the region's purity from profane eyes? No, you fool! How could you believe such a thing! Culture is a book with a red cover. Astonished and opening it up, you ask what kind of book this is. Do you believe it is the Bible that everyone travels with? No, my friend, culture is Baedeker.[41]

These people stand here and stare. Yes, they stare. Maybe they are looking at the mountains hoping to find the God who lives there, or perhaps they're looking to the glacier's depths for answers to the questions plaguing mankind since time immemorial. Or, staring into infinity, they turn away violently from the glory of the view, as a tourist turns from the glare of the snow glimmering in the sun? Look how they open their mouths and how their lips are full of words. Surely they are going to stutter something about holiness with reverential words; that the ineffable will cast its splendor onto their words. They will praise the One who dwells above the hills and who permits his glory to roll over them when the morning light shines. Their stuttering will speak of the freedom and nature of God, and those honored to see the holy will consider themselves blessed. They will grow by measuring their smallness against the enormity of these surroundings; and they will become silent, because they have learned to know this enormity! You who have prophesied falsely according to the measure of your folly and are strong in your lack of reason, you climb onto a high mountain and cast yourself into the chasms over terrifying stones. You know nothing about the world that opens its jaws here and that serves God in its own manner. These people don't look at nature to see its beauty; they look in the red book that teaches them the thoughts that cultural mankind has had on this spot. At the end of the valley is a cliff with a glorious view. The book places a star next to it. Checked off. They don't see the glacier with its blue crevasse. They don't realize that tomorrow this crevasse will close up, and another will open up at a different spot. They don't realize that their lives are like the glacier. What marvelous views of the Hüfig glacier, they think (it takes between 7 and 8 hours to walk its length, and has retreated significantly recently, and connects up to Claridenfirn). Indeed, this is what they think and read about out loud. But there is no angel that descends from the mountains with a fiery sword to drive them out of the paradise they have desecrated. The mountains don't rumble down onto the desecrators. Haven't they defiled God through their silence about him on this place of his throne! And yet the earth does not open up to swallow them!

When Sabbatai Sevi wanted to prove to others he was the Messiah, he went to the marketplace in Smyrna and, with his head uncovered, uttered the name of God.[42] There was a popular legend according to which no one except the redeemer can mouth the name of God without an angry bolt of heavenly lightning striking him down. Because nothing of the kind happened, Sevi believed in himself, and the people believed in him. These days, it's the same old story with people, who continue to sink into their own madness. They talk about the mountains, though not of their glory and not of their beauty. It's enough for these people to know the names of the mountains! Vocabulary pours out from their lips, and they praise themselves happily for their rich vocabulary. After they have—as they say—"completed the program," they repeat once more, "Really quite lovely," or they throw in some ejaculatory prayer, before they turn to leave. Back home they speak in grand tones of what they saw, and they mock those who keep their experience hidden inside their breast by saying, "He doesn't have a feeling for beauty. . . . He shouldn't travel without Baedeker!"

. . . Mist and fog still hang over the mountains; a few hills emerge sleepily from their white veil. It was just half an hour ago that the sea of stars protected its princes, and now the clouds to the east are turning red. On the mountain meadow stir some four-footed beasts; they look at the person passing them with eyes of whose language, since the days of King Solomon, nothing more is known.[43]

The sun shines over to the east. I can't see it but can only sense it. Its rays, breaking through the fog, give a clear sign. Here and there a gap in the wall of clouds opens up, and golden masses of light break through and cast reflections on the snow. This is not the great sunrise of the mountains. Not in the least. But isn't the humble beauty that reveals itself from the east, day in and day out, even more substantial than the quickly passing beauty of an exceptional day?

In *Emanuel Quint,* Gerhart Hauptmann describes in various places how God's holy idiot threw himself down before the setting sun and allowed the ecstasy to fall upon him.[44] Surely this Quint served his God better than those who build special houses to lock him up in because they can't find him in nature. . . . Why do they build churches and chapels in the high mountains? Isn't every mountain a church and every hill a chapel? Hasn't God called out to them, "Heaven is my throne and the earth my footstool? What kind of dwelling can you erect for me? Where is my place of rest?"

You, though, you come into the mountains from far away in search of beauty. After making your way here, aren't you asleep at sunrise? When is the world a beautiful place if not when it appears in its youthful splendor? When are you young if not in the early morning? When is your world so if not at sunrise? Your cows and oxen, animals you call lacking reason, they stand watch. But you, as someone who's been endowed with reason, you sleep. How do you expect to find beauty if you don't seek it out!

A storm rages high up in the mountains! A black wall of clouds looms threateningly over a glacier. Shreds of fog fly and break apart against the crags. The snow in the distance sparkles in a strange darkness, like the ocean swallowing up the last beams of light before a hurricane strikes. In the valley below and in the mountains above, the wind howls. Humans crawl out before the storm like Adam before the voice of God. Water gushes down from heaven as in the days of the Flood. [. . .] A wild army stalks above my head, and the God of the mountains rises up in the storm. "You lonely creature, why do you stand here? Doesn't the thunder call you to repent? Won't the spirits and the elements rise up against you for disrupting them and spying on them in their battle?" No, I will not retreat! For I have come here because of the storm. For you are the chaos now, out of you alone shall the Eternal Will bring renewal. God can be found only in danger. [. . .]

Though we don't know, we shall pave the way for the angel who will

come, so that another Herzl may arise for us, too, the later-born, someone who is complete in his path and can guide his fainthearted brethren.
[. . .]

NOTEBOOK 2

Notes on My Insignificance

November 15, 1914–December 7, 1914

November 15, 1914

Søren Kierkegaard![45] I am looking for him, and I'm finding him! (I've
decided to read Brandes's book on him,[46] though I suspect, without being certain, that Brandes doesn't entirely understand him.) What a seeker
of God! Very few have had such a massive religious feeling as he—
and by this I don't mean piety, or what Brandes calls senseless religiosity. Surely, the only Christians since Jesus himself have been Augustine, Francis of Assisi, maybe Meister Eckhart (though in a very limited
sense), Kierkegaard, and Tolstoy. Paul de Lagarde, David Strauss, and all
the others are nothing more than nuisances.[47] Someone once said that
Kierkegaard has a bit of the Old Testament in him. There may be something to this. He is *absolute,* and that's what makes him so colossal. He
once again dared to make demands that lead to the renewal of the spirit.
He is the death of rationalism. "Christianity is paradoxical," he says. Indeed it is.

In thinking about myself, I'm always comparing myself to him. In one
of his fantasies Kierkegaard said about himself (in the guise of King Solomon), "He was a thinker, but didn't pray; a preacher, but didn't believe;
he could help many others, just not himself." This is spoken directly to
me. I would like to pray, but can't. I notice it every time. Who has seen
me pray in the synagogue? And how? I think and I try. Naturally, I don't
yet deliver the sermons I would like, probably because I don't know what
to preach. But I'm no believer, and this is what's so horrible. I can't utter
the thing that always brings me back to Kierkegaard: his *Credo, quia absur-
dum est.*[48] Where is the God I believe in? Who can give him to me? I
preach Hasidism, mysticism, Buber, and socialism as a new religion. But I
have no idea where the God I speak about dwells. I don't know if he's
there. I can't even say *I believe.* No, I can only hope. *Utinam!*[49]

It's odd that this fellow Kierkegaard was always walking around with plans he failed to carry out. [. . .] He wants to write novelettes and dramas, and then what! Yes, this is what makes his personality so extraordinary. That makes him into an Either-Or Man.

And me? I run around with fantasies. Either I think about Jettka[50] or about my own future (yes, yes, my future!), or I want to do something else. Instead, I can only manage to muster a few thoughts or a title. What have I written until now? Nothing until now on Hasidism. The only exception was the travel impressions I jotted down four months ago. And these impressions are also the only thing that seems to me to have any merit. They aren't mendacious, which is rare for me. I really believe that if I had any genuine poetic talent I would have already serenaded Jettka. My relationship with her was destined to be put into song. This is the way it is. You want to say something and then you realize that you're choking on it, and afterwards it won't come out. At least, it won't with me. The words escape me. And why do I read Stefan George if not to learn the *Word*. The gentlemen from the faculty were right on the mark: I lack a sense of harmony. Youth. With all their pitying scorn, they'd like to carve their judgment into stone. What do they know about my lack of harmony? Herr Professors Meyer and Röhr—philosophers of history! They can have it!

Röhr undoubtedly put his finger on it when he asked me what I know about the philosophy of history. Excepting the philosophies of Hegel, Marx, and Chamberlain, all I know is what I think about all the views of these professors. What is the philosophy of history? It is the attempt to capture the flow of life in an iron box. Just look at the Bible etc. As a Jew I should be closer to the philosophy of history than anyone else. But we have been dragging too much history around with us. We can do without a modern Steinheim or Krochmal.[51] Here's to life! It's good that we don't have to justify ideas and movements out of such opinions, which are the most beloved of all. Socialism and Zionism. One doesn't need historical materialism to justify socialism: personal experience suffices. That one cannot prove Zionism is clear to anyone who has ever felt it. *Dixi*. Phooey on the historical mode of observation!

Kierkegaard had a magnificent experience that governed his entire life: he had a father from whom he not only inherited his abilities but who also influenced him personally, and in the most personal way possible. How mightily he influenced him! I'm of the opinion that without his father he would have been unthinkable. But these days we, or rather I, lack something to give me a goal and direction. As a result I waffle around aimlessly. And there is no one in my immediate vicinity with a stronger mask than mine. I allow myself to be driven about by my choices, and I end up putting one person after another on a throne, only to knock him off again. I don't have someone to lead me, nor can I because I would never have any belief in him, or at least not in his value judgments. And what about a family? As the Hebrews say, God forbid!

Forget my family! Is it my fault I was born into these surroundings? If I had been born as a worker or the son of a poor but ambitious Jew (and who cares if his name is Yitzhak the Rag Dealer) I would have the world at my fingertips. But as it is! Ugh! The fights that are going to break out in our home over the coming years are going to be fun. Either-Or.[52] [. . .]

What shall become of us young Jews if we build our lives upon lies? Do we need such lies? Is it really true that society cannot live without them? Either lies are permitted, or society itself is forbidden! What is a lie? Is it dishonesty against oneself or against others? To be dishonest to yourself is without question mendacious (and this is, among us Jews, a very important point: honesty directed against ourselves. Jewish humor). What about deceiving others? Jews not only trick others commercially but also pull the wool over other people's eyes in their attitude. They scream out and play the hypocrite with feelings they don't even possess. And then they go around peddling their insolence and want other people to reward them for it. What a lovely lot they are! [. . .]

"On the Psychology of Socialism," Herr Dr. Oppenheimer's article in *Der neue Rundschau,* is outstanding.[53] A bit later I'll compile a list of all his philosophies of history; for now I'll just say this: as he said quite rightly, utopia is the reality of tomorrow! And reality is yesterday's utopia. [. . .]

It's amusing how this publication promotes a racial theory that Oppenheimer demolishes. For me this is new proof that Montaigne's mother was a Spanish Jewess, just as Saenger claims someone has proven.[54] This is the source of his tolerance!

[. . .] Here I sit and read in my cloud-cuckoo-land. I have to read because I have nothing besides my ruminations. What good do they do me? Everyone has an awful lot of respect for me—as someone who's highly educated, and other such lovely things that may even be true (and what does it mean to be educated? To know more than what's written in the headlines?). But for me, none of this matters. I'm incapable of attaining nature or freedom or life (and I don't even think they would help). I thirst after life, but where can it be found? [. . .] Now I sit on a pupil's stool, later I'll go on to the university. And life? I may really end up studying philosophy, which is the rape of life. If I had a good spirit, a guardian angel, I would beseech it to protect me from this. And yet sometimes I still believe that a good bit of life hides away in books. I've certainly gleaned a lot from books such as the Bible, *Zarathustra,*[55] and piles of wonderful poems to life by seekers like Buber, Jakobsen, Sudermann, and last but not least Frenssen (even if people consider him passé, as if one can outgrow longing).[56] This is the very reason I've never learned a thing from writers such as Anatole France[57] and the myriad of other so-called classical writers who've stopped seeking, even if they've made, and still make, a mighty impression on me. Blüher's *Wandervögel,* hardly a book by a first-class genius, has obviously given me a lot through its immeasurable youthful longing for Romanticism and the enormous lust for destruction.[58] What is my goal? I made my way to Rilke[59] and Stefan George. I believe in all things that have yet to be uttered, and above all I believe that "I am the one, and I am both."[60] That is my goal. Maybe I should thank God (which God?) that I haven't yet achieved it. [. . .]

Through our long wanderings we've lost everything except the Tantra and the money sack (and sometimes they are the same things). We've left God out in the cold. How does Dehmel put it? "It's a beautiful wild world."[61] We are unable to find this. We know too much about the world. Regrettably. We are no longer innocent. Sun, sun, who will give us some sun? "Blessed is he who comes in the name of the Lord" (Ps. 118:26). "And he will give us the sun."

It is our fate
Never to rest.[62]

Was Hölderlin a Jew? Is this line to be found in a song by Ahasver?[63] No! How then could he have written something like this? With these words he chose sides. No wonder he went mad. Only the Jew can put up with *life*. What about Nietzsche? He too gave himself up to blessed lunacy.[64] Why didn't we go crazy 1,500 years ago? If we had, we would have spared the world and ourselves a great deal of evil! [. . .]

I've been at Tauber's, who's still only permitted to get up at night. After talking about it back and forth for ages, and after an ocean of words, I've returned again to Judaism. [. . .] I spoke to Tauber about the beauty of our customs. How lucky are those who grow up in a household where tradition is lived out in a meaningful way! Is there anything more beautiful than a Friday evening? What kind of impact the two menorahs must make on a sensitive soul, lit in a festive chamber, and with the father with his head covered, the cup lifted up to heaven. Or when the mother stretches out her hands to bless the candlelight. That is *our* beauty. If our Seder evening isn't beautiful, what is? I showed Tauber that it's precisely these ceremonious observances, this patriarchal simplicity, which makes such a mighty impression on me. He considered what I said too binding. I put forth my view of the Torah as the national law of a people. But there is no renewal with him. And I seek it so much. [. . .]

I imagine its being so beautiful one day to introduce my children to our much maligned—and by the Orthodox so terribly misused—rituals. As evening approaches my wife lights the candles and says the blessing over them. When I arrive home I lay my hands on their tiny heads, black as the night, and say the blessings. This is a Jewish Friday evening. No one who earnestly seeks renewal can leave out beauty. [. . .] I'm fantasizing again. When will I finally stop creating heaven on earth in my dreams? When will I finally step into quotidian realities? People often say that the true poet can experience daily life as a gift from God and has no need for the "uplifting of the soul." This is the romanticism of the bourgeoisie, as Stefan Zweig has said so correctly of Dickens. He has tried demonstrating this, for instance, in *Stories from the Land of Children*[65] and "Burning Secret."[66] Superb.

I read *Werther*.[67] I like the book, which I certainly didn't expect. There are very beautiful things in it, and not only about God and the world but especially about youth. I certainly like Goethe. He's a rebel. Oh, what a superior kind of rebellion Werther communicates! This is a Wyneken of 150 years ago. [. . .]

Because of the victory at Kutno (with 28,000 prisoners taken!) there was no school today, only a celebration.[68] [. . .] I finished reading *Werther*, and it made a mighty impact on me. The translations of Ossian's songs at the end are wonderful and of far greater value than Klopstock's collection of songs.[69] This book is in fact miraculous. [. . .]

I'm reading the Bible. There is no book in this entire world I read more. Each time it hits me with something fresh. This is the reason I nearly always return to the same passages. My favorites are the Second Isaiah; the beginning of Isaiah; the Torah; and some passages from the prophets, such as Jeremiah etc. But the Second Isaiah hovers above them all. I'd like to call him the prophet of our renewed Judaism. His enormous personal religiosity and these wonderful images serve as a symbol for us all. Is there anything that approaches the beauty of the passage "Who is he who comes from Edom?" or of the two final chapters (Isaiah 65:17)? "Behold, I will create a new heaven and a new earth. The former things will not be remembered, nor will they come to mind."

This is the most beautiful saying in the entire Book of Isaiah. It contains the entire future of coming generations and all their promises. I'm finding that I get much more out of the Bible than any Orthodox Jew. The reason for this must be—as Buber says—because I understand and honor it as a subject, rather than an object, of religiosity. To take the Bible as an object would be terrible! By contrast, true pleasure and beauty is to allow the personality and the people's extraordinary fullness of God to work on you. Where can you find a book of such longing? I'm hoping to find one in Lao-tzu, if in a very different way. And what's so wonderful about *Zarathustra?* The other books I know by Nietzsche, *The Anti-Christ,* the book on Wagner, and the *Untimely Meditations,* failed to make the slightest impression on me.[70] Yet *Zarathustra* is in fact a new Bible, regardless of what one thinks about the ideas it propounds. To write something like it is my ideal. That's it! But who can write a *Zarathustra* of the Jews or a *Hilligenlei* of a modern Jew (in the deep sense of the word)?[71] For the last six months I've done nothing but try to get a total perspective on the different kinds of poetic longing. This is the reason I traded the Agudah for Buber and why I'm now checking out Tolstoy and the like. I've even looked into Mauthner, whose *Critique of Language* contains a great deal of religious longing for something new, not-yet-experienced, and not-yet-heard-of, a longing for, shall I say, a new synthesis.[72] This is also the reason why someday I'll have to take up philosophy seriously, just as I'll need to read up on Romanticism and above all Novalis.[73] Peter Hille called him the "Goethe of the soul," and Karl Joel can't say enough about him.[74] All of this gives me grounds for ascribing to Goethe the quality of longing. But in general I'm going to need a much wider and freer perspective.

This evening I'll study Gemara Schir with Bleichrode.[75] I'm eager to know what he'll say when he finds out I'm no longer Orthodox. Still, I'm going with a good conscience, and not because of religion but to learn the Talmud thoroughly. And whoever wishes to do so has to go to the Orthodox. Strack also studied with Israel Hildesheimer.[76] I go as a friend of the Talmud, not a spy or an enemy, otherwise I'd certainly never listen and engage in a discussion of the "firstborn who fell into a hole" (Beza, section 3). I have one year behind me, and 27 folio pages! Yes, this business is far from easy, even if I've learned a great deal from Bleichrode. If only all my friends had my energy in penetrating Jewish literature instead of allowing others to fritter away their time. If you want a thing done, do it yourself. If I had the energy I'd write this diary in Hebrew. *I will write in the language of our forefathers.*[77][. . .]

November 18, 1914

[. . .] By order from above, it seems there were special services today, even in the Catholic churches and synagogues. On the way back I heard the bells ringing from Saint Michael's church. Thoughts turned to the likelihood of a World to Come. Sometimes I really don't know what to think about it. Anyway, I don't believe in it. It's not impossible; it simply doesn't matter. We were created for this earth, and we've denied ourselves of it for far too long. If there is a just God, what can he say against someone who seeks him here on earth and not in some irrational or imaginary crystal ball? I of course don't go along with the people who dismiss the belief in the World to Come as mere pessimism or flight from the earth. Jewish rationalism is obviously optimistic and yet still adheres to this belief, or at least claims to do so. Nietzsche tripped up on this point, unless of course he wanted everything for our world and detected in the idea of a World to Come traces of world-flight and world-dissatisfaction, which he immediately fought against. I'm of the opinion that the World to Come is the object of our longing; it is perfection and fulfillment, and as such, it's hardly a bad or even pessimistic notion.

There's a difference between a "Preacher of Death"[78] and a preacher of the Beyond. These days, at least as far as I can tell, the idea of the

World to Come is synonymous with the idea of eternal life of the soul or the spirit, or that which we cannot explain. He who admits to one cannot deny the other, and if you say A, you have to say B. Or at least this is the case when you see the soul as a mythological monster with terrifying powers and gigantic wings, great talents, and just a dash of consciousness. In *my* opinion the soul is that which exists between things—that which communicates to me the impression and knowledge of things. When I see Theodor Herzl's picture hanging opposite me I have the impression of "Theodor Herzl," along with certain memories and associations. At some point along this material transmission there is something "between-the-things" that itself cannot be identified as a material force. It may be a force we humans lack the ability to recognize. Moreover, this "something" doesn't operate mechanically, as a very large percentage of our perceptions—I suspect it's a majority—never reach us, which is to say, they never reach the remarkable site where our mythological "Self" resides, the place where perceptions are registered and are taken up into the possession of the "Self." [. . .]

November 19, 1914

I read an awful portrayal of the proletarian life of Jews, Juschkewitsch's novel *Ghetto.*[79] Misery and death stare out with glassy eyes from these pages, and the author's laconic remarks are even more terrifying and devastating than the speeches of Zipla and Jerochim. If everyone knew that his description of blind Jerochim's misery isn't fictional, he would shudder before this corpse, this uncanny cadaver of the nation, this degeneration. Oh if only it's not too late to give them and us new blood and new life! The hour is very late indeed. What would I say and what would be my facial expression if I were to come into such a proletarian family and learn firsthand about these people and their suffering? [. . .]

Mauthner describes our highest objective to be pioneers of godlessness. If Jewish history had any objective, he says, this may be it. If not exactly godlessness, transferring heaven to earth certainly wouldn't do us any harm. Our forefathers thought this way, too. When you don't have your own place on earth—as has been the case during our Exile—it's understandable when someone projects his own personal heaven into Heaven. [. . .] Give us the earth back, ye gods and men! You've taken it away from us long enough. We want our property back! . . . Is it foolish to expect an answer? . . . We believe that we'll get one soon, in our lifetime—and from a God who dwells behind our houses or an angel hovering above us. Soon, and in our days. . . .

November 21, 1914

[. . .] Werner's friend Jansen was killed in action. [. . .] The old men should be shipped off to war. They can kill one another if they want, they just shouldn't rob youth of its blood, which is a vicious act against the future of society. We shouldn't tolerate it. But the youth think "you have to go along," otherwise you're a contemptible coward. Of course you can't fight against this. What is the stupidity of the gods measured against the slyness of men?

November 23, 1914

[. . .] It's taking me a long time to do, but in the end I'll convince Heymann of the madness of Wellhausen's historiography.[80] He told me he's beginning to agree with me that Wellhausen's hypothesis is a product of scientific anti-Semitism and Christian insolence. On the one hand, Wellhausen wants to date the rise of Judaism as recently as possible, while on the other, he puts Judaism in as poor a light as he can vis-à-vis the New Testament. I've found the most elegant and decisive evidence of this in these Christian theologians' so-called "history of the religion of old Israel." It's absolutely shameful. Now that I've completed the first stage, I'll go on to acquaint Heymann with my view of the creation of the Bible. I'm really enjoying myself. [. . .]

November 26, 1914

It's absurd to write a journal like this—like a chronicle, like something out of *Werther,* or ruminations from Berthold Auerbach.[81] It deserves to be hung up in the lavatory. What do these idiotic daily events have to do with my life if they don't have any special meaning for me? [. . .]

At least Experience still exists. Yes, at least you can still have experiences these days. What is vital is personality, not strife and foolish discussion, or in the German philosophic parlance, "speaking-round-the-object." Three cheers for August Strindberg! Till now I've read only his *Abu Casem's Slippers,*[82] which is all well and good, but now here's something else: *The Gothic Room* with its fin-de-siècle scenes. [. . .] What Strindberg says in this book is Life itself: from beginning to end, it's Life. There's not a trace of vacuous style and bathetic pondering, just Life. It's mysticism as revolution. He has grasped the nonsense of a "world mechanism without a mechanic." The book stimulates anthropological myths and dreams of God; for "freethinkers," it's more dangerous than Bergson, Buber, and their ilk all rolled into one. I'm going to devour his novel. I've been caught up in a storm. It's a new *Hilligenlei*. It's a *deed*.

"To my people," says the voice of a messenger, "Woe unto those who have sucked up culture and education into their rankling hearts, who have introduced education to their nation, and who have caused ruin and death to their brothers. Your God calls out that if you wish to die, you should continue on this path, ever farther, all the way to the gates of perdition. Woe unto those who seek to take their nation, standing as it is on the grave's edge, and enliven it with education. You will never succeed, says the Spirit, and your hands will rot. For you have robbed my people of creative power, stripping them of their blessed certainty of God." Thus speaks the God of coming generations. "I wish to curse those who lead my people into bewilderment by seducing them onto an ignoble path. I will make no peace with the educated," says my God.

Stay far from the altars of culture, you peoples and nations who desire to remain healthy in body and soul. Their ways are not your ways, and a holy war is now in the works against them. O you from the house of Israel, this is your mortal disease: that you partake too much in education, and too much from the evil ways of the people around you. Be what you once were. Be natural, which alone can bring you salvation and redemption. "Cursed be he who desires to give this nation the blessings of culture and who leads it astray from its straight path. And the entire nation says, Amen."

You are Orientals and not Europeans; you are Jews and humans, not Germans and degenerates, and your God is named *Ha-Shem*[83] and not the belly. It is because of this that you should not wander onto their path. What for you is light is for them darkness, and what for you is holy they consider an abomination. God says that you've had your fill of Europe and you should get out. Don't you have enough within yourself that you have to borrow from strangers and forge your weapons with your enemies? It has been your doom that you haven't been able to use your own heaven against the sun's rays breaking through from a foreign world. You are bankrupt. Even worse, you've made compromises. As the saying goes, if you ram your head into a wall, the head suffers the consequences!

We of the coming generation think that what's needed is to rouse ourselves, allowing something new to sprout out of fertile ground. We believe that we must ram our heads against the wall, and that the wall, not our heads, will split asunder.

As we see things, he who holds the former opinion is assimilated, and he who holds the latter a Zionist (someone who crashes into walls, who's a fanatic).

We maintain that a people can remain alive only to the degree that it knows nothing of culture. Decadence and culture are synonyms. Hanukkah is the festival honoring fanatics who first rammed their heads into the wall and were victorious. They were complete men who weren't decadent because they had their own heaven with which to counter Greek civilization, and at a time when the Greeks had already lost their way!!

Our task is to leave European culture behind, in its repellent sense, and to create over there, where our hearts are, a true nation free of lies and deception. Our task is to bring to completion a deed, a redemptive deed (and only deeds can redeem). It is to ram our heads into the wall, and to know (not only believe) that the wall will come crashing down. "If only you desire it"[84] are words of heroic desire bequeathed to us by the man who has given our movement but one thing (and he gave it unconsciously, for what he gave us consciously we can't do anything with). To inspire actions for the sake of our people, he told us to desire.

We as a people believe that the Messiah will arrive after all Jews are gathered again in the land of their fathers (or the other way around, after the Messiah comes, all will be gathered together). Yes, the moment every single one of us has performed the deed—and once we all have forced back the night because the morning beckons—the Savior will come as a sign and seal, and he will speak of what has been achieved, pointing the way to a new future. The deed itself is not the Messiah, but he will come by virtue of the deed. It may be that the new heaven and new Jerusalem will find a new God, a renewed God. The glory of God wanders with his people, and *his glory* changes with his people.

We do not wish to be the generation that perishes in the wilderness. We want to see the Holy Land from the hills of longing. We wander in darkness, though we believe in the light behind the forest-covered mountains. Where is the angel that leads us, and where is God's messenger who directs us? We are tired of wandering; it has been too long; and we've lost everything of value along the way. Our forefathers beheld a heaven and the stars. They did not stumble along the way; they knew their goal, which was God. But we—we have lost everything for the sake of strangers and the laws of the goyim. . . . Yes, a foolish generation that doesn't know its way or direction is Israel's future and her hope. This accounts for our disparate aims.

Aestheticism! Oh this word, an abyss on whose opposite side is nothingness. Aestheticism, by which of course is meant self-conscious aestheticism, is the dying man's last shivers and final attempt at life. Every natural nation is in its very essence aesthetic. But a cultivated and decadent nation has lost this natural aestheticism, and as a result—as with everything one lacks—it becomes a science, the science of aesthetics (or just look at the "Science of Judaism"!!). This is evil because in life the word "the" can no longer appear; it disappears. New standards must be discovered in order to name what is new. This is the method of Marx Brod and his comrades.[85] They are worshippers of ugliness as a result of coquettishness and the need to be original. Sometimes it's tragic when someone truly desires life only to arrive at aesthetics. Hofmannsthal,[86] Nietzsche, George. It's a disaster, also called a *Kismet*.[87] God spare us from aesthetics! [. . .]

November 27, 1914

[. . .] God protect us from the scientific study of the Talmud! They take everything away from us, and we're stupid enough to bravely help them do it. Oh this systemization! We should just kill off these Jewish systemmakers who use the European method. They want to examine the Talmud "scientifically" because they are no long able to study it properly.

[. . .] We are the coming generation into whose hands everything has been given. We are the future. We are different, completely different, from those who preceded us. We have made our decisions, and we've made no compromises. We charge into walls. The deed depends on us alone, no one else. Excuses count for nothing. *B'lewav Scholem b'chol nefesh'cho.*[88] We refuse to put on costumes and organize Zionist congresses. [. . .]

Are we the generation that will die in the wilderness? We don't want to be. Before we exit this earth we want to see the Holy Land. We will take care that this land once again becomes holy, a Promised Land in the true sense of the word. [. . .]

With Nietzsche we say that the child's land is the land of the future.[89] The future is not to be measured or oriented according to what has been. Indeed, we have our ancestors' blood within us, and this blood gives us enough historical connectedness. There shall be no return to Judaism, which would be the romanticism of decay. This here is a great and earnest danger for Zionism. We seek not the old but a mysticism that is young and that was born with us. We'll let Europe keep its Strindberg. Ours is a new and uncharted path. Where is our Moses? We, the bewildered sheep from the House of Israel, need one. *The myth of exile!* Exile will have to become for us a myth. And we will allow the philosophers to decide whether we will take this myth, which was born in exile, along with us.

Today's mood is like in the days of Jesus of Nazareth. A new hero is coming (his name just mustn't be Hermann Cohen).[90] [. . .]

November 29, 1914

[. . .] I paged through Tolstoy's *Confession,*[91] I'll read it next week. I'm anticipating the book with enormous excitement and desire. I can't say whether his picture of Jesus will become mine, or rather whether his view will change mine. He makes it difficult, extremely so, to be a Christian, which puts him in the league of very few others. He's one of the chosen. Tolstoy has a marvelous understanding of the essence of Christ's teaching. That one should not resist evil he shows to be the key to the Gospel. He too recognized that "only one thing is needful."[92] I finally have proof that Jesus said so; until now I've only guessed that he had. All of this awoke in me thoughts on early Christianity. I'll have to try to differentiate and clarify early Christianity more. Wasn't in fact Christianity, in its mystical understanding, a progressive force in its time? Is it not the renewal of the prophetic call for the uncompromising life? How can I militate against anti-Semitic tendencies of biblical scholarship when it also seeks to present the Christianity of the New Testament as a revolution against atrophy? It's a very difficult issue I'll have to look into more closely. [. . .]

December 4, 1914

[. . .] I discussed the Bible and Jewish racial pride with Briese.[93] As someone who understands the thought patterns of Orthodoxy better than anyone else, I really think I can appreciate these issues. I'm able to understand that the notion that the Bible has a divine origin isn't at all stupid. Why do people laugh their heads off when they read Genesis? It contains simple, ordinary tales. "This stuff" is celebrated as having come from

God! Today's "intellectuals" know better. They say that God would surely have come up with other stories besides shepherd yarns and peasants' tales. From here they go beyond poking fun at the origins of the Bible to ridicule the Bible itself. People have forgotten how to read the Bible. It's in every home and on every bookshelf, yet no one reads it. For the first time in history it's "outdated." No one can be bothered with it. But the way people treat this book is silly and perverse. I would love to teach people to read the Bible for its own sake and not for dogma—and for the sake of men who will have to give up so much because of the Bible. In my mind the biblical stories are the mightiest kinds of myths, the likes of which no other nation has ever created.

What does the Book of Genesis teach us? It reveals the greatest discovery a human can make, which is the divinity of daily life. This is the reason why it's not at all stupid to deny humans the ability to come up with such myths, and to see God as their primeval source. These tales recount not monumental things but completely normal everyday life with a few festive interruptions. That is what's so fabulous about them. They present common life as being truly divine and ideal. Beauty is uncovered from amid endless repetition. In Genesis the reason we still read about simple peasants and commoners with such relish is that they are always surrounded by the divine glow. No other nation on earth has ever thought to bring heaven down to earth and to recapture it in daily life. The greatest men our nation has ever produced are these unknown poets who first composed myths as parables for all humanity. What kind of uncommon and uncanny loveliness and depth inhabit the holiday myths? There is surely more in the first nine chapters of the Bible than in many entire libraries and literatures—not in science and scholarship, but in sublime beauty and the primal power of imagination. No other nation can easily match this wonderfully complete world-myth that we've created. Till now no one has. Is there anything more beautiful than the famous story of Jacob wrestling with God? Volumes are contained within these five verses; they are truly packed with content. Genesis is one of a kind.

Children live in the Tao. They always do the right thing out of inner compulsion, without cogitation. All children believe in a personal God. With trust they talk to him, and they would never dream to question his existence. This is really quite unusual, and the Sophists could use this as a

proof for the existence of God. Only in school, when the child falls under the discipline of adults and when he learns systematically to tell lies,
does he begin to doubt. There are ten-year-old atheists out there, which
is no laughing matter. These are the ones who have suffered deeply and
who know what it means to have a God snatched from their hands. A
child can quickly imagine the most difficult and abstract things. He
imagines God as a friendly old man who spanks him if he is naughty and
who lives with him according to a kind of contract. Every child has an
Old Testament view of God.

Children are the greatest creators of myths of all. They have the immaculate conception. You can't disprove anything to a child. Jesus would
have become famous alone for saying, "If you are not like these children,
you will not inherit the Kingdom of God." We have lost our childhood.
Shall we seek it out? [. . .]

The Liebknecht affair in the Reichstag has stirred enormous anger
everywhere, though no one wants to admit it and prefers to make him
look ridiculous.[94] Upon hearing about it I said at once to Jahr that
he must have his reasons. Someone then interrupted me angrily and
snapped, "Nonsense!" When I go home today I'll get a letter from
Werner containing as a postscript a tribute to Liebknecht as the only
honest man in the German parliament. I'm supposed to give Werner his
address so he can send his tribute to him. [. . .]

Werner writes that there's a great deal of anti-Semitism in the party,
even if no one's aware of it. This interested me a great deal. It really made
me think. I don't know which circles Werner means, the proletarians or
their leaders, though I suspect it's the former. This is definitive proof for
the correctness of Zionist teachings. The Jews get kicked out of everything, even if they were the first and most involved. And it doesn't matter
whether it's with the capitalists or the workers. [. . .]

December 7, 1914

[. . .] Stefan George's *Star of the Covenant* is extremely tough going but
sumptuous. He too has the ethos "Only one thing is needful." Has he
studied Swedenborg?[95] His conception of women is astoundingly similar
to what Swedenborg wrote about marriage. He speaks of the temple of
material. Man is spirit, the woman material. [. . .] I'm having doubts on
mysticism and on Martin Buber's conception of Judaism. Is everything

really so spiritual and celestial as one would like to think? Or is this just prattle? I'm in a severe crisis and everything is vanishing from under my feet.

NOTEBOOK 3

From the Workshop of the Spirit

Winter 1914–15 to May 21, 1915

January 4, 1915

[. . .] Today I've discovered another genuine human being: Arthur Bonus![96] He's someone who came up with the doctrine of myth before Buber, a man of integrity who can justifiably call himself a German. I'll have to see if I can get a hold of his key book on religiosity. I came across some of his aphorisms in his small book *German Belief* published by Diederichs Verlag,[97] with the epilogue defining the editors' notion of "German faith." As far as I can see, however, there's nothing "German" about it. It's all the purest and most cosmopolitan mysticism—and in our time!! And it can't be anything but this. Religious souls from all the nations have taught the same thing, which is also the doctrine found in Lagarde, Fichte, and similar minds. What's specifically German in all this is not the crowning idea—for this is the same everywhere, as the fundamental experience is the same—but rather the substructure, the path the thinker takes. But this is what the book's editors have left out. They shouldn't pretend as if what they offer in their books is something inseparable from the nation. Fichte's manner of thought is no doubt very different from Buber's (I don't know him!), though at the end they meet, as well they must. At its apex, national thinking overcomes the national spirit. The highest fruit of every nation is cosmopolitanism, while to be cosmopolitan requires you to have a national substructure. Some other Asian thinker or mystic could just as easily have thought up the ideas of Lao-tzu, which are not national-Chinese. When I write a book on Jewish mysticism, I won't describe the *Siwwuga* as a specifically Jewish-Zoharian doctrine.[98] *Siwwug* is the ultimate crown of the Zohar's intellectual system and as such is present among other nations, which indeed is the case in Oriental thought, Sufism, German mysticism, and so on, while the substructure, such as *Zimzum,* is Jewish.[99] [. . .]

[. . .] I've been reading Vischer, Strindberg, and some others. Vischer has made the greatest imaginable impression on me.[100] He has the magnificent idea—which he doesn't even state openly—that the world was created not by God, who doesn't exist, but by the devil. Yesterday this inspired my speculation into the religiosity in German literature and elsewhere, including inside myself.

It's now obvious that I don't believe in a personal God, even less in a being embodying the idea of morality! My God is but an ideal generated by dreams of a fulfilled human life. I can no longer believe in unchanging moral laws. Over the past century the old heaven has been so completely torn to bits that it's now gone forever. I view the development something like this: following a period of Romanticism that still propped up the old dreams, there have been two major periods of attack, followed by a transition. The first one is represented mainly by three names: Schopenhauer, Karl Marx, and Max Stirner,[101] whereby Stirner can be substituted with Comte, Hegel, or Saint-Simon (who shouldn't be underestimated). Schopenhauer was the one who murdered the absolute God. It's just as Nietzsche said: God is utterly dead, even if his murderer limited himself to metaphysics. Marx, the mightiest, most calamitous, and most important man of all, is next in line. By destroying the old heaven for the masses, Marx has forced on them his new religion. Marx, like no one after him and only Stirner before him, paid no attention to heaven and hell. And Stirner, who unlike Marx and Schopenhauer does not number among the most influential attackers of the Pearly Gates, is unknown, even though he's the one who said the horrifying Kaddish[102] for the deceased God.

All three men agree that their task, the essence of their revolt against heaven, is to use reason to snatch heaven away from people. In any event, it seems to me that a common thread runs through the last forty years, after which a second generation—Strindberg, Nietzsche, and Ibsen—came on the scene to rattle heaven with their romanticism. For the upper classes they created a lot more stir in the dubious region of heaven than the other three. Next come Søren Kierkegaard and Tolstoy, two giants who, no doubt unwittingly, destroyed heaven through their deep religiosity. We today have nothing left of the heaven of the past. Proof? Henri Bergson, Stefan George, and Jakob Wassermann.[103] [. . .]

Our guiding principle is revolution! Revolution everywhere! We don't want reform or reeducation but revolution or renewal. We desire to absorb revolution into our innermost souls. There are external and internal revolutions, the former mainly aimed at family and home. We are "enthusiasts" and "provocateurs" like few others. We should be revolutionaries and always and everywhere say who we are, what we are, and what we want. For the sake of Judah we want to fight it out with our foes. Above all, we want to revolutionize Judaism. We want to revolutionize Zionism and to preach anarchism and freedom from all authority. We will go to battle against all autocrats and all other miserable miscreants! We wish to rip away the formalistic facade from Zionism.

In doing so we've arrived at Herzl, but only taking from him the force of his personality. We reject him. He's *to blame* for today's Zionism— a movement that instead of going forward looks backwards, an organization of shopkeepers that grovels in the dust before the powerful! Zionism is *Mauschel!!*[104] It has taken up the Jewish problem merely as a form instead of in its inner essence. Its only thought has been the Jewish *state*. We preachers of anarchism reject this. We don't want a state. We want a free society, and Herzl's *Old-New Land* hasn't a thing to do with this![105] We as Jews know more than enough about the hideous idol called the state than to bow down and offer up prayers to it once again, nor will we deliver up our progeny to be willing sacrifices to its insatiable greed for possession and power. We Jews are not a people of the state, nor are people from the other nations. We do not wish to go to Palestine to found a state, thereby forging new chains out of the old. O you miserable little philistines! We want to go to Palestine out of a thirst for freedom and longing for the future. The future belongs to the Orient. [. . .]

January 23, 1915

[. . .] Our Zionism is the doctrine of ramming ourselves headlong into walls. It is the doctrine of revolutionizing the Orient. It is the loftiest teaching of anarchism out there. In the greatest possible way we insist that the Zionist deed take precedence before organizational speeches. This means that we demand emigration to the Orient, if possible to Palestine. We reject whatever there is of Europe within us because it's not total. People may mock us as doctrinaire, an insult we gladly accept. In times such as ours it's a bitter necessity to be doctrinaire. That is to say, we need a race of men to educate themselves for the sake of a principle and for the future. [. . .]

It's the Kaiser's birthday. I'm up again after lying in bed the entire day, and I can now descend back into human landscapes. The Kaiser's birthday doesn't cheer or move me in the slightest. I'm not touched at all. After all is said and done, the man is one of the best out there, as I believe in his honest intentions (just not in his abilities). He's not to blame for everything. He's no genius and can't do much more than repeat tired phrases and bore people with his eternal God, whom he always has by his side. He has this disgusting habit. You don't boast about such things, it only rubs against the grain in today's pagan state. [. . .]

Martin Buber, the man we'll be talking about this evening,[106] is next to Ahad Haam contemporary Zionism's most important personality and one of the movement's greatest spiritual forces. He was the first one to proclaim a Zionism of tomorrow, a Zionism of both inner and outer revolution. [. . .] I believe that today his victory has been decided. He has the youth on his side, for he has articulated in his writings their deepest longing. His ideas are being compared as equal to Herz's, Zollschan's,[107] and Ahad Haam's.

What lies behind his victory, however, is neither the youth nor our contemporary juncture in history, or whatever else one may point to; it is Buber himself. His entire focus has been directed at uncovering within the spiritual heritage of Judaism—and even more so within its deepest longing—the possibility of "renewal," in particular religious renewal. His discovery of Hasidism was for western Europe something of monumental importance, because Hasidism is the most outstanding example of religious revolution and of Jewish mysticism. Within Judaism, a religion that has hitherto been the quintessential religion of rationalism and of the spirit of calculation, he has discovered the irrational emotions and desires that are the mother of renewal. He has presented us with deep and wonderful conceptions of the essence of Judaism, and he has uncovered the deep streams of inner connection that bring us together with other creative peoples of the Orient. And where others have seen only death and decay, he has seen life and rebirth; where others saw graves, he has seen resurrection. Slowly, over a long process of maturation and after much pondering and searching, he has become what he is today: a voice calling out in the wilderness, a prophet of a God who has yet to be born. [. . .]

Snow swirls down in front of my window in minutely small flakes. The smaller snowflakes put up resistance: they don't want to sink down, though they must. They are being pulled down. Earth is a snowflake's destiny. Or the wind is. For snow, fate is an unknown, inexplicable, and "terrestrial" power. I can apply this to humans. Snowflakes don't believe in eternal life. Nor is there any reason—besides megalomania, which is hardly a strong argument—why we should think differently. Yes, we're no better than snowflakes. We also put up resistance when we plunge into an unexpected abyss, and we also melt. We are snowflakes with a bit more distinction. They probably have as little reason as we do.

Rationality is a longing desire without any reality whatsoever. Reason is a stupid man's longing. These people think that in the messianic age everything will be rational. God forbid! I just had a lovely dream of the future. In the messianic age everything shall be humane to the highest degree. This is rational. Everyone can be rational, but the Messiah is something exceptional. He is irrational. [. . .]

To Theodor Herzl

He was the first to pronounce the words
That lifted us to the heights of light,
He was the first to dare a new world
That rose unsuspected before our eyes!

He preceded us with steps that gladly moved ahead
And showed untrodden paths to those in doubt!
To us who suffered from the past in dread
He pointed to a better springtime, a new way out!

He spoke for those who had repressed their longing
And for those devoured by silent grief,
And they all bowed their heads, now belonging
To him who had come to slake their disbelief.

We shall never forget what it was he meant,
Who gave us this dream so rich, so glowing,
And who restored what we had once possessed
And what we had lost—without our knowing![108]

March 25, 1915

[. . .] Today Liebknecht was drafted into the militia. Great fun. [. . .]

I am falling ever more into the arms of nihilism. For quite some time now I have no longer believed that my friends have honest intentions toward me. Türkischer, Heymann, Czapski, Klein, Levy, and his cohorts (not including Horowitz!) look at me as inferior and in a certain sense crazy.[109] Every time I see them I have powerful doubts about my Zionist effectiveness and my work for the future. They wouldn't mind getting rid of me altogether, if they could only pin something on me from a Zionist standpoint. They can't, God knows they can't. Still, I'm no believer. I have to admit to myself: I no longer believe in anything, not God, the world, parents, family, friends (girlfriends!!), or any ideological and material humbug. [. . .]

March 27, 1915

[. . .] This afternoon my brother Erich arrived home from Ghent.[110] May God protect him! Arthur S., Mr. Big Shot, was overjoyed.[111] This year there won't be a Seder meal, as Herr Scholem says he's "had enough of Judaism." He's always talking about his plan, the minute the war's over (why not right away?), to cut his ties with the Jewish community that can find a place in its ranks for such a young good-for-nothing as me. Regrettably, this is just empty sound and fury. He'll never expose himself to a boycott by leaving. Lord knows I wouldn't stop him. [. . .]

April 4, 1915

[. . .] Today I've read the entire Gospel of Mark, and it made quite an impression on me. There are wonderful things in it, despite its being so totally muddled. I'm going to read the other three Gospels so I can have the subject at my fingertips. (In Jewish circles there's a total lack of decent knowledge of the New Testament.) Perhaps then I'll have a clearer idea of Buber's justification for his interpretation of early Christian sects.[112] There are some things I simply can't grasp, above all the Gospel of Mark's extraordinary emphasis on driving out demons. Along with Jesus' words, the author pushes it into the foreground. With great relish he lists all the cases of it, with the other miracles taking a backseat. It would be good if I had a different translation in a modern language. Luther's translation makes it ten times harder to understand. [. . .]

May 8, 1915

For the first time in ages I'm back in the mood for Buber. I'm in a deep Buber spirit. I've been toying with the idea of writing him a long letter. What will come of it?

Since I've started attending lectures at the university I've often had exceedingly productive moods and days. At some point I'll have to start finally jotting down the fragments of my philosophical musings. This could be of some help to me in my spiritual concentration. [. . .]

Italy is now on everyone's mind in Berlin. Everyone, myself included, is convinced that war is imminent. Everyone is cursing. What's the point? A German U-boat just sank the *Lusitania*.[113] I feel but a light shudder and horror at the German barbarians who celebrate attacking and furtively torpedoing a ship as an act of heroism! It's good to have Buber around for such an occasion. [. . .]

May 15, 1915

[. . .] Recently I've been greatly inspired in my spirit, and I've been full of ideas that are not merely for the present moment. One of these days I should compose a monumental essay for *Der Neue Rundschau* titled "Martin Buber: A Chapter from the Depths." Given my comprehensive study of *all* his writings and dealings, I should be able to come up with a detailed portrait. Besides the introduction, I'd write on Bergson, Landauer, Joel, Simmel: contemporary mysticism and Judaism's role in it;[114] and on his spiritual predecessors, who in Judaism are the Baal Shem and Luria (whereas in philosophy it's mainly Søren Kierkegaard, who even had the doctrine of Decision). Next in line would be a description of Zionist and spiritual conditions: formalism, evolutionism, and racial theory. In contrast to these, we have Buber's "renewal" and his Zionist activities. This would be the place to bring in his philosophy, and not only *Daniel* but also his books on the Jews and, last but not least, his introduction to *Ecstatic Confessions*.[115] Then comes Buber's teaching of myth as the most essential form of knowledge of the world; his attempt to describe the mythic materials among mostly unknown peoples; and his description of the Jewish myth. (Is he an accomplice to Berdyzevsky's collection of Jewish tales?)[116] Next we have the Chinese myth of Chuang-tzu, Finnish mythology, and Celtic mythology, all of which point to a seminal study in which Buber will give a complete synthesis of his work. I'll also add a note on his position on the World War, which is deduced from his glorification of the Self. An example is, "The decisions of war come to those / who today your heart beats through."[117] This is written entirely in the spirit of *Daniel*. Finally, there's Buber's influence on the coming generation of Jewish youth: redemption of the Zionist idea among academics. A mysticism of race? One sees how this could be a good and wide-ranging book. But I know too little about Buber's life, his family tree, etc.

May 21, 1915

[. . .] Together with Grisebach's biography of Schopenhauer, I've been reading with great relish the German mystics.[118] *Lux divinitatis.* I'm also reading the skepticism of Sextus Empiricus. Modernity isn't just Hume but also Poincaré and Mauthner. Hamann's *Socratic Commentaries* didn't exactly overwhelm me.[119] Though it's droll and biting, I expected more. I'm finding more and more of Buber's thoughts in Kierkegaard's *Concluding Scientific Postscript* and *The Present Age,* which by no means puts into question Buber's originality.[120] Kierkegaard's *The Present Age* is one of the most fabulous books I've ever read. His sneering is unbeatable, his consistency unrelenting, his Christianity honest. Kierkegaard uttered something I've often said even without knowing his work: that there have been only individual Christians but never "Christendom." The figures I know include Augustine, Saint Francis of Assisi (who experienced poverty), Peter Chelezizki in Bohmen,[121] Martin Luther during his years of rebellion, possibly Hamann,[122] certainly Tolstoy and Kierkegaard. Meister Eckhart[123] isn't a Christian, Buber's more of one, though he takes a different path, that of community. He's a Jew. He's more of a Jew than those who are merely spiritual Jews. Kierkegaard *is* a Jew!

I'm becoming increasingly aware of the fact that I have ample ideas of my own, but these cannot arise out of my treasure trove without some external catalyst. I always have to be *against* someone, I present my own viewpoint in response to his. I always need someone to stimulate me, someone who provokes me and arouses me to contradict him. It is in this sense correct, but *only* in this sense, when people claim that being in opposition is for me an integral part of life. I need someone whose thoughts are different from mine but ones I've already entertained in some other context. For this reason Kant and Frischeisen-Köhler challenge me as they do.[124] Do people really want to reckon this as a flaw on my part? [. . .]

NOTEBOOK 4

Notes in a Large Notebook

May 22–August 15, 1915

And who is this dreamer, whose name already marks him as the Awaited One? It is Scholem, the Perfect One.[125] It was he who equipped himself for his work and began to powerfully forge together weapons of knowledge.

—Diary entry from May 22

May 22, 1915

[. . .] It was in those days that the power of symbols rose up again and armed itself against folly, as a young and aimless generation in all countries looked for the path leading to an unknown land that they sensed was on the other side of the mountains. It was then that the first herald of Zion emerged on the scene, calling for repentance from the ways of others. In those days I was born. I come from a well-to-do family that has become torpid due to running after practical affairs, a family in which there seemed no way back to the path of the few who wander to heaven. My parents worked long and hard and thought only of getting ahead. There were relatives who decorated themselves with scraps of idealism and scientific sham so they could stage parades before astounded nephews. The young man remained alone and avoided the others. During the turning point of his childhood, he permitted only a few people near him: the dark and quiet Edgar Blum,[126] who—proud and lonely—hid within himself lofty hopes for the future. Then there was Jakob Jahr, who has seen too much poverty not to long for the wealth of the soul; and some others who were quiet and stood to the side and who remained in place because they did not want to be disturbed from their stargazing. . . .

In his early youth he already went over to Herzl's Zionist movement, and from that point on he has immersed himself in the writings of the Orient. *One* stupendous passion has henceforth flared up in him: the *Jew-*

ish State[127] and the Bible. And he discovered that the Bible has a soul, a soul that by necessity had to get lost in the storms of the ages. There was no longer any soul in Herzl's writings . . . only the desire to have one. This shy youth began to dream dreams of the soul of his people, which he believed to be in books. With immense speed and desire he took books and began to drink in the wisdom of all ages. He felt compelled to search from China to Wales. Those who watched him from the outside began to respect him as a bookworm and a scholar. In Young Judah, a group of like-minded Zionists where he found his place soon after his turn to Zionism, he was regarded as a walking conversation lexicon. This group was a pathetic and wretched lot. To the poor questing youth, most of its members at first appeared to stand miles high above everyday life as idealists and wall-bashers. For this reason close friendships grew up in the first years of their acquaintance. But soon he noticed that among them there was neither searching nor finding. As they grew older, most of the participants adopted the shopkeeper's spirit that threatened to turn the Zionism practiced in their own camp to *Meucheln*. They became "rational" and began to poke fun at "Scholem the Buberian." They did so at first behind his back—and finally, uninhibited by friendship and other such "ideals," they did so to his face. This greatly puzzled the wounded youth. So, as he also recognized their barrenness of spirit, he embarked on his own path to Zion.

This was an unusual time when the dreamer awoke and got to know his own longing. It was an absolutely wonderful time! All who burrow deep turn from the wisdom of their age to lonely ruminations. The best men of science, of practical life, and of journalism—Henri Poincaré and Fritz Mauthner—arose and used new weapons and means to give fresh life to the old notion of "not knowing" and of the impossibility of knowledge.[128] Dissatisfied with the endless blabber that has spread out to all places under the sun, poets such as Christian Morgenstern and critics such as Hermann Bahr[129] went the way of theosophy and followed the banners of enthusiasts and God-seekers. They teamed up with Rudolf Steiner.[130] Theirs was a secret movement, and the few who participated weren't even aware of its existence. It was a distant rumbling.

A melancholy spiritual drowsiness has seeped into the Zionist circles that, at the end of the last century, had lined up behind Herzl's Zionist flag. During congresses and similar meetings they began to split hairs over the minutiae of Palestinian mini-colonization. No one gave any

thought to the soul of the desert-bitten, neglected land awaiting liberation. No one! But we mustn't exaggerate, for there was one man who
thought about that which others refused to address because they lacked
the wherewithal. It was Martin Buber, the preferred philosopher for
those who worship culture, a man who intuited and comprehended the
meaning of the new generation better than his blindly loyal disciples.
When he looked at his nation he saw something horrible and empty,
with seemingly nothing joining its scattered members other than the inexorable, enslaving, and demonic power of racial instinct; the dull compulsion of historical memory; and the external, formal laws of association
that other people, strangers, have forced on our people.

Buber saw that for far too many people, "national Judaism" was something forced and unreal, a mere Judaism of defiance. He saw that these
messengers of new life turned to others in order to strengthen their
spirit, but that they no longer knew anything about the primordial
power of Jewish religiosity and the creation of myths—not to mention Jewish beauty! Now, the messengers were still Jews, and the poor
Galician peddlers were their brothers and sisters. But in the framework of
the Jewish idea, one had to inculcate in them enough modernity to be
able to parade around with them. They had to be changed! But Buber,
this Galician Jew who absorbed everything from European culture, still
had one thing they lacked: he had longing—longing for unity and longing for beauty, longing for freedom, and longing for reality. He realized
that nothing but superficiality swam on the surface of political and external life. He looked for depth instead. He took the plunge! He dove deep,
very deep, and not just into his own people but into the entire Orient.
For he had a dark and indefinite premonition that it was there that the
affinities and secret streams are to be found that can bridge the chasm
separating us from the nations of the East. He intuited something that he
later unforgettably restored and renewed as a "doctrine." And with his
submersion he was led by a great belief in a deep religious feeling, and in
the unchanging mystical facility of his people that he found in himself,
and therefore went searching for it in others.

And he discovered mighty and overpowering things! He found in his
nation—in the despised and pitied charity cases of eastern Jews—beauty
and reality, religiosity and unity. Out of the ruins of a century he rediscovered Hasidism. He discovered how, through the youth, the bonds of
Jewish mysticism and a national myth join his people together. He wrote

down this myth, and not only as he found it. No, he did so as he found it in himself. That is how he wrote it down. So he wrote it, so he stuttered it. The light from his longing casts a faint beauty on all the occurrences of myth.

Longing is the mother of renewal. This man who senses enormous inner emptiness teaches that longing fills up this emptiness. Fullness comes out of longing, like the clouds that form out of drops from brooks. Just as Buber felt longing, he also desired to make tactile his desire, and so he cried out, "Renewal must come." But he was not the redeemer. . . . He only wanted to prepare the way for someone greater than he who was to come. He sacrificed himself for the others, for those he did not know but whose blood he shares. He was not the redeemer. . . .

The quiet youth living within the walls of a Berlin home felt how the embryo was growing within him. He had read Buber's peculiar *Books of Heroes* and its account of the deeds of the modern-day Baal Shem.[131] Beyond searching and the crying out, fulfillment also stirred in him. At first he didn't yet recognize this fulfillment, nor did he yet know its object; he only felt its reality. He had to mature. Through the books by seekers of all nations and times he fed on longing and the desire to perform an act of liberation. He, as it were, drank the books dry, taking so much of their spirit inside himself that there was nothing left. On his bookshelves you can see the volumes from which he has taken and purloined life's longing. They look terrible. Go to them and you'll see.

This young man went alone through the world and looked around to find where the soul of his nation awaited him. He believed deeply that the soul of Judea wandered aimlessly among the nations and in the Holy Land, awaiting the One who would have enough audacity to free it from banishment and from the separation from its national body. Deep down inside he knew that he was the Chosen One who was to search for his people's soul, and to find it; that he must equip himself to pave the way for the soul's discovery. To do so he needed knowledge of the nations that would enable him to go to them and inquire, "Have you seen the Jewish soul anywhere—that timid royal spirit of my people?" He also needed power to clear the way between the soul and the people, and he required longing to convince the timid and to compel the hesitant. To ban evil desires from regions of holiness required a quiet royal soul, and to drive out knowledge with its own instruments required tremendous powers of knowledge. For as long as knowledge ruled the nation, it was unable to find its soul. This was an old prophecy. But knowledge, having found a happy abode among them, could be vanquished only by means of a very systematic death blow. The simple man's way is the path of redemption. And who is this dreamer, whose name already marks him as the Awaited One? It is Scholem, the Perfect One. It was he who equipped himself for his work and began to powerfully forge together weapons of knowledge.

June 29, 1915

A critique of Kurt Hiller's[132] lecture:

A professor of philosophy once thought he could disprove materialism by calling it "shitty philosophy," as if his characterization proves its inadequacy! Unfortunately, the same can be said about Herr Dr. Hiller's deliberations. He believes himself to have polished off the contemporary system's school of thought by venting the full force of his bile, and to have eliminated all of its representatives by calling them "idiots." It doesn't sit right with me to see something carried out in this ugly manner when one can perhaps do better than insults and verbal acrobatics. It casts a bad light on Dr. Hiller's deliberations when he delivers insults instead of offering proof. Dr. Hiller fails to grasp that there are problems out there that other people have tackled with integrity. It's not necessary to go into additional detail. It was unpleasant for all of us to see our enemies suddenly so degraded.

The worst thing of all for me was that Herr Dr. Hiller was so awfully superficial, and that for him everything seemed so simple, so obvious. Strangest of all was that Herr Dr. Hiller didn't sketch out any problems, polarities, and tragedies. For him, everything speeds along one grand highway, with clever people on one side of it, idiots on the other; we are up front in heaven, and the idiots back in hell. In short, it bothered me that someone could judge everything to be so trivial, so insipid. Things are in fact very different from this. The path of youth is full of abysses, and difficult contradictions cannot simply be passed over silently, but in one way or another they must be actualized. I would like to demonstrate this with a problem that seems to be the most important one of all, even if Dr. Hiller, unaware of its gravity and its urgency, ignores it: that of history and youth.

Herr Dr. Hiller makes it simple for himself: History? Why, it's all nonsense! For him we live without history, so why bother with millennia of rubbish? We live with the generation that was born with us! Yes, it's all very simple! I have a headache, and Herr Dr. Hiller says: "My dear friend, you don't have a headache; you mustn't have a headache; thou shalt not have a headache." But none of this will do anything about my headache. The state of affairs is as follows: we drag oppressive volumes of history around with us. History is a fact, it exists; we feel its weight with each step we take. We carry the burden of history in our blood and in our consciousness. We feel some kind of connection, some sort of responsibility. In this sense we're old, ancient, as old as the experience of the nation whose history we carry around in us. And then comes our youth, our own sense of life's fullness that cries out after completion and confirmation. *We* are here, and no longer as a link in a chain but as uniquely individual. We are young, and we desire to re-create the world out of our spirit. All youth must contend with the tension that is within themselves, namely, the tension or contradiction that obtains between daily occurrences and longings on the one hand, and history and the slumbering longing of the millennia inhabiting our blood on the other. What is needed is to make this tension fruitful, to perfect this antinomy. Leaping over the chasm is no solution to the problem. We can't leap. [. . .]

July 4, 1915

It's around ten P.M. and I just read an apathetic letter from Blum. I walk to the window and look out at the street and the sky. The street is empty of people. . . . Directly opposite is the one glaring streetlight whose light spreads out ray-like on all sides like the dusk. This is the only bright point in the entire uncanny scene. The houses, these tall black human creations devoid of feeling, stare with their unredeemed souls into the heavens. Black lines demarcate the earthly realm from the surfaces of endlessness. Everything is so dark, so absent of humans. Up from the Wallstrasse I hear screams and bad piano playing. But above the houses there is something else—nothing but a dark blue nothingness uninterrupted by shadow or any other color. There is nothing but dark blue. No human could have done this: it's so pure, so atmospheric, a liberating power. Is blueness all there is, or do worlds hide behind it? Or is there a God up there on his inscrutable throne? Venus alone sparkles with its luminous and shifting light. No other star has risen. It is lonely in heaven.

At this moment I cannot but conclude that there is no God who directs it all—everything is so lovely and its harmony so completely impersonal that I couldn't endure there being a God. We are flying through the eternal blue of the heavens, and nothing that is existing rests for us, not for an instant. Everything happens so quietly and as such a matter of course that one could think that the stars have decided among themselves to keep to their tranquil course. Nothing here calls after God. One feels happy and liberated not to have to think always about an unknown Being behind the stars and the worlds, a Being who—regardless of whether or not he has influence on the world—could disturb the correct harmony of these gigantic proportions by his indefatigably gargantuan size.

God is insufferable. One sees the world and that there is no end to it, and that there is eternal creation and eternal change; that maybe, but only maybe, the worlds seek rest—just as God is at best the aim of deeds we seek to achieve, but not something that is, that exists.

When I gaze into the sky, I'm always reminded of the magnificence of the mechanical view of nature: everything is so necessary when seen in the proper dimensions. It's just like the law of large numbers that makes sense only for large dimensions and sums. All our paltry laws of cosmic necessity work only if projected onto the scale of entire worlds. Hence it is abundantly obvious that they can't apply at all to humans or to any other small chunk of the universe, which is analogous to the statement that Stirling's[133] formula for "n!" does not apply to 100 but only to infinity. Applied to us, it can only yield nonsense. We have to admit, however, that it doesn't follow from this that we are exceptions in the universe, but just that everything is wonderfully harmonious, if the properly large dimensions are taken into account. One of these days someone should create a system, or an anti-system, that uses the law of large numbers as its leitmotif. This system will justify the deterministic viewpoint for infinity while showing that it is only a rough formula for the parts, and that the formula must necessarily contain mistakes at certain points because we are dealing here with large, though not eternal, factors. [. . .] The fundamental idea is this: *A law becomes more accurate the larger the dimensions that are observed and employed in its operations.* This is what has occurred to me this evening as I stared into the skies.

July 13, 1915

It seems to me that the functional connection (in the mathematical sense) between the physical and the psychic realms is an argument against the notion of a psychophysical dualism. If dualism were correct, either there wouldn't be a functional relationship between the soul and the mind, or the relationship would be one of cause and effect. It may well be that the physical is the source for the psychic. If the relationship between them is not a mathematical one but rather a function in the sense of the natural sciences, then we're once again back at a materialism that has been rejected precisely because it doesn't harmonize with our experience. [. . .] Brauer[134] and I are planning a new magazine called *Blue-White Spectacles: A Journal of Intrigue.*

A poem will be the first thing to appear. I'm going to pressure Brauer into finishing the magazine by August 15. [. . .] If only we find enough people to help. I would include a large essay "Us and It," in other words, the Zionist and the war.[135] [. . .]

July 16, 1915

[. . .] I began reading Mach's *Knowledge and Error* in the Adalbertstrasse.[136] It spoke to me directly from the heart. This afternoon I went to the university library to browse a bit through the books. I went to the card catalogue room and there stood my Herr Benjamin. He looked up and he couldn't take his eyes off of me. I did what I had to do, and he left. Good, I thought, you're gone. But I saw the door open up again, and Herr Benjamin returned directly to me. He made a perfectly formed bow and asked me if I was the gentleman who spoke during the Hiller evening. Yes! Now he wishes to discuss what I had said, and he asked for my address. He said he would write next week. I wrote it down for him, and he trotted off again. One sees what can happen when a youngster opens his mouth. I'll just have to see what happens next Wednesday or thereabout. No doubt we'll discuss the war. I'm eager to see what his position is. I read *Tristram Shandy* to the end, also *One for All.*[137] [. . .]

July 23, 1915

The day before yesterday, on Wednesday afternoon, I paid Benjamin a visit. He has a handsome room with books in sufficient number. It gives off the impression of a philosophical hermitage. Immediately we got down to business. He's thinking a lot about the "essence of the historical process," and he has some historical-philosophical ideas about it. For this reason he was interested in what I had to say, and he requested that I tell him what I thought about the problem. I therefore began to present my ideas—namely, how in our blood is a heritage that gives us spiritual substance along with certain proclivities. Moreover, that every individual also has spiritual ancestors who don't come to him through the blood, but who fashion his nature: Friedrich Theodor Vischer and me, for instance. (His *Auch Einer*[138] also sits on Benjamin's reading table.) In addition, I brought up our individual will and the like. A long discussion ensued on the heritage of blood and spirit. Then came my solution to the antimony that Benjamin considers synonymous with the historical process in general: socialism (which, after going back and forth, he accepted, just as I gave a speech on anarchism) and Zionism. He was satisfied and admitted that these are two paths. We discussed Buber and Lao-tzu. I was completely his equal in the knowledge of literature. Thank God.

Then came the war! He stands wholeheartedly on the side of Liebknecht. I unpacked my personal drama of getting kicked out, and so on.[139] This interested him greatly, and he immediately wanted to do something with the opposition. Tomorrow afternoon he'll come here to read the *Internationale,* etc.[140] I was at his place from 5:30 to 8:30. [. . .]

July 24, 1915

This afternoon Benjamin was here. We became considerably closer. We spoke about *The Beginning,*[141] and I gave an oppositional speech. I gave him the *Internationale* and lent him *Beams of Light.*[142] Then came some comments on Kant. He was quite honest and said that he's never gotten past the "transcendental deduction," which he didn't understand. We also discussed synthetic judgments and mathematics. He knew Poincaré, if only superficially, along with Schelling's[143] solution to the question. Many interesting matters were discussed. I then accompanied him all the way to Unter den Linden,[144] and he told me how he managed to get free of militarism. He made a sympathetic impression, and at times he spoke almost buoyantly.

July 25, 1915

[. . .] This morning there was *Don Quixote.* Incidentally, yesterday Benjamin really marveled at my library, where he found some things that were of great interest to him. I read Klemperer's essay on Schnitzler.[145] What struck me was how, like Buber, this man wrangles with the problem of "history and us," though without suggesting a solution. He's re-

signed to being a skeptic. I'm making a lot of effort with my *Spectacles.*
Benjamin wants to come to Young Judah to hear me stir up some opposition!! He takes a middle-of-the-road Zionist line. He's still ignorant.
This week he can't come. Next week I'll have to see if I can squeeze
something fruitful out of this. I hope. One must only maintain one's balance. [. . .]

July 28, 1915

[: . .] *Blue-White Spectacles* will have to propagate Jean Paul.[146] One must
read him, read him, read him! [. . .] Mauthner's *Critique of Language,*
vol. 3.[147] Benjamin is *against* Mauthner.

July 29, 1915

[. . .] Some comments on Foerster's[148] lecture that ended today:

The life of the community should—and must—be founded anew according to foundations that from the start exclude the use of force. Indeed, the common life of men must be based on the Good, and we
should always remind ourselves that in the universe there is harmony,
that a violence-free cooperation obtains among revolutionizing powers,
and that we on earth must usher in a new age that constrains the ca-
prices of the spirit with ideas that can last. But how to do so is a difficult
problem that you, Herr Professor, have shied away from addressing. We
need the courage to draw consequences and to think out our thoughts
through to the end. We have to pull the rug out from under the rule of
violence and authority. Just as you quite rightly and honestly noted, we
must act to prevent butchery and murder. This means that we shall not
serve violence. On the contrary, we pioneers of a higher freedom—
which is nothing other than the awareness of cosmic necessity—must
work against it whenever we can. [. . .]

The state is violence, from which follows that we have to extricate
ourselves from it, resisting every form of patriotic dogmatism and all ob-
sessions of a non-organic nature that all too often arise. We must oppose
the war, Herr Professor Foerster, for otherwise we are only talkers.

For three thousand years we've seen how priests have exploited their
exclusive possession of cosmic knowledge for violent ends. We have to
be on guard that the priests don't return and destroy what we've built out
of our dreams of humanity. We hold that the life of community shall not

merely develop out of economic or any other forms, which are nothing other than forms of inorganic violence; it shall grow organically, just like the harmony of the heavens in its course.

No, Epimenides[149] shall not awaken to be a servant of power but rather of a new and harmonious life that drinks from the sources of Being and finds itself in everlasting harmony with heaven and earth. Epimenides, Herr Professor, shall not be the German Goethe. He shall be the higher Goethe, a mythic man of a new life. Goethe knew what he was lacking and so made Epimenides awaken to a new Being, a true Being living among the stars, which are just as free of violence as the thoughts of the coming generation. Epimenides is utterly and entirely the future.

I'll have to read Plato's *Timaeus,* also *Wilhelm Meister.* I'll have to compose the myth of the coming reality, a reality that arises out of our own needs like fog out of steamy water. There were ten people, nine males and a female, in the room. The entire lecture has been this way. The other sex comprehend something only if it's exaggerated; they prefer to steer clear of anything that smacks of subtlety. [. . .]

August 2, 1915

[. . .] I gave a grand speech at the dinner table on the question of volunteering for military service. I did so to avoid suffering the fate of dying a hero's death for the German fatherland. [. . .]

August 4, 1915

[. . .] Joel asked Benjamin to work with us, to which he gave detailed reasons why he couldn't.

He had high praise for the *Internationale.* In particular, he was mightily taken by the high degree of objectivity to be found in the essays. This and the essay by Gustav Landauer ushered in the main themes of the afternoon: socialism, Marxism, and the philosophy of history.[150] The upshot is that we basically have the same views on the work of history and what it would look like if it were really history. He too *does not* admit to any laws of history. On the contrary, history is that which is "objective in time, an objective object that is *knowable.*" This leads to the possibility of scientifically proving the work of history. He admitted that until now he hasn't succeeded in pulling this off, indeed, that he's only proved the exact opposite. But we both said the same thing: "In the end you'll agree with me, I'll agree with you." We want the exact same thing, and we both think that there is room for a common rejection of psychologism (Lamprecht)[151] and also of Buber, whom Benjamin accuses of having a schematic psychological theory of history. I pointed out the inadequacy of this prejudice and tried properly to assess Buber's manner of taking what he has found in himself and looking for it in others. Buber has no intention of doing philosophy of history. He aims at matter-of-factness, and in a higher sense. [. . .]

August 15, 1915

I was at Benjamin's on Friday evening. He read to me four poems from *Flowers of Evil,* in both his and George's translation.[152] The result was that in each case I thought his translation was George's. In two cases his were plainly superior. In sum, he did excellent work. I told him about my work on the Song of Solomon, and he said that this translation is by far the more difficult of the two, as his translation is child's play in comparison. I talked at length about the Bible and its current sorry state, and he showed me some of his valuable acquisitions: Von Gerstenberg's *Ugolino,*[153] a (wonderful!) first edition of Klopstock's *Oden* from 1771,[154] and a number of other similar things. He lent me his edition of *Ugolino.*

Like Werner, he also has a "woman." Sunday he'll travel to Lake Arend for fourteen days. I let him borrow Buber's *Chuang-Tzu.*[155]

NOTEBOOK 5

Book of Vanity: Metaphysical Tales of Physical Ego

September 11–November 17, 1915

I march bravely through the primordial forest in the firm belief that there is light at the other end. I don't even realize how happy I am.

—Diary entry from November 15

September 11, 1915

[. . .] On Friday evening, which was yesterday, I was with Benjamin from 7:30 P.M. till 12:30. We discussed a number of subjects, in particular we launched into the problem of Palestine, and the Zionists' historical perspective. This led to unbelievable difficulties and antinomies. It'll be continued. I discussed a number of other things with him. He hopes to get a summa cum laude for his doctorate, and in the winter he'll go to Mu-

nich—if he doesn't get examined again along with the others unfit for
service. [. . .]

I'm in a turbulent mood because of the risks of taking my lay sermons
into wider circles.[156] I can land in prison if someone betrays me.

Hölderlin's poetry is very difficult to understand, but it's music, music,
music. [. . .]

September 13, 1915

I went on a walk with Löwenthal[157] and then picked up Blum from
school. Today Blum's parents called him in for a talk. It's come to his attention, said the old man, that Scholem often spends time in front of the
school, and he doesn't know why. Mr. Blum doesn't know me and
wouldn't recognize me if he saw me. He asked if I picked him (Blum) up,
or if I have closer contact with others in the school. Blum replied that I
only pick him up. He asked if Blum has any political opinions. "No, none
at all!" Now, his father said that he doesn't want to say anything against
our friendship, if indeed there is a friendship, but that I shouldn't wait in
front of the school.

The outrageous impudence! I can stand on the Sabastianstrasse if I
want, which hasn't the least to do with the school. Nevertheless, I'll have
to be cautious in my relationship with Blum, otherwise they will ex-
ploit it.

I began Jean Paul's *Titan*.[158] I can't get over the feelings of astonishment. [. . .]

September 15, 1915

[. . .] Today *Blue-White Spectacles* came out, and with a rather successful
look to it. About twenty copies have already been snatched up. [. . .] I
later went to Young Judah with Heymann, Brauer, Türkischer, Freund,
Kalischer, and Klein.[159] Once again we went back and forth discussing
our work. I was very irritated at Brauer after he tactlessly let loose his polemics against Freund. Afterwards he began to make some comments
about Calvary.[160] I spoke about bonding and dignity as formal elements
of Judaism, namely, that not having bonds has something non-Jewish
about it. This does not imply the negation of freedom, which has content
but no form. The idea is powerfully forming within me to come up with
a new and higher Zionist ideology someday, which is sorely lacking. This
is a lofty ideal.

For the second time I've read some of Kierkegaard's *Philosophical Fragments*. I'm now beginning to grasp some things better than I did the first time around. Maybe I'll slowly make some progress. These are very large and deep thoughts, and since I haven't grasped them in their entirety, I still can't take any stance on them. I've read a lot of Buber on Hasidism. [. . .]

September 17, 1915

[. . .] Yom Kippur began this evening. Dressed in white burial clothes, the Jews stand in long rows. With sounds as if from a broken violin, with the Kol Nidre they force their way into heaven to find a God who can snatch them up.[161] The degree of sanctity and longing down here below shall be entered into the books on high. In the morning the accounting of sins will be made, and—being "mindful of his covenant with Abraham" (Exodus 2:24)—the book of guilt and memory will be sealed. On this day my sole desire is to be among the eastern Hasidim, as I cannot endure the fumes of godless perfume in Berlin's well-maintained houses of prayer, where the custom of repentance is made so easy, and where being a Jew is so degraded.

I'm fasting for twenty-four hours just as the Law dictates, from three stars to three stars.[162] But I can't do more than this. I can't go and pray, not to myself, not to God. I can only seek God out (and I could never pray to *the* God). Still, I'm surrounded by the sanctity and dignity and sheer greatness of this day. [. . .]

September 19, 1915

The newspaper finally reported that the *Berner Tagwache* has published the appeal made by the socialist congress in Zimmerwald. It probably won't be published in Germany. Ten nations along with the English delegates were prevented from attending. Certain newspapers are palpably irritated. Strangely enough, the *Vorwärts* wrote nothing about it.[163] Did the censor prevent it from publishing what others were permitted to do? [. . .]

It astonishes me time after time that, with the exception of Herder, I haven't the slightest relationship to the German classics. It already says something that among my books there isn't a single volume by Goethe or Schiller (excepting poetry). I'm not praising myself, but I cannot stand men who seem to me to live in the clouds. Aristotle, Leibniz, and Goethe are not my cup of tea. I have gone in an entirely different direction, where the word "classicism" does not appear. Even though I'm unable to put my finger on it, I can't read Goethe without feeling somehow irritated by him. But when I read Novalis, Vischer, or Cervantes, my inner strings sound out their melodies. To put it trivially, I belong to Romanticism. (It could be worse, since Romanticism is revolution out of the longing for better spirits.) Apart from the clear and fixed lines of what directly repels me, it can't be denied that absolutely nothing in me is firm, but for the time being contradictory opinions dance around my brain. What a difference, a world-spanning chasm, there is between Vischer and Kierkegaard! Yet both abide together under my roof. I shout with joy over both—and not just after their bathos. Did Vischer know Kierkegaard? What did he think about him? He occupied himself intensively with mysticism. Mauthner's *The Last Death of Gautama Buddha* is a disappointment.[164]

Recently I've been thinking more than usual about the reasons for my Zionism—not its justification but its foundation and its yawning abysses, and how to trumpet the idea of a new national culture. Occasionally I have a deeply sad feeling of being a tired and burned-out Jew (though I still can't say what's behind this feeling), and then a reaction immediately sets in, and with desperate effort I conjure up a sense of joy. I don't seriously believe that one day I'll really go mad, even if I'm altogether certain that melancholy lies in store for me. How many others are like me? I'm now less certain that I *won't* die from suicide. I don't play with the thought of suicide—I first thought about it on April 1. I do know that I'm not secure against such thoughts, and that the only thing I have to defend myself against them is my reflections, with which I set sail with great power onto the waters of life.

At this moment I no longer believe as I once did that I'm the Messiah. Which is sad, because the minute I recognize my inability to bring about renewal—my own renewal—I cease being a Zionist, or at least a Zionist in the sense I consider necessary. But I won't allow myself to sink into melancholy and brooding. Bad thoughts give birth to even worse ones! Just think about the Athenians, my good sir![165]

Religious Jews have it easy. In business, an inventory is taken every January 1. Yom Kippur is the soul's inventory. They are lucky. With the snap of the fingers, on a particular day the scoundrel must take an inventory. [. . .] They are truly the lucky ones. They know everything in advance, while I know nothing. I can't do an inventory of the soul. Recently, that is, for the last two months, I've been in a distinctly anti-God frame of mind. I've even gone so far as to tell those people who don't understand a thing (Arthur Scholem) that I've broken off my relationship with heaven. This set off peals of triumphant laughter. They never had any such relationship. "I'm an atheist," says the "educated man" named Arthur Scholem. "One" must keep pace with the progress of science. Once he heard Haeckl speak.[166] These vermin should be killed, their necks snapped. As dead as dead can be. I can't put up with this anymore.

A question: what is your favorite book? Answer: the Bible (I'm a Jew).

September 20, 1915

This morning I met with Löwenthal, bought tickets to Busch's Circus, wrote a letter to Benjamin, and continued reading *Titan*. This afternoon I discussed the topic of "kitsch" with Arthur Scholem, a topic brought on by Heilmann's so-called "Art Pages" in the *Lustige Blätter*.[167] Blum, now in this new situation of his, came by at 2:30 to see my room for the first and last time. This morning he got his military orders to appear early tomorrow at seven A.M. in Königsberg in East Prussia! Briefly and warmly we said our good-byes. It really shook me up, and as hard as I tried, I couldn't read again after he left. I had to go to see Tauber in order to get some fresh air. All of us are very sad; we really belong together. I discussed *Blue-White Spectacles* with Blum. The military is now threatening to get Löwenthal and me.

In the evening I went to Busch's Circus. This isn't for me—everything was so tortured, and then came all the inelegant bows. It was a waste of time.

Of all the people I know, I like Blum most. Today I realized clearly how much I'm going to miss him. But he won't trip up. [. . .] Still, I can't write a thing, otherwise the entire story stirs me up too much. I don't want to think that Blum will go to battle for Germany, and . . . It's all too monstrous to think about.

Sept 21, 1915

Zarathustra: "The gentlest words are those that bring on the storm."

"The decision takes place not during the upsurge but in the recesses."[168] This means that the great event takes place without sound; the eternal goes the way of depth. This is the case not only in an evolutionary sense in which the beginnings of world-changing storms emerge where no one notices, or that, as the old truism goes, the antithesis is already a part of the thesis. No! The *most essential thing* resides down below, and not on the Leipzigerstrasse. Where is it, then? We can't say anything other than that it takes place in secret. Just as a poet cannot be observed during his greatest hour, no one sees or hears the creator during the hours of decision. All "movement" is subterranean. *Emanuel Quint*. [. . .]

Remarkably enough, Nietzsche apparently didn't know Kierkegaard, not even the monograph by Brandes.[169] But listen to what's written in "Of a Thousand and One Aims" (p. 86): "First nations were creative, and only later were individuals. *Truly, the individual himself is the most recent creation*."[170] Isn't this astounding? In the truest sense of the word, the "individual" was indeed the most recent creation. [. . .]

At the latest, we'll be called up for the military examination on November 1. I hope Father will go alone and they'll turn him away. That would be the best. I'll have my turn soon enough. But I'm so depressed because of Blum that I don't care about anything. Today long rows of nineteen-year-old troops marched through the city. Everywhere the 1896ers are being called up.

I finished Jean Paul's *Titan*. I still don't know the original, though at least the abridged version seems decent enough. I'll certainly buy that as well. I'll first read his *Siebenkäs,* followed by *Flegeljahre*.

Curses on the military and militarism; crush them like a cockroach. Do you hear? Three cheers for the revolution and for Judah!

If somewhere there was a self-respecting revolution, I'd be there, but everyone only bows down silently, stupidly, and hopes. And I bow down with them! What a disgrace! Why don't we run away and flee from all this hubbub? It's of no use; they'll chase you down. The earth is too small; you can't hide anymore. Everything is madness. And the gods laugh at us. They are all sitting in some enormous dining hall and rolling in laughter on the floor at these idiots who are murdering one another—idiots who offer up their prayers to them. Idealism!

I hear everywhere from these sons of bitches, these filthy, slobbering pigs, that the youth shall be idealistic. That is to say, the youth shall be stupid enough to allow the knights of filth to stuff their mouths full of shit and murder one another. But we don't want this, we don't want this, we don't want this. You people! Yes, we say that the youth shall be idealistic, but without any of your smutty undertones. To be an idealist means to be *against you,* against everything that is lowly and impure—and to be for the holy war against this petty-bourgeois war that is draped with the mask of a holy war. Youth is idealistic, in other words, it throws your rubbish back in your face, for youth has *different* ideals from yours. But this isn't what you mean by being idealistic, which is anti-idealistic, just like you. This ideology of filth will drive a person insane unless he can lift himself up, make an about-face, and go in a different direction from the others. One has to enter into deep, burrowing, subterranean paths, and it is there that the older generation will be toppled. [. . .] If only someone could understand our rage (but we are so alone). [. . .]

I've been thinking about my thoughts. Isn't this a touch exaggerated? Should one reflect upon reflections? And do my thoughts contain more dreams than reflections? When I go to bed I'll dream about it. I always dream. Good God, what else am I supposed to do? [. . .]

September 23, 1915

Everything was settled with satisfaction. Yesterday Father was in Wusterhausen, where he was told that the entire regiment isn't permitted to accept volunteers under the age of twenty, and that at best there's a chance that Verden or Frankfurt will still do so. Letters went out to the people today. With luck they'll reply that they regrettably can't either. Then Father will be satisfied, and so will I. I have no desire whatsoever to volunteer. Let's hope this is the way it will turn out, or otherwise I'll have to swallow the bitter pill. [. . .]

Later I went to the Old Synagogue with Heller for the beginning of Sukkoth.[171] At the end I looked up and who did I see? Herr Alfred Rabau.[172] I didn't care, but afterwards he let me know that he wanted me to wait for him. I waited, and sure enough the young Herr approached me and made some tactless comments, such as that I've become even crazier than before and so on. I turned my back on him. [. . .]

September 24, 1915

[. . .] I know of no other group that has experienced in two years such upheaval as Young Judah. It is even more on the way to dissolution because of its aristocratic selection process, and last but not least its rejec-

tion of propaganda, which is after all my work. I'm now beginning to believe that Brauer's reforms won't survive long. What we need now is
some great event or a great personality in order to come back together.
There's too much bitterness, and there's still personal animosity. Heller
is very openly against Türkischer, while deep down I'm also against
Türkischer. [. . .] At the very most there's a basic agreement between
Brauer and me, which—thank God—has developed through mutual influence because we got together and talked things out. Otherwise, everyone goes his own way, and everyone thinks that this way will lead to
Zion. They seem to think that this individualization is a consequence of
the notion that Zionism is basically a personal issue. But this no longer
holds for those who have understood and decided that, at the very least,
they must join together as a community of people filled with the same
spirit. They must forge a movement. [. . .]

October 1, 1915

[. . .] This evening at Benjamin's we talked about rendering oneself unfit
for military service, about parents, and about the great humorists. It was
Simchat Torah,[173] and the service at the synagogue was extraordinary. I
told Benjamin all about it. We were together till one o'clock in the
morning. I promised to keep him company during an evening of making
himself unfit for service. [. . .]

October 2, 1915

[. . .] One of these days someone should say something about Wassermann's *The Dark Pilgrimage*.[174] Without question it is the most extraordinary Jewish novel yet written. Something should be said about the
book's atmosphere, which rises up from a sphere of subterranean life and
goes directly into eternity, absolutely directly. We are all in this novel, all
of us young Jews—though we are not all like Agathon.[175] It's truly a Hasidic book, though Wassermann didn't have an inkling about Hasidism
when he wrote it. Together with *Der Grüne Heinrich*—which is its opposite in every way—it is our great song of the future. We have no choice
but to share Heinrich's longing. Heinrich is rooted; at every moment,
even the most abandoned, he has, so to speak, a fig tree and a shack. Now
we still need Agathon, who has no other home than eternity and no
other roots than the tattered soul of the Jew. The book is the bible of our
disgust with Europe. It's wonderful that the most "Jewish" character in

the book, the liar Gudstikker, has to be a Christian. He's rooted in an—admittedly very complex—lie. Don't most Jews do the same? Don't we all do this? And don't we need to free ourselves from the false and unreal native soil in order to find ourselves?

All of us search for none other than this Agathon.

I read the two mighty chapters of Ezekiel 36 and 37. I was astonished at the sounds of the Hebrew. Why do I always start singing when I read? [. . .]

October 4, 1915

Yesterday I had an absolutely unpleasant discussion (because it was pointless) with Dr. Hirsch over the war and the opposition to it.[176] Since this war hasn't been going exactly as people had wished, but has become seriously drawn out, they now suddenly discover something none of them suspected during its first six months: namely, that *they* (!!) are also "against the war," and that we are the rational ones who know that the war is useless. Who isn't like them? [. . .] Dr. Hans Hirsch managed to make the grandiose remark that the entire antiwar "philosophy" (the *real* antiwar philosophy) was invented by a handful of people to benefit people in the printing business. Now that's what I call historical materialism.

October 17, 1915

[. . .] Yesterday evening I met with Benjamin. It began at eleven at the Café des Westens. After one o'clock we were in his apartment, where he said that I had come to get clarification on the end-of-school exam (!!!), which lasted all night. This fellow had a thermos full of cocoa without sugar, and I swear downed an entire bottle of Benedictaner. We played a game, and I won 2 marks. We discussed his essay and the free student movement, whereby he was very pleased with what I had to say about it.[177] After reading it for the second time in the afternoon, I unwittingly stumbled onto the right points. We had breakfast and left. In Café ABG he read the brochure "Who's to Blame for This War," which I had copied down over the last few days, and liked it a lot. [. . .] We were together for precisely twelve hours.

I read *The Legends of Saint Francis* (Insel-Bücherei), which is very lovely. In the last few days I didn't manage to get to Jean Paul. Incidentally, Paul Scheerbart[178] just died! This man was another God: he too could have created the cosmos in six days.

October 18, 1915

This afternoon between five and eight o'clock I passed my exams, completing the so-called leap out of the first epoch of life. The Scholem family is exuberant!

I read Bonaventura's *Nightwatches.*[179]

October 26, 1915

[. . .] I'm planning a crazy novel called *The Strong Hair.* Holiness is the rustling of madness in our blood.

Following Schwarz's lecture[180] I spent most of the day writing a letter to Julie Schächter.[181] It grew to ten pages. The concept in it is fairly precise. The letter is far too good for this girl. Besides understanding it, she should learn to have some reverence for people seeking greatness.

October 28, 1915

Brentano's fairytales are delightful, and I've been reading them with joy and pleasure.[182] There are motifs in them that seem related to the Grimm-like tales from my childhood. For instance, the central theme of Klopstock[183] reminds me of a fairy tale still darkly present in my memory. [. . .]

I've read George's *The Seventh Ring,* his poem on time, along with a few others.[184] [. . .] It seems to me that his most beautiful works are *The Carpet of Life* and *The Year of the Soul.* [. . .]

[. . .] I've been in personal contact with Benjamin for three months now. It's undeniable that his acquaintance has influenced me spiritually and will continue to do so in the sense of attuning me more to knowledge. This summer has already demonstrated this. It wasn't long ago that I damned knowledge, just as Julie Schächter still does.[185] The transformation is now very rapid and totally unconscious—without any awareness of having placed myself in spiritual discord with myself. What I know is I've managed to ponder the possibility of Gerhard Scholem parting with Zionism, an unthinkable act one year ago.

Anyway, the foundations and abysses of my Zionism are not nearly as clear as they appear, and there is no way to make a satisfactory decision one way or the other with the tools I have at hand. I had already started during my first meeting with Benjamin, when I set forth my variation on Buber's teaching—and this is what one can call my argument, which isn't identical to Buber's, though related and first made possible through him.

I still have to get over the comparison of Orthodoxy with science as two equally unjustified jackasses, which is a standpoint that, for the time being, I continue to maintain, though as the result of the completely honest skepticism that had launched my quest for knowledge, and which to overcome would initiate a uniquely individual spiritual phase. To this point, however, I've found no need to make any corrections in any area, particularly not in the history of philosophy. I still don't know whether or not the study of mathematics, to which I will devote myself, will allow my range of ideas to take on a mathematical foundation (for my own sake, I hope so). At least for now, science remains closed to me. The skeptic is either eighteen years old or sixty. [. . .]

October 30, 1915

Yesterday came the highly welcome news that I have to begin service on the twenty-first instead of the eleventh. This gift is a stay of execution. [. . .]

October 31, 1915

The last day of October! During the summer I heard lectures by Foerster, the astronomer, who during one of these splendid lectures talked about the precursors of modern natural science, as both individuals and groups. He described how ideas that first emerged in the Orient among a closed circle of men, the "Order of Pure Brethren,"[186] were later developed by Copernicus and Kepler. Apparently, it was a circle of men with enlightened and intellectually refined sensibilities. How remarkable! Today, after finishing the *Siebenkaes,* I picked up Scheerbart's *Tarub: Baghdad's Famous Cook,*[187] where I discovered a very clever and sneeringly ironic treatment of this theme. A good picture of tenth-century Baghdad emerges in the depiction of how the Order of the Pure Brethren was founded by a group of very impure fellows. The poet Safur is well sketched, especially toward the end of the book. Scheerbart's cheerful disposition along with his famous love for the World Spirit (admittedly, it appears only once as Safur's Experience) come to the fore. The book focuses on the overwhelming craving and love for food, describing with great precision the different courses served up during the various banquets. It is as if the au-

thor probes his fantasy, and with all the splendor and desire he can muster, because in real life these are the things he altogether lacks. He stuffs
himself by thinking about all the beautiful things that Tarub sets before
his lover. As a personal book, it's good. Strong. [. . .]

November 11, 1915

Today I actually should be enlisting in Verden.

In reading Jakob Böhme's *The Way to Christ,*[188] I am astonished how
even I am still caught up in the wisdom of titles and of literary history. Only now am I gradually learning to know something about all
the greatness I had previously spoken about so arrogantly, but without
knowing a thing—based only on my intuition of the power of these
things. This was also true with the Romantics, the humorists, and the
mystics. Everyone thinks he knows enough about Jakob Böhme if he
knows the titles of his books and Deussen's speech.[189] But I know there is
far more. It's tough to read, for it combines the old-fashioned manner of
expression with a ringing passion for formation. [. . .]

November 15, 1915

Today is the one-year anniversary of my diary. I can still see how I began it, a year ago on a Sunday sitting in a streetcar and reflecting on the
enormous misery I was destined to have because of the spirit burning within me. A year has passed, full of events, both outer and inner.
While some progress has been made, I want to look to the future, not the
past.

I'm fully aware that under certain circumstances it's perfectly justified
to keep a diary; sometimes it could also be quite wrong. When a person
is lonely he has the right to speak to himself, and to go into battle against
himself, to work on himself. During these months I have written only
during moments of loneliness. [. . .] Others must regard me as far more
pulled together than I actually am, which is the reason why I need a
place of honesty where there is no statue in my honor, but where I'm
honest, incomplete, half reflective: the way I am when I'm alone. One
year ago I was searching, and it was the search of discovery, above all discovery of that which is complete and not fragmentary. I have searched
diligently (and in the future I'll continue to do so) for the lofty songs of
desire, the songs of a sacred land—irrespective of when and where and

who sang them. I believe that one cannot get enough of this, and that the search for related spirits is preparation for renewal. My family is not my parents, uncles, and cousins. I'm related to restless people who derive their knowledge from the roots reaching down somewhere into their essential self, and who go off searching for these roots. Nor can I ever get enough from these relatives; they are more fertile than Goethe. For one has to bring them to perfection, one must take up the thread that they have dropped. I want to keep my Judaism holy.

Everything that is finished is mythic (everything that is unfinished is religion).

I won't write a diary when I'm in the military, which will probably begin on November 21. They will scarcely permit me to get out of it. Instead of keeping a diary, I'll keep my eyes open. I'll look at the people, even if I don't believe I'll find anything. The Germans curse too much. This is the reason why there is nothing to hope for from them.

[. . .] We are Jews, which is a statement that must be properly understood. That we are also humans shall be called out with a full voice because some (or many) of my friends have forgotten it. It is no proof of one's Zionism to think that being Jewish is to occupy oneself *only* with Jewish matters. Someone can be Jewish and be with Jean Paul, Gottfried Keller,[190] and Friedrich Nietzsche. You can't crawl out of your own skin, and for a Jew who knows something about his Judaism, there is nothing non-Jewish that can do damage to him if it's not damaging to other people. It's nonsense to assume that pursuing something else could lead you away from Zionism. Zionism is the presupposition for this pursuit. [. . .] This is a lesson I've experienced and have understood over the past year.

I'm happy that I haven't stood still but have continued to grow. I've continued to grow organically. For the revolution is not unnatural, it's just another way of understanding organic growth. I can say of myself that I have forged all of my paths on my own, following no one. I've been forced to track down all of my relatives on my own.

My hope is that the various paths I've embarked on, with their sundry directions and waves, will eventually join into a new synthesis. This will be the synthesis: a New Jew, or Gerhard Scholem. I march bravely through the primordial forest in the firm belief that there is light at the other end. I don't even realize how happy I am.

NOTEBOOK 6

Marginalia to a Daily Book of Experience

November 27–December 26, 1915

Lurking over me is the sneering face of the angel of insecurity, and it whips me through the silent valleys carved into the depths of my life. It's anyone's guess what my life would look like without this angel, who is for me both fate and doom, but also a severe master and stimulus.

—Diary entry from December 18

November 27, 1915

I had to leave already at 7 A.M. on Saturday, the twentieth of November. With a suitcase in my hand, Father—delirious with emotion—accompanied me to Lehrter Station. I was given fifty marks, but otherwise I took as little as possible. The wounded heading to Rathenow sat in my compartment till we reached Stendal. They cursed the war horribly, even though they seemed to be "Germans." The issue of food has pulled the rug out from under everyone's feet. They had been shot up in northern France and are supposed to be released now. In Stendal I lounged around the waiting hall for an hour to get a close look at the people in Lower Saxony. Then in the train till Langwedel I traveled together with a farmer's son who had to go into the marines. In Uelzen a group of schoolgirls boarded the compartment next to ours. They were traveling back home from the school for Sunday, talking twaddle about school, classes, and homework. I didn't have much to say to the fellow across from me; we each had to repeat a sentence three times before the other understood it. I don't know a thing about this fellow's background. In Langwedel I took the Verdener train. Upon arrival in Verden I asked a young man on the street about a hotel; I told him I had to join the ranks in the morning and needed to spend the night. I found out that this young fellow from Verden also had to join the ranks of volunteers tomorrow in order to avoid examination. He took me to the Hotel Germania, where I took and paid for the prince's suite (he told me, "Every other room will be just as expensive"). After dinner I had to sit in my room, huddled in a buttoned-up jacket and mittens, because the owner didn't heat it. After a stroll through Werden I knew there was nothing to see, at most cheap comic novels in the bookstores. Except for one street, everything was completely dark and unworldly.

The next morning at ten o'clock I went to the administration office. The acceptance papers were taken from me, and I had to wait with a number of others, all volunteers. Thank God I didn't have to wait long. As we were eight in all, two people soon appeared to lead us out into the main road and to the recruitment office. On the way the soldier who accompanied us asked if I was also a volunteer, and when I said I was, he replied, "My God, how could you commit such a crime?" "I certainly have sound reasons," I replied. "Yes, to get into the infantry," he said. We waited awhile before being ushered into the office to receive our papers. Finally we could go into our barracks, which were rather large and roomy. I was one of the first to arrive and therefore managed to find me a good closet and mattress frame. I didn't even unpack because the barracks sergeant told us we would stay there only a few days until we got divided into units. The entire day I got to know the others, among them a terribly stupid Berlin goy and first-year recruit, a young fellow—an 1898er—who only wanted to talk crap as if he were a professor of smut. He disgusted me, and he's from the west of Berlin, from around Bayerischer Platz! There was also an assistant postman from Diedenhofen. I quickly struck up a friendship with him because he was a jokester. The fellow with the most seniority in the barracks was an aspiring officer, an 1896er who was a really nice Berliner. At 9 P.M. we had to go to bed, but we told jokes for an hour, especially the postman and I, since our bunks were next to each other. I earned the reputation of being a philosopher. I slept till 2 A.M., and then I shivered awfully through the rest of the night, as did the others. We had only one blanket each, which was of course far too little. Periodically, the watchman marched past the window in an impressive silhouette. Two fellows snored atrociously.

We got up at five-thirty. Washing with ice-cold water went well. We drank coffee quickly, and afterwards we sat and did nothing with the exception of the usual Sunday cleaning of the barracks, which seemed a very useful exercise. Occasionally a junior officer came into the barracks, and everyone still behaved humanely enough. On Sunday we had a specialty for lunch: potatoes cooked together with beef, which I nearly wolfed down. Around ten o'clock all the volunteers went into the courtyard, where after our names were read out we headed into the canteen, and those who had already been examined were sent home. The rest of us waited. Finally, the word went out that the first ten of us were to be examined.

I promptly went with them, and we got undressed. Those in front of me were measured and admitted after they gave satisfactory answers. As for me, the doctor asked, "Parents healthy and alive?" (You're expected to answer always with yes!!), to which I replied, "Father has a heart ailment, but mother is healthy." The doctor: "You've always been healthy?" "No! I'm nervous, and I've been in the sanitarium three times. I also faint during long marches." He discussed my case with the staff physician, who asked me, "When?" I replied, "In the three years before the war." At that point I was supposed to breathe in once deeply, and I breathed as poorly as I possibly could. He said, "You can get dressed." I was thus declared unfit and released!

December 7, 1915

Yesterday! On my way to the physical examination I said to myself that the child I shall bring into the world will have to have a name. If I had said during the examination that I'm nervous, the absolutely most the fellow would have thought is that I'd get over it in the infantry. So I punctiliously came out with "neurasthenia," the lovely, one-of-a-kind, and vacuous word that I wanted to clobber him over the head with. I was lucky, as after only twenty minutes of waiting all the "Sch's" were called together and led upstairs. There I sat in a shirt for half an hour. I was in the third department. After being weighed, I had to go into a room with civilians and two doctors. As I entered the room, an eighteen-year-old was sent home because of syphilis! At that age! It was soon my turn. The occupation I gave was not only a student, which would have sufficed, but also a student of mathematics—which I said so they wouldn't be surprised at what came next. I call this a prophylactic measure! I was supposed to breathe in, and I executed the art of breathing I had devised so well. The doctor was completely stunned, and he called over the other doctor. "Look at this mathematician's breathing!" I put on a very severe expression and breathed exactly as before. They didn't know what to do with me. "Do you have a disorder?" "Neurasthenia." "We can see that." I was temporarily sent home! Such was my examination!

December 11, 1915

[. . .] I've been reading Schnitzler's *The Way into the Open*.[191] It's always been so awfully difficult for me to recount my moods when reading important books. This goes for Schnitzer, whose books—those I know, but this probably applies equally to those I don't—are full of melancholy. No, this is going too far: they are full of the spirit of melancholy. It's no accident that in reading *The Way into the Open* my mind turned to the other important work by Schnitzler, whose more appropriate title would be *The Lonely Way*.[192] What occurs in this book, both within the characters and in the outer actions that spring from their inner natures, is not the "way into the open" but the great bustling movement on a street where one person does not see the next. (At this instant I'm forced to think about an image from Hirszenberg's *Exile*.)[193] In this book it isn't only the Jews who are in exile, though they give the book its particular sense, but a few non-Jews such as Georg, Fabian, and Anne are as well. They are all pure wanderers of the night; and the writer permits them to walk together along the same stretch, and he stands behind it all with a smile. It means nothing because they remain born to the spirit of melancholy. For me, it says a lot that everything occurs in Schnitzler's books, that is, everything except joy. Some passages in the pages of the book give the impression that it's there, though all of the characters know that it's senseless, and that their belief is just an impossible longing for an escape from themselves.

There's been a lot of talk about the book; supposedly it's been criticized for actually being two books: a romance (of dying!) and a novel about Jews. I have to say that for me the book seems quite unified. It's in truth only *one* novel. For it poses only one problem, and it's a cardinal problem determining the question of the book's unity. The question at the heart of the "Jewish" novel is the same as the death of love among non-Jews: and this is the great, the massive solitude of all men, as if confined and forced to stay on an island. Everyone stands on his own island, on which there are multiple canyons and abysses, towering peaks, the firmaments of heaven and the depths of hell. People call out to one another, "Listen, comrades from the other side, we wish to build a large bridge out of magnificent stone, the heart's blood, and the human spirit. Come, let's erect it together so we can reach one another over ocean storms!" Some things in this book are truly remarkable. Sometimes subterranean streams of deep understanding flow between people who otherwise seem so insanely lonely. Someone utters a word (deliberately?), and someone on a different island feels struck, as if by an arrow. Sometimes it seems as if Schnitzler really doesn't know where to leave people metaphysically: in isolation or in community. Maybe there is a massive

rock formation under the ocean that works as a connecting road between the islands. Perhaps these lonely creatures are in truth only confused, and in the end they'll find their way back to the path that leads
through the human heart back to the human community.

To the characters in this book it's unimaginable that a Zionist would
really go to Palestine, which is a common attitude among Schnitzler's Zionist circles, especially in Vienna.

What must and will be written is a novel about a young man who
travels to the Land of Israel and is shattered because it is not yet pregnant
enough to bear him. Still to be written is the history of someone who
seeks the soul of his people among the mountains of the East; still to be
sung are songs about the new God. There is no point in writing a novel
about Palestine in the year 6000, or about an Old-New Land (which was
for young people a great disappointment, a really soulless book). Worthwhile is speaking about the Holy One and about the tragic dramas that
are in the communities, and in the loneliness of those who travel over
there today, or who will head out tomorrow.

If someone over there *doesn't* find redemption, it may be his fault, or
that of the country itself. True Zionism, whose ideology has yet to be
written (and not Buber's Zionism that blames the *person;* or political and
practical Zionism that blames the *country*), points a finger at both. There
is an undeniable correlation between the maturity of a people and the
development of their land, with one ripening the other. "Oh, my friend,
he was born as one who will return, and the hand of the Lord is over his
roots so he can be brought back at the right time for him, and the right
time for you." Buber.[194]

Do you, Gershom Scholem, long for Palestine? Do I have the right
and—inwardly—the duty to go there? It's a difficult question, and each
of us should be able to answer with a resolute "yes." It's obvious that I
want to get out of here, though wouldn't I just as soon go to Arabia, Per-
sia, or China: to the *Orient?* A great love for the Orient stirs within, and
only in league with the rest of the Orient do I believe that the Land of
Israel can celebrate its resurrection.

I still think I'd like to travel to the Orient but live in the Land of Israel!
Herein lies the difference between the two. I don't want to go there to
see Jerusalem in its splendor, or to have seen an "interesting" country so I
can shamelessly boast about it. I want to become a son of the old earth

and a citizen of the future. A great hero must arise, and a great deed must be performed in this land and in this earth—a land that remains virginal with the streams of the millennia in its womb, and a place that in these difficult days awaits fertilization and the sprinkling of seed. This is how I dream when I think about the future, and what I long for when I look at the lost condition of Europe. I would love for this land to be my son, for I am a man who lives his most beautiful reality through silent dreams—dreams that no one has yet heard of, and of which I will never speak. [. . .]

December 12, 1915

Sunday! It's now six o'clock, and at seven-thirty begins Gustav Landauer's lecture on Romanticism. This morning I spoke to Buber for the first time in person, or rather over the telephone. He knew right away what it was about and invited us on Thursday morning. Excellent.

Today I picked up Blüher's *Wandervogel* for the third time and read the entire first volume.[195] While not everything in it is true, it is *truly* extraordinary. Notwithstanding all its truisms (Wilde and Suttner),[196] it is a book with a grand undertone. It strikes every young man in the heart. German youth has in it a magnificent song to its beauty. No one can take from it this song.

[. . .] I still haven't decided whether or not to join the Social Democratic Party. In truth, I've already answered the question with an affirmative. I'd do it tomorrow if nothing stood in my way. But wouldn't it harm me if perhaps I ended up as a government employee? It's a weakness of mine to make so many concessions to Germany. I should join the party precisely to prevent my being able to stay here. I am not the way I should be.

December 14, 1915

[. . .] I finally read Tolstoy's *Death of Ivan Ilyich,* a very beautiful book. At first it reminds one of *Ugolino,*[197] and then the theme—how, at the hour of death, the recognition of a failed life brings salvation—disappears. Tolstoy's prose is remarkable, completely simple and straightforward, lacking in pictures and sounds; and only through the author's fury does some non-objective melody blend into the tone of the whole. Otherwise, the book is the quintessence of objectivity. Nor is Tolstoy an artist of words, as he talks only about content. He makes no concession to a "poetic beauty" that would detract from the astringent rhythm of the whole.

In the pages of *Blue-White Spectacles* I'd like to write something about "ideology"—why one needs one; how its detractors are misguided—and about the reigning confusion on the issue. Youth has no ideology that can give voice to what youth has *recognized*. Buber has written about what youth has experienced, not about this. Ideology is about knowing. No Zionist ideology can be based on Experience. I had once thought otherwise but have changed my mind. There must be knowledge. [. . .] What shall constitute the new Zionist ideology is a question neither I nor anyone else can answer, because it is not yet here. Our first task is to open people's eyes to the fact that an ideology is needed. We could perhaps point out its salient ingredients: a burden of history that cannot be swept under the rug; a social conscience vis-à-vis humanity; despair at Europe; spiritual distress. [. . .]

December 15, 1915

[. . .] Today Benjamin replied. He seems to be doing well, and his longing for Berlin seems to have fallen to a minimum. I'll send him a humorous report. If I should succeed at some point in traveling to Heidelberg, I'd also be able to meet up with him. That is, after peace arrives, or if he's not drafted into the army and therefore can't get back to Munich. But I believe he'll manage to get himself off the hook on October 1. *Prudenter!*[198] [. . .] Now I'll have to get some sleep to prepare for Buber.

December 16, 1915

What a day! Besides a bit of irritation and disappointment, I'm completely shaken up, half out of irony and mockery, half cheerful knowledge. [. . .] I overslept and rushed off to the lecture, and with great repose I pursued scholarship for an hour. Then I went downstairs where Brauer was waiting. Counter to expectations, he looked properly bourgeois, dressed in his famous new winter jacket. We journeyed out to Zehlendorf [. . .], and at 11:45 we arrived at the last house on Annastrasse. Up the second flight of stairs was the holy abode of the great *Zaddik*.[199] He was speaking on the phone just as we arrived.

The salon was very elegantly decorated, just like the office where we ended up. There were large artworks on the walls, an oil painting of him, and mystical cultic objects. Then the door to the room opened and Buber greeted us with a very brief, formless introduction, after which we went into the very orderly office. For me, the only piece of bad luck was, because of decorum, I had to sit on a stool the entire time, though I would have preferred to wander around the room. Up close Buber looks very good, despite his horrifying, utterly bloodless white tint, shockingly tender hands, and almost entirely bald head. After looking at us lovingly for half a minute, he told us that Leo Herrmann had mentioned something to him about *Blue-White Spectacles,* and had shown it to him, but he had only flipped through it without reading it carefully. He said he was very pleased with it because we had done everything ourselves, had written it, the works. Things you print yourself make a better impression, he said. He told us how "his friend Gustav Landauer" initially produced *The Socialist* by making the editor do all the typesetting![200] Among other things, he liked the "antibourgeois courage" with which we tackled issues in *Blue-White Spectacles,* and how it was presented.

Gradually, we entered into a conversation. We spoke about the friends and foes of the volume, and of its rhythm. Buber said he would prefer to see it less literary and intellectual, which was of course not a fundamental criticism. He then asked if we had heard of his new journal, which he said had been an old idea of his already in the year 1903. He showed us this in a prospectus he wrote. Now it's become a reality, even if in a different form from the earlier one. He explained how he had taken over the editorship "as an emergency measure" because younger people were in the field. At that point a discussion began over a position on present tasks.

[. . .] It turned out that Buber wanted to be less ideological than political and "matter-of-fact." He said that the possibilities for solving urgent tasks of the present should be discussed in an open and positive manner. "Polemics should aim only at preparing for objective things. I believe that objective things operate out from themselves." This was a clear rebuff if we had thought that *The Jew* wished to be a banner for opposition. I told him my concerns, and he replied that there was no danger of confiscation and the like. We spoke for a while about collaboration, and Buber made some sharply critical remarks about Jewish art. "Anonymous artists have the disadvantage that no one knows who they are." Finally, someone telephoned him, a sign that we had to go. He said we should send something as soon as we have something to say, asked for a copy of *Blue-White Spectacles,* and said "good-bye," adieu. We were on our way after an hour and a half. [. . .]

In the Royal Library I read the first act of *The Great Love,* Heinrich Mann's new drama that's appearing in *Der Neue Merkur.* I unfortunately had too little time to read it all in one sitting. Scarcely was I home for five minutes when Czapski and Heymann (the latter for the first time in six months) showed up and stayed for an hour. Heymann informed me that there is a place free in Arje Rosenberg's Hebrew class and asked if I wanted to participate. I agreed immediately. I'm overjoyed to be able finally to make a connection with modern Hebrew. [. . .]

A Jewish disciple of Schopenhauer is the perfect paradox of assimilation. And to further accentuate the paradox, this Jewish Schopenhauerian is a Zionist. Ye shall know them by their fruits! [. . .]

I'm again reading *Zarathustra,* a book that simply cannot be exhausted. Every time you begin at the beginning and open it up to some random page, you find sentences to surprise and strike you at the deepest level. You are constantly astonished at the power of his images and the force of his language, which screams out at you. There is no doubt that this is a holy book (if "holy" is understood properly). [. . .] So it is. It's a holy book because it speaks of man and the overcoming of man, and because it's revolutionary. I love it. [. . .]

I nearly became a member of the Social Democratic Party. Suddenly, something came over me, and I headed to the building where Werner had once enlisted. If I had found the fourth electoral district's cashier, I would now be a party comrade. Later came the skeptical rumination that I would never join a party during peacetime, and that my interest in oppositional novelties is really driven by mere curiosity. Is this so? What business do I have in the party? Almost none.

Today I wrote Blum, tomorrow afternoon I'll write Benjamin. I visited Uncle George, and brought to my aunt a copy of Micha Josef bin Gorion.[201] Pretending it really existed, I told her about a book compiling all the typical comments made about me, in the full abundance of their contradictions. (I like to amuse myself with the idea of piecing it to-gether, though of course I haven't done it.) In hilarious fabrication, I told her how the book contained the expression "Scholem's icy shard of skepticism" (in reality I had just thought it up), which she liked enor-mously and asked who had come up with such an expression that was so extraordinarily on the mark. I couldn't praise myself, so I said noth-ing. [. . .]

Lurking over me is the sneering face of the angel of insecurity, and it whips me through the silent valleys carved into the depths of my life. It's anyone's guess what my life would look like without this angel, who is for me both fate and doom, but also a severe master and stimulus. Insecu-rity is an eternal womb that gives birth to action—action as flight from the flaming sword and as an attempt to reach salvation in the meadows of paradise. Action is quite simply the daughter of adversity. We don't know what the structure of action would be like if we lived in security—whether amid sloth we would be overcome with longing for power and the beautiful life, or whether under such circumstances we would never have thoughts of action.

The crudest and worst type of uncertainty—because the most ubiqui-tous—relates to money; a different sort is when the soul waits impa-tiently for the Messiah, shivering every day and each hour before the birth of God. An additional type is the spirit's insecurity that leads it to lift itself out of its own saddle because it's an uncertain rider (and by its own nature, the spirit cannot be certain because it has a bad conscience). The strongest insecurity of all is what one can call being-cast-out-into-the-world. This insecurity doesn't operate visibly but, as a special blood-stream, grieves or celebrates and ponders away in our arteries. [. . .]

December 19, 1915

I just sent a long letter to Benjamin. I told him all sorts of things.

Given the terrible locust plague, it would be a worthy deed to build a hermit's hut on the Jordan and to live off locusts.[202] To me, however, this doesn't seem to be the foundation for a new national community. We can live in lonely isolation once work has been done and renewal has been brought about; but in the current circumstances, seeing that we haven't even properly started, to pretend as if we've achieved this final state is hardly an action taken for the sake of the future. Even if it could be good for me, I mustn't go there now because it would not be driven by the thoughts of resurrection. The way for the Jew of action is fight, not flight. [. . .]

December 20, 1915

[. . .] Over the last three years I think I've made a complete about-face. If three years ago someone had shown me a picture of what Gerhard Scholem would look like today, I would have totally rejected him. Back then it was precisely *this* type of person I so resolutely despised. What has remained constant between then and now is the enormous thirst for knowledge, along with the radical position taken in opposition to what once passed for knowledge. Beyond this point, it'll be a matter of suspenseful research for my successors to decide whether there's also a similarity in content between then and now. Back then, with my one-year military service before me, I considered myself—even if purely theoretically—to have taken up the loftiest spiritual command post: that of Orthodoxy. At least then I was totally and utterly Orthodox, offering no justification for small acts of apostasy, such as carrying a bag on the Sabbath. Already by October 1913—I know this very precisely—I was internally forsaken, and I knowingly went to the Agudah as a heretic. [. . .] The process began with opposition—not, however, against godliness, which I still acknowledged, but against certain aspects of the oral tradition, such as bending the rules of godliness and our duties to the Law.[203] Within a year I was following Buber, and now I'm following myself. No! I am on the way to myself.

December 21, 1915

[. . .] Yesterday evening I made my way to a rather empty office with a small room in back at Kaiserallee 99–100 in Friedenau. [. . .] There were six people already there; a seventh arrived a bit later. Counting me, we were eight in all. Among them was someone I'd often seen before, a very young fellow by the name of Feldner. Everyone gave me his card, and I in turn handed out mine. They were members of the Free German Youth and did not belong to the Wandervögel. [. . .] I liked the way they were all so natural and open. We saw things eye-to-eye, and we knew who we were: they were Germans, and I was a Jew. When I uttered the word "Jew," no one showed any embarrassment. Instead, they honored my different national heritage, just as I honored theirs. They considered my Zionism to be completely natural. The wholesome consequences of this division—each working in his own way—is that one doesn't consider himself a *burden* but can draw closer to oneself. These young people want Jews to show dignity and become aware of their own culture, thus creating the path to understanding.

[. . .] Recently something new and unknown has begun to stir within me. I experienced it as a quietly budding self-disgust at my actions and my manner. This journal rankles me, and I say to myself that this addiction to experiencing everything twice is decadent. But it doesn't matter, I must write. [. . .]

December 24, 1915

[. . .] Yesterday evening something occurred that happens very rarely: I dreamed. It was in fact a remarkable dream, for in it my father strangled me to death because I didn't want to become a soldier. I thought long and hard how I came to dream this and finally decided that it was as a response to Leonhard Frank's novel *The Cause*,[204] which I had read the previous day. I must have been unbelievably involved in the book for such images to appear in my sleep.

Tonight all the others are celebrating Christmas, but what do I care? I'm now sitting in the Adalbertstrasse and reading newspapers. On such holidays we Jews are subjectively total outsiders. We know only that tonight is sung "Silent Night, Holy Night," and that we don't study Talmud. Everything else drifts into unreality.

An objection to Buber's ideology: he begins with Experience instead of leading up to it or laying a foundation for it. He has only an apparent objectivity, while in reality his ideology is a concealed form of subjectivity. This is all very nice; it's just not ideology. One takes a shortcut to the ultimate aim. His Zionism doesn't allow itself to be grounded universally, which is what an ideology is there for in the first place. Or from a different angle, Buber wishes to make repairs on a bad racial theory by substituting a racial mysticism. [. . .]

December 26, 1915

This morning I planned to read the Eichendorff volume from the series *Bücher der Rose*.[205] I really enjoyed it. I read his *From the Life of a Good-for-Nothing* for the second time, but it was like the first.[206] It is such a lovely book that it keeps you in a perpetual state of joy. By reading it one sees clearly how deeply we belong to Romanticism. The movements and emotions of Romanticism are able to fill us fully and entirely, with all their color and a great halo of joy.

I have set aside the coming year 1916 to make the acquaintance with the choicest fruits of German Romanticism. I believe in it. [. . .]

I'll buy the Eichendorff book, though I already have the *Poems*. In the afternoon I once again straightened up my things, and to give myself a bit of order I threw away a very large heap of old notebooks and diaries.

Naturally I have it much better than those forced to fight in the war. I can work in ease and can win a year or years of valuable time. Yet the mere fact that I've made out like the owner of a munitions factory or that I don't pay a special war tax is no reason for me to judge the war more positively. I didn't seek such advantages, and my mood—which doesn't come out of my experiences but from my longing for different and better experiences—is independent and uninfluenced by all these things.

NOTEBOOK 7

The Voice of Silence during Unobserved Moments

December 29, 1915–January 30, 1916

What else is there to talk to myself about other than me? I am the sole object of my experiment and of my science.

—Diary entry from December 29

December 29, 1915

My knack of losing myself in dreams, always the choicest part of my lonely conversations with myself, has been racing out of control. I have an inexhaustible capacity for coming up with fresh variations on highly romantic themes for my life. Lately I've been preoccupied with the question of moving to Palestine and mostly of marriage, mornings and evenings conjuring up a new novella.

This morning's is a continuation of the one I began last night. Recently, for example, I hit on the idea of meeting a countess with an educated father who likes Jews, and to marry the goy. That would cause a great stir among the young men of Judah. On a different occasion I thought up the novella of my suicide. With shocking ease everything played itself out in my spirit (not with my hand): I would shoot myself after concluding that there was no solving the gaping paradox in the life of a committed Zionist. In a detailed explanation, I described how my suicide was delayed by two months!

I'll never be able to come up with a story in which I'm not cast in a very central role. Which is preposterous, or rather it's not! What else is there to talk to myself about other than me? I am the sole object of my experiment and of my science. I surely won't disturb the circle and adorned lines of my dreams; for me they are the ongoing sign of my development. If I were to jot down in a book all the strange novellas I've experienced in my spirit over the last six years (none have endings), people would be more than confounded. I still know most of them, even if they've lost the burning colors of life that the craziest of them have had—like the one with the deluge and my journey at sea.

The day before yesterday, while in bed, I gave an entire—and superb—lecture on the theme "the Jewish youth movement." One of these days I'll most certainly deliver it. When I crawl inside myself, I know I'll end up finding all sorts of wonderful things. [. . .]

December 31, 1915

These have been incredibly dreamy days with the most indescribable dreams!

[. . .] The fruit of madness is knowledge. The fruit of life is the longing for a beautiful life. The fruit of the quiet nights of my youth is ultimately ecstasy, which is something I've experienced. When I take lonely walks, particularly alongside water and wide streets, I scream out speeches I usually deliver in whispers. Some people look at me with surprise, and I blush. [. . .]

Mysticism is . . . This is a good question. So what is mysticism? Or better yet, what *isn't* mysticism? What isn't mysticism is everything *spoken out* with a lack of reverence—that is, everything that doesn't concern the divine. What follows from this is that mysticism occurs whenever someone speaks about the divine. [. . .] Mysticism is the experience of reverence. There is nothing more unfathomable on earth than reverence, and yet no one can say anything substantial about it. The mystic has witnessed reverence—and who can imagine what this means? The philosopher knows something about what exists or what will be; the mystic has witnessed something that doesn't exist and also never will. He has quite simply seen the impossible (and only the mystic knows that God *doesn't* exist): he has seen reverence. He has seen the holy. [. . .]

[. . .] The coming generation will, I hope, receive more honest instruction. Then it will go something like this:

"Who was the greatest human being ever?"

"No one knows."

"Who was the greatest poet?"

"No one knows him because he never said anything that could have singled him out."

"Who was the greatest rogue and profiteer?"

"You mean, who *is* he? God!"

"Bravo!" says the teacher, to which the pupil replies, "Nonsense. This was just ignorance. I haven't learned anything."

"Yes, but science and hunches are in agreement. This is even better than good!"

"Fine with me! Fine with you, Herr teacher?"

Let's be honest. The Talmud is not a palace with many passages, to use the metaphor people like to use out of phony romanticism. The Talmud is a heap of ruins in which occasionally magnificent fragments can be discovered and upon which one can build something again. Still, it's a field of ruins, a gigantic structure that has unfortunately caved in. Ritual law is not an amphitheater; it's a field of corpses. The corpses whisper like spooks, as if they were alive. It's a heroic book, with an unusual object of heroism. The main point of this heroism is not what's being fought for (as an absolute) but *that* a struggle is being waged for something recognized as absolute.

Kierkegaard is a palace erected out of the stones of the Talmud. One gathers the stones of the Talmud together, and out of them constructs Kierkegaard. This is the reason he's so colossal. He is the mediator between God and Israel, something the Talmud has never become. *Food for thought!!!* Indeed!

I spent the day on all sorts of superfluous things. I read Hoffmann and dreamed about what's coming in the future.[207]

. . . And it will come to pass in those days that a new Zion will rise up, and a new sun will rise over the mountains of the East. Luminous waves of light wander over the land, covering it with the colors of reconciliation. For this reconciliation will be between the land and the people, once they go out in search of the soul that has been lost. A massive flag will be fashioned that will always be at hand, and on it will be the stammering sounds of an unborn future and the echo of unsaid words.

And then the flag will be hoisted, and three times a year it will be carried through the entire land and through the forests growing on the edge of green plains. Joy will be spread throughout the entire earth and among all souls. And the soul of my people will be bursting with joy, for it has found a home, and its children will be born in joy. It will be utterly free, liberated from the manacles of domination. Gardens and garrets will be in the colors of reconciliation. When people speak of Zion, all lips will smile, and they will no longer think of past suffering that came from longing and the tension of preparedness. Redemption will burst forth out of the lamentations of echoing words spoken out in the past: it will be a glowing dawn with a crown of joy. Joy will be over the entire land as if it were a temple, and over the deserts, calling out after the wide seas. For the center of the world will be in Zion—Zion built out of the suffering of humanity, blessed with the longing of the abused.

Zion will be nothing less than the humanity that existed at the beginning of time. In the beginning was *humanity!* [. . .]

January 4, 1916

[. . .] It seems a paradox (*is* it one, or does it only seem so?) that someone like me, a sworn and implacable foe of Europe and a follower of the New Orient (which will carry a new Judah on its mighty shoulders), will temporarily have to make do with journeying to Palestine as a teacher of a very European science. To this crazy paradox there is but one possible solution, and one path to the Orient: to become a farmer in Palestine (which is precisely what Heller plans on doing). This is the only thing a person can do with a clear conscience for the sake of future generations, or for his own inner challenge. Zionism demands a grand life in the Land of Israel. If the grand life allows itself to be lived only in the Ur-forms of human society, then the Zionist deed demands that one sacrifice the thing people have held up to us as essential throughout our entire youth: analytic knowledge.

The Zionist deed requires the sacrifice of the ego because we recognize that, on our own, we cannot meet the demands; we cannot belong to the Palestinian soil and hence give our children a free path into the liberated earth. The Zionist deed would then be suicide. Between these two radical positions—going there as a corrupting agent because you're not yet Jewish enough on the one hand, and suicide, which represents the outer left of the Zionist "movement," on the other—is a farmer's radicalism. The last has won the most adherents because it demands the least amount of reflection. The first position demands the most because it's the hardest line to hold; the other, however, requires the courage to draw consequences that are no less difficult to hold. The problem is hardly simple. More light![208]

I've read Kierkegaard's extraordinary *Stages on Life's Way*.[209] The first section, "In vino veritas," is brilliant. The parts on women and the comedy of being in love are absolutely on target.

January 5, 1916

[. . .] Kraus really hits the mark and exposes a lot of grief when he says that the greatest experiences of today's literary youth are always literary.[210]

How right he is! Someone calls Nietzsche, Tolstoy, and Wagner his great experiences, and so it goes. When asked, everyone is ready to name a person and a book title, though the title doesn't mean a thing, even if it's from Marx or Nietzsche. But that someone really experiences life is the most unusual and unheard of thing of all. And yet we all seek this—not that we wait for it or that we conduct some special research into new foundations. But we all have something that gives us hope in life, hope that perhaps someday, while we are asleep or in broad daylight, life will appear to us as in a vision. This would be a mystical experience, though it's nonsense to expect to "experience" rather than "read" about this in Kierkegaard or Buber, or Lord knows whatever other mystic.

This is the reason why especially today mysticism among the youth is such a deeply slumbering hope and melody, just not a reality. This literary predisposition makes us blind to things that are not to be found in Tolstoy and Marx. And there can be no doubt whatsoever that between these two, *not* everything can be found, not even everything essential. To have a literary experience is to experience something secondhand, which means that it is no experience at all. It can be fruitful, but only to the degree that it awakens in me dimensions that prepare the way for a primary experience. The literary experience is only a way, and a finite one. [. . .]

If someone were to write the history of mysticism, he would have to take an unusual leap. In observing mysticism's primary and fundamental phenomena (the history of mysticism would be somewhere between philosophy and mysticism itself), one would have to start with Lao-tzu, Plotonius, and Meister Eckhart, and jump to the theme of humor, where until Jean Paul the most essential mystical development has always taken place. (Naturally, the expression "mystical development" has to be taken with a grain of salt, for mysticism has no development: by its very nature it is full of discontinuities.) From Cervantes and Shakespeare to Jean Paul, humor is an essential form of mysticism.

At this point one would have to turn to Romanticism, mysticism's successor. Then there would have to be a transition to Schelling, Kierkegaard, and finally to today. The study would conclude with Nietzsche, Rilke, George, or Buber. I would choose Buber because through him, Jewish mysticism, which is still so neglected, could find its place. And Buber is a specifically mystical phenomenon; he is *essentially* mystical. This doesn't seem to be the case with Nietzsche. And thus is the plan ready. But who will write this book? [. . .]

Evening. [. . .] Most likely I won't join the Social Democratic Party. I would only end up walking around in confusion in a place I don't belong: namely, by representing the interests of a nation I don't feel I have the right to represent, and a nation which one of my essential tasks is to separate from. I am not a Marxist; in fact, the "scientific" socialists would no doubt number me among the "utopian socialists of sentiment," whose only virtue is not having fallen for the war. In any case, the way things are looking I wouldn't contribute much to the opposition by joining. In Berlin the party doesn't need this support; no one in Berlin supports the majority. [. . .]

January 6, 1916

[. . .] I borrowed Harry Levy's copy of Wyneken's *School and Youth Culture*.[211] Already at the beginning of it I was annoyed at the nonsensical conception of history, namely, that someone could fail to grasp his time. Drivel! Historical materialism notwithstanding, every period of time can be great or small. The only thing that's important is to awaken greatness and to remain on guard. Wyneken was also possible earlier.

[. . .] The cuffs of my dress shirt are the cornucopia out of which my idiocy flows, as if from a bubbling spring. This idiocy is the mother of bourgeois respectability, or rather her daughter. Mental confusion is not always claptrap!!

When Gideon, the son of Jacobus P. Sleepy-Brain, came to visit the Scholem family, he was most astonished to have met only Scholems there! Those who were least wanted were the ones most present. And as Gideon began to say something in his lucid human speech, all the members of the family chimed in with their Scholem-speak (each member in his own way, but always Talmudic-dialectical), and told him to be reasonable. Gideon was most astonished. He looked around until his eye fell on the picture of the father hanging in the family's dining room. He then understood everything and began to laugh out loud, and left. There was the general sound of stools moving in outrage. Once downstairs he vomited out the air he had breathed. Back home, however, he said to his father, "Today I've seen humanity." At that point Jacobus P. went out and hanged himself, as that was not what he had expected. [. . .]

In reading the prophets this afternoon, I noticed repeatedly how one breaks into song when reading them aloud (I always read Hebrew aloud). One doesn't even know how it happens. It's strange: I always read the same passages; I've probably read them seventy-five times by now, and the last chapters of Isaiah, Amos, Zechariah, and Joel continue to hold me in their grip. I don't think I've ever read five chapters of the original in Ezekiel; I'm always caught somewhere else, being swept into a state of half ecstasy. Then Hedwig[212] approaches me from behind because she loves to listen in, and I can't continue.

Only alone in the solitude of my room or in nature can I do those things that are for me utterly holy and personal. When other people hear me read such passages, by necessity I do it poorly and with stammering so as not to reveal too much. This doesn't happen when I read *Zarathustra;* only with the Bible and *The Legends of the Baal Shem Tov* do I always feel compelled to read aloud.

Reading the prophets is for me prayer and religious service, all wrapped into one. What it is not is a literary study, which is what most people, and nearly all non-Jews, see in it. When it comes to the Bible, I don't have any literary thoughts whatsoever. I don't, as it were, count the

Bible as literature—because it belongs to me, and is entirely different from any other book, even the best and most sacred of the lot. I believe that even among today's Jews the entire Bible resides within us as something innate, as the inherited property of a tribe you may not be aware of, but that at some point appears in consciousness. And from this hour forward, the person who has this experience knows that it's a holy book, and that it has nothing to do with God.

For me at least, I've known for quite some time that the Bible is a holy book, whereas the Talmud isn't. This is the major difference. Yes, within these entirely trivial comments resides the main difference between the deepest strata of Talmudic wisdom and the religiosity of the Bible—and this is the sense of being holy, the sense of something personally being born into us. It may be that we're born with the legalistic Talmudic spirit, and with a legalistic dialectic, and all other such advantages and disadvantages. But deep down we know perfectly well that none of this is holy. What is holy is only that which is intact, and only the Torah and the prophets are holy. This is the entire Bible, and if everything else were lost and gone, we wouldn't miss it. Only scholars would, and they can have it.

There are parts of the Bible that we know only through tradition rather than by reading, as we never read them. Nor is it necessary. You can know the Bible after reading fifty lines from some essential passages. And this selection would be completely different from what some "modern" Bible anthologist could ever imagine. This selection would leave him astonished. "What's so great about this?" he would ask. The Bible is precisely that: trivial! It is Jewish. Try to figure that out! [. . .]

January 11, 1916

[. . .] In reading more Kierkegaard I found the following: In self-reflection you can always spot ugly self-love.[213] This really took me aback. At first I was baffled, and only afterwards did I have to agree with him. A rotten character uses contemplation as a wall of defense, behind which he can creep furtively to enter all the more easily—as if with a visitor's pass—into a fortress. Contemplation is a double-edged sword. We use contemplation to get a serious philosopher with a lot to say off our backs by trashing his words and shooting them to pieces, thereby rendering them palatable for home use. But this is the shameless, ever-recurring triumph of cowardice and addiction to security we all have, but which the words of seers and prophets threaten with certain death. The bourgeois man is enamored with every type of certainty, just not the certainty of death.

At the moment I feel a familiar sense of physical nausea at myself. This is the clearest expression of my loathing for the Gerhard Scholem who at the moment is such a braggart.

As I was young and radical, I considered it necessary to have a Jewish name, and I thus called myself Gershom Scholem. I wrote this name into some books I had bought back then. Even if this wasn't quite silly, it was wrong. When I want to think Jewishly, there is nothing wrong with embarking onto the right path from an obviously un-Jewish milieu (the name Gerhard reminds me of this!). [. . .]

I'm puzzled why Benjamin doesn't reply. Is it that he doesn't want to?

January 17, 1916

[. . .] I read the first twenty Psalms in the original. A few of them utterly astonished me. [. . .] From this point on, each day that I don't learn at least a bit of Hebrew will be a total loss. I must energetically wage the decisive "battle for language." Doing this will enable me to attain my goal before my deadline—my twentieth birthday. I must do this. I can. [. . .]

Benjamin is really stubbornly silent. Without definitive proof that he hasn't received my letter, I'm no longer going to establish contact. I don't hang on to anyone's coattails, and not to his. [. . .]

January 18, 1916

All the people from the Wandervögel missed the meeting last night and attended instead a discussion of military preparedness with Walter Fischer and other members of the Wandervögel. They have all become completely *meshugge,* as they all support it. The entire leadership of the Wandervögel is for it, which is what I call bankruptcy.

There's no point in protesting against the government—and only the opposition groups do so—as long as the respectable citizens listened to by the government don't join in. From this perspective, protest only shows the government that it's on the right track. The upshot for me is that the state of the German youth is really pathetic. The Jewish youth could certainly do more, but unfortunately it makes no sense when the Jews, of all people, are the only ones protesting, for we have no right to do this. It's simply impossible to launch out on our own after the German youth have brought disgrace upon themselves. Jews don't need to add extra proof of their anti-patriotic sentiments—that is, that they're the only ones who don't want to go along. No, as a Jew in Germany I have no choice but to keep silent if, by doing something, I'm opposed by the German youth. [. . .]

At the moment I'm reading Kierkegaard's *The Present Age.*[214] It offers truly inexhaustible variations on its basic theme that Christianity is the death of Christendom. But it's an excellent book, even if as a Jew I see where our ways finally part. Kierkegaard's irony is unequaled; even Nietzsche couldn't make a tenth of the accusations against Christianity that the Christian Kierkegaard does.

There is no doubt that future and upright generations will name Kierkegaard among the greatest and loftiest of men and thinkers. Even if not inscribed upon the flag of a new desire to religiosity (Kierkegaard is no help here), it's certain that his name will be etched onto the brain patterns of future thinkers, and so indelibly that it will be impossible to erase. If immortality really exists, then those who deserve it are the seekers (those who seek more than God), not the great intellectuals and "harmonizers." Kierkegaard has earned eternal life, in our sense of the word. [. . .]

January 23, 1916

Over the last few days I've put in some good work on my Hebrew. I read the biography and the first story in Steinberg.[215] I glanced at Tschernichowski,[216] though I'd prefer to read Bialik first.[217] I've also been continuing work on mathematical equations. [. . .]

This morning I went off to the Wahnsee with Brauer. For the first time in ages, beautiful weather accompanied our tour. The sky was blue, and it wasn't too cold; only in the late morning did the wind pick up a bit. We made our way slowly down to the cabin where the group was gathered, and we stayed there till evening. We experienced and observed some things—especially during the "song hour" after the meal—that would have been enough to scare off any novice wanderer taking part in the journey.

Instead of taking in the sun between 2:30 and 3:30, the loveliest hour of the entire day, the "Leader" Hirschfeld ordered everyone to sit in a cramped cabin and sing German songs.[218] It was so outrageous that Heller and I sat speechless. Finally, these gentlemen agreed to the suggestion that we go outside, and Heller, Freund, Brauer, and I turned our backs on this entire singing business.

It was a wonderful trip back in the evening sun through the Nuthe-wiesen. No one in the group ahead of us noticed anything unusual. But this generation of young Jews is really in bitter need of "discipline." Naturally! In *Titan* there's an excellent passage against wandering in a group.[219] [. . .] There was a wonderfully lovely sky on the way back, full of stars. They all sparkled and glittered, and the edge of the horizon was completely lonely and empty of stars, as the depths of the earth sent out its light to swallow them. In winter Orion is surely the most beautiful constellation in the sky. [. . .]

January 24, 1916

[. . .] I went all the way to the zoo with Heymann. As a matter of course we spoke in Hebrew, and the person sitting opposite us, apparently a Jew as well, asked patriotically what language we were speaking. "Oh I see, are you rabbis?" "No, dear Herr, we are Zionists." [. . .]

January 27, 1916

In the evening I spoke to Beermann about life in Palestinian schools. Finally we had another lovely evening. Running through my head the entire time was the thought, "Oh how we've squandered our youth in German schools." By the age of eighteen, students in Jaffa have every-thing I've had to obtain at a later age, and with such great effort. Above all, as citizens of Palestine they've acquired a native homeland. They have become Palestinians. [. . .]

Today the Germans celebrate the Kaiser's birthday. They can have it. [. . .]

January 30, 1916

I sit here and sleep away my days because, as they say, I am working. And what is happening in me, around me, before me? Nothing? It's like this: the world becomes just the way one imagines it, with events utterly de-pendent on my will. When I flee into the halls of silence, the clamorous voices from outside grow silent, and all that remains are the quiet whis-pers of the many books piled up along the perimeters of my room. At home I lead a quiet "scholar's life," interrupted by gatherings and meet-ings, and still more gatherings and meetings. But nothing happens. It may be (I'm in fact convinced) that something's about to happen. One of these days I'll have to cease from all this writing for half a year, and afterwards I'll surely be able to sing songs of the great battles that draw their powers out of the present silence.

I'm not even working in any directed way; I'm tackling Jewish things as they come my way. As for other subjects, I haven't yet bothered with them in the least. Momentarily, I am once again ensconced in the wide home harbor, where one rests for a while within the sources, until some new and mighty windstorm whips up (I have nothing to fear from it), and I sail forth again into the vast ocean. In this manner I'm waiting to be thrown once again into Jean Paul. I haven't dared approach him the entire month of January. [. . .]

I haven't a clue what Benjamin is up to in Munich. If he didn't receive my letter, he could at least have asked about it. Overall, the entire business is very murky. After these six weeks I can't expect to hear anything from him. [. . .]

PART II

BLUE-WHITE SPECTACLES:
MARCH–DECEMBER 1916

In the spirit of the Kabbalists, one can say that all genuine study of the truth is basically the study of language, by which one investigates the "heavenly alphabet" (Zohar II 130b) along with the spiritual powers that are reflected in it.

—Diary entry from November 18, 1916

FOR SCHOLEM, the period following his initiation into Walter Benjamin's thought was turbulent. Edgar Blum, his closest childhood friend, was shot in the abdomen in battle and died of his wounds; some of his other friends stopped writing. His diary records a steady shedding of childhood alliances. Meanwhile, Scholem's literary forays took him to Benjamin's essay "Life of Students"[1] and a book on the Kabbalah by Franz Joseph Molitor, an eccentric nineteenth-century Catholic theologian who had studied with Friedrich Schelling and Franz von Baader and who had devoted forty-five years to studying Jewish mysticism.

Gerhard saw his friend Walter a good deal less after the latter left for Munich at the end of 1915 to study philosophy and literature. At the University of Munich, Benjamin studied with the phenomenologist Moritz Geiger. More important, he began to ponder the problem of myth, historical existence, and history. For this he turned to the esoteric works of Franz von Baader, Johann Georg Hamann, and, at Scholem's suggestion, Molitor. At the university he took a class on ancient Mexican culture, in which his fellow students included the poet Rainer Maria

Rilke and Felix Noeggerath, whom Benjamin simply referred to as "the genius." For him the only other interesting course he took, together with four Benedictine monks, was on medieval penitence.

But it was less the university that intrigued Benjamin than where he was now living. If there was anyplace in Germany that still had a medieval spirit it was Catholic Bavaria, which was for many German writers what eastern Europe was for Buber: primal, non-Prussian, still premodern, and full of magic. Surrounded by the city's Baroque monuments, Benjamin turned his attention to an obscure body of Baroque plays.

These seventeenth-century dramas, mostly anonymous and largely composed of recycled biblical tales, had been gathering dust for centuries. But Benjamin spent his time in libraries poring over them, sniffing out subliminal messages few had ever noticed. The essay Benjamin then wrote on Baroque tragic drama, "Der Ursprung des deutschen Trauerspiels," was also his allegory for his own battle against the philistines who were destroying European culture—and who had already destroyed the life of his friend Fritz Heinle.[2]

In the seventeenth century, Germany was split up into countless states and dukedoms, many of which were ruled by tyrannical crackpots. So at a time when the English, French, Spanish, and Italians were spreading out to explore and conquer the globe, and the French comic genius Molière (1622–1673) was entertaining his aristocratic audiences, German Baroque writers withdrew into "inwardness," writes Benjamin in his essay.[3] In their quietly subversive way, using symbols laden with hidden meaning, they transformed biblical "ruins" into a subversive message of spiritual freedom and renewal.[4] Their obsession with biblical myths was only apparent, for these unknown authors were actually challenging the reigning doctrine of princely sovereignty. Through hints and allegory, their passion plays and morality tales raised "questions of the most pressing present urgency" and sneered at the despotic political powers that ruled their outer lives.[5]

Scholem first saw Benjamin again in the middle of March 1916, when Benjamin arrived in Berlin for a six-week visit. Diagnosed by a family doctor as a neurasthenic, in the summer of 1916 Scholem left Berlin and went to Heidelberg and Oberstdorf. During the fall term back at the University of Berlin, he met Grete Lissauer, a thirty-five-year-old woman who introduced him to a number of other women—Toni Halle,

Käthe Holländer, and Valeria (Wally) Grünwald—who appear frequently in his diaries.[6]

The two friends saw each other again while Scholem was in Oberstdorf undergoing treatment for his neurasthenia. Walter was now engaged to Dora Pollak, the daughter of a wealthy Zionist, and he invited Gerhard to visit them at Dora's father's villa. It was during his three-day visit that Scholem spoke about the "breakthrough and transformation" in his relationship with Benjamin "from being an acquaintanceship to friendship."[7] It was also in Oberstdorf that he daydreamed about forging a secret society of "fanatics" to save Jewish youth.

Their conversations on history, philosophy, and religion continued, as did the chilly Prussian formality that had until that point characterized their relationship. While Benjamin addressed some of his coterie of followers with a friendly "Du," Scholem had to make do with the formal "Sie."

One evening Benjamin allowed Scholem to read his essay on Hölderlin. In a journal entry Scholem writes that Benjamin considered him "worthy" of receiving it, adding that it was "extremely tough going."[8] What Scholem noticed in the work was how his friend concealed a hidden personal dimension that led back to Benjamin himself. "Hölderlin" reaches the highest order of abstraction, pushing language to the very edge of comprehensibility, and yet expresses a terrible personal loneliness and grief. What appears to be abstruse speculation about truth in fact lays bare the violence of war, the love and death of a friend, and the true historic role of the poet, more powerful than cannons. It is a theory of how a moral and intellectual genius attains eternal life by entering silently (and frequently unnoticed by all but a select few) into tradition.

A far more profound discovery for Scholem was how Benjamin had managed to write an "esoteric" tribute to his friend Heinle.[9] What may have tipped Scholem off was an inconspicuous line that the dead poet "must remain unforgotten, without a monument or keepsake, and even without a witness."[10] In any event, Benjamin's essay celebrates his friend; he bestows on Heinle, now hidden and unnamed in the work, cultural immortality.

Scholem, after having sharpened his philological and investigative skills on the detective novels his new friend had recommended, was skillful enough to unravel the various meanings woven into Benjamin's insular, self-contained world of esoteric reflection. Scholem was able to enter into the inner sanctum of Benjamin's intellectual world because he managed to see the luminous personal message behind the essay's arcane density.

Back in Berlin, while still deciphering the Hölderlin essay, Scholem received in the mail an eight-page handwritten letter, later known as "On Language as Such and on the Language of Man."[11] Esoteric in the extreme, Benjamin's essay turns to the mythic origins of language. The work was heavily influenced by both Molitor and Johann Georg Hamann (1730–1788), a friend of Immanuel Kant's who grew to distrust reason as a tool to reach the truth, and who thus preferred to write between the lines, using myth, irony, fragments, and hints in need of interpretation. Benjamin wrote in the same vein.

"On Language" is a web of myth and philosophy, fantastic claims, and seemingly indecipherable speculation. Benjamin uses the biblical myths of Adam, Original Sin, and the Name of God to attack the "bourgeois" and pragmatic theory of language, which attributes no inherent meaning to words but sees in them merely a product of convention. The essay made a particularly enduring impression on his young friend because of Benjamin's ample use of Jewish theological terms and metaphors. It also intrigued him for other reasons, not least because it was addressed to him as a personal letter, which in turn made it something much more than a speculative study of language.

Coming on the heels of their time together in Oberstdorf, this was enough to cement the young man's deep and abiding love for Benjamin. As his teacher's official scribe, he transcribed and typed up the essay on language, then handed out copies to selected friends. When he tried to translate it into Hebrew, he felt overwhelmed by a series of "miracles."[12] His first serious literary effort, his translations of biblical lamentations, he called a sequel to Benjamin's essay.[13]

Particular terms that appear in Benjamin's early written works and in personal conversations and letters—such as "Name," "History," "the Teaching," "Order" (a synonym for Kant's notion of "category"), and "Tradition"—began to crop up in Scholem's diary and correspondence.[14] With palpable excitement, he dressed up his friend's thoughts in expressions drawn from his own Zionism. "Torah" replaces the "Name" or "History" as the world of absolute meaning: he writes, for instance, "Torah is in everything, just as everything contains both speaking and silence."[15] "Zion" is the image of the just society, and the faithful Jew becomes the bearer of language. ("Each and every young Jew today, if he has a sense of true reverence, passes down the Torah; he develops and expands it.")[16]

Gerhard's old messianic dreams were now given form, a program, an anchor for his increasingly unstable mind. His loathing of Buberian "experience" was now matched by a new appreciation of Judaism's hermeneutical tradition. He now predicted with confidence that "the Messiah will be the last—and *first*—philosopher of language. He will deduce Judaism from its language."[17]

NOTEBOOK 1

After Breaking Out to Myself: En Route
March 1 to 11, 1916

March 1, 1916

I can't see any reason why I shouldn't be writing in this notebook. [. . .] I had the good sense, totally justified, to take a month's break. As in the oral tradition, I've used the time to take a good look at myself. Properly speaking, nothing has "occurred"—until today, that is, as will soon become clear.

On this day, the first of March, 1916, all of the 1897ers designated for the infantry were unexpectedly drafted. Löwenthal was sent to Hagenau, as was Harry Heymann [. . .] and, or so I've heard, the poet Gumpert.[1] There's a general dismay in the air. Of course, everything now will be twice as empty as before. I'm eager to see how many people will be missing from the Knopp seminar. [. . .][2]

In February I worked a lot and did it well. I began Arabic with Lubmann, and I can now read it with a bit of confidence.[3] Most of all, I've been studying Hebrew and mathematics. The persistent use of the language has already had its intended effects. This afternoon I was invited to the Young Judeans at the Herzl Club, who want to create a Hebrew club.[4] Arabic lessons are also held in Hebrew, even though mathematics (some people call it philosophy) and not Arabic is what I'm most focused on. Schwarz[5] says that a philosopher once responded to the query "What is philosophy" by calling it the systematic misuse of a terminology specifically created for this purpose, and which is abstruse in the extreme.

A variety of factors have led me to reflect on mathematical issues, above all on the question of foundations. In my fantasy (which recently has been powerfully stirred up) I thought up a truly devastating lecture, subsequently held on my way between here and the university. It was on the foundations of mathematics. In a letter to Benjamin I've made a few intimations about it, as I have in conversations with Frau Lissauer (who's someone I still need to write something about).[6] And yet I'm still completely at the beginning of my cogitations, and I feel more the potential and rhythm of mathematics than its substance and truth. [. . .]

March 2, 1916

[. . .] If we had a political party, it would need to be the party of "honest radicals," in contrast to the radicals who after 35 years still drift around Germany without having dared to do a thing! Exactly one year ago was the trial at the Luisenstadt Gymnasium.[7] Contrary to all predictions, since this friendly warning I haven't become softer and more agreeable than on March 1 of last year. I have almost entirely purged myself of memories of school years; they aren't worth remembering. Today if I see my former teachers, I can walk past them with indifference. They are factors in my life I can permit myself to neglect. It's baffling how these people live out the days allotted to them, stupidly and quietly. There are very few revolutionaries among the teaching staff, which explains why there are so many nihilists like Goldschneider.[8] [. . .]

As I was recently again thinking about Wyneken, and I wanted to get a clear grip on his mistakes, the most decisive inspiration came to me as if in a flash. It concerned what Buber possesses and he lacks. To get something great out of the cauldron of history, a person has to experience history over and over. Nothing must be allowed to stand between him and history; as in Kierkegaard's relationship to Christianity, he must be confronted by it as a terrifying totality, naked and unconcealed. Only out of this sense of horror is a liberating renewal possible. Wyneken lacks this; he's too much of a pedagogue to pay any attention to it. Nor does this Hegelian have any intuition. On this score I think Buber deserves some credit, since he once wrestled with history as a category of life. Though he may have created out of it an objectively false construction of history (indeed most certainly has), this struggle has given him something that bears the visible mark of great horrors that must have surrounded his birth. This is what attracts the youth. The fact that Buber has descended into the depths while others wisely remained on the surface necessarily speaks in his favor—even if he's not the one able to compel the depths, as is needed for a decisive action. He isn't strong enough. A mystic will arise who knows that he himself is lost and who preserves a new religiosity within the bosom of his prophetic message. No one can follow Buber now. He has—as he said so himself—given his undirected soul up to ecstasy. Nevertheless, unlike all other ideologues, he is great because he has truly experienced history, and because the duality Buber-History was once a reality. And this is also something Benjamin will have to prove one day: that he has seen history in a new and fabulous way. Otherwise, he has no justification in wanting to build something completely new. No one has a right to speak who, in the midst of thinking, hasn't been overcome with the experience of *glimpsing the essence of history.* [. . .]

A scene from the underworld: the persons involved are the ghosts of Goethe, Jean Paul, Hölderlin, Bodenstedt,[9] and Fritz Mauthner. A tug-of-war pits Goethe, Bodenstedt, and Mauthner against the two others. As the latter are victorious, Mauthner takes a magical formula from the *Critique of Language* he borrowed from Landauer and throws it into Hölderlin's face. Hölderlin, from the force of this empty negation, is pinned to the wall and remains stuck there like a poem by Morgenstern. Meanwhile, Jean Paul uses *Hesperus* and *Campanerthal,* as well as *Flegeljahren,*[10] in a fencing duel with Goethe and Bodenstedt. "He's a philistine," Goethe vomits out, while the other one blabbers bosh. The spirit of Stern rises up and gives the blue crown to Jean Paul (who could have become more universal than Goethe if he had found the courage to be myopic). [. . .]

March 3, 1916

It's indeed welcome news that Benjamin is returning to Berlin (for at least six weeks). Now nestled in my refuge, I can discuss out loud—really discuss—questions I'm preoccupied with. It's not that I consider loneliness to be an inferior state of being. Quite the contrary: the legitimacy of revolutionary critique has been demonstrated through loneliness, and through my ability to act as my own opponent in discussions. For good reason I acquired this talent in earliest childhood. Still, it's a thrilling thought to establish community with someone so productive and awe-inspiring. I can't discuss these things with Brauer,[11] or with any of the others. It's depressing for everyone involved that I can't reveal my Zionist concerns to the Zionists, just as I can't talk to them about anything else because they lack the doubts and desires to really think. I have to go to Benjamin, the non-Zionist and non-mathematician, for this. He has a voice, whereas most of the others don't even respond.

Today I read Plato's *Symposium* and, just as I had expected, I loved it. What's so completely shattering is that Plato, with all his matter-of-factness, really can't say what true Eros is; he can only allude to it with pictures and metaphors. All he can do is drop hints to someone who, through previous discussions among friends, already intuits or knows what it is. Through sympathy, he knows that Eros is the love of one's own life. But even this is only a metaphor. This book could only have been written by a mathematician who knows something about the impossibility of speaking concretely outside of mathematics (mathematics being the only region where knowledge can be communicated). It was for this reason that Plato chose this remarkable language, which for me still has the hues (yes!) of mathematics. [. . .]

March 6, 1916

The most amazing thing one discovers on vacation is a strangely heightened receptive ability. The longer you rest, the better you're able to look around. Despite its being Father's birthday (an event in itself), and all his children were present (predictably, the older he gets, the more he wants to have his children around), yesterday I read Voss's book which had just arrived, *The Essence of Mathematics*.[12] [. . .]

So, dear sirs, is it better to think for yourself, investing the effort without perhaps coming up with such great results, or to read books by great minds that are so foreign yet familiar? Who is better, Jean Paul or me (there can't be the slightest doubt that Scholem *is*—not I am—better than Goethe), the progenitor or the progeny? It is here that a marriage must be performed, or in the worst case, procreation must be performed alone. Benjamin's essay touches this issue as well.[13] The way has to be found between the creative and the generative Eros. Speaking is to see oneself in the mirror of language. Silence is always proud.

March 8, 1919

[. . .] Surely man's deepest stratum is reverence, and reverence is also what I believe forms the essence of holiness. "Good" and "evil" part ways here. Good people are those who are soaked through with reverence for things, for all things. "Evil" people lack this. [. . .]

Yesterday a good piece of evidence again fell into my hand backing up my conception of writing history: Thomas Mann's *Friedrich and the Great Coalition* (in Fischer's series "Texts to Modern History").[14] Historians should use this extraordinary attempt to say something essential—and original, of course—about Friedrich the Great as a model. "Oh that you fellows could also be like Mann—an artist without the claim to 'science,' that is to say, without the truth." Thomas Mann of course knows that his book is anything but science, but it is precisely here that we see what it takes to fill in, or leap over, the abyss of historical skepticism. What psychology! What grandiose subjectivity! What irony! And his German! Thomas Mann takes a look at someone (and he sees him exceptionally well) who has some apparent or genuine similarity to Friedrich II, then calls him the king of Prussia. Naturally, he isn't. He *could* be. It is a possibility among other possibilities, a possibility that, in this case because of its unique process, awakens our favorable prejudice (that it's the truth). It does so in the most audacious manner by standing all the "original sources" on their head, which Mann dismisses as hypocritical (and there's a lot to support this), and then tries to grasp Friedrich the Great, the king of Prussia, with pure intuition. This may be the outline for a unique piece of fiction. History it isn't, nor does it pretend to be. Moreover, it's replete with such mocking and irony that one grasps Mann's intention, which is the notion of different possibilities. It could have happened that an overpowering devil sat on the throne and fooled fate, fooled himself, and fooled the entire world. He makes an excellent comment when he writes on pages 112 and 113, which are extraordinary both as psychology and fiction: "If someone has a sense for horror, then 'the old Fritz' is a horrible name, for it's clearly awful that a demon becomes popular and is given such a jolly name." [. . .]

It is a proof of the spirit's power and expansiveness that the spiritual life of man has come up with mathematics and religion, two things so different and essentially unrelated (which makes them easily juxtaposed). People say I'm not artistic, which I readily admit. I'm not. But my lack is not only in the sense that art is supposedly an independent arena of life, in which case I have no business doing it. It is also possible, however, that art could exist outside of art. If one excluded the other, which they don't, I would much prefer being mathematical than artistic. Religion and mathematics are more substantial than art, and one can safely say that the poet, to the extent that he is a man of substance, should be counted not among the artists but among the reverential and religious, though rarely the ultra-religious. The poet who is an artist has no value, except for entertainment. Look at Arno Holz![15] Stefan George is, by contrast, considered to be religious. [. . .]

March 11, 1916

[. . .] In thinking about mathematics, I've come up with sharper formulations of the idea that, excepting mysticism, only mathematics can know something in its essence. All knowledge is thus mathematical and deductive. The greatest criminal and jackass is someone who has access to mathematics and then misuses it by applying it to things that are utterly foreign to it. Take the "problem of substance," for instance. Such things cannot be known by means of mathematics. It's possible that eventually Benjamin will also end up in mysticism, or he's already there. [. . .]

I've often thought that if someone were really to know my books and look at what's behind them, what's hiding in the corners, he would know me completely. Maybe it's a drawback or shortcoming that I express myself through a library, which makes me truly superfluous because the library can take my place (which isn't the case, and is a false inference!). But this much should be clear: all that could be discovered is my longing, and knowing my longing is what I call knowing me. Clearly, one wouldn't know what I think but only how I'm basically put together. Which is enough. Besides me, no one has ever attempted to study my library. It's difficult work with too little payback: me.

If nothing earth-shattering occurs, which I'm always prepared for, I'll probably put my diary aside and store up what's happening in my memory and brain. It'll be spiritual rest for the sake of spiritual labor. I'm an elevator that's stuck in place. [. . .]

NOTEBOOK 2

Zion and Youth: Reflections on Myself

June 15–August 1, 1916

June 15, 1916

A paralysis is now following on the heels of a time of creative joy, which is what happens every time I set my sights on something. At the moment,

I can't get back to writing the essay—that is, to prepare it for print. I'm caught in a curious state of laziness. I'm now living out the ideal I demanded of myself this summer. For hours and days on end I can hike and rest without thinking anything in particular. During a fabulous hike I again sang old songs to myself, along with a great number of things from the old Jewish prayer book called the Siddur. Recently, each time I've been in a joyful mood, I haven't been able to express it better than through prayer. I still can't. With great passion I've said the prayer "Eighteen"[16] three times a day. [. . .]

I visited the Jewish cemetery in Ulm. It's brand new and situated next to a beautiful old Catholic one. Besides this, there's a large festival full of amusements taking place. In Munich I was afraid that I would be so preoccupied with Benjamin that I wouldn't write a thing on the essay. My provisional conclusion is that there can be no Jewish youth movement because it lacks *content* and *greatness*. [. . .] Without the courage to myopia and dogmatism, and lacking *Blue-White Spectacles,* everything's a waste of time. [. . .]

June 18, 1916

After we finally got a day of beautiful weather, the rain hasn't stopped pouring down in the most hideous and paralyzing way. Early tomorrow morning I'm heading back to Munich, and from there I'll go directly to Oberstdorf. I've followed Benjamin to his friends' here because we wanted to talk this morning, which we succeeded in doing only to a very limited extent. (In Munich we were together for just a day and a half.) At least it's now becoming clear that Benjamin has arrived at Judaism, and it won't take long till he experiences for himself the necessity of learning Hebrew. In discussing *The Jew*[17] I told him a lot about Judaism. Just as I had rightly suspected and told Buber, he has no ability or inclination to collaborate on *The Jew* because his current position precludes any literary activity. Given the circumstances at present, he has no other option but to express disapproval that someone should create journals at all. [. . .]

June 22, 1916

Jean Paul's *Die Flegeljahre* is indescribably lovely! "The Persians believe that on the Day of Judgment statues will demand souls from their sculptors."

God is the only true bourgeois subject; he alone has no forebears! *Die Flegeljahre* is in many places even better than the utterly magnificent *Siebenkäs* (though it can scarcely be compared to his *Titan*). The richness of Jean Paul's spirit (which to me is more a palace than a field of ruins) is so astounding that you could imagine this genius to have single-handedly composed the Talmud (which he frequently cites). A person could easily spend days ruminating over the epigrams he, out of his superabundance, comes up with by the thousands without ever coming to an end.

To be a Hebrew Jean Paul!! What a desire! This would require two ingredients: first a translation, and then a spirit like his, only translated into Hebrew! [. . .]

The final and gravest original sin of our youth, which was their reaction to the outbreak of war, only goes to prove one thing: it is impossible for a Jewish youth movement to arise among those who considered it conceivable and even a matter of duty to absorb Jewish ideas and who nevertheless gave themselves over freely to Moloch. Some even did this just for the sake of paradox.

It may be that they have longing, as does everyone else. But it cannot be emphasized enough that you can't build a movement just to be talking nonstop about *desire,* as if desire were the content, form, and expression of a movement. Life must arise out of longing, *and longing must bear fruit.* Out of true Jewish longing there must spring forth a true devotion, an act of entering into and up to Judaism. Longing must first and foremost lead us to work on ourselves and to enter into marriage with Judaism, and to do so requires far more difficult and sacrificial work than listening to a lecture. Longing must produce content, and this has until now not been the case. The movement has been prepared by a handful of young people whose longing has truly awakened life, and for whom Judaism isn't just a flag but a marching order. Since the movement lies *within* these young people, a movement between them can arise.

You can't erect a house out of desire, but only out of the fruits of desire, in the same way that you can't eat seeds but only what the seeds produce.

[. . .] The new youth has been impelled forward in its development by the war. The earlier youth, which has fallen apart, is both spiritually and physically gone, nor will it be back. A new generation, my generation, now stands before the overwhelming dimensions of the task. It may well be appropriate here to reflect on this task, a task that I believe must be undertaken for the movement, that is to say, for the future.

June 25, 1916

[. . .] Today I finished Jean Paul's *Flegeljahre*. Like every other reader, I'm only sorry the book's not three times thicker. It's really fabulous. Just as Anatole France later did in his books, Jean Paul carves out of himself silhouettes, and whatever he comes up with—Walk and Vult, Albano, Roquairol and Schoppe, Leibgeber, and Siebenkäs—has eternal validity. Jean Paul venerates friendship throughout his novels; it's always at least as important as the love of woman, which also plays a part in his books (in *Titan* it even carries the action). He would have gotten along well with Plato. It's superfluous yet necessary to comment on *Flegeljahre*. Best of all would be to have a newborn spirit like Jean Paul's.

Youth Movement. Among the most serious shortcomings of the youth "movement" is its lack of a unified orientation: of a single goal. For people are too preoccupied with other things—they are "working"—to see the goal. People haven't paid any attention whatsoever to Judaism, but rather to "Judaism *and* something else." And all of these "ands"—and everyone picks his own, sometimes more than one—prevent people from reflecting upon themselves. I don't accuse the youth of having no goal, which surely would be a serious accusation; nor do I say that their *goals* form a confusing multiplicity. What I'm saying is that they bring with themselves nothing essential, *not even and above all themselves.* They carry around a lot of good things, which is no contradiction to what I just said, because they have left behind their true self, their true personality. We have yet to learn how to give power to ourselves and our ultimate Being. [. . .]

June 26, 1916

My conception of a Jewish youth movement is this: young people moving as a whole and in their wholeness toward Zion. The key conception here is wholeness. All individual demands must be derived from the conception of wholeness—wholeness of the dedicated person, wholeness of the way and the goal, wholeness of the demand and of the sacrifice. Though I had previously thought I had a pretty good understanding of

Benjamin's essay "Life of Students," it was only last night that I believe I truly grasped it *creatively*.[18] It was while I was in my own train of thought and I finally arrived at the concept of wholeness that I discovered that wholeness is nothing other than what Benjamin calls an acting person's "totality." I've now thoroughly translated this essay into my own language. I've come across the problem and the solution by thinking the article through afresh, and then thinking it through once again from within my own linguistic forms and my own spirit, the spirit of Zion. [. . .] (How many times have I done this by now?) [. . .]

June 28, 1916

[. . .] Among the numerous documentations of confusion, the most recent examples that come to mind are Heinrich Margulies's essay in the *Jüdische Rundschau* (May 11, 1915, "The War of Those Left Behind"),[19] and Alfred Lemm's "We German Jews" from February 1916[20] (which is sky high above the first essay because it searches for something better, even if in the most decisive points it also succumbs to confusion). Especially noteworthy is Dr. Fohlen's intrinsically and profoundly scandalous and repellent eulogy to his fallen comrade Jacques Bing (*Jüdische Rundschau,* June 16, 1916).

I read the eulogy yesterday evening, and one can only imagine the mood it put me in! At once I wrote a card to the author and asked him for more details. This is unimaginable in days like these. And the editors accepted it! [. . .]

I could sum up everything I now desire as an epigram someone could in all honesty inscribe on my gravestone: *He Was His Name*—which is to say, he was total, he was *Scholem*.[21] By living out his name, he was what his name required of him: like it, he was complete and undivided. The upshot is that he who is total or wants to be total cannot be confused, or he cannot want to be confused. The true solution is to "remain unconfused." I'm thankful to Alfred Kerr[22] for really giving it to the Krauts. To hell with these people and their shepherds who are confused! [. . .]

June 29, 1916

For thus saith the Lord of hosts: Yet once, it is a little while, and I will shake the heavens and the earth, and the sea, and the dry land, and I will shake all nations, and the choicest things of all nations shall come, and I will fill this house with glory, saith the Lord of hosts. Mine is the silver, and Mine the gold, saith the Lord of hosts. The glory of this latter house shall be greater than that of the former, saith the Lord of hosts; and in this place will I give peace, saith the Lord of hosts. Haggai 2:6–9.[23]

July 13, 1916

On a tour of Einödsbach over the last few days I was once again completely overtaken by enthusiasm, which was accompanied by a swarm of ideas for the next volume of *Blue-White Spectacles.* We'll have to decisively "bring it back to life" with a tremendous series of editions as genuine documentations of the movement. And at the end of volume 12 we will write: "We hereby declare our work to be over; let the work begin!"

I'm now constantly caught in a mood of such lofty enthusiasm for the new *Blue-White Spectacles* that I want to reach an understanding with my friends in Berlin about it, and the sooner the better. Now I know exactly what I want, and I have more than enough to say. The plan for a series of essays and commentary includes: "Manifesto of Youth" (which will no doubt be written soon); "What Is Radicalism? An Attempt at Drawing Borders"; "Revolution: Over a Necessary Spiritual Stance for the Youth"; "Buber and Us: Remarks on the Jewish Movement" (which in one way or the other will settle the score with Buber).

Feeling so utterly complete and anchored religiously in the thoughts of Zion, I can now allow myself "subterranean screams." It is in *Blue-White Spectacles* that *our* youth will herald its manifesto. Art is seeing life through spectacles. Radicalism is when the spectacles become so much a part of one's existence that the two fuse to determine *everything*—action and idea, things both on the other side of the world and next door. [. . .]

Epilogue of a Pessimist:[24]

We had believed that the youth had something to say, that they had *a lot to* say out of their strength of will, their lofty goal, and their unfathomable path. Because of what we knew we wanted to cry out, to call forth until those we had been waiting for—who were our friends from afar, the youth of tomorrow like the night watchman waiting for the morning—found their way to us. We have carried around a dream of a new brotherhood, and in this dream the calling of a new-old truth has become alive within us. We have appeared before you, and not because we were under the illusion of superiority, nor out of arrogance and delusion.

We have done so because we have had the feeling of a true calling: that so long as we were the only ones, it was our duty to share what we know. We *had* to issue the call. We beseeched you to join the brotherhood of a new youth.

But you, the youth, did *not* come. You never showed up. Why?

It is not allowed to speak about this, for we are biased. But still, perhaps you didn't come because *we* weren't the right ones to awaken you, though it is also possible that *you* didn't want to be awakened. But as long as the jury is still out, it is our inward duty to regard *ourselves* as the guilty party.

Within you still lies the full range of possibilities. We will go our way, and yet we still demand of you that you come *now*. If you don't, we will know that it is not our fault that this call has been unanswered. It is yours. And once this uninvited crier has withdrawn, the knowledge of this will be terrifying, and not only for us. We will then know that you will not to be the ones to build Zion.

Where did you go? A clear call has pierced the fog to reach you, but the call did not stay with you, and it didn't want to be absorbed into the fog. You have stayed where you were: in a state of confusion. We have issued the call for you to make a decision for life or for death, and you should have chosen life. But you didn't make *any* decision *at all*.

No one can overcome confusion for *you;* only you can do it for yourself. For this reason our call is superfluous. It is worthless. It can't help you in the least, for you have not yet recognized the misery of your own soul. We just don't understand one another: we the awoken ones who scream at you on the streets—and we too are young!—and you that live in confusion. Our languages will continue to remain different until our experiences have converged, and *until you have found the way, the way to Zion!*

July 15, 1916

To Werner,[25] on Simmel and Weininger:[26]
Simmel's typical intellectual discourse makes both of his books (especially *Religion*)[27] enormously difficult. Simmel is one of the exceptions among German professors of philosophy, and yet I consider him just about the worst of the lot. He's a man who has succeeded in *dissolving himself entirely into a terminological system.* He has created a machinery bearing the name "Simmel" that functions as follows: one inserts a prob-

lem, the "Simmel" machine moves and reacts purely mechanically, it translates the problem into a foreign language, and after a bit of time elapses a book or an essay gets spat out—which, if people consider it valuable, then has to be retranslated back into the original. There is surely some greatness here, but for me it's not worth talking about. If you knew Simmel, you would agree with me. With the possible exception of Hermann Cohen, nowhere is the fullness of life so completely translated into a system of the most difficult and, for my taste, purely mechanical abstractions. It took me *four attempts* to understand the small (and lovely!) volume published by Goeschen.[28] If language has to be abstract, I'd much prefer the Upanishads. Simmel is the most extreme sublimation of the language of the Talmud. It takes 1,500 years of intellectual culture to produce such a man.

There's an anecdote Buber told me in Heidelberg that relates to the connection between Simmel and Weininger. In the course of his and Simmel's discussion of Weininger, Simmel exclaimed: "If Weininger had known me—Simmel!—he wouldn't have committed suicide!!!" It's rather naïve to think that anything could have changed Weininger, whose disease was curable neither by men nor by philosophers because it came from himself, or rather from his Judaism. Weininger is one of the most terrifying representatives of the type of man (Blüher[29] also numbers along them) who is plainly tragic and for whom problems inexorably lead back to himself. Usually this results in suicide. Though I've frequently denounced the method as false or unjustified, I can only analyze Weininger from a psychological rather than an evaluative angle. It's impossible that "he got many things right." It only appears that way. *For me,* he was neither right nor wrong, as his mental attitude is no longer accessible to me. I have to confess to being of the opinion that the future task for the Jewish nation is to produce as few such people as possible—people full of issues I'm still unable to grasp. Compared to this, everything "sensational" about Weininger is secondary. I'm not interested in his view of women or the like but only in *him*—or, if you want (and as *he* wanted), his view on Judaism. He fell to pieces internally because of Judaism. He could have easily been a hero of a story by Perez, for whom the world and humans become a question mark because he has become a question mark to himself. "Who am I?"

A comment on *Das Ziel:* it is not of primary importance to change

the world but rather to change Herr Rubiner.[30] Zionism; Platonism; the
French Revolution: Benjamin!

July 23, 1916

[. . .] With irrevocable lucidity, truth, and clarity, I've gradually yet finally
come to the realization that I don't fit in with these people here, these
German Jews. I cannot meet with any of them, male or female, without
something compelling me—be it the beauty of the topic at hand or an
unconscious troublemaking streak—to be frank with them, completely
frank. Without exception, I've noticed a chasm as wide as the sky separating me from these people. The entire lot of them—whoever they are:
be they named Cohn, Scholem, Huth, or Hirsch—pretend to be far-
sighted, but it's obvious that they haven't the slightest understanding of
the greatness and anti-bourgeois nature of things. Our relationship is
permanently destroyed the instant they realize this. They now "know"
me to be an intolerant fanatic. Thank God! In the vocabulary of the
bourgeoisie, there is no more accurate or necessary description. From
this comes the bourgeoisie's "shocking" consensus in their judgment of
me: with sound instincts, they've all felt the same thing after having seen
into my inner self. [. . .] Instinctively, they arm themselves against this
hostile destroyer of their peace of mind and comfort.

If I can't shake the habit of speaking with these bourgeois types about
things that are for me essential, I'll soon be a failed human being. What
compels me to give these people—for whom salvation has been denied—instruction in the way of Zion? One mustn't speak to the bourgeoisie about God. There shall be no peace with them, says the Lord. For
its part, the bourgeoisie is also by nature very much opposed to God!
This is the truth.

What I've always experienced as particularly monstrous about these
people is their universal hypocrisy toward one another. Immediately after
her arrival, Frau Scholem told Frau Cohn that she's always alone and isn't
one for a lot of company, which is a shameless lie that sprang forcibly out
of Frau Scholem's psychology. Frau Cohen replied in the same vein. And
what happened? These "ladies" are walking, standing, and sitting with
each other every possible minute of the day. And this too is a lie because
they don't know what to do with each other. Good grief! What a paradoxical bunch of Jews! How angry they are when you hold a mirror
up to them! "Now, please, don't criticize me!" is my mother's stock for-

mula. Or she looks pathetically to her friend, and both—equally under threat—agree that Frau Scholem has a hard life with such an undutiful son! If the gods could only hear this!

July 24, 1916

In my more arrogant hours I sometimes think that Athens, the city of philosophers (not to mention Königsberg),[31] fares miserably in comparison to Zion and Göttingen. This may be mere vanity, and it's probably not even true. But when measured against Zion, everything disappears; being immeasurably small, everything else can be neglected. And what about Göttingen . . . or perhaps Port Royal?[32]

In the temple for all my demigods and Caesars I'll erect in Jaffa, Herr Plato and Herr Gauss will rotate places daily; Herr Pascal, Newton, Leibniz, and Kepler monthly; and Herr Husserl will be sacrificed to every ten years.[33] All others will have to make do with special mention in the book I've yet to write, *Jerusalem for a Thinking Humanity or a Large Measuring Rod in the Vest Pocket.* The book goes all the way up to the father of the Messiah. For the religious, it'll be something special!

July 28, 1916

[. . .] Pushing it a bit, one can distinguish among three classes of ideologies: Berlin, Heppenheim,[34] and Zion. Berlin is the ideology of the politician, the tactician, and the phony; Heppenheim is the ideology of confusion; while Zion, our Teaching, is the ideology of dogmatism, truth, and *one necessary* standpoint.

Berlin requires Zion for logical reasons; Heppenheim out of experience and desires; Zion demands itself. Why? Why indeed! One *major* difference separates the position of Zion from the others. The Berlin perspective exists, as does that of Heppenheim, and all the others, too. Zion is a perspective that does not yet exist. So where do the demands of Zion come from? From itself! Is this verging on nonsense? Not in the least, for it's the only adequate expression for our way of thinking. [. . .]

These three possible classes of ideologies are at the same time three different perspectives: one demands something foreign, the other experience, and the last itself!

The necessary perspective is the one from which the movement receives its eternal impetus and which makes it impossible to stand still. From this point one can see and then ascend directly into heaven. We must also stand where the prophets and Moses stood. Out of this follows the necessity of *the most extreme* position and most extreme demand.

Those who herald the demand are still on the path—and the fact that they do so at all is itself a stage on this path. They wrestle with the path; they move on it. With the utmost clarity and undisguised honesty, it is at some point a matter of duty to proclaim this on the streets we can reach, even if these streets are down in the depths. Screaming is an act. A magnificent motto for a commentary on screaming is Isaiah 57:1 or 40:8.

The prophets were screamers in our sense of the word. "Get thee up into the high mountain, O thou that speaks good tidings to Jerusalem." Or: "Cry aloud, spare not, lift up thy voice like a horn."[35]

July 29, 1916

[. . .] In number 4 of *The Jew* there's an article that merits a lot of attention, no matter how objectionable the views it propagates are. It is on our relationship to German politics. [. . .] By contrast, I was very pleased with Elias Auerbach's essay on our position vis-à-vis tradition, in particular how it relates to the education of the coming generation.[36] I could have literally written the essay myself, and it's the same line I've always taken in dealing with Orthodox Judaism. This position is the only possible one for someone who *knows* tradition and who wants to turn loose its creative forces so that they can be active within the youth. The best way to do this would be through a religious Zionism (as I imagine it and as I have possibly even attained) that can be achieved without bending the rules of the religion in the slightest. I'm realizing increasingly that Zion is a religious symbol. Of what? It is a symbol of the *Jewish* concept of redemption, a concept not corroded away by Christianity. I'm of course no slave of tradition, and I would handle it freely. I wouldn't require my son to put on phylacteries, but eventually I would strictly observe the dietary laws (this would depend on my wife). Above all, I'd work to bring life into our fabulous and inimitable holidays: the three Passover feasts, Rosh Hashanah, and Yom Kippur. [. . .] I would naturally teach my children to follow the Jewish customs of Yom Kippur. All else will find its creative outlet in the Land of Israel, where everything that is beautiful and is at all available to us will be created anew, and where new symbols will emerge the instant a seeker of Zion, full of mystical fervor, charges into the life there. The Torah will come alive as it rarely has in the past because we—we Zionists—will be religious. [. . .]

Today's the anniversary of the European funeral.[37] Europe has abdicated, opening up the way to a better Orient. (Today's Turkey is *not,* of course, what I mean by a "better Orient.")

What should one do for today's jubilee? One wants to make peace, peace at any price, but can only let out curses. Oh for a few sticks of dynamite!

The "holiday spirit" is so depressed that even the "weaklings" are astonished. The German people are paying a bitter price for the crimes of their masters, the miscalculations of their military leaders, and the contemptibility of their professors of history and philosophy. Oh, what a dark pit of wickedness.

Today Eduard Bernstein and Hugo Haase, both *Jews* (isn't this symbolic?), are going to speak out publicly against the war.[38] Joining them will be Herr Harnack,[39] the so-called "Mr. Thick and Thin." People in Berlin no doubt have more sympathy for Haase than Harnack.

What about us Jews? Here I won't say a word, otherwise I might violate my neutrality. *Blue-White Spectacles* (and in truth all other newspapers and periodicals) should appear with a black border around the text. The content should be a few obituaries to (1) our silent brothers and heroes in the East; (2) our butchered victims who were forced to serve; (3) volunteers (with an extra curse thrown in); and (4) our intellectuals *à la* Wassermann.[40] The conclusion will be an appeal to the youth to emigrate and to establish a better humanity.

It's surely of great consequence and importance that my most decisive intellectual development over the last two years has taken place during wartime (another year will certainly be added to these), which has forced me, in total subjective and objective harmony, onto the path of radicalism. Two years ago I had arrived at the juncture where I could embark on a path that could lead to Zion. Now I've made my choice, clearly and decisively. [. . .]

Today in heaven a mighty Kaddish[41] will be said for Europe. Will it be the "Kaddish of renewal," as in cemeteries during funerals? No, it'll be the *Kaddish of condemnation* against the servants of Moloch. Calling out from Zion, God lifts up his voice against the seducers in Berlin and the wretches in St. Petersburg.

It's around eleven o'clock in the evening. The heavens move silently in circles, and with such musicality that the human spirit is said to be incapable of hearing and comprehending it. Stars hang in the heavens above me; they are glittering sparks from souls, each one a fallen angel. Occasionally, shooting stars lose their way over the high rooftops and are extinguished in the endlessness. Surely these are souls that have merged forever into godliness, having found their goal. Without a doubt, the evening star world is but our inner life, projected outwards. And the star group of godliness and the Milky Way of desire orbit around the two hemispheres of good and evil. [. . .] The Milky Way divides itself into two parts, and its orbit encompasses an island. God dwells on this massive island full of mystery, in the womb of our souls' unborn light. He who believes in God is an astronomer, and a good one, too. It goes without saying that the star of Zion, by virtue of its own laws (and they are indeed strange ones), beams out in its evening movements across lonely stretches under the heavenly stars that are within us. Its brightness is amazing, incomparable to Sirius, and rises on the horizon of the inner skies. [. . .]

The Messiah will be an astronomer in Asia. The Zohar is a holy book, a shooting star. These days it flashes bright only in the memory. [. . . .]

NOTEBOOK 3

Miscellanea from a Mechanistic Picture of the World

July 11, 1916

Our age has completely forgotten to honor and understand the greatness of the mechanistic picture of the world. In times like these—when the "organic" way of seeing has become so entirely dominant and in which everything is spiritually animated and ostensibly non-mechanistic—it has become a matter of duty to reflect on the true value and deepest meaning of mechanistic thinking, which appeared to such great minds as Kepler, Galileo, and Newton as the final possibility and factual form events take.

How did this revolution and renunciation come about? People quickly discovered that the mechanistic picture of the world only really worked in the very limited arena of "pure mechanics," where it was possible to express all events without exception through the operations of mechanics and through a finite number of second-order differential equations. Here there were no gaps. But already in other areas of physics, in electromagnetic and other phenomena, for instance, this explanation didn't suffice. As for the appearance of life and of spirituality, the mechanistic point of view, which submits everything to mathematics, seemed to fail altogether. It wasn't only that such phenomena would have to be placed under different mathematical categories than second-order differential equations, or that perhaps the discovery of a new "mechanism" with new functional relationships would be able to explain life's processes. No, the mechanistic view was fundamentally denied the ability to serve as an explanatory and ordering principle for the richness of phenomena and of *World Events. History in its widest scope was exempted from the mechanistic worldview.*

When the attempt was made to point out "laws" with a supposedly different structure from mathematical-mechanical ones, they were entirely novel and differently construed. This was the upshot of the entire organic philosophy of history. That it's nonsense is obvious, as the concept of *Law* is nothing other than a functional and mathematical relationship, otherwise it is no longer a law. $Y = f(x)$ is quite simply the form of a law, nor is there *any* justification to make a distinction here between "natural laws," whose formal relationship is $y = f(x)$, and the "historical laws" whose structure is supposed to be different. How then? In light of the impossibility from the human perspective of understanding history scientifically, it must be conceded that two sorts of *possible* a priori sciences must be *fundamentally* distinguished: one is mathematical, mechanistic, and cognitive, while the other is historically determined. Factually, however, only laws of the first order exist and are feasible; by contrast, the second class of laws inherently fall victim to a form of skepticism directed against the possibility of historical knowledge.

We too want to admit that mundane sciences and mathematics cannot deduce and establish necessity for spiritual processes, by which is meant all processes outside pure mechanics. The realm of spontaneity, of spiritual and organic realities, will provisionally be recognized. The only question is whether some entirely new perspective—of a completely different sort from all previous models—will enable us to understand and deduce the world process as a mechanistic necessity (and this has been the final goal of intellectual thinking since prehistory). The aim being that every detail, each event in the life of a fly and every thought in the brain of a philosopher, will be completely explicable in mechanistic terms.

It's obvious that till now no one has come up with such a purely cognitive picture of the world (and we can debate the reasons for this later), and everyone who has tried has violated this principle at some point (Hegel constantly violated it, and at every point) by sneaking in a teleological, moral, and finally mystical way of seeing. To be sure, they filled their world with life; but their ambition was not fulfilled, and the world has yet to be comprehended by exclusively intellectual means. It seems that this preliminary work will be the task for a new mystic, who will forge different ways of knowledge [. . .] in order to give his ideas a foundation as deep as the world. [. . .]

This mathematical mystic, or mystical mathematician, will surely be a Jew. He will be the Messiah. The idea of mysticism is Zion, and that of mathematics is Torah. As it is said, "And out of Zion will go forth the Torah."[42]

NOTEBOOK 4

Myth-Mongers

August 14–December 30, 1916

We young people are all in some way myth-mongers, some of us very strongly so.
—Diary entry from December 18, 1916

August 14, 1916

Over the last fourteen days, after weeks of enthusiasm and elation, I've fallen into a state of laziness and incapacity to work. The time has come to look for help through forceful means. Since receiving Brauer's last letter, I've made it my primary duty and intention to write my essays for *Blue-White Spectacles,* volume 4.[43] But then I slipped suddenly into a state in which I couldn't work, even with the best effort and greatest desire. You go for a walk and say to yourself: "Yes, tomorrow morning I'll surely begin my work." You then go home, sit on your bed, and dream about the magnificence of future *Spectacles.* In the morning you're simply not spiritually fit to do a thing; you feel no motivation other than torpor, and you put off the entire business till the afternoon. In the afternoon the sun is burning so hot that you just can't get a thing done, and hence your sloth continues over days on end, till you reach a point where the spirit finally rebels. All my grandiose notions are still with me, I just can't give them a satisfactory form. The lovely weather over the last three weeks does its part in preventing me from gathering my forces. How often I've silently longed for the return of bad weather, which will force me to stay home and write. [. . .] The time has come to do something: to do my duty.

Walter Benjamin's invitation and prompt retraction has had a hand in wearing me out. I was really looking forward to being together with him, having already firmly decided to embark on a new epoch. Namely, to do something. And then all my calculations got upset. I still don't know where Benjamin has gone, but I'll certainly hear from him soon. I don't know if we'll see each other, it may be that he'll be away for a long time. Apparently he's really ill; he's not as skilled a faker (or hypocrite) as I.

I haven't been totally inactive, just in the arena where I have moral obligations. Otherwise, I've been doing all kinds of reading, the most important being Werner's two thick war diaries (each one is like this journal) that he wrote between September 15 and November 2 (which is also Mother and Father's silver anniversary). He gave them the lovely title "My Life's Nocturne." I sensed in these diaries such tremendous desire that I only barely repressed the urge to make a copy of them. They are a first-class *documentum humanum.* If anything is left of the belief in the Germans' right to wage a "war of culture," Werner has totally smashed it. Indeed, if it weren't for the love of neutrality, reading this could make a person into a first-class enemy of the Germans. There can be no doubt as to the truth of the diary. I had thought it next to impossible that the face of the Krauts would look like this. Now documented, every rape of a Russian girl can be broadcast out into the world. By the way, I wasn't prepared for these kinds of stories. At first I thought that the general barbarity of the Krauts would be highlighted, but never did I imagine that such Cossacks dwell in holy Germany. Involuntarily, I often had to laugh out loud at what he recounts. I hope that Werner's monument in honor of the German soldier continues all the way up to the time he was wounded.[44] It would be hard to beat this journal in battling one's inner bourgeois. Werner is completely on target by saying that this is the diary's main intention. [. . .]

I've recently purchased two serious books (both published by Insel): Flaubert's *Madame Bovary* and Humboldt's *Letters to Charlotte Diede,*[45] which I've nearly finished. The accusation of "quietism" that, according to the foreword, has been made against the letters is completely justified. Wilhelm v. Humboldt is someone I hold in exceptional esteem, and in my opinion he ranks among the greatest minds ever. Still, not even old age is an acceptable excuse for this embarrassing quietism that, according to Humboldt's own account, was already in his youth his inward attitude.

But what I noticed most was not this but something that was predictable: his absolute individualism and the exclusive value he sets on the individual spirit. As a Jew, I can't go along with this. It's not as though I have any sympathy for the way the Germans in particular regard the state; their absolute obligation is repellent and strikes me as unspiritual. The problem is rather that, broadly speaking, Humboldt lacks what we call Zion. The aim of life is individualistic only to the extent that Zion is in everyone. The meaning of life is not to give your spirit the highest, most harmonious degree of cultivation, leisure, and perfection, but it is Zion— to build up Zion both internally and externally (and not *only* symbolically). The meaning of life is to call forth the Messiah, and to build Zion. [. . .] Humboldt never mentions Zion, or any similar notion translated into German. [. . .]

Recently my dreams have been about something that is perhaps not entirely a delusion but could only be carried out by a generation inflamed by truth: "a fraternity of fanatics." The idea is to join together a small group of young Zionists of both sexes who are inwardly governed by Zion and for whom Zion has become absolutely religious (admittedly, what I'm saying here is how I'd like to be myself). This fraternity will be just as in Jeremiah's prophecy, going forth to the Land of Israel in purity, laying the foundation for a new life. This New Fraternity will be like ha-Ari's circle of mystics in sixteenth-century Sefat that brought forth revolutionary changes in the life of the entire Jewish people.[46]

A few people living a Jewish life wholly devoted to renewal could have incalculable consequences for the entire nation. You just have to think about it and it all becomes abundantly clear. If news came of a group of a few young Jews who have turned up in the Land of Israel to make Zion the central point of their religious (and every other) vision and to lead—in silence and the highest acuteness of mind—a life of sacrifice and devotion, [. . .] is there the slightest doubt that, together with some other young Jews, I would at once venture forth to the Land of Israel to start a new life pregnant with the future, even if we had to crawl on all fours to get there? [. . .] Why don't we in Young Judah create such a fraternity? Why don't we redeem Judah through our actions?

In my waking dreams—which since childhood have been my life's greatest therapy and truest revelation of my being—I see it all vividly before me: the laying of foundations and putting together the membership list. (It's kind of funny, but being the way I am, I always seek to achieve the utmost—and most sacred—possible with whatever materials are at hand, even though a "fraternity of fanatics" would obviously be a lot easier to get off the ground in Poland or Russia than in poisoned Germany. Here it would immediately become a Jewish version of the George Circle, and would develop out of the total break and separation from the *Volk* rather than the unification with its deepest longings.)

The next step is to go somewhere to purify myself, followed by making a difference through immigration to the Land of Israel. This is how I imagine young people going out "among the people" and eagerly building up Zion, and not just in symbols but in truth! The problem with symbols is that they have so little substance that people try to take them "literally," which would turn Zionism into nothing more than a gigantic simile. By contrast, I seek to make Zion into a very palpable reality. Our intellectual life will not be a symbol lacking material, a watery soup like what's dished up at the Fasanenstrasse.[47] My *positive* Judaism comes down to my desire to give symbols a factual, real content. For me, the Messiah is the Messiah and not the socialist social order, just as Zion is Zion and not just another name for agricultural colonies in Palestine. [. . .]

August 15, 1916

This morning I sat myself down, firmly determined to launch into my work, and wrote out on a piece of paper in large, beautiful letters, "Big Mouth." This was intended as a commentary in praise of screaming. After all, doesn't the Torah say, "You shall *speak* of this while you sit in your house, when you walk upon a path, when you lie down, and while you get up"?[48] It doesn't tell you to keep quiet! Next I wrote that because of the immorality of the nations and the arrogance of men, those who speak, sing, or shout on the street or in the markets normally shouldn't be allowed to stand on their soapbox, whereas those who know something about the truth and who recognize the sacred duty to announce it, regardless of whether anyone listens or not, mostly sink into a haughty silence.

At that point I simply couldn't bear it any longer, and an irresistible force drove me outside. I had to take my walking stick in hand and embark on my usual morning jaunt through the fields to Tretach, where I began to fantasize the way I do, though naturally I didn't get down to business. I had wanted to come up with some mighty words for the "screams from the heart" and for the religious propaganda of the future Zion. Screaming is a necessary stage before a person throws himself into work. In this way Zion must be proclaimed *at least once*. Being a big mouth is an extraordinarily essential and vital weapon of youth, whereas buttoning your lips is a German perversion. "Silence is golden" is poppycock. *What needs to be proclaimed is the essence of truth.* Truth that can't be proclaimed may be fine for the stars in the sky, just not for us. We would deny the right to scream only to benighted fools or those who are confused and blabber out clever rubbish. A prophet goes beyond *seeing* by speaking. And don't we all want to be prophets? Stand up and shout into the ears of these Jews racing all around me, "The truth has *arrived!*" [. . .]

This afternoon, as I walked across the market square and went into the book dealer's, I thumbed through the second issue of *The Reich,* which I had seen in Heidelberg.[49] Back then I had no reason to buy it. Benjamin asked me about it afterwards. He had nothing good to say about the first number, but he also added that he could easily imagine *only* being able— or wanting—to publish certain things in *The Reich*. I bought the second number; for the sake of scholarship, I'll also make it a point to pick up the first issue (not to mention the third, where the article "The Mysticism of Martin Buber" is due to appear, which for obvious reasons I'm eager to read).

The Reich is quite unusual, and not at all a purely theosophical publication, even if the disciples of the modern Plotinus, Rudolf Steiner, set the basic tone. The poets Else Lasker-Schüler,[50] Klabund,[51] and others are also given a right to speak, just as they are in *Weissen Blätter.* There's a mass of theosophical remarks and elaborations that for me remain totally incomprehensible, and I'm unable to assess their value, or lack of it. The pieces that make the most sympathetic impression on me are the poems by the editor, "Opening Song for a New Era." A few of these pieces, like "The Apocalypse" and "The Pre-Socratics," are not lacking in greatness and depth. These poems' rhythm is like a hammer pounding away at the conscience. In a certain sense they are like George's. I don't care for Carl Unger in the slightest, while Swinburne's "Choir from Atalanta" is without question fantastic.[52]

I'd like to know whether Buber, who certainly has been asked, has agreed to contribute to the series. For here are the "bearers of secrets" of whom he speaks in *Daniel*. They are the ones who say, "Come with us and we'll take you to a transcendental land," but when you think about the trip afterwards, you realize that you're still in the same place as before. Buber has intuited, and in *Daniel* tested out, the "mathematically exact" mysticism, which is what makes him far greater than Steiner and his natural-scientific mysteries. For the deepest mysteries can be found in each one of us, and their solutions are in Life, writ large.

To find the mysteries requires a moment of introspection. It is there that one will discover that there's plenty to do right down here, and that the mystery of human life is deeper than that of the apocalypse—unless the apocalypse is just another word for the mystery of human life.

Someone who thinks he knows more than one single, true, and essential mystery is surely no mystic. There is but *one* mystery, which can never be comprehended or hinted at in words or through words, because this mystery is not the "mystery of God, mystery of life, or mystery of unity."[53] It far transcends all this. At the very most, it can be grasped through a word—this word having been invented only to give a name to the ineffable, to the "mystery of infinity"—which is incomprehensible to men. No wonder that the Kabbalah describes God as the Ain-sof.[54] Existing beyond all borders, Ain-Sof is that which *cannot* be named. Mysteries inspire reverence, though there is only one thing that deserves reverence, and that is really the only true object of mysticism: the "great abyss" which only God's judgment can bridge. (In the Siddur it is written: "Your justice is like a mighty mountain, your judgment is like a vast abyss.")[55]

Reverence is basically a mystical feeling. It is the intimation that behind everything yawns the "great abyss" and that one must surrender to the power that animates it. For this reason, the feeling of reverence is directed not to any man (unless he is the Messiah, *who is a human being!*) but at the revelation that is within him or that works through him. The sensation of reverence must therefore be a mystical experience. The connection between God and reverence is similar to the way *The Crown of the*

Holy Name beautifully equates the Shekhinah with prayer.[56] The experience of God and the experience of prayer are inseparable. [. . .]

August 16, 1916

Yet another great joy has come my way today: Benjamin has reissued his Friday invitation, this time without withdrawing it. Now that I've been punished for my first impure joy, and having had to practice renunciation as a consequence, the next great joy has arrived. He doesn't write how long he'll be visiting, though I assume it'll be two to three days, till Monday. We'll meet on Friday afternoon, giving us ample time to talk about everything. For him, no doubt, our relationship has also turned into something heartfelt and friendly, which is what makes me happier than anything else. More than any of his particular opinions, his spiritual being has an inestimable influence on me. It's just as likely that he's gotten something from me. Relationships like ours are always reciprocal. Today I have the same impression I had when we met a year ago: he's just like me, only five years older. And this makes him a good role model, the paragon of the way one should struggle and wrestle.

It's a pity I can't take the Bible with me to Seeshaupt! One really should read to him passages from the prophets and the Psalms, in particular Psalms 120–134, which is better than literature.

The Bible isn't divine because God dictated it, or as especially run-of-the-mill Reform rabbis like to say, because it came about in some other way. The Bible is divine because the totality of its contents is so overpowering, and the depth of its expressions is so unequaled and in such a class of its own that it can serve us forever as an arsenal of divine longing and divine security (and both are equally present in the Bible). What is certain is that in *no* other people is there such a stupendous quantity of religious geniuses as with the Jews. Not even the Indians come close. Down to the last man, the "people" who wrote the Bible—that is, those who experienced it, even Kohelet, not to mention the "late" Daniel—were religious *Übermenschen,* incomparably greater than even Kierkegaard, in whom one can detect a faint trace of Old Testament humanity. [. . .]

I know from the turning point in my own Zionism how at first—I can't even put my finger on when I stumbled onto it—I was completely unaware and had no clear conception of its deeper meaning. The *decisive* change occurred later, around 1914, with the declaration of total revolution. This took place already *before* the war. Back then (and I recall very well my first days in the Agudah) I was an Orthodox Jewish national-ist and only rarely did I unfurl my revolutionary banner, and when I did, it was without the awareness of a contradiction between Jewish nationalism and Orthodoxy. One reason for it was perhaps that while back then I wholeheartedly accepted the Orthodox notion of the Torah, at the same time I already had my present conception of the Torah, even if it was some sort of convoluted mishmash. An example of this is Deutschländer's[57] lecture on Samson Raphael Hirsch in March 1914, and how in the discussion afterward I decisively attacked and disputed the relevancy of Hirsch [. . .] and I flirted heavily with Marxism. Hirsch—I said back then—can be accepted only historically; in our contemporary situation he cannot claim any validity. And even when he was alive he was already behind the times: his *Nineteen Letters* appeared twenty-five years too late.[58] [. . .]

I can still vividly recall how in those days I had a long Sabbath after-noon discussion over the sacredness of the Halachic dispute between Abaje and Rabba, or over the Prosuls.[59] Despite the fact that I readily ac-cepted the concept that "Halacha was given to Moses on Sinai," at the same time I utterly and vehemently denied its sacredness, for it dishonors the human spirit altogether to deny a person the right to authoritative thinking.

For this is the upshot of the doctrine of sacredness: that one doesn't concede to the human spirit the capacity of making independent nor-mative judgments about life. For this reason, in order to secure recogni-tion, everything that supposedly has the force of law is connected up with God. Already back then I rejected, and in fact never accepted in the first place, an idea that otherwise has no place in Orthodoxy and that val-ues the human soul so *little,* at least in its capacity to think. [. . .]

I have always conceived of the notion of the Torah as a continual act of creation that—as the Orthodox would say—may well take place in the mind of God but only by way of the thoughts of men. Only thus conceived does the Torah receive its true value as the quintessence of all Jewish religious traditions from Moses all the way to Israel Hildesheimer or the little Rau and Harry Levy[60] as the most profound human creation imaginable. For the Torah to have its true inner authority—and not for the purpose of external obedience—it doesn't need a stamp of divine dictation. The Torah is the eternal revelation not *to* Judah but *within* Judah. Each and every young Jew today, if he has a sense of true reverence, passes down the Torah; he develops and expands it.

August 17, 1916

Today I read a couple of lines in the newspaper that put the fear of God into me: in Niederbarnim districts I and II orders have been given for all years to appear for examination. While this doesn't affect me personally, I fear that examinations in Berlin are imminent. If the examinations take place in September, I'll have to cut short my stay here. This would be most unpleasant, as it wouldn't give me enough time to get rid of my suntan. I would still be under the influence of my restored health and would make too good an impression on the doctor. [. . .]

August 18, 1916

[. . .] I'm sensing a great longing for my library, my best friend, even though it's wrong to give your love to the Torah and not to another living being. Broadly speaking, my library is the Torah. Even the writings of the anarchists belong to it. Everything that is not the Torah is condemned to stay outside. Oh, if could only sit again at my table and let my eyes wander along the row of books! [. . .]

August 23, 1916

I barely arrived home from my trip to find the draft order, or rather the report of such an order. It's good I was away, otherwise I would have had to appear already on August 22, leaving me no time to get rid of my suntan. They've moved it up to September 5. I wrote home at once and asked them to send a telegram if they agree I should return at once. I'm certain they do, in which case I'll leave the day after tomorrow. This will give me nearly two weeks in Berlin to get rid of my suntan and to see how things go. I *hope* they don't take me. My weapons haven't yet grown dull. The idyllic summer is over, and it's going out on a high note: my visit to Seeshaupt. [. . .]

I should say a few words about my visit! I departed with a lot of inspiration, which I'm now trying my best to preserve so I can reflect on a number of things.

I'll start with the superficial details. After my arrival in Munich, where we missed each other because my train was delayed, I ran into Benjamin purely by chance in a greengrocer's on one of the streets near the train station. It was 5:45 P.M. We sat in a café in the station, and he told me that he's not going on his trip because of the call-up, which he expects any minute now. He said he'll be returning to Berlin next week, and that I should stay in Seeshaupt till then. Long ago he stopped reading newspapers; he gets news directly affecting him from Berlin. He told me how in the library that afternoon he had been browsing through *Die Weissen Blätter*[61] and other journals when he realized (and he's absolutely right) how, while the contributors naturally aren't writing the same way they did on August 1, 1914, the divergence between them and events hasn't changed since the first day of the war. Or to put it somewhat differently, the difference between these "radicals" and all the local newspapers, dailies, and Aunt Vossischen[62] has remained completely constant. It was at a certain level on August 4, 1914, and today it's the same.

At 7:15 P.M. we took the train to Seeshaupt during a downpour that only let up on Monday evening. Today is the first day sun has broken through the clouds. During this entire time I was outside for only half an hour, on Monday evening, otherwise I was indoors. On the train Benjamin told me he really enjoyed my letter because of the way I had understood his essay in *Das Ziel*.[63] With that I announced to him my "conversion" to Kant, in other words, to the need to study Kant. We then spoke about *The Reich* and about literature by men of vision. He wants to read *The Flowing Light of the Godhead* in Latin.[64] (He knows the work of Dr. Pulver in *The Reich*.)[65]

By the time we arrived, we still had half an hour's walk in the pouring rain ahead of us. After dropping off our things, we went into the music room, where people were awaiting us. I had a very attractive and decently appointed room on the first floor, whereas Benjamin and the lady of the house slept upstairs in far less beautiful rooms. Dora Pollak is a daughter of the well-known Professor Leon Kellner-Czernowitz, who's the executor of Herzl's diary and the publisher of his collected works.[66] It was only on Monday evening that she told me this. She was raised in a Zionist environment in Vienna, and she already knew Buber before he arrived in Vienna. All of her siblings are Zionists; she's the only one who's not. Or at least she's not a part of the movement.

She made a very positive impression on me, and till one o'clock in the morning we discussed Zion, in particular the concept of "screaming." Benjamin then read aloud from his letter to Buber (he's yet to receive a reply). Benjamin challenged Buber to direct his language and that of his journal "to the innermost core of silence," which *The Jew* obviously doesn't do. In passing, a few weeks after writing the letter Benjamin found in Schlegel's *Philosophy of History* a section on language that uses different words to say the same thing.[67]

The next afternoon Benjamin and I inspected the library, which contains some magnificent books, for instance, Hölderlin's collected works (in Schwab's 1846 first edition); Bothe's translation of Pindar from 1808; Brauer's edition of Jean Paul in a wonderful old single volume; Voss's translation of Horace; and many other things, including plenty of philosophy. Mach's *Knowledge and Error* was on the floor, and Dora said she wanted to sell it because it's really nothing of great importance. When I appealed to her conscience to sell it to me, she told me if her man had no objection, I could have it as a visitor's gift. I was in full agreement. Let's see what happens.

In the afternoon Benjamin read me an ode by Pindar, in the original, that made a deep impression on me. These songs have a divine emanation. Hölderlin's translation is also good. It's colossal.

Afterwards I read from both of my essays, which Benjamin liked. "I think they're good," he said after a long pause.[68] Both he and Dora made a lot of fuss about my getting an honorarium. They said I shouldn't do things so childishly. "To have the truth is enough to deserve support in life," Benjamin stated. I have no idea if *The Jew* pays honorariums, though I think it does. [. . .]

During the entire time we were together, we discussed Judaism a great deal: about going to Palestine, "Agricultural Zionism," Ahad Haam, and "justice,"[69] but mostly Buber, and after four days there was nearly nothing left of him. As we were saying our good-byes, Benjamin told me to give Buber a vale of tears next time I meet up with him.

It's not as if Benjamin taught me anything; I've been thinking the same things for nine months now. In only one point have I come to some linguistic clarity, namely, on the rejection of the value of "Experience." In this regard the question becomes (one could call it the fateful question): "Have you already had your Jewish Experience?" Rather than saying "I've gotten to know" Judaism or "I've seen Zion," one says, "I've experienced my Judaism." Vision and Experience are *entirely* different things. Vision is spiritual, and everything depends on it. Here it becomes clear how close Benjamin is to Ahad Haam, which is something that will become clearer in a central point, namely, the conception of the role of "justice" in Judaism. Benjamin pushed me in my essay to make a clear renunciation of this Experience business. Down with Experience! I'll even take this further by saying that the notion of "Experience" is Buber at his most grotesque.[70] [. . .]

Buber philosophizes about religion instead of leading religion into philosophy. The worst thing of all is to compose *essays* on the philosophy of religion, to use the essay form to write about things that can be dealt with only in a system or, as it were, in a thick tome. I've always believed that the most monstrous thing about Buber is that he somehow has the truth, but he conceives of it falsely. In no way can you disprove Buber, but you have to overcome him—just as I have overcome him, because my Judaism has not come to me from Buberian sources. [. . .]

August 24, 1916

I just got news from Blum.

On our first evening together Benjamin and I discussed whether Zion is a metaphor or not: I said yes (only God is not one), Benjamin said no. From there we continued on to the prophets, at which point Benjamin maintained that, if you accept the divine authority of the Bible, you mustn't use the prophets metaphorically. The prophets howled when they screamed, which is the only sense in which "screaming" should be used.

We read Plato's *Symposium* twice (Socrates' speech was in the original), and we discussed the strange doubling up of the Greek pantheon of gods, and the remarkable fact that some older Greek gods can be directly translated into an idea, like Necessity. "Socrates is Plato's argument and barricade against myth." We discussed the historicity of Diotima[71] and of the commentaries.

On Saturday evening the conversation turned to Hegel, which led to a long discussion. I maintained, as did Benjamin, that Hegel used a language that we no longer—or far more likely not yet—comprehend. Maybe in a century the natural sciences will arrive at a place where they will understand Hegel and Schelling. We took up a couple of sentences from Hegel's *Phenomenology*. Benjamin did such a good job of interpreting the line "The nervous system is an organism's resting point in its movement"[72] that it really made sense. We also looked at the definition of action, juxtaposing it with Lichtenberg's assertion that it makes no sense to distinguish a man from his actions.

At this point we arrived at general philosophy: mathematics, philosophy, and myth. Dora Pollak denied that Hegel wants to deduce the world. Then Benjamin and I piped in. Benjamin only accepts myth as "the world." He does not yet know what the point of philosophy is, for the "sense of the world" does not need to be discovered because it's already present in myth. Myth is everything, and all else (mathematics and philosophy) is but its dim reflection, a mere illusion. I replied that, for me, besides myth there is also mathematics. [. . .]

Benjamin's mind circles round and round the problem of myth, looking for an approach from various angles. He's been going at this for a long time. In terms of history, he approaches myth from Romanticism; from poetry, he comes at it from Hölderlin; and from religion, his starting point is Judaism and justice. "If I developed my own philosophy," he said to me, "it would somehow be the philosophy of Judaism."

In Berlin he's going to give me both of his essays on Hölderlin, which he considers the only things of substance he has done till now. This proves that he considers me worthy. The essay is extremely difficult.

We played four games of chess: Benjamin and I played two, and I won both; the third pitted Dora and me against him (I triumphed brilliantly); and for the last game the two of them played against me. I lost. Benjamin plays remarkably slowly and "blindly." It is, as it were, always his turn, for I play much faster, and I make my moves immediately after he makes his. Nevertheless, he does the most that's humanly possible for a blind chess player.

Zionism has to get over three things: the whole business with the agricultural settlements, the racial ideology, and arguments based on blood and experience. It isn't at all the case that you can go to Palestine only as a farmhand or a peasant. He who goes there for the sake of the *Teaching* has perhaps an entirely different profession. [. . .]

Dreams of Walter Benjamin and ghosts. Ghosts exist only in China and Scandinavia. Benjamin recounted unbelievable things from certain dreams, and signs that constantly recur in them: like the large, empty house in which a ghost dances in midair, and the window (which is a symbol of the soul). You can't research these things because everyone is *afraid* of ghosts. Judaism has no ghosts, and a Jew is obliged to research them.

The man of myth knows no fear.

I could take more than the entire winter to think about what the two or three of us grappled with in the course of our extensive conversations.

One has to build up Zion over an entire lifetime. I can't deceive myself here: to truly follow Benjamin would require making some extraordinary revisions. In four weeks I would have to break with everyone and to resign from the organization. But first I have to conduct some tests. My Zionism lies too deeply within me for anything to rattle it. The upshot of Benjamin's critique is that I'd have to repudiate the sort of Zionism other people proclaim, which is quite possible once I go over to his side.

The word "somehow" is the mark of an emerging opinion. Never have I heard anyone use the word more often than Benjamin. But one thing he's already settled is that he is no longer "somehow" a Jew. Dr. Hiller is "somehow" Jewish, not Benjamin. After Hiller learned that Joel[73] got baptized, he wrote to Benjamin, "Are you also baptized?" One consequence of baptism is a muddled state of mind. Dr. Hiller wrote this on the back of an open postcard! Hiller is supposedly a decent fellow, and Benjamin goes into great detail to defend his dealings with him. In today's Germany, he said, decency is reason enough to respect a person. [. . .]

September 5, 1916

I returned on Saturday, eight days ago, and over the last week I've been busy. Yesterday afternoon I was with Benjamin, and on Thursday, Levy and I took an evening stroll to Drewitz. This morning I left for the military examination armed with well-laid plans.

From 9:00 A.M. to 12:30 I had to stand around downstairs, and at 12:45 I was finally able to take my place upstairs. Height: 1 m. 76. My eyes apparently couldn't do better than 5/8 and 5/24, which I wasn't aware of. Then I stepped up to the doctor, who listened to me take in air. I told him the story about my breathing. He asked me what sort of disorder I have. Neurasthenia and a nose disease, I replied. The major chipped in, "Yep, this fellow makes a rather strange impression, like a sleepwalker." The doctor then explained, "This man has neurasthenia," at which point I was released. This is the short story of my military examination.

Moloch's first attack has been thwarted! Victory! Victory! I now have six months of work ahead of me. [. . .]

For my philosophical reading materials I've made up my mind to read Keyserlin's *Immortality* and Franz von Baader's *Theory of Sacrifice*.[74] I borrowed Kierkegaard's *Stages of Life's Ways* from Benjamin. Zeitlin's writings on the Hasidim are excellent.[75] The plan for my development is as follows: beginning with pure vocabulary, I'll move on to getting acquainted with the titles of books and chapter headings, and from there I'll train my instincts in making judgments. Afterwards I'll give my hunches some substantial content. This is what I've been doing for the last three years, and not without success. *I* also regard Hebrew as purely and simply content, as the form of language. *It is no accident that the Torah was written in Hebrew. The concept of Torah is completely Hebrew.* [. . .]

September 10, 1916

After the Arabic course on Thursday evening I went with Türkischer to the Volksheim.[76] [. . .] Lehmann was in the middle of delivering a lecture, and as soon as I heard that Hodann[77] was also in attendance, I decided to join in. As I marched into the room, I was happy to see Lubmann[78] in a back corner. Schragenheim[79] had a pained expression on his face, the reasons for which became immediately clear. There was also the little Zadek,[80] and as a pleasant surprise Fräulein Halle[81] stood in front of me, along with the entire chorus of young girls from the youth group from Marke. Out of the room echoed noises, and Lehmann obviously was speaking about Hasidism, and gave one half-baked citation from Buber after another. Buber was being "interpreted," that is, Buber's interpretation of Hasidism was being interpreted. Like dew dripping from his mouth, Lehmann spoke of "Avodah," "Kavanah," "Schiflut," and "Hitlahabut."[82] If Buber had by chance written two hundred pages instead of forty about these subjects—which would have given him the opportunity to delve seriously into the central Hasidic virtues, above all "Simcha" or "joy," and "Devekuth" or "dependence upon God"—one would have heard "Simcha" and "Devekuth" similarly dealt with. Of course, nothing of the kind occurred because Lehmann didn't consider it important to have expert knowledge. One reads Buber, gobbles him up, imitates his use of German, and delivers a lecture on Hasidism. People treat Hasidism in a way they wouldn't dare do with anything else by speaking before an assembly without having studied its sources. And those gathered, caught up in an *aesthetic ecstasy,* were nearly whispering the words, "Oh yes, oh religiosity, religiosity."

This is unspeakably shameless. To be sure, Buber knows something about Hasidism, but he pulls out only one aspect—its subterranean side—and speaks about it.[83] He has faith in Hasidism; in the depths of his heart he ascribes to the truth of the mystery of Kavanah; he believes in magic; and he writes a book whose only flaw *is* its *beauty* (and given the massive consequences of the book, this is a flaw). Hasidism is thereby made socially acceptable, and the aesthetes pounce on it like wolves. [. . .] They confuse beauty with truth, and do something forbidden by establishing a cult of the Baal Shem. For them, it's nonsense to study the sources or even to delve into *other* writings of Hasidism or mysticism. They speak without having any understanding of the totality of their subject.

None of these people has heard a thing about the *total* Hasidism. And this is because Buber (for a very specific reason that can only be touched upon here: his hatred of "visible" Judaism) leaves out everything connected to the deeply Jewish conception of Torah. He has completely hollowed out the notion of man becoming Torah, which *does not* refer to man becoming God but means that man lays hold of the deepest sense of Teaching in word and deed, that he comprehends the conception of the Torah. Buber robs Hasidism of its totality, the consequence of which is that none of these people has an inkling of the deepest conceptions within Hasidism. [. . .] Where Buber gets it wrong, they are ridiculous; and even where Buber (seen in his context) gets it right, their second-hand interpretation (exponentially, as it were) turns it into nonsense. The people in Charlottenburg worship Fichte,[84] and here they worship Buber. And the Jew *shivers* in abhorrence at this blasphemy. I was in full agreement when Lubmann cursed *these people* horribly. *I don't recognize the Zionism* of people who haven't the foggiest understanding of Judaism and who waste their time with "religiosity," which is an aesthetic game they play in front of girls and the goyim. [. . .]

I just started Baader's *Philosophy of Sacrifice*. It strikes me as a very difficult book.

October 6, 1916

When the LORD restored the fortunes of Zion, then we thought we were dreaming. Our mouths were filled with laughter; our tongues sang for joy. Then it was said among the nations, "The LORD had done great things for them." The LORD has done great things for us; Oh, how happy we were! Restore again our fortunes, LORD, like the dry stream beds of the Negeb. They who sow in

tears will reap with cries of joy. Those who go forth weeping, carrying sacks of seed, ·Will return with cries of joy, carrying their
bundled sheaves.

	Psalm 126

October 8–9[, 1916]

I read Ahad Haam together with Benjamin this evening. [. . .] The following comes from a notebook I borrowed from him, "Notes on an Essay on the Philosophy of Justice."

Every object confined to the dimensions of time and space carries
with it the characteristic of ownership, which reflects its temporality.
Possession, however, caught as it is in the same finiteness, is always unjust.
It is for this reason that no system based on possession, regardless of how
it is built, can lead to justice. Justice, rather, lies in the nature of an object
that cannot be possessed. This alone is the object through which other
objects become freed of ownership.

In conceptualizing society, one tries to give an object to an owner
who then eliminates its character of ownership.

Every socialist or communist theory fails to achieve its goal because
the individual has a claim on every object. Individual A has a need Z that
can be satisfied by X; and one thinks he's doing the right thing by giving
Y, which is similar to X, to individual B to satisfy his need which is similar to Z. But it doesn't work this way. [. . .]

The thoughts hinted at here lead to the following supposition: justice
is not one virtue among others (humility, neighborly love, faithfulness,
and courage) but forms the foundation of a new ethical category that
one perhaps cannot even define as a category of virtue. It is a different
category, of equal status to virtue. Justice does not appear to relate to the
goodwill of the person but creates a condition in the world. Justice denotes the ethical category of the one who exists, while virtue denotes the
ethical category of a person on whom demands are made. [. . .] The plea
in the Lord's Prayer, "And lead us not into temptation but deliver us from
evil," is the request for justice, for a just world order. [. . .]

October 11[, 1916]

[. . .] *To a critique of the present age:* I see the nation not as a thing that happens to exist and in whose framework we do our best to realize human
conditions, but as an essential determination of the inner form of Juda-

ism. It is an *absolute*. It is possible that with the coming of the Messiah nations won't exist any longer, though the Jewish nation surely will because the very essence of the religious conception of Judaism requires its existence, and *especially at that time*. I believe that the Orthodox conception of Judaism's "nationality" has a kernel of truth, deeper and more necessary than the common conceptions of Zionism (which I even think could be disproved). *The purely national conception of Judaism leads to the Land of Israel as its final destination, while the true conception of Zionism leads to Zion* (Zion conceived of here as having an inner connection to the Land of Israel). If I didn't want to go to Zion, I wouldn't go to the Land of Israel. And because I know that Zion *is the absolute truth* (the same cannot be said yet of the Land of Israel), I measure all things against it. My credo is that *Zion is the measure of all things*. [. . .]

Grete Lissauer gave me the Bolzano book,[85] which has a gorgeous binding. Sukkoth starts this evening. The Kabbalistic idea of the soul having three parts (Ruach, the mid-region of the soul; Nefesh, the lower part; and Neshama, the highest) is astonishingly profound. Mathematics belongs in the intellectual part (Ruach), though it also has a metaphysical ur-image in the central sphere (Nefesh), which I once identified as reverence for thinking. Nishama, the last part, is the magical center, the unmediated divine. Its central form as well as its inner form—in its endless identity—is constantly being produced. There is an *inner center of the soul*, which is language, or at least the Hebrew language. And in the connection between Nefesh and Neshama (as the "inner center") lies the foundation of the magic of language. This magic is hence far removed from translation or rendering into another center.

[. . .] In Judaism, love and justice do not belong to equal categories. Justice is higher, closer to God. *A person can't use justice to cast spells; with love he can.* Judaism is an ongoing triumph of magic through magic itself, through the Torah. It is an ongoing victory of the historical over the mythical. Myth uses magic to bind men; Judaism does it with history.

The equation History = Torah perhaps expresses this essential issue: Torah is History. The history of the Torah is the inner history of the world, with the historical process playing itself out in the unfolding of the Torah. *Historiography is the science of the inner laws of the Torah* (which is a history, to be sure, yet to be dealt with and explored). Molitor had an inkling of this, but he saw it Christologically, whereas one must see it as a Jew. *This would be a genuine ideology of Zionism.* It would be the inner relationship between mathematics and history—in Zion. Otherwise, there is no relationship.

October 12, 1916

[. . .] *If Hasidism were the Jewish truth, it would have to develop out of an investigation into the Hebrew language.* I suspect that is what Markus was up to.[86] These days, psychological elements and interpretations of language are either mocked or unknown. Samson Raphael Hirsch, who was aware of this, was uncannily on the mark when he grounded his thinking in a theory of language (in his commentary to the Pentateuch).[87] People today, however, have dismissed this theory as "false" and unnecessary, which is a very big mistake.

The Messiah will be the last—and *first*—philosopher of language. He will deduce Judaism from its language. Benjamin told me that Ernst Lewy holds very similar views.[88]

Man's holiness lies not in moving from possibility to reality but in transferring one reality into another one, into the highest and most divine reality. A holy man meets someone on the street and says, "God will be happy if you repent," and then the man repents! This is the conception of holiness mentioned above. The righteous man's holiness you see; a mediocre man's you can't; and with a frivolous man all you notice is absence. [. . .]

October 16, 1916

There are detailed descriptions of the Kabbalah in the sixth and ninth volumes of Graetz's great work.[89]

In the end, historical skepticism can be overcome only through the Jewish conception of Tradition. *Judaism is the embodiment of history.* Judaism also supplies the historical standards that can truly be applied to *everything:* to China as well as to the dukedom of Castillo and the Iroquois.

October 17, 1916

[. . .] If one of these days I had to (and could) write something, it would perhaps be a "Bible commentary from the perspective of Zion." It'll be a Rashi[90] authored by Gerhard Scholem. My explanation of Isaiah 2:4, for instance, is certainly original, and it's good. I know a rather large number of verses and proverbs to which I can give novel explanations. According to Gematria,[91] the mystical Shiloh in Genesis 49 equals the number 345.

"Messiah" equals 358, which means that the difference between the two is 13 (which means "one" or "a single one"). Shiloh will bring the Messiah through unity—Shiloh *is* the *one* Messiah. There is no second or third.

October 25, 1916

Over the last few days I've been reading the German translation of Zeitlin's *Shechinah.*[92] I'm thinking about writing an article on "Torah and Experience." I bought a book by Pascal.

October 27, 1916

[. . .] My two-year-long flirtation with Orthodox Judaism, or rather with its deepest inner core, has really been remarkable. While I had once fought against Hirsch and flatly rejected him, I now see how much immeasurable gratitude German Jewry owes him. For a long time I went to synagogue only because of Jettka Stein; now I am able, and driven, to go for inner reasons. The opposite is now happening: my friends prevent me from going. I can't pray because there are people at the synagogue I'll have to speak to afterwards. The Talmud is another factor in all this, as I'm finding my way back to it after having consciously abandoned it. This is happening because I now understand such things in a deeper and better way than two or three years ago. From nothingness I went to Orthodoxy, and from there I continued on to Buber; and from Buber—by *giving him up*—I arrived at Zion.

Now I know that the driest "juristic" deliberation in the Talmud is religious. In a word: it is religious because Judaism desires justice. The Talmud's doctrine is not of right and wrong but one that contains justice.

Is the Bible's divinity rooted in its humanity, as I once thought? No. Its divinity goes far, far deeper. It is *not* in myth, but in its view of history—a view that is never hinted at or discussed in the Bible. [. . .] Judaism is the embodiment of history, and because Judaism is the *absolute* truth, it follows that the Bible and the Torah are divine. For this reason, one can employ the Bible as a proof. This also means that the Jewish "tradition" is unlike any other tradition. Jewish literature is directed at the "truth," unlike any other literature. This places it beyond literature and turns all biblical studies into something nonliterary. [. . .]

At the very core of Judaism lies the belief that there is a revelation from God, and this is something no modern man can grasp. This is the point that Kierkegaard never understood, which comes out clearly in his brand of Christianity. I erred grievously when I believed that Kierkegaard had been a Jew. He is like Plato, his only precursor. Kierkegaard was the quintessential Western Man. Like Plato, he was Oriental, which is surely part of the problem with him, as it was with Nietzsche. For he approached philosophy from the question of history—and he was the greatest in the crowded field of those who have tried to take this route. He too tried to overcome historical skepticism by going to its source.

Kierkegaard is among the righteous of the nations appointed by God to serve as priests. That a generation has "outgrown" the Bible says nothing about the Bible but about the generation. There is absolutely nothing more devastating than the scientific study of the Bible by people who have dragged their own relativism into their research. Science has taught us many things and can teach us many other things, but what it definitely can't do is prove the antimodernity of the Bible. Or rather, science is correct: the Bible is out of step with the modern world, because it has *always* been antimodern, from the days it was written until today. The Bible is the eternal *Untimely Meditations.*[93] The Messiah will come during the generation in which the Bible is also "externally" relevant.

The liberals are correct with their claim that Judaism's structures have changed over time. Where they are decidedly off the mark is that Judaism must "snuggle up" to European structures. Judaism cannot be modernized without robbing it of its soul. Only from Zion can the real reformation of Judaism take place. Reformation is God's business, and God alone speaks to us from Zion.

Indeed: for us Zionism is Judaism.

October 28, 1916

[. . .] I read the story of Noah with Hirsch's commentary. What particularly caught my eye were his extraordinary remarks on the Tower of Babel and the development of a multiplicity of languages, and I also found particularly revealing what he said about the "divine presence" or *Shekhinah.*[94]

Time and time again you have to marvel at the measureless dimensions of Hirsch's mind, as well as the extraordinary manner in which he reads the Torah. According to Hirsch, the translation of the Hebrew word *jezer* as "drive" says a lot about Christianity.[95] *Jezer* is something created in the mind; it isn't active but passive. *There is no evil drive.*

For Jews, God is not a problem of metaphysics. Or at least he's as little a metaphysical problem as is life itself. Hirsch lashes out at "fanatics" as well as pantheists and the like. But I too am a fanatic. And Hirsch was perhaps the greatest fanatic of all. For every commentator on the Torah is a fanatic.

Or perhaps Hölderlin's famous comment on the "holy solemnity" also applies to him.

October 29, 1916

According to Duprel (as cited by Markus in *Hartmann and Hasidism*), "mysticism is a person's magical relationship to himself."[96]

November 6, 1916

[. . .] One of the deepest roots of "German Judaism" and the humbug of "Experience" is simply that if a person wants to "experience" anything in Germany, it has to be as a "German-Jewish" Experience. No wonder that the purveyors of "Experience" are so German-Jewish. The most important thing, however, is not to experience but to *know.* This is difficult, so extremely difficult that it's far too unpleasant for most people. If a person had knowledge, he would never fall into the arms of "German Judaism." He who "experiences" a landscape, or his fellow man, or anything else, escapes from the ultimate Jewish imperative. With Experience he'll always remain a German Jew—and never get to Zion. For once make it hard on yourself: *know!* You'll then discover that all the forbidden mixing and adulterations from the realm of Experience will sink down into nothing, with only the Jewish soul left over. [. . .]

November 9, 1916

On October 9 Blum was wounded in the pelvis, and he died on November 1. Edgar Blum is dead. I couldn't even give his mother one word of comfort, because what killed him was the most horrific thing imaginable, the absolute Satan. I'll have to keep silent on how all of this affects me. The time will come to erect for my best friend a living monument. [. . .]

[. . .] It could be a really intriguing exercise, and not at all frivolous, to use function theory and analytical geometry to come up with a *mathematical theory* of truth. Is truth constant? Can it always be differentiated? That is, does everything have a concept, and every truth an inner form? What is the function of Being? *Can* history be *examined* as a boundary concept? All this would be the ultimate textbook on logic and on the theory of science that only the Messiah will write. It will be both the most objective and the most metaphysical book in world literature. [. . .]

Heidegger's essay on historical time[97] is really quite ridiculous and unphilosophical. Benjamin really got it right with his assessment of it.[98]

[. . .] Benjamin writes that Judaism's concept of Justice is essentially the "striving to turn the world into the highest good,"[99] which comes out clearly in the extraordinary (and *entirely* untranslatable) Words of the Wise in Genesis 24:1. Hirsch's translation goes, "The righteous will prepare the land for the coming of the Shekhinah." In the words "The just will prepare the earth to make it a shrine of Godliness," Hirsch's beautiful translation captures a *part* of the meaning, a nuance (it sounds as if Benjamin knew this passage).

The definition of justice is to make the earth into a dwelling place of the Shekhinah by drawing the Shekhinah *down* to us. The phrase "the head of the Shekhinah is in the earthly realm" can sensibly be applied to justice. If I'm still composing Hebrew aphorisms when I'm a teacher of the Torah, I will say, "The essence of the Shekhinah is justice." As a result, an increase in justice is in truth only the increase in the revelation of justice and an increase in the divine power on earth, which is the Shekhinah. Justice is hence the highest form of God's revelation and the highest form of reverence we can give him. The *righteous* ones cry out for the Messiah, and for him alone. [. . .]

In the concept of the Shekhinah, the Jewish people have transformed that which is subjective within them into something objective. Through the Shekhinah, Jews objectify their *suffering* and Exile. [. . .] The Shekhinah is in fact the transformer through which we seek to objectify that which is most human within us, and through which our humanity wishes to rise up to God. [. . .]

My last letter to Blum came back today. [. . .]

I wrote to Benjamin and sent him the translation of Zeitlin's *Shekhinah*.

The philosophy of language is a science that in every way has yet to be created. I have in fact a very strong affinity for its fundamental thoughts. Surely, to do this doesn't require knowing many languages: a person needs to only know *one* language intimately, be it Chinese or Hebrew. Besides this, he has to be an extraordinary philosopher to be able to ferret out all the vexing problems from history, mathematics, and a handful of other nonscientific spheres. The philosophy of language will be the only science that can rightfully be characterized as "intuitive."

The task of this philosophy is to examine language as the revelation of the truth, thus determining the truth content of language. In this context one can say that Wilhelm von Humboldt was a philosopher of language in the pure sense of the word. Perhaps Herr Mauthner—who wants to prove the impossibility of such a philosophy because he says language isn't a suitable instrument for transmitting the truth—is also one. That he does this superficially proves nothing *here*. I suspect that during the Renaissance there may also have been some philosophers of language, even if they are unknown to me.

Judaism's philosophy of language is entirely concealed (yes, entirely) within a disguised core that is always active wherever the Torah is studied and transmitted. It is in the Torah, as a divine book, that the philosophy of language appears least problematic: as the language of God it must necessarily be the language of truth, of *every* truth. The truth, which is expressed in every verse as a general and specific truth, must perforce be a function of the applied words, with different truths ensuing from different words and circumstances. Just look at the interpretations done by Talmudic scholars over "synonym" verses that are "the same" despite having two different manners of expression. Here it is naturally assumed that a different truth arises from a slight shift in the word order and language. With complete justice one can say that *truth is a constant function of language.*

Truth is the inner form of the sentence or the word, and once the word is changed, even if only slightly, the truth also changes, becoming the inner form of the new word. In this way, the *affinity between roots* can be understood: according to the law of the constancy of truth, if the root changes even minutely (say, by replacing one letter with another), the truth it expresses also changes only slightly. It's still possible to identify a deeper common center tying both together (tangents of both), which is the common *concept* underlying both. Necessarily, the second word must express a *different* truth, though one with a *relationship* to the first. (It is here that Semitic languages show their superiority over other languages in which the law of constancy doesn't apply, or at least not in the absolute form that it does in languages ruled by the root.) If one so desires, this kind of analysis can be done in relation to individual letters, but also with words, sentences, and entire books seen as a composition of functions. [. . .]

"The letters, *which are the expression of spiritual powers, have their roots above*" (Molitor I).[100] (Word for word, Hirsch could have written this in his commentary to the Pentateuch!) That is to say, the letters' roots are in the truth. In the spirit of the Kabbalists, one can say that all genuine study of the truth is basically the study of language, by which one investigates the "heavenly alphabet" (Zohar II 130b) along with the spiritual powers that are reflected in it. [. . .]

November 21, 1916

Yesterday evening Cassirer made the remark on Pythagoras, "We shouldn't get lost in our own reflections."[101] Thus speaks this philosopher. No, a philosopher does not speak thus! Nevertheless, this is a commonplace—if entirely unconscious—theme. What has philosophy come to, Herr Cassirer, if it can save you from the trouble of thinking? This may work for you, but not for the philosopher.

I'm disgusted by this entire business of the history of philosophy these days, which is the reason I can barely stand Cassirer, who's just like the others. (Unfortunately, I didn't hear Simmel lecture.) Philosophy of history is done with such a shallow and hence wrongheaded approach (logically, its superficialities are not "inherently" false, but metaphysically they are absolutely so) that it is quite unbearable for anyone with some vision.

People get accustomed to bringing the history of philosophy into a system that doctoral students study and get to know, but whose core [. . .]

has the journalistic character of a feuilleton piece. Without any major adjustments, Cassirer could easily become the chief editor (or, even more appropriately, the editor of the feuilleton section) of *Berliner Tageblatt*. Certainly, he may "know" more than the current editor, and he has more of a "timeless" point of view. But what difference does this make? What proves this is his method of taking what is difficult and making it so cheap and easy that students don't need "academic philosophy" (as Troeltsch[102] says) to understand, but it becomes a part of their "general humanistic and academic education."

I'm astonished when I think about lectures by great thinkers, such as Franz von Baader's *Theory of Sacrifice* (which were *lectures!!*). Back then it was possible for a lecturer to appear before students and treat such truly difficult and essential things, and to have people understand. Either the student body has in the meantime gone metaphysically to seed (which is what I tend to think), or the professors who have anything to say have been driven away by general disapproval. If one of these days Benjamin were to deliver lectures on the history of philosophy, no one would understand a word. His seminar would be unbelievable—if people would really question rather than stupidly and superficially play along with the traditional etiquette (such as when Edith Henschel asked me yesterday who the modern Heraclitus is, by whom she "naturally" meant Henri Bergson, which is the most horrible nonsense that is only especially pernicious because it sounds superficially so correct. One discovers one connection or the other and therefore is doing the history of philosophy. This is what the history of philosophy has become today: it is not a system genuinely moved and carried forth by the holiest dogmas of truth, but scraps of information, such as who at the time of "T" developed or fought the philosophy of the renowned "A." To sum up in *one* formula the philosophy of history in Berlin, which unfortunately is *all too* ubiquitous: "The renowned 'B' was the 'A' from 'T'").

Benjamin's seminar would be unimaginably difficult, making students constantly sweat by stirring their passions. The precondition would be an entirely philosophical structure, without which everything remains mere babble. With such a structure, students would find themselves on a truly suitable path.

The real problem is when people ask tirelessly why problems aren't made easier than they were "the first time" a thinker thought them up. Where the devil do people get the right to spare themselves angst? Who has granted them permission? Where do they get the right to approach and treat a problem with any less struggle than the famous A felt at the time of T? [. . .] It's palpably obvious that people who do this give away something that has become a matter of indifference. *Because* they give it away—and as cheaply as possible—they leave the spirit out in the cold. Something with *spirit* can't be gotten on the cheap; one must pay *full* price for it. It is the fault of both professors and students that we've come to this. I, of course, can't do a thing about it yet, and only God knows if I'll be able to in twenty years. The one thing I *can* do and know how to do, however, is to be on the side of purity. I also have a better concept of philosophy than those people in the lecture who already knew what philosophy was when they were in the cradle. [. . .]

November 24, 1916

Harry Levy's lecture was awful, or at least entirely open to refutation. He justified the use of the expression "Torah Judaism" and not Orthodoxy or "law-abiding Judaism" because he claims that Judaism is far, far more than the Law, even if a very large portion of the Torah is legal and the Law is the Torah's shibboleth. Levy's deliberations concerned mainly the issue of modern education and culture. In the discussion we forced him to take a somewhat more Jewish position and more Orthodox views than he did throughout the entire heretical lecture. Heller asked him how the Orthodox regard other Jews, to which Levy replied, "Even a sinner is still an Israelite."

According to Levy, Judaism's only true and absolutely decisive dogma is "The Torah is from heaven,"[103] because if the laws of the Torah were created by men, they would lose their absolute obligatory status. The main problem here is not with the expression "The Torah is from heaven," which is but the shell, but with the problem of truth. How do we know that the truth was not *invented?* The truth, if absolutely valid, is still binding. The statement "The Torah is the absolute truth because in it man has succeeded in identifying the final truth" would be just as absolutely binding as "The Torah is from heaven." Orthodoxy doesn't trust man's ability to discover valid truths. Metaphysically, the standpoint for the study of the Torah is not that the Torah is divine but that it is the truth. If he wants, someone can maintain that the truth is always divine (though I wouldn't characterize *every* truth as divine).

"One cannot prove Judaism in any ultimate sense; you have to believe in it." *Not so.* If Judaism is *the* truth, one must be able to prove it. The fact that it can't be proven is the fault of the gentlemen who hold sway over this particular juncture in history. *They can't* offer up proofs, and hence they turn to faith. Briefly, the Messiah will *prove* Judaism through the Hebrew language. [. . .]

The Torah is not a law, just as Judaism is not religion. Torah is the transmission of God and divine things; it is the principle of the gradual rediscovery of the truth that is hinted at in writing but whose understanding has been lost. Torah is mathematics and language. *There is* no concept in German for Torah; and even if such a concept were as thick as a book, the concept of Torah—which is *Judaism's conception of truth*—could still be explained only through itself. Torah is Torah, and whoever considers this a tautology is wrong. (Or he is right, but only wrong if by this he means that there is something *un*fruitful about it.) He who understands a concept in its innermost sense can explain it only by using the concept itself. [. . .]

November 25, 1916

In Schwarz's course yesterday I had ample opportunity to be dazzled by my fellow mathematics students and the full range of their spirit. But it was ghastly to listen to them. I have no relationship whatsoever to mathematics students. [. . .] I have no doubts what Blum would have said had he ever gotten to know German mathematics students. To avoid self-disgust, I'll have to be completely different—to do more, to work more, to think more. I have to work on behalf of my dead friend. I must work as a *Zionist.* The others are not driven by an ultimate power whose demands constantly prod them on. With us, however, a magnetic force pushes our powers in *one* direction.

[. . .] I haven't heard a word from Herr Erich Gutkind in ages. If he's so preoccupied with settling his inheritance and other such affairs, I'm inclined to think that nothing much will come of his Hebrew studies. Still, I'm astounded by it. After all, he has *spiritual* reasons to want to learn Hebrew. Can death stand in the way of this? I'm very rarely in the habit of thinking about my father's death, but *one thing* is certain: it will hardly derail me from my spiritual track. The two of us—Herr Arthur Scholem and I—don't have that sort of relationship. Can I help it if I never felt any affection for him, or if my relationship to the man is basically a material one? How could it be otherwise with someone whose exilic Judaism, in the very worst sense of the word, I'm forced to stare at every day? Is this my fault?

November 26, 1916

Late in the morning I was at Löwenthal's, who was here on leave from Glogau. He hopes he'll soon get a twelve-day leave to come back. Till yesterday he didn't know about Blum's death. He was completely beside himself and kept coming back to the subject. The impression Blum left us is rooted in deep spiritual sources. Though the living, physical memory of his corporal presence—of speaking with him face-to-face—may become weak and unclear, this spiritual impression will unquestionably be strong enough to stick with us in the coming years.

In every way he had only just embarked on his course in life, and no doubt he had gone through a lot. Still, in him we had someone who carried around inside an inner formation of the strongest potential, a true harmony that can only be described with the great Hebrew expression *Tikkun*. Through this he exercised a large but invisible influence on his own life as well as on everyone who crossed his path.

I have no question in my mind that the source of his inner calm, which remains for all of us also his strongest outer characteristic, was that he was a Zionist in the true sense of the word (to the extent that one can be in Zion before it's built).

Zion is alive and active in us as the highest requirement imposed on us by practical reality, and as the root of our thinking and feeling life; it is represented in us as the highest truth there is: that we will not be scattered to the four winds but will, together with our hearts, be gathered together in the center. Blum's life was determined by the same spiritual Orders as mine, and along with everyone else's who carries in his heart an inner connection to Zion and to mathematics. In this sense, he didn't die *so* young that we are unable to learn the lesson of *reverence* from him. There are so few people who truly embody the "world of formation," of *Tikkun*, that when the wicked foe—the "other side," the violent men of Europe—destroys some of the few *(and may we not have to wait till the Last Judgment for the day of retribution!)*, he cannot easily vanish from the thoughts of his fellow seekers.

It may well be that Professor Goldschneider was very saddened by the news of Blum's death. But it has to be asked what *right* he has to tears when he has made his lazy peace with the murderers of his students. It's easy to say on a postcard, "I am for a prompt peace," while at the same time submitting to the nihilism of an academic system that doesn't permit a person the right to complain over what hits him, or at best he can complain to the provincial school board. With the butchery of Blum we have suffered a truly monstrous inner loss. But what has Goldschneider lost, who isn't young and who doesn't come from the world of *Tikkun?* God spat him out 59 years ago.

On the Talmudists' method of research: [. . .]

At least at first glance, the human spirit has discovered various means in its quest to transform the truth into a sphere where it can be made fruitful. Here we cannot address the question whether these means, or at least some of them, are *absolute* from the perspective of a divine mathematician (even if to nail down the character of truth, this problem may have to be carefully examined).

The two most important means for such a spiritual deduction are *experience* and *language.* The regulative instrument through which the Talmud organizes and decisively enriches its reflections has an intimate relationship to language. This instrument is the Torah. With the Torah the problem of the relationship of language to truth does not need to be raised, or in any case is easily solved because the Torah is assumed to have arisen from the divine center. It is placed outside of experience because it precedes it; with its help heaven and earth were created, and experience was first made possible.

The law of noncontradiction is the purely formal regulative instrument of logical schemata. Similarly, in the realm of spiritual induction, certain basic assumptions are made, and among these the Talmudic assumptions are of a completely metaphysical nature. The astrologist has Newton's laws as his most powerful research tool in ascertaining truths about the cosmic objects. He can then translate these things back into the language of everyday experience and hence make a verifiable assertion. The *regulative* instrument of astrology is a necessary corroboration between past research and present observations in the cosmos. If one of these were to diverge, one wouldn't assume either Newton's law to be wrong or the observations to be faulty, but rather the presence of something that could never be thought up in a pure logical model: that there is a new cosmic object that until now has never been observed. This method can to a very high degree be characterized as Talmudic.

The two most important rules of the Talmudic method are (1) *kal wa-chomer,* or to infer the easier from the harder. This has the form: If already during A1 the event X1 occurs, how much more so must X2 occur during A2, which somehow falls under A.

The second rule (2) is *gezera shawa,* or the inference by way of analogy. According to the Talmud, the specific characteristic of this rule is grounded in the inner nature of truth.

Both of these fundamental rules have a regulative form that guarantees an ongoing creation and discovery of new relationships and truths over the divine and earthly things, which are the subject of Talmudic deliberations: that which is inferred and explored must agree with the truth as revealed to man in the *Torah.* If the application of *kal wa-chomer* or *gezera shawa* leads directly or indirectly to a contradiction with the Torah, it follows necessarily that the person making the inductions has overlooked something, which will then clarify the matter or—more commonly—demonstrate the impossibility of the induction. This can happen, say, because the two objects being compared are shown to be fundamentally different. A very good example of this is in Baba Kama 3 b.[104]

The Torah can thus be characterized correctly as the spiritual experience of the Talmudists, all the more so because the Torah's validity is never put to question.

The exploration of such contradictions naturally assumes a very major role in Talmudic deliberations; it is the constantly flowing source out of which emerges the spontaneity of thought unique to the Talmud. [. . .]

It follows inexorably from the law of the *constancy of truth*—the tacit and ubiquitously visible foundation of all methods through which the Torah is studied—that when two verses use the same terms, the truths they express or hint at must perforce be related. This is an extraordinary source of Talmudic learning. [. . .]

The point here is that for Talmudic Judaism the Torah has been in the spiritual realm (that is, for Judaism) what the physical world is for modern science: a place in which everything has a meaning, where nothing gets lost, and whose study—with the help of certain basic assumptions and regulative instruments—can go beyond logical schemata to produce an unending series of factual truths. Our conception of tradition comes out of Talmudic Judaism. Tradition has been the *Torah,* and Judaism has seen in the Torah the eternity of the spiritual world as formed through a dynamic relationship to daily life.

December 3, 1916

[. . .] For my birthday Father has finally, if delinquently, printed up a hundred copies of my translation of the Song of Songs. It's an aesthetic horror: the dustcover and title page with the association's garland are absolutely deplorable. Far worse are the complaints I have against myself, namely, that it's not at all clear to me if this kind of translation, while quite literal, is still too free—and free in a forbidden way. Some places are really good, others really questionable. In any event, I can hardly make it public; to do so would require completely reworking and improving a second edition. [. . .]

December 16, 1916

This afternoon we began some readings with Max Meyer. Braun joined us. It was a real delight. It amused me to discover that he has also been poisoned by Wellhausen.

It's quite interesting to follow the development of higher criticism. The president and prime minister of all criticism is de Wette.[105] He operated out of a particular historical-philosophical construction, for instance, that the choice of Jerusalem must have been a late development, from which one deduces that the "Song of the Sea" must be recent, and hence the language must be recent, and hence the ending "-emo" must also be recent.[106] And wherever the ending "-emo" appears must be an early passage. [. . .] Today a critic says with a slight smile on his face, "But it is a general and certain observation that '-emo' is a recent linguistic form," and yet the same critic avoids admitting that this assertion is possible only *within* the Christian-critical world of thought. This is not a certain "observation," but most likely is a sham.

The tragic story of the Bible in the nineteenth century belongs to the saddest examples of the confusions of human cleverness.

Without a historical-philosophical assumption on the development of Israel, the critic can't establish or prove a thing, *nothing.* This assumption is not the *result* of research but *precedes* it. Like a shut door, the assumption even constrains research. The undeniable cleverness some people have employed to prove nonsense could have been used more productively elsewhere. Moreover, the Jews in general are very receptive to this critical humbug. They seem to think that they are not fully human if they don't join in—which *also* means ignorance of both Hebrew and history.

December 18, 1916

[. . .] Benjamin has announced his arrival, which is welcome news indeed. Let's hope it'll do us both a lot of good. [. . .]

How can Zionism alone bring healing? Through secret societies! Yes, this is my absolute conviction. A few young people should join together, pledging themselves to the religious duties of the Zionist life. Only from such a small community, kept together and permanently constrained by a great truth, can a catalyst to productivity shake off the physical and metaphysical lethargy of a "working" (and not only pseudo-working) group. The "band of fanatics" I dreamt of in Oberstdorf is urgently needed.[107] *Only* the religious truth—which is to say, a compulsion coming from the truth—has enough strength to hold up over time.

It's astonishing that we have no community, even among the handful of us on the extreme left, and this is because we lack the will to *totally* bind ourselves religiously—to be active in Palestine as simple people dressed in white robes. What everything hinges on is not the world being our stage, but that new human beings shall grow up in Zion. What we are lacking is twelve people who know what Zion is all about, and who are willing to go there to translate their knowledge into action. Why, O Heller,[108] should *we* not be among the twelve chosen ones?

What is needed is purity, and lots of it. What mustn't happen is for someone to go there to become someone else, which will only rarely take place; but his entire youth must be offered up, and he must enter into marriage with the *Volk*. He shall be a "bridegroom of blood"[109] for Judah. The sacrifices that we bring to Zion are more powerful than anything our fathers can come up with, as we sacrifice our broken hearts. And our hearts *are* broken because we have been raised in Exile. [. . .] *The secret society is the stage of fertilization.* The *Volk* can be fertilized only in small doses. Afterwards, there will naturally follow another stage at which point Zionism appears, or better yet, when it breaks through to the surface.

We young people are all in some way myth-mongers, some of us very strongly so. We could easily create a mythic garland to celebrate Zion and the coming of Herzl out of the East (whose name won't be a pseudonym but will have to be in absolute truth: Ahad ha-am, One from among the People).[110]

Zion is what nourishes and nurtures our fantasy. Nevertheless, it seems to me that God won't permit his name to be muddled with new and outrageous myths. He wants to spread messianic clarity. The Messiah will not propagate any more new myths, but will lure old myths out of hidden granite gorges, and will pass mighty judgment on them. He gave Buber the task of preparing the way, but Buber proved to be an unfaithful servant by turning all the values upside down. What does the Messiah care about the judgment of his chamber slave? The Messiah will keep his silence and bring forth a better judgment. Tomorrow is Hanukkah! Scholem!

December 21, 1916

[. . .] *Dogmatism is an urgent necessity.* We need fanatics! [. . .]

December 30, 1916

[. . .] To the great surprise of the gods, Benjamin has been declared fit for agricultural labor. Until he's actually drafted, he'll naturally be robbed of his peace of mind. As for what will become of him afterwards, we can only cross our fingers. I'll only be able to speak with him after my return. [. . .]

PART III

THE IDIOT: JANUARY 1917–APRIL 1918

Walter once said that the messianic realm is always present.

—Diary entry from November 3, 1917

IN 1917 GERHARD'S relationship with his father, never good, worsened dramatically. Tensions began with Arthur's indefatigable and entirely futile admonishments to be practical. "My son the gentleman engages in nothing but unprofitable pursuits. My son the gentleman is interested in mathematics, pure mathematics. . . . My son the gentleman is interested in *Yiddishkeit*. So I say to my son the gentleman: All right, become a rabbi, then you can have all the *Yiddishkeit* you want. No, my son the gentleman won't hear of becoming a rabbi. Unprofitable pursuits."[1]

This was playful banter when compared to his bile over Gerhard's and Werner's opposition to the war. In early 1917, after Werner had been arrested for taking part in an antiwar demonstration while in uniform (he was charged with "insulting the majesty" of the Kaiser), Gerhard hid his diaries and prepared for an explosion, which came one morning over breakfast in the form of a registered letter when his father, Arthur, apoplectic with rage, demanded in writing that he move out.

Gerhard ended up in a hotel in a working-class neighborhood whose inhabitants were mostly Russian Jewish intellectuals. There he met a number of Hebrew writers, including Zalman Rubashoff, who would later, under the Hebrew name Zalman Shazar, become president of the state of Israel. (Arthur Koestler borrowed his name for the hero of *Darkness at Noon*.)

In March 1917 a military examination declared Gerhard fit for service. In May he got his orders, and on June 20 he began his service. Meanwhile, Benjamin had been released from the military on feigned medical grounds—he went so far as to use hypnosis to produce symptoms of sciatica—and had arrived in Switzerland with his wife, Dora.

Scholem soon began receiving mysterious letters from his friend, which he interpreted as support for his own efforts to get out of the army. Benjamin sent one missive first to Werner Kraft, a poet who was serving as a medical orderly fit only for garrison duty. Kraft passed the incomprehensible letter on to Scholem, rightly assuming that it was really meant for him. Gerhard realized that the letter contained a "secret code for any delicate communications to be sent to Switzerland."[2] What must have seemed to the military censor like a harmless if obscure literary conversation contained a secret code:

> You are mistaken if you think that the cryptogram is a recent device, for there is a cryptogram in *The Count of Monte Cristo,* and in the Middle Ages entire systems existed—putting numbers in place of words according to a key, for example, or letters instead of words, or numbers instead of letters. If fact, I recently read about systems so ingenious they do not look like secret writing but appear harmless to the uninitiated. . . . For example, 42345, which means first the fourth word, then the second, then the third, then the fourth, then the fifth, then the fourth again.[3]

While reading and rereading Walter's letters, trying to decode them, Gerhard set about getting out of military duty. Eventually it worked. He told army psychologists about his "visions," and the army doctors diagnosed dementia praecox, a form of schizophrenia characterized by delusions. After having been declared mentally ill but before ending up in the military psychiatric ward, Scholem had plenty of time on his hands: his job at the base was that of postman. He spent his free hours writing letters to potential members of his planned "secret society," or *Geheimbund*. "That Zionism exists is something everyone should know," he wrote to his friend Aharon Heller, "but no one should know that the society of Zionists exists."[4]

Between the end of July and the beginning of August, Gerhard was assigned to the psychiatric ward, where he continued firing off his missives. (To his friend Gerda Goldberg he tried vainly to explain what he meant by Torah, Tradition, the Messiah, and History, naturally raising more questions than he answered.) And from the mental ward he was released from the military.

Back in Berlin in August 1917 he tried to bring some order to his unsteady psyche. Suicide, he decided, was out of the question because it required a "completeness" he still lacked.[5] Benjamin sent him suggestions for some light reading, including the novels *Rosa the Beautiful Policeman's Wife* and *Creative Indifference* by his friend Solomon Friedlaender, who was loosely associated with the expressionists and later with the Dadaists. He also suggested Louis Levy's *The Onion-Man Named Kzradock and the Spring Chicken Called Methusalem*.[6]

Already by the winter semester of 1917 he was back at his studies, this time in Jena. His mental condition, still precarious, was helped somewhat by the friend he met through Benjamin, Werner Kraft. Kraft, often on the verge of suicide, needed psychological help, which Gerhard was eager to give. Another thing that spoke in Kraft's favor was the way he felt about Martin Buber, now Scholem's archfiend: he hated him with all his heart, Kraft assured him. Gerhard in turn related to him the mysteries of Zion which he had been practicing to battle his own sadness, anxiety, and suicidal fits.

Another lifeline for Gerhard was Erich Brauer's sister Grete. Though entirely absent from his autobiography, she was Gerhard's first true love, an older woman whom he compared to Walter in the power she had over him. In his own awkward and bulldozing manner, he tried to declare his love to her through letters and during visits back home to Berlin, where she lived.

Uncertain of Grete's love and faced with tragedies, both his own and those of others, Scholem took the mighty Hölderlin as his model and translated more biblical and post-biblical lamentations.[7] Here we see the budding master at work. In these seemingly straightforward translations he infused Jewish tradition with a motif of death, yet also a naked youthful yearning for intimacy, couched as love of man for God. For Gerhard, mourning became a divining rod to the truth: through it he understood the world, the past, and the future.

Lamentation is in Scholem's hands not about mourning for the dead as much as it is about transmitting the Teaching and Revelation. Lamen-

tation is endless because the longing for intimacy is based on a messianic
hope that cannot be fulfilled in real historical time. ("All truly profound
talk about the past is lamentation.")[8] Lamentation is hence the motor of
Jewish history, an unfulfilled longing tying together past, present, and future, a timeless space in which the interpreter enters into intimacy with
others.

The autobiographical dimension, however esoteric, comes through
clearly in these translations. Voices from the past suddenly become animated because Gerhard filled them with his own memories and feelings.
"I have borne witness to my love and to my present stage in life," he
writes.[9] Upon completion of the epilogue he titled "On Lamentations
and Dirges" he writes similarly, "This translation has revealed to me the
most fabulous things. [. . .] I have laid out things in the epilogue that
come from the extreme depths of my heart."[10] His translation of Samuel
1:17–27 was a tribute to his fallen friend Edgar Blum; another recounted
his longing for Grete.

What did more than anything else to snap him out of his melancholy was
a small essay that arrived in the mail from Benjamin in November 1917.
It was Benjamin's short study of Dostoyevsky's *The Idiot,* which Scholem
recognized immediately as an esoteric commemoration of Fritz Heinle.[11]
Deciphering "The Idiot" came to him as an epiphany because it touched
upon what he called "the Teaching." Shortly after reading it Scholem
wrote in his diary:

> It seems that a person needs to experience an eternal life in order
> to find it again, for how should the average critic find an idea in a
> book that no one has explained to him before? How should he
> praise Dostoyevsky in any other way than for his "psychology" if he
> knows nothing about the Teaching—if the Teaching has not been
> transmitted and taught to him, regardless by whom?[12]

In the same entry Gerhard states: "Walter seems to have had the
Teaching transmitted to him from a teacher, namely, from his dead friend.
He saw in him the essence of youth. He also saw in him how youth dies.
It is unimaginable, monumental, how Walter Benjamin has survived the
death of his friend. I'm breathless that he was able to give up his own

youth (and this is the first miracle) and yet to continue living with the *idea* of youth."[13]

Having made this discovery, Gerhard dashed off a letter to Walter, declaring his understanding of "The Idiot." His letter did not survive; Benjamin's response has. On December 5, 1917, while he was sitting at home and thinking about himself, the response arrived. Gerhard called it the only "perfect" letter he had ever received, a missive inspired by love. Benjamin writes:

> Since receiving your letter I have often found myself in a festive mood. It is as if I have entered a holiday season, and I must celebrate with reverence the revelation in that which has made itself known to you. For it simply is the case that what has reached you and you alone must have been addressed to you and has entered our life again for a moment. I have entered a new phase of my life, for that which severed me from all people with planetary speed and turned even my closest relationships except for my marriage into shadows unexpectedly emerges and establishes a connection at a different place.[14]

Gerhard experienced Revelation, and the source of it, his friend Walter Benjamin, assumed the stature of a mighty prophet.[15] Scholem was still battling his mental and physical problems—friends were dying, others regarded him as a madman, and Grete didn't seem to be responding to his amorous overtures—and yet Benjamin had written him the extraordinary words, *you alone.* He soon received a raft of other secret writings from Benjamin, including "The Diary." What is more, Benjamin soon invited him to visit him and Dora in Switzerland.

Scholem was euphoric as never before. Walter had learned the "Teaching" from Heinle, and now Gerhard was receiving it from him. He was now confident that his and Benjamin's lives were "grounded above all in Revelation," that is to say, a mixture of silence and words, deliberate concealment and written texts.[16] In Jena, Scholem set up a sort of shrine to Benjamin by propping up his photograph on his desk and carrying on imaginary dialogues with it.

His metaphysical "system" further matured, even if much of what he learned he hesitated to put into words; it was so sacred that it had to be "gleaned immanently; like the rays of light emanating out from it, it just can't be written down."[17]

Revelation—through which alone words gain meaning—occurs through the Teaching, and is an ongoing affair, unfolding as interpreters, variously called prophets, poets, mystics, critics, philologists, and translators, create and give life to Tradition.[18] Tradition is hence the "effective operation of a word in each concrete situation that occurs in a given society."[19] In one of the most beautiful passages in the diaries Scholem writes:

> In each text lurks countless linguistic armies, lined up and half asleep, and the most curious operations are at work in language and in its relationship to the outside—what is commonly called its *influence*. Within us, words are silent or speak in an inexplicable succession. They speak to me, and to you they are silent. . . . *The canonical word is lusterless;* it holds back the abundance of its bright rays.

The messianic act intentionally refuses to address quotidian political issues, no matter how vital they seem. It operates through deferment—*Aufschub.*[20] Nor does it shout. Transmission takes place in silence. "Torah is in everything, just as everything contains both speaking and silence."[21]

There is a moral and "messianic" imperative behind the work of the interpreter. "The messianic order of time as the eternal present corresponds to justice as something concrete and existent. If justice weren't there, not only would the messianic realm also be absent; it would be altogether impossible."[22] Driven by a vision of a better world, the interpreter reinterprets the past for his generation and thus helps continue the ethical Tradition. The works he interprets may ring out from a vanished society, such as Pindar's Greece or Hölderlin's Germany, but they nevertheless continue to reverberate in language and as such are still present. Concealed within their words is a range of linguistic possibilities that, working on the imagination, render them timeless.

NOTEBOOK 1

Before the Lord

January 4, 1917

[. . .] On Monday Benjamin has to report for active duty. Heymann wrote a long letter, partly directed against me,[1] though not in any fundamental way. I'm still hoping to win him over. Over the past few days I've been watching Werner a lot, and I haven't held back my opinions from him.[2] He's essentially bourgeois. Werner was furious when I claimed that Liebknecht was above nationalism and that he was beneath it. Basically, he's not the brightest at grasping difficult or spiritual concerns; he clings to the surface, and probably in his heart of hearts he thinks I'm a hairsplitter. [. . .]

January 5, 1917

[. . .] I spent the afternoon with [Jakob] Jahr, who's really down. [. . .] I spoke to him about the philosophy of language, about Benjamin's and my work, and about experiments on this subject. In the evening I was at Hedwig Scholem's.

Sometimes I notice that I tell too many *lies!* I'm running the great risk of supporting a historical legend about myself—and of creating, then sanctioning, something that is superficially (though not inherently) mostly legend. By *no* means can this be justified. [. . .]

January 6, 1917

At the Royal Library this morning I read Werfel's article in *Die Neue Rundschau,* "The Christian Mission: An Open Letter to Kurt Hiller."[3] With the exception of some confusion in terminology, it's marvelous. Both activism and politically minded men really get a thrashing. One could hardly better him at this, though it's wrong to talk of "the Christian mission," because it's the *Jewish* one: it is the *Teaching.* What Werfel should know but doesn't is that Teaching is a Hebrew concept. It is Torah. Someone should tell him, but how? [. . .]

The false bourgeois conception of language (which Buber shares) says affirmatively that language exists so people can communicate (Jakob Levy, for instance, used this formulation in a discussion against me); negatively, it denies it has any inherent content.

All superficial notions of philosophy, and hence the inability to see and feel problems, arise essentially out of this accursed notion of language. All true philosophers who really think things through have absolutely nothing to do with such notions. There is no language so mired in Original Sin that a person can't uncover its non-bourgeois dimension through which he could potentially return it to its linguistic Orders.

Like the biblical narrator, I interpret Original Sin as the confusion within the spiritual orders of language. All modern languages have this Original Sin, possibly due to metaphysical mechanization; only Hebrew has escaped it.

Only from this profound and ultimate conception of language is it proper and permissible to say, "Judaism is the religion of deed," whereas in M.B.'s mouth (Martin Buber's or Marx Brod's) the statement is both shallow and wrong. This evening Grete Brauer and Erna Michaelis were here. We read the Psalms together.

January 7, 1917

[. . .] I've finally reread Benjamin's fabulous letter thoroughly.[4] In grasping what Benjamin has to say, the same astounding thing always happens to me: at first I'm standing somewhere on the wide earth while Benjamin's in heaven. Then what is said comes closer to me, and suddenly I am in the center. Each time I feel the exact same instantaneous jolt. Now these things are no longer difficult for me, and I can completely identify with his views, and I can expand on them. More than anywhere else, this applies to his reflections on the philosophy of language (to which I am not an entirely innocent bystander). Some things he writes simply can't be added to. On the theme of mathematics I could have a lot to say. Benjamin seems to have articulated one of my most important thoughts, just in a different form: to wit, that mathematics as such is a primary infinity and that *individual* facts about mathematics are generated through thinking. While Benjamin of course has a lot to improve on here, I can hardly imagine working on mathematical questions with anyone as well as with him. Mathematics belongs to the order of the Teaching.

[. . .] A highly significant remark—which in my view follows necessarily, and which immanently operates *very* powerfully in Benjamin—is that *definition is a form of knowledge:* it is *knowledge.* Everything else is the interpretation of the definition. (There was a time when this notion was considered to be trivial, which was *also* shallow and wrong, and then it was considered to be nonsense.) [. . .]

January 14, 1917

[. . .] In summer of this year, while I was away in Heidelberg, a discussion about me took place in the highest court of heaven. Furious debates broke out, which also extended to my future wife. They then sent down an angel to ask what I want. As a result of my proper metaphysical progress, the angel looked like Benjamin. (Reliable sources tell me that the celestial spiritual beings set just as much importance on this progress as on not pocketing silverware, et cetera.) I said I wanted Order. During a second hearing in October it was decided to grant me my desire by gradually revealing to me this winter the *vocabulary* of divine science—the Torah or the "Teaching"—which I could then develop further. At the prompting of the angel Gabriel, they also seem to have decided to grant me upon my arrival in Jaffa (if I prove worthy) a goblet woven of spiritual Orders.

Hence, they revealed to me the concept of science as the Teaching of the Torah's Order or the spiritual Order of things, which alone deserves to be called the introduction to the Torah. So I can better study the Orders of Judaism, it was also revealed to me that I'm a fool. They revealed to me heaven's immense indignation at the Europeans' "Experience," and that God has grown weary of being experienced, day after day, by the bourgeoisie. I also learned that I have been called to be a witness for the truth! Onward!

February 3, 1917

[. . .] The *Foundational rule of the mystical conception of language* is that all languages consist of names of God. It seems that from here it would be (comparatively!) easy to establish the foundation for a theory of language. Like the Kabbalah itself, the Kabbalah's theory of language has yet to find a person worthy to work on it. O Gerhard Scholem, what you have yet to accomplish! But *when* will you have time? Surely not in Palestine, where you'll have to work rather than think.

May 15, 1917

I'm taking a break, for as one says, I've "experienced" something. I now live at Uhlandstrasse 100/11, where I feel better than I did at Grünstrasse 26.[5]

On March 28 I was placed in the Infantry Division.

NOTEBOOK 2

*Exemplum non datum: The Example Not Given. Truth and Lies
of a Young Man and Zionist by the Name of Gerhard Scholem.*

May 16, 1917

[. . .] No one has the right to have "reasons" to become a Zionist. The
same goes for Hebrew: nothing is gained if someone has "reasons" for
learning it; otherwise he'll at best become a Hebraist. *You learn Hebrew in
order to keep silent in Hebrew. This makes sense.* Even if the person doing the
learning doesn't know anything about this, the immanent content of
what he's learning will prove it to him, and with an inescapable clarity.
Hebrew is the Torah, or you can also say that only he who learns Hebrew
for the sake of the Torah is a pupil, a student of the Teaching. For only he
who has attained the sphere of silence can enter into the sphere of the
Teaching.

The Teaching is the only permitted argument for Zionism, its only
true and *compelling* reason. [. . .]

May 17, 1917

[. . .] Benjamin, who was here for four months, got married on April 17.
My wedding gift was Scheerbart's *Lesabendio,* a book of important depth
and clarity. I've read Dostoyevsky's *The Idiot* for the first time. There will
be a lot to say about this.

The definition of philosophy as the Teaching of the spiritual Orders
demonstrates its importance and its full connection to a large and final
unity: that of the *Teaching,* pure and simple. Torah is not the Torah of
something. The Teaching of Orders is immense, but Torah is more. Torah is the sphere where all things become substantial—substantial from
the perspective of God and substantial for the life of people.

Sometimes out of pure enthusiasm I have so much to say that I can't
say anything properly. I can only throw everything together and give it
over to a future master craftsman. [. . .]

I've been giving a lot of thought to *commentary* as the conception of
Order in the Jewish world of spirit. It follows logically that if commentary is truly the ultimate task, as Benjamin says quite correctly, then the
world is made up of script and language, which would be a fundamental
insight. Important in this regard is a treatment of the spiritual essence of
commentary in Judaism.

Rashi's masterpiece is both very easy and extremely difficult. The oral Torah can be advanced only through commentary. *Commentary is the inner form of the oral doctrine,* its legitimate interpretation. Ultimately, only the Bible can be commented upon. It is the *absolute* written text. Every commentary, according to Jewish law, is a commentary on the Bible. In today's Judaism, the knowledge of the deep meaning of commentary is still alive.

May 19, 1917

[. . .] I am completely unsuited to be a member of the board at the Beit-Wa'ad,[6] as my entire sensibility militates against this sort of activity. Just think, I'm twenty years old! (Sometimes I question whether Strauss[7] is really worth his salt or if he's a phony. Terrible!) My current problem is that, sitting around the table with people in the hostel, I frequently sink for hours on end into the nastiest moods. Nothing "happened" today, but thirty minutes before the meal I was so disgusted by my landlady Frau Struck that during the entire afternoon and evening not a single word passed my lips.[8] Everyone now thinks something has happened to me, but no one suspects the real reason, which is *that this pension repels me every bit as much as my parents' house.* I loathe the proprietor and her insipid blabber. What stirs me up time after time is her despicable habit of preferring some people to others during meals, and her indescribably conniving behavior (which I sense so deeply and entirely, even if I can only express it poorly). All the people in the pension, with the possible exception of Rubaschoff,[9] are deeply corrupt petty bourgeois. I've gradually lost every scrap of respect for Kitain,[10] just I have for all these other gentlemen and ladies. So this is what the famous Pension Struck looks like! It's shocking. It is only in my room, where I don't have to look at these people, that I can calm down. My problem therefore cannot be *my* spiritual disposition.

Here in the pension the conflict is not as open as in my parents' home. On the surface, I am polite and immensely kind, while at the same time I despise this Frau Struck, who describes herself as a "fine, cultivated lady" and bears a close resemblance to Aunt Viechen.[11] *I'm such a fraud in this place that it puts me to shame.* And I'm too smug and bourgeois to spit in these people's faces and leave. *Never again in a pension!!!!!* I've learned the lesson *well.*

Once upon a time there was a fellow whose life was a failure but who didn't find the courage to put an end to it; the coward couldn't bring himself to do it. He therefore played a game with the things most apt to prevent him from fulfilling his duties. He was extremely radical, so radical that no one could impress him with any demand. Far surpassing all demands, he didn't need to fulfill any. He discovered a science that allowed him to hide the emptiness of his heart behind the fullness of his spirit, and—desecrating something very respectable—he called his science Zionism. I know this young man well: sham is written all over his face.

Nothing is wrong with me, nothing in the least. I'm so lazy that the most I can aspire to become is an old bookworm like Steinschneider[12]— just not a genuinely creative scholar. I could easily pass my time in a large castle with an old library filled with interesting things. There I could sit out my days in leisure and idleness, without a trace of Zion. If one of these days I abandon my "spiritual center," I'll be washed up. And then what will become of me? By pretending to have an ideal that I've in fact abandoned long ago, I'll join the gigantic swindle, becoming just like everyone else. Perhaps everyone was once like us before they turned into ghosts, stalking around their own graves. [. . .]

People say that I make such disgustingly disparaging remarks about everyone else, and that I consider everyone around me to be an idiot. Pardon me, but can I help it if people are idiots. *God help me, they are!*

Cohn[13] the big shot wanted to know what I intend to write. How should one answer someone like him? Maybe I'll say, "I'm thinking of investigating Truth."

If I were a young man with some integrity, I would put a bullet through my head and let dear God do the rest.

Woe to those who sit on a high throne because when they fall, their plunge is all the more terrifying! In his journey among men, he who wears the garment of pride will be tossed into chaos the instant his pride abandons him. I would go to my death if someone came to me and said, "Listen, if you die in honor, you'll get a great necrologist." [. . .]

May 24, 1917

Fundamental objections to my second and third translation:

1. The lack of dignity in the language.
2. The murder of the original's stringency through the arrange-
   ment of words and a versification bordering on kitsch. [. . .]
3. The lack of literalness. [. . .]

May 29, 1917

I began to read Dostoyevsky's *Brothers Karamazov.* One of my worst mistakes is that I'm not doggedly consistent, which is obvious in my dealings
with my family. I wouldn't have failed had I not succumbed to their stupid babble. Father is right now. Why don't I just turn my back on all of
these Hirshes and Scholems! [. . .]

I don't have to conceal from myself that *I'm uncertain.* My Zionism is
still not enough to give me the ultimate security with which I can appear
on the outside as a Zionist and a human being, which will perhaps be a
reason for some people to value me. I'm a coward (and it's no excuse that
other people are *even* more cowardly).

May 30, 1917

I've been godless in my life, as godless as they come, a genuine frivoler.
Buber's totally right when he says that a person confesses God with his
lips and betrays him with his life.

Am I a Jew? No. A human being? No. An upstanding youth? No.
What am I then? A nihilist who, spurned by God, goes behind God's
back because He's rejected him. All the piety in the world isn't enough to
wash clean all the inner sins I've committed in my nineteen years of life.

There is nothing more repellent than the holy swindler, the spiritual
hypocrite who tries to make a career out of his earnestness. Bookworms
with the instinct for power could degenerate in this direction. This is the
kind of person I am. I could sit my entire life in a library and devote myself to Jewish books, yet something compels me to go beyond pretending
that I'm doing so for "spiritual" reasons. *This is one big hoax! That's what it
is: a hoax.*

June 3, 1917

[. . .] The Jewish people *today,* who carry around Exile as a kind of
karma, no longer form a living community. This must be said with great

emphasis. From the time our banishment began determining also the inner structure of the Jewish people, the life of the Jewish people no longer rests upon a community but upon *Jewish souls,* upon individual Jews. Among these Jews there has been a higher, binding order: this was the Torah, which in Exile was the nation's only permitted and legitimate bond. Where the Torah has vanished, all that remains is the anarchistic Jewish soul. This soul cannot be helped by "work" because such "work" does *not* operate within the community.

The decisive question is how Zionism can be introduced to such Jews. The possibility of winning over the youth to a deeper truth through some kind of mass effort, which I define as the influence of two or more people, must be denied. Every such effort deceptively pastes over the abysmal difficulties involved in this by creating for individual Jews a fictitious community and thus making it seem possible that they could do the most difficult thing of all. The various German-Jewish youth groups have done just this. But as long as we are in Exile, there is no other way to have an influence than this: to work among individual Jewish souls, one person at a time, and not to make life easy for anyone, "not to pause from hard work." We can't build any bridges to make it easy for those who come to us from the future. The conditions for Zion will only be fulfilled once every such bridge has truly been torn down.

So long as this does not become general knowledge among the youth, the deep confusion that has been sown in the hearts of Zionists by "activity" cannot be overcome. But if you work and educate yourself along our lines, there can be no doubt whatsoever that out from among the Jewish youth will come the strongest actions imaginable. Only once we have become *lonely* will Zionism also reach the sphere that it absolutely must attain if it is not to sink into the spheres of indifferent concerns. It will attain the sphere of Torah.

Our national education is this: education through friendship and the necessity of loneliness, which alone will make possible a community in Zion. [. . .]

Our duty is to make the youth worthy of this stage. If we can do this, Zionism will flow out of our spirits into our *legs,* and actualization will truly be just around the corner.

We have to admit that here in Germany we are sitting on a sinking ship. It cannot be our task to save the masses but only to win over some individual *souls* and to snatch them away from the bane of corruption. What we are really up to is a kind of *inner* work that has never been done before. Anyway, we Zionists especially have no need to stir up trouble. We must give up on the public, and the only thing we have to say to them is our confession of sin. [. . .]

August 9, 1917

Yesterday I wrote Benjamin. [. . .]

There is no propaganda unless it is for a prophet. When the Baal Shem spoke, everyone believed that he spoke directly to him. *He* was able to grip ten men in their souls. *We're* not able to do this.

On June 18 I was drafted into the 18th Reserve Infantry in Allenstein. From June 20 to July 6 I did my service. I was released till July 25, and till August 8 I was assigned to the psychiatric ward. Now because of psychopathology I've been given leave and am dressed in civilian clothes pending my final release.

I will not leave any written account of my time in the military. This, the central test of my Zionism, has proven that Zion is stronger than violence.

Undated [August 1917]

So Gerda Goldberg is an atheist![14] She can't make heads or tails out of Revelation, by which she obviously means the verbal inspiration of holy books such as the Bible. Great. She builds what she has to build on humanity, apparently as opposed to on God. Here I'm going to go into a far more essential question, and one that means a lot more to me than the so-called denial or affirmation of God's existence: namely, whether the spiritual essence of things is formed according to certain scales and Orders, and whether she concedes that Being (the "Order of Creation") is formed *centrally* and not from the periphery. The affirmation of this question, which is something I demand of everyone with whom I have a fruitful conversation, makes it for me at present entirely unimportant whether or not the Center of Things "exists" or "does not exist." (For me this is the least interesting question posed by the atheist.) What's important to recognize is that things are fashioned by this Center. It makes no difference if a person is an atheist or a skeptic. What's important is that he acknowledge with a fanatical decisiveness the Law, the Order of

Things, in other words, the Torah. The proof for the existence of God can be carried out only from a fresh perspective. What is certain is that at the end of the day, the meaning of thought is trying to do this constantly. This is what one calls thinking justifying itself.

I demand no return to eastern European Judaism, though not because this would be *going backwards*. When a person repents (the Hebrew expression means to "turn around"), he turns away from his evil ways, in other words, *he goes back to the place where his evil ways began*. What he doesn't do is *continue* walking straight ahead. If we Jews need to turn back, and we surely do, we have to go back to the spot in the road where we began. I'm all for regression (though of course not politically or culturally) to the extent that it is an inner necessity. As far as I am concerned, *Kultur* can go to hell. We can return culturally by approaching the *Center*. But Judaism's Original Sin is as old as Judaism itself. It began the minute the Torah was not *taught* but was acted out. [. . .]

August 27, 1917

[. . .] One can see particularly in Benjamin's remarks just how absolutely abominable Original Sin is. If it implies that "heredity is sin," it's a metaphysical heresy, for sin implies an immediate relationship to God, whereas heredity signals a mediated relationship. Only in the pagan imagination is sin also a mediated relationship. Not so in Jewish circles, and for this reason the concept of Original Sin is (serious) dialectical nonsense. For us, the concept of tradition is something *good,* and here there is heredity without sin (admittedly, in a very profound and non-biological sense). Within Christianity (just as with all things and all Jewish Orders) an internal degeneration of this concept has spawned the doctrine of Original Sin. [. . .]

Tradition says that human society has an immediate connection to God. Perhaps the question can be raised whether the individual can even *have* such a relationship. The answer to this is *sin*. Without sin there would indeed not be such a relationship.

During the psychological examinations, everyone was asked if he believed in God. I said I did.

I see my thoughts but I have no visions. That was a hoax on my part. I only have a very lively fantasy in my thoughts. I haven't even had a vision of Zion. The psychiatrists are fools, all their cleverness notwithstanding. They believe everything they want to hear.

[. . .] *After a visit to the Sturm exhibition.*[15]

Chagall's pictures made the most powerful impressions. His Jews are of colossal greatness, free of any trace of kitsch and absolutely perfect in their own way. Two portraits in particular deserve singling out as opposites: I call them "The Zionist" and "The Anti-Zionist." The latter has already appeared in *Sturm,*[16] with the full abyss of Jewish rottenness and sacrilege in his eyes. No color that exists can oppose him. His opposite is the perfected Zionist (who's painted green).

Like everything he does, Chagall's colors are purely metaphysical. The division of space (in the magnificent paintings *The Birth* and *The Dead*) is astonishing. A question to ask this very Jewish figure pertains to the Christian nature of his mystical symbols. What is the meaning of the animals sitting at his table?

Reflections pro and contra the cubists: here's an irrefutable argument. Spiritually, cubism expresses the essence of space by dissecting it. Fantastic symbols are the functions of their knowledge of the world (the half-circle, the perpendicular and horizontal lines, especially the "\," and to a lesser degree the "/," all of which have the highest metaphysical symbolic meaning). This brings these symbols in close proximity to mathematics (or at least the way I understand mathematics).

Beginning with Picasso all the way down to the worst painters among the cubists, the decisive objection against them is their use of color. I can imagine someone (Chagall) using color to know the world symbolically, or how someone like him in his magnificent pictures can damn the use of lines. This is the *pure* way. The other way is that of the *pure* cubists, who use line to communicate the essence of space (especially in Picasso's *Woman with Violin,* with its unprecedented perpendicular and slanting horizontals). When forced, Picasso proves contra the cubists that at some point in his world color must be allowed; he cannot use lines to know the world, which means that his cubist metaphysics is incomplete, and hence *impure. The cubist work of genius cannot have color; it clearly has to be formless.*

A picture such as Picasso's *The Woman with the Fan* is kitsch, first because the woman and the fan are *visible;* they are formed and not truly absorbed into the cubist system (unlike, say, *The Woman with the Violin,* which can be seen *only* by those who can see symbolically-mathematically, who can see it at once). The other reason it's kitsch is that the colors are used in manifold ways. This picture testifies to an entirely immature knowledge of the world. *Nothing* is known *spatially.*

The Woman with the Violin is completely different and is among the finest pictures in the exhibition. Yet one is forced to raise this decisive objection: the two sides of the painting have different colors. In the perpendicular middle of the world stands the woman, who is crafted as the motionless creature of space, and in her spiritual center is the center of the violin. Music is brought into deep relationship with space, which separates it into parts. In other words, on the right side is the world without music, and there are *no* lines, especially no *perpendicular* lines.

As mentioned above, Picasso's main instrument is the perpendicular line. The woman *plays the violin,* and the music flows over to the left side. On the left side is the world with music, and this side is magnificently dissected. Nevertheless, for Picasso the symbols were not so powerful that they could exhaustively communicate the world. And here begins the slide into sin. The world without music is light, and the world with it is in a dark Dionysian hue, otherwise everything is gray on gray. *This is unbelievable kitsch.*

How could Picasso prostitute and really defile his "knowledge of the world" by taking something that is metaphysically intuited and dissected and mixing in a colorful world, where it doesn't belong because it is a-mathematical! If I wanted a synthesis between color and line, I'd go to Rembrandt, not to the cubists.

My demand is total purity of spheres. I would never paint a cubist picture using color, let alone many colors (and perhaps I tend strongly toward cubism, to the extent that I can speak about it). One can and must insist that the magnificence of the mathematical symbols also includes color in its knowledge. *Color must not be an element of this world in which space is divided up into metaphysical cells,* otherwise the entire dualistic observation a priori becomes bourgeois kitsch. The notion that space has color is a viewpoint, an observation, with no relationship whatsoever to the cubist worldview. Indeed, insofar as cubism demands to be taken seriously as world symbolism in the highest sense, it is out of the question.

In the pure cubist approach, identity is dissolved. Space is no longer identical (because space means the absolute essence). In painting, however, identity is won back through color—which, philosophically, is due to people's stupidity. I too can *produce* identity, but the real challenge is to put it systematically to question in the manner of *The Woman with the Violin.*

Picasso may be on his way to colorlessness, and then he'll be good. Klee is occasionally good. [. . .]

One of the greatest symbols is that of a half-circle with tangents. One picture is composed out of only a few of these symbols (six or seven). It succeeds completely. Cubism has overcome form and will overcome color. Then it will be *true knowledge.*

August 31, 1917

Cubism is the artistic expression of the mathematical theory of truth. Without question, there are mystical materials introduced here, presumably in the horizontal "\," which must have some relationship to the rays of the sun, and which divides space up in the most remarkable way. The real challenge, however, would be to put the symbolism of the straight line on an entirely new basis, which is what Picasso seems to be up to.

From this standpoint, futurism has to be energetically opposed as utterly impure. The minute the line is used as an instrument for knowledge of the world, the purest blue also becomes reprehensible because it is, to the known world, irrational and incommensurable. I don't have any idea what futurism wants, but if it seeks to establish a synthesis between, say, color and line, then it has an entirely different view from cubism. It may have more linguistic possibilities, though it is less sublime.

Chagall is an entirely un-mathematical man. His attempt to go in a cubist direction (in *Two Men under a Tree*) is inherently objectionable and bad. Poor splattering of paint and half-circles without final importance don't produce magic.

Jewish art (from the symbolism of the Tabernacle and the mystical symbols of the Kabbalistic tree etc., all the way to its more recent pinnacle in Chagall) seems to me to rest on the symbolic division of space. This is particularly clear in the Kabbalah's "Tree of Life," which almost has a cubist feel to it. The menorah separates space. The "orders of creation" divide up space symbolically. The deep relationship between Judaism and mathematics is revealed here. Zion is the medium of space. The Spaniard Picasso's *Woman with the Violin seems* Jewish. The prohibition against "likeness" in Judaism leads to the division into symbols. Jewish art depends not on likenesses but on rigid, thick lines. Jewish art resists the creation of new forms and seeks mathematical-metaphysical knowledge. The *Jewish* image of a man *must* be cubist.

September 2, 1917

I am such a liar that I may have to make believe I live a heroic life because I'm too dishonest to kill myself. Suicide requires completeness.

I'm no psychopath, I'm just bourgeois. It's because everyone thinks I am anything but bourgeois that they think I'm crazy. If they could just take off their spectacles for a moment and look at me, they would know. Gerhard Scholem performs a dance—around Zion. How disgusting!

Do you believe in God? Yes! "I don't believe you do," said the psychiatrist. He didn't say this to me but could have easily.

Mathematics is the Jewish art. Jewish art is the symbolism of the Teaching. Jewish *art* begins with the number 3, Jewish *Teaching* with 1. Their circles cross each other at real and imaginary points. The number 7 is a real point. All European art is sham and vulgarity. It wants spirit through the flesh. Jewish art is cubism, which has managed to abandon flesh. The Messiah will be a cubist in the abovementioned sense. And he will know about the grand synthesis of divided space: the words of the Torah. [. . .]

September 9, 1917

[. . .] Upon careful reflection, I have no reason to be well disposed toward myself. This would be worth considering only if I could be the way I want to be, and how I generally present myself. As it is, I know in my heart of hearts that I'm a swindler. I desire something great, but I'm not great. None of us is capable of the true greatness of sacrifice, because in reality *all* of us, without regard to health and the like, would have to become agricultural workers in order to redeem the land. Harry Heller is no hero either. He allows the looming dangers of hypertrophy to prevent him from becoming a farmer. This is wrong. This totally pernicious and mendacious generation of ours won't end up building Zion.

The only argument in my favor is that I'm ugly and lack even the slightest trace of style. My ugliness seduces me into using my spirit to accomplish something: it turns me into a blasphemer. [. . .]

September 14, 1917

Life in *Jena* began for me yesterday.[17] After walking around somewhat pointlessly yesterday, today I found a very lovely room on the Fürstengraben, in the home of a museum employee. It has a clear view, and is large and bright with four windows. I'm now sitting here at my desk as if at home.

I am in love with someone, I just don't know with whom. Isn't this farcical?

I've been reading Ahad Haam's forth volume, *The Torah from Zion*.[18] His thought is a typical example of a thinker who's deeper than what he writes, someone who inevitably comes out with twaddle when he speaks, while the soul—the center that isn't expressed, which is enough and is essential—is the only thing that ultimately counts. Hegel spoke his mind; so perhaps did Kant. *The Jews have never manifested themselves in speaking.* In this sense, everything we create is related to Ahad Haam—to Moses and the prophets, all the way to Ahron Marcus and even Buber.[19] All are incapable of uttering the most important matters residing *within* written and writable language.

To continue on this theme, an important question would be: could one express all languages in writing? Are they writable? Is it thinkable to have a language whose very nature excludes the written text? Or are the inner principles of language and script so related that the principle of expression and that of script are identical? This may in fact be the case.

Is Walter Benjamin really a Zionist? Isn't there truthfully an immense chasm between us? Isn't he only *for* the *centered life* and not for Zion? Has he really already accomplished the great Zionist synthesis, which is the establishment of a standard in the Teaching? He is the purely theoretical man. Is he able to understand those of us who want to work in the Land of Israel for the formation of our *life?* I sometimes have my doubts. I would like to speak with him now. This would be good.

September 25, 1917

[. . .] Religion is the consciousness of the Order of Things. Here is the point where one can see that, in an *ordered* condition, there can be no Buberian or modern separation between religion (dogma) and religiosity (the living relationship to the "Absolute").[20] This consciousness is both the religiosity of man and his religion; it is his primary formation of life.

Every movement unique to the individual is magical. This movement articulates a particular relationship to the Orders.

Christianity and magic. Mythology and Love. Judaism is the consciousness of the *ethical* (and not sacral) Order of Things. Christianity is the mythical reaction against history by means of a new conception of love. [. . .]

Yom Kippur begins today. Gershom Schalom,[21] do you have any inner relationship to this terrifying day? Do you really intend to mortify yourself because of your sins and shortcomings? I don't know. I have to admit that I neither deny nor accept the traditional ideas on practical Judaism. I am a complete and total skeptic. I don't know the truth of the value of all these things. I am fasting, though without any inner connection to it. It is incidental, not a part of *myself.* A nice, pleasant custom. No, the Jewish religion isn't mine!

September 26, 1917

[. . .] To Meta[22]

I left Berlin during a fit of antinomianism. It's good but also terrible you're not here. The most we can achieve in Exile is absolute clarity and purity, out of which grows a core accord. I have succeeded in establishing this sort of relationship with a few people (Walter and Aharon),[23] though never with a girl. All the girls I know have question marks smeared all over them. [. . .]

I understand all too well the disinclination to learn Hebrew in a classroom. This just confirms my view that you can only learn the *essentials* of Hebrew—like all essential matters—alone or with one other person. To be sure, Hebrew in the classroom is better than no Hebrew at all. Yet everyone who takes it seriously will find in every class a fly in the ointment. He will retreat into loneliness, though he had earlier cried out for "community."

Only the relationship of the *Teaching,* which occurs between two people, enables positive work. And as with all the most foundational things, this "other" is God himself. As it says with monumental wisdom in one of our blessings: he is the one who plants the Teaching in our hearts. Just think that there are people out there who, in their concept of science or art, have found an ultimately valid relationship to the Order of Creation. Zionism has been presented to these people as an imperative, which also means to bring it into an inseparable union with the Center of which they are already aware. Clearly, these days this is a task (which concerns a *mystical* relationship) that cannot be performed by people. God is the teacher here. Having fundamentally recognized where we must fail is precisely the most important point for someone who wants to do Zionist work. [. . .]

[. . .] I've had an important experience in the pure heights of the idea. Until now the great gateway to Kant has been closed to me, but now I've passed through it. I read the *Prolegomena* to get an understanding of the basic ideas of the *Critique of Pure Reason,* and I believe I've grasped it. I finally have the great aggressor in front of me. It would be immensely significant if what he asserts in the *Prolegomena*'s first few paragraphs— and ostensibly proves—were true.

I have no right to think about continuing my development as long as I don't know Kant or haven't proven him wrong within me. My innermost convictions will have enormous question marks over them. A terrifying attack on metaphysics (and I *know* that metaphysics is possible and is the beginning of philosophy) has never really taken place, and is scarcely imaginable. Someone may come and say, "These metaphysical views of yours are all well and good, but regrettably I must refuse to test them as long as you haven't proven to me your right to apply rational conceptions to metaphysics! No, I will use the transcendental deduction to offer irrefutable proof that the fundamental categories you use in both metaphysics and the normal sphere aren't at all *explained* here. Rather, it has meaning only by enabling experience." He will offer ample proof of this. But I am convinced that the *proof is wrong,* no matter how clever it is.

As long as metaphysics is not disproved, the pure vision of the Teaching remains in the center. [. . .]

Can it be true that our metaphysics, which is the Teaching of Orders, isn't a science at all but belongs somewhere else entirely? Yes and no. Certainly it belongs somewhere else—precisely in the massive association of the Teaching. Still, it cannot be excluded from the arena of its science. Properly understood, science leads exclusively to this ultimate center of the Teaching. Walter once wrote that "the genius"[24] is doing research in the mathematical theory of truth. How can he do this? He is a Kantian, after all. Or perhaps the Kantians have found a way back to the path of the grand truth. I would love to get to know him immediately.

Surely *one thing* Kant could not question, because it cannot be affected by doubt, is Zion. But doesn't this knowledge or this doubt, which is applied to other things, split the *Teaching* of Zion in two? [. . .]

Is it true that there can be only *one* Zionist in the world?[25] Or that Zionism is something completely different? *No,* it is not true. The entire world is bound up into the bundle of life.

Love is magic, love is forbidden. Or is there a very deep love that does not cast a magic spell but, in inner coherence, brings things together and binds them? Couldn't this be a deeper conception of love? Or is love also an antinomian thing containing both love and magic? The love of a people as a nation is not magic; it is Order. But isn't the love of people as individuals magical, as is all experience? [. . .]

October 1, 1917

Good heavens, why *must* there always be creatures like this Grete Krämer, a pathetic fool who worships fools and who can put up with everything except when someone lets loose on authorities, be it official Prussiandom or the pseudo-Zionists.[26] She calls herself a *radical* Zionist! Yes, we really have *this* coming to us! Why do our leading women and men have to be people like her? Grete Krämer has what people shamelessly call a "future." Of course! She is tolerant! My God, how the insipidity of this tolerance stinks to high heaven! She is tolerant only because she lacks strong principles, and all principles are consequently the same for her.

I'm the idiot! *Why* do I get myself mixed up with this girl, who would be happiest if she never had to set eyes on me again? What kind of interest do I have in her? Surely none. This reptile doesn't want to learn Hebrew because she would have to do it with me—she claims to be *afraid* of me. And she's not lying. To be sure, anything's preferable to the danger of learning a *proper* and anti-bourgeois Hebrew. [. . .]

It's all so much claptrap with these people here. What do I really want? Halle, Krämer, Holländer—they all irritate me.[27] [. . .] And what *are* these girls to me? Nothing. Absolutely nothing. The truth is that they're just a bunch of barmaids for me. This is the truth about them.

NOTEBOOK 3

On Metaphysics and Logic, and a Few Areas of Phenomenological Reflection That Don't Belong to Them: Dedicated to Myself.

October 5–December 30, 1917

I cannot recount to you what [Benjamin] wrote, as silence prevents this, but I must tell you and no one else that these words have made me great. No one on this earth could be a prophet of God besides him; he has purified and refined my spirit the way only a prophet can purify and refine.

—Letter to Meta Jahr, December 5, 1917

October 5, 1917

Last night Kahn[28] came over with three fellows and spent the night at my house. In the evening we had a long discussion of Blue-White,[29] the final result being that *they will all resign*. They are about ten people in total. [. . .]

October 15, 1917

Werner Kraft[30] *was with me from Friday evening till yesterday afternoon.* There were many *very* important things to discuss. I only wish I could get him to come to Jena.

Kraft says that the German heart stands against the Jewish spirit, that silence is against the word. *No, no, no.* The Torah is in the heart, disproving his entire argument. What kind of injustice is it to go against your own soul and to *think away* your heart? He doesn't have a *clue* about the Torah. How can he dare throw away Judaism? I told him this. He was silent. No, Rudolf Borchardt also can't bring the German heart any closer to me.[31] *The Jewish conception of the word includes silence.*

Kraft said to me that only because I am a German do I want to be silent in Hebrew. "If you were a Jew, you wouldn't strive for this."

It's not so. The German usually doesn't keep silent in German, but is just silent. What we seek is the rhythm of the Torah in silence, and *this* is what we mean by being silent in Hebrew. A part of the *Torah* is silence, but not silence beyond the Name. The Torah is silent in symbols and speaks through being, while the German speaks in symbols and is silent in being.

Kraft said: "I feel you're lacking something, and I know I can't give it to you." *No, I lack nothing, for the thing he misses in me is what I have re-nounced.* [. . .]

To Mirjam Fuchs:

Joy is contained even in the profound insight that God hasn't destined us to be joyful—which is the only source of joy for today's Jew.

You ask whether I have also been educated for mediocrity. In the tru-est sense of the word, I haven't been educated *at all*. No one has told me what is good or evil, valuable or abhorrent. I have lived for a long time in an atmosphere of complete inadequacy. The place I stem from hasn't managed to pass any ideas down to me. I have long lived a double and disjointed life, which is the fate I've wanted to spare others.

Externally, my life was senseless: I went to meetings and heard lectures that gave me nothing and only wasted my valuable time. Parallel to this I led a completely different life of study. Back then I was Orthodox and found within Orthodoxy something total. Surely this has left some traces on me. But none of the dealings I had with the stuff of ultimate impor-tance was taught to me. Only as I had nearly found my way did the greatest experience of my life occur: I came into contact with a man of absolute and magnificent greatness. He exercised the deepest influence on my life—and not through his Teaching but his essential being and the reverence I continue to feel for him till this very day. This man was not a Zionist, and it may be that he only came to Judaism through me. But he was the miracle that occurs only once in a generation. In him spoke out the deepest, most absolute Judaism—all without his having the foggiest idea that this was what he was doing.

This man is the only one who has fundamentally changed me to the core. I would never have found him had I searched him out. Since then I now know the truth of youth. He has taught me that we must give up our youth (not to give up on other youngsters but to give up ourselves: on our own youth we don't deserve because we lack innocence). He never told me this, but he did it before I did. Never has anyone played such an indispensable role in my life.

I am not a German Jew. I don't know if I ever was one, but now I speak out with absolute certainty: I am not one. It may be risky to say this, yet I do it with a clear conscience. I live in the freedom and the law of an idea. I know of no corner of my life that does not get its life from this idea. [. . .]

God is not interested in our origins, only where we are heading. I'm not—in the deepest sense—responsible for my parents or for my birth, though I am responsible for my death. And everything depends on this. It is a harsh judgment against us all that we are not able to die justly at every moment, that today we still cannot answer for our death. The reason for this is that we are not yet in Zion, even though Zion may already be here (which is easy to say). Today our death would be only symbolic. Woe to the life whose end is *merely* symbolic. Theory can justify *everything*, just not a theoretical death. This is a terrifying point.

"Theory" and "Torah" share the same consonants. The smallest abysses are the greatest. In this wordplay I'm hiding a racing series of thoughts I dare not point out. They sound out only when I'm thinking.

October 16, 1917

When I went over to Valeria Grünwald's I really only wanted to study Hebrew. She sat there with a totally miserable expression on her face. I asked her what was wrong, to which she replied in a most despairing voice that she had experienced something so indescribable, something so indecent, that I couldn't imagine it. She didn't want to tell me what it was. I thought to myself that perhaps Agnon's behind it,[32] so I asked her if she had heard from him. What came out was that on Thursday her sister had met with him in Weimar without telling us a word about it.

Valeria maintained that this was just *one* of the things bothering her. I can't say whether this is true or not, but what I do know is that her mood was contagious, and I walked around the room for ten minutes in stone silence. I then declared (which I saw on her face really irritated her) that I no longer wanted to study with her, and in fact I left. I really didn't have any reason to be irritated because I didn't, and don't, have an intimate relationship to Agnon. I'm extremely irked at Anne Grünwald, however. There is a kind of silent jealousy between the two sisters, and I derive hardly any pleasure out of the relationship. She knows that both of us wanted to be together with Agnon in Jena, and now behind our backs she made all sorts of arrangements. Humanly speaking, this is really shabby—unless she's in love with Agnon and wants to be alone with him, which one can understand. It's all too familiar for me, however, how in a certain sense we parted without saying a word. I have no mastery over my moods. [. . .]

To translate the Bible, a person needs to write it all over again from scratch.

Maybe women have been given symbols that we men lack. This is *certainly* how it works. Maybe they are wealthier than we. As *mothers* they also know our symbols. Women don't perceive the same way as we. But the ultimate spiritual differences between men and women are to be found in these symbols—which they received before us.

The symbols of the woman cannot be learned; they constitute the *language of a woman,* whose essence we cannot know and whose translation always leads to *human* symbols, while we are barred from the things that interest us in these symbols. [. . .] *A woman cannot betray her essence even if she wanted to.* (I use the word "betray" literally: that is, if she wanted to betray her sex she would never succeed because we would recognize the symbols in the *other* spheres.) This could lead to the supposition of a feminine Torah, a supposition that is not justified, not least because this Torah would *mis*understand the essence of the Torah's symbols—even before it could *understand* them.

It is not true that the woman is closer to mythic connections than the man.

I'll take the risk—without being trivial—of uttering again the eternal truth: the spheres of man and woman are different. The public sphere is not that of woman. I don't want to see them in public. I am no defender of woman's rights. [. . .]

There are books that man must read a priori—or not read. To the former belong detective novels, but doubtless also books by the great Frenchmen. You can't convert to them; one is born for Balzac, Flaubert, France, and Mallarmé. Jewish literature doesn't have such books. Is this bad or an advantage? [. . .]

Insight into the art of poetry implies symbolic skepticism about its truth. The theory of poetry is either a stillborn child or the Messiah himself. *There is nothing in between!* Poetry is destruction. I'm just a bad poet because I'll never be prepared to give up my life for a poem. I would never risk ruin for a poem.

[. . .] Listen to me, Werner Kraft, it doesn't matter in the least whether or not someone knows what he has![33] The most silent of things (that is, something going toward silence and not only coming from it) belongs to the essence of the Teaching. Or is the Teaching *babble?* This is a prejudice. There are things that one doesn't know and yet still work. I basically don't need communication where there can be none.

There is a chasm separating Kraft and me. Is it the chasm of youth? I daresay that he is much younger than I, even if chronologically the opposite is the case. It's just that my youth is different from his. Shouldn't this be an abyss that, while perhaps unbridgeable, can at least be drawn from? I've thought a lot about what makes up his particular stage of development, and one thing is certain: it can't be determined intellectually but has to be experienced elsewhere. He says it's the heart, and that "the smallest abysses are the largest." This is one *truth!* But the abyss separating us isn't at any point the "smallest."

Kraft distinguishes language from the German language, while I distinguish silence from Hebrew silence. This is indeed quite remarkable, as a superficial glance would lead one to expect the opposite. But this distinction is the Torah. That Kraft makes this distinction—in *this way*— demonstrates both the abyss and its inner unity. Torah is where Hebrew's silence overtakes simple silence. [. . .]

Torah is in everything, just as everything contains both speaking and silence.

One of the deepest truths of language is how speaking passes from silence to silence, with language lurking between them as the medium of silence. Silence takes place *in* language. [. . .]

October 19, 1917

[. . .] Are God's messengers poets? No, that is to say, they aren't *yet,* or are no *longer* so. But they aren't. Or maybe they *should* be. I don't know if this is the case or not—or only in the sense that *every* person is God's messenger in the world, that God speaks through everyone. Only lamentation can turn someone into a poet who is not one already. [. . .]

October 21, 1917

This morning at around 5:45 Wally[34] and I went out from my apartment into pitch darkness, and we walked to Naumburg. At nine o'clock we expected to meet up with the others. At first only Kahn showed up, for the two Fuchs girls didn't make it for female reasons.

We walked through the *indescribably* lovely fall forest and went to Koesen and up Rudelsburg. It was exceptionally beautiful, and in every imaginable way. [. . .]. Incidentally, after hearing from Kahn, I'm afraid

Mirjam Fuchs misunderstood my last letter. A girl who has infinite passion is never too young for *any* truth. She can understand everything,
even if she doesn't fully comprehend it—rather, if she doesn't grasp it
conceptually. Some girls (there are so few that one mustn't say "each")
have a genius to a very high degree. There is a lot of conventionality in
all these girls, lots of secondary things, and it may be that girls talk too eagerly and too much. They really must—and can—be broken of this, just
not through an academic, Platonic discussion of the knowledge of Being,
but by discussing things whose justification as objects of discussion must
first be proven through actions. One can and shall talk about God and
the Teaching for a lifetime, because if someone begins at all, he'll never
arrive at a conclusion. [. . .]

Among the most difficult of questions, but one that has to be asked, is
why Buber must be repudiated. Lately (it has already been a long time
now) I've developed an increasingly categorical enmity against him. It's
simply not true that I'm not *against* him; I am. Why? There are certainly
a hundred serious objections of a personal and objective kind, yet all
must have *one* central source. Can someone really say that the author of
the postscript to Tchung-tze lacks the Torah? Ultimately, I don't believe
that a pantheistic (or a *modern*-pantheistic) Torah is a Torah at all, and all
the most moving and supple language in the world can't hide the fact
that the Law has been taken out of it. When the heavenly court con-
venes, the following accusations against Buber will be made:

1. He lacks Torah. Buber lacks the ultimate earnestness he pre-
   tends to have, especially in his language. This is obvious in everything he does, but mainly in his use of language. He's not a
   mystic but a mystical novelist. He doesn't understand that for a
   true Torah, the Torah of the heart and the Torah of tradition are
   identical.
2. He's a liar. This is a terrifying accusation against him. [. . .] Just
   look at his preferences for poesy, his enormous craving for
   power, and his vanity. He's certainly proud to be today's most
   famous and recognized German Zionist. Yet one word or sentence can sum up everything: *Buber is a teacher of heresy, someone
   who teaches the truth but does so falsely.* He knows the truth, but
   his soul has twisted and distorted it.

October 22, 1917

I first noticed during Hebrew lesson the monumental greatness of the Hebrew language. I derive the greatest joy in presenting before girls the system of language. Everything is so clearly and logically ordered. And afterwards in discussing the doctrine of forms one is delighted with the perfect conformity to rules. The moment someone understands the fundamental principles of Hebrew, he understands everything. [. . .]

October 24, 1917

[. . .] During a seminar on the philosophy of history in Heidelberg, Grete Lissauer agreed to lead a discussion on "Freedom and History." Rickert[35] (this supreme idiot!) said, "One has nothing to do with the other!" He didn't understand. She replied, "One has a lot to do with the other." Excellent, because in fact one has *everything* to do with the other.

One could call "freedom and history" the introduction to the Torah. The question is where freedom exists in history and how freedom is history. This would be a Jewish seminar discussion. [. . .] For good reasons, the Russian Orthodox party calls itself the Party of Tradition and Freedom—that is, of history and freedom.

At what point is man free in history? This is the fundamental issue, which is to say: at what point does he leave *loneliness (which is always without freedom)* and become creative by freely binding himself. This occurs after he, in loneliness, has gleaned his creativity from out of the depths of history. *Loneliness is history and bonds are freedom*—and not the other way around, the way superficial observers think! In the unity of loneliness and bonding, of loneliness and community, is to be found the deeper unity of freedom and history, all within the concept of the Teaching, of tradition. He who wants to pass on tradition must live both alone (for how else will he know the tradition?) and in community (for how else could he transmit tradition?).

Three phases traverse his knowledge: binding himself to the things that happen; loneliness in history; and binding himself to freedom. It is from loneliness that he sees history, because he fights against it. And from bonds in freedom one has a view into history because one stands at its center. One of the fundamental insights of this view is the knowledge that history is a *good* (which is a view that flows out of the Torah and that takes ethics *seriously*). Everyone has known for a long time that freedom is a good. But that history is also a good was more difficult to recognize because to know this, one would have to exit history (the same way one became acquainted with freedom when it was just an *idea*). The question whether history has a yardstick for quality can be addressed only by ethics.

The basic question of all metaphysics of history can be thus formulated: *does history happen?* If so, where and how? The reply that history takes place in time needs to be demonstrated, because freedom, for instance, doesn't (namely, it doesn't *occur* at all).

Freedom and history condition each other to the extent that if there were no history, there wouldn't be freedom. For this reason, the movements of the planets, *though* occurring in time, cannot be counted as part of history. It has been known for ages that it's silly to define history as that which occurs in time. [. . .]

November 1, 1917

[. . .] Today is the first anniversary of Edgar Blum's death. May we at least learn one thing from this immense mourning, so distant from the Teaching: reverence.

There are people who believe in God (in a Jewish sense) and are yet skeptics. Are they unhappy? Aren't we all like this?

I've read Buber's *Occurrences and Encounters*,[36] and a critique will follow. It's disgusting. I'm gathering such books for a museum of hell (and not Dante's).

November 3, 1917

The greatest image of history is to be found in the idea of the messianic realm. (History's endlessly deep relationship to religion and ethics arises out from this thought.) Walter once said that the messianic realm is always present, which is an insight of *stupendous* importance—though on a plane which I think no one since the prophets has achieved.

Revelation and the messianic realm are the foundation of the Jewish conception of history, and history's unity is created through the Torah, which is history itself.

Barthel's writings resound with hatred against infinitude; it's a hatred rooted in metaphysics.[37] I am convinced that the lion's share of his Teaching is concealed, which is the reason I assume it is of a mystical nature.

[. . .] A critique of Martin Buber's most recent deeds, accomplishments, events, and encounters: Buber has compiled into one book the
various essays he has written in the *Weissen Blättern,* articles on God, the
world, Frank Wedekind,[38] the body, Grünwald's altar, and whatever else
he tossed into his saucepan, all cooked up according to the recipe found
in his book *Daniel.* But compared to the babble from hell found in these
essays—even Dante couldn't imagine this inferno—*Daniel* is gold from
Ophir.[39] *Daniel* thrilled me, and I bought it as an eternal keepsake. But—
don't do the same thing now! One book is enough. In all seriousness, this
book is repulsive, and in *every* way possible. [. . .] I am *very* sad. It didn't
have to be this way, for Buber has plenty of pages better than the ones
you'll find here. Certainly there doesn't seem to be with him anything
more that is *un*written. Just like a pathetic lunatic who has the need to
write all over every piece of paper that falls into his hands, Buber doesn't
seem to be able to stand silence. As he puts it, everything has to be "actualized"; he applies his "Daniel" formula to whatever he touches. Is
there really no hope of saving him? Could it be that what we have here is
a terrifying example of the spirit turning against itself? [. . .] That working under the glimmer of mystical talk is the publisher's finely honed
technology that works with greater precision than a calculating machine? "You are a mystic," someone from the *Monist* said to Buber. "No,"
he replied "ironically" (on page 23), "I am a rationalist." This is only too
true; on second thought it's not true at all! All the great rationalists would
have turned their backs in horror on this perverted form of rationalism.
Can it really be that there are some people whose conception of reverence has become so twisted that they are compelled to *speak* about *everything mystical,* regardless of what it costs? And the price is high. My hunch
is that Buber is a miserable man. This is the only way I can explain it. He
has been seduced by the fallen language, and in the most ghastly sense
possible. [. . .]

November 4, 1917

[. . .] Grete says that she isn't sure if my approach can solve ethical conflicts.

Apparently she meant by this that such conflicts are not objects of reason, and they surely aren't. On the contrary, one deed always depends on
inner, magical relationships to other deeds. But more is meant by knowledge here than the ruminations of a rationality utterly lacking in dignity.

I don't know *what* knowledge is, but we *can* know some things (Walter says we know things because they have a language).[40] And if today knowledge has been robbed of clarity and value due to reflection, mediation, and other such forms of confusion, the task for us becomes that of recapturing the dignity of knowledge as an immediate relationship.

Somehow knowledge also includes feeling, to the extent that a feeling is legitimate and hence *worthy* to be included. *I will never believe that there are things that inherently cannot be understood by a form of knowledge worthy to be God's knowledge.* The fact that we've yet to know God proves only something against our generation, not knowledge (or even God).

It would be an important insight that women have a more ingenious relationship to knowledge than ours. Why is this? A boy or a youth can only guess. Yet the opposite side of this is that women lack all the means to communicate this knowledge to us, a fact that constitutes the most important problem in the metaphysics of the sexes. Even if Grete had known the truth, she couldn't have communicated it to me in the way I would have to her had I known it. *Idiots* have concluded from this that women can't know at all, and even greater idiots have based their anti-feminism on this. The only proof against the latter is that anti-feminism contains the deepest metaphysical heresy imaginable.

This does not apply only for *Strindberg,* who had encountered perverted women.

November 5, 1917

The content of history should be freedom. This can only be taken figuratively. Do history and ethics really have the same subject? Could it be possible that history doesn't have any object at all? Is history the exhibition of ideas? Can ideas be exhibited? Maybe history is itself a form, namely, that it is religion. How then can it have a different content than religion? Is it really true that "religion is the consciousness of the Order of things"? How can one say that history is its form? How does one go from this to tradition? Can a consciousness (also in a mystical way) be *taught?* This is the point at which the Teaching leads to wordlessness.

To the extent that the Teaching relates to consciousness, *the Teaching is passed on in silence.* The passages in which the Teaching breaks through silence are double points of the Teaching. It is there that the Teaching's relationship to *life* becomes dialectical. A Teaching that is kept silent *encompasses* life; that which is uttered doesn't, but at best can only attain life. It's possible that at its deepest core, life is not something that happens. The opposite can also be true: that it is precisely here that life becomes meaningful. The laws of the Torah—"the Teaching of life," as they're often called—are intimately involved in life. [. . .]

Zionism would be realized this very day if all Jews were pious.

I shouldn't deceive myself: am I really in love or just stirred up, which may be perfectly natural among young men of my age? Recently I've learned a few things about girls, things that are possible to know only if you've loved. Do I owe this more to Grete or to Meta? I can't decide. What is certain is that I have loved Grete, and still may, even though Meta has become closer to me. Where this influence has come from I can't say. [. . .]

There's one test for love that can show if I'm serious about it: this is *absolute* chastity. Woe to me if I touch her, even with the lightest kiss. I must know if my love is only out to seduce a girl. God forbid![41]

One thing I have no doubts about is that Jewish love isn't like a goy's love (and I love like a Jew). Jewish love doesn't cast magical spells. It could, of course, and herein lies its abyss. This is the essence of seduction.

The Order of love means that two people embrace the world when they are aligned to *each other*. Friendship does not embrace the world. I don't *believe* that it's ultimately possible for someone to have a relationship to a girl other than one of love. Somehow, polygamy has something deeply true about it, even if it is wrong. Basically, though a man can perhaps love many women, he is aligned to only one (either at a particular juncture of time or for an entire lifetime, with the church adopting the latter position and hence banning divorce, Judaism the former). If the friendship with a girl is not a close second to an ultimate relationship, then it's a sham. Friendship means the knowledge of symbols. But among women such knowledge is possible only through love; without love we cannot know women (and even in love they remain enigmatic for us!). How are we supposed to have a friendship with them?

Love, alone among the spiritual Orders, has its place solely and permanently in the soul. Love is not in the world, where all the other Orders have their place. Christian love is also in the world. It creates chaos. [. . .]

November 6, 1917

Lord, is this Werner Kraft a great fellow! What, for God's sake, have these great men found in me? Why have they given me such friendship? No, even more: what have I done to deserve the kind of reverence issuing forth from his letters? I can't conceal the fact that *I just don't know.* It's just a brute fact.

But I'm not great. I swear to God, I am not. It could be that at some point in the past, at some seminal moment, I gave up on greatness. Yet can this have lasting effects?

He writes that he sees my life as miraculous.[42] But do I see it this way, too? God, oh my God. [. . .] If experiencing oneself as great is a part of being great, then I know I'm not. In my very best moments I am ruled by the insight that the greatest thing I can achieve in the spiritual world would be to be a *soldier,* taken in the deepest sense. I may have my short-comings, a lot of them. But the main flaw other people think they see in me—conceit—is the very thing I manifestly lack. I've never been con-ceited about anything. I've never had cause. No one has.

It is an utterly devastating fact how *few* people these days believe in God, how *everyone* has become a skeptic, or worse. How can this be ex-plained? Many believe in the spirit, but in God? God has been silenced by our age. One must ask over and over how this is possible. How?

How? Is it because God could no longer endure this new world? Or is it really true that this generation has *rebelled* against its creator? A revolt against God is hardly unthinkable. Yet today there is something *more!* No one rebels any longer. People are *silent* about God—not because they have the Torah in their hearts, but because they don't have it *at all.* [. . .]

Nov[ember] 10, 1917

This afternoon I delivered my report. Bauch[43] acted like he was bored, and that the discussion was worthless; no one said a word.

What good does it do me to be recognized if no one helps me? Ulzen dismissed me because of dementia praecox. O you gods in heaven!!! It's only temporary, and I'll be able to make it up.

November 13, 1917

From yesterday evening till this evening the three of us were together with Grete Lissauer in Weimar. I got to know Goldstein.[44] It was really quite pleasant. We led a bit of a wild life.

Three years ago today I began this diary. Over these three years I've failed to become a real human being. Will I do so in the following three? *Above all,* I have fallen from what I had considered back then to be great and holy. Then I was reprehensible, and in the meantime my Zionism has changed, root and branch. Admittedly *this* is a good thing. I won't always be so dumb.

The Maximalists[45] have made a peace offer. This is the first official document in world history that each single decent person could sign. People are just going to make excuses and do nothing. . . .

November 21, 1917

Phenomenology has something of the Teaching of Orders to it. It questions the identity of concrete objects. [. . .] Concrete objects, be it a dog, the special quadrant, or myself, also have a problem of identity. If a thought of an object is necessarily identical with itself, is an object as well (taken as all meaningful thinkable objects)? For when I say that the thought of an object is identical with itself (Walter), it follows that this thought is an *object* in our sense. [. . .]

November 24, 1917

Am I any better because I've been lying to myself about love? This is more than unlikely. My language bears witness against me. If being young means to be prepared to sacrifice youth, then I'm not young.

I'm completely mixed up. When I look inside myself I see an irreparable chaos, and I won't be able to master it because I'm silent about it. Oh what an abysmal lie it is to deny that a lie is *absolutely* immoral. It is! Oh the influence a lie exercises on the Order of men who use it to appear ordered! Every kind of chaos is more moral because from chaos there is no way to repent other than to chaos. I believe (or I fear) that I am no longer capable of repentance.

Greatness is an element you must have, and I'm lacking it. I recognize this clearly because I know my own lies. Am I any better than someone who becomes a political hypocrite in the worst way imaginable because he's afraid of not passing his school exams? And this is what constitutes my deepest depravity: that I can *live,* and even become famous, while knowing that I am a reprobate. God, why doesn't anyone *see* it! How can my lie be so successful that *everyone* falls for it? What kind of abyss, what kind of unspeakable and unsalvageable lack of order it is when someone, with a cool demeanor, multiplies the power of his nothingness into infinity, and through the most unimaginably mysterious magic of evil (even *I* find it unimaginable, which is guaranteed only through success) is also able to derive something *good* out of it! What potency this magic has!

Henceforth, I am convinced, as I *must* be, that magic exists, and in the most terrifying way. What kind of reality could correspond to the illusions I generate? If God existed—*oh this if!!!*—I would be swallowed whole. Sitting for eternity in hell, I would only wonder at this God's limitless forbearance at allowing a life to continue unchallenged, a life that by acknowledging God puts him to shame. But does he really allow this life to continue unchallenged? Isn't my doubt killing me? Is there any worse punishment *imaginable* than the autonomy of my conscience?

I have a conscience. God help me, I do. I can't kill it. It pursues me, not in actions and not in speech, but in my heart. My conscience takes out its revenge on me—on my life's frightful love affair with babble. There is no grace in the world; there is only irony. One should found a religion based on irony. This would certainly be a catholic religion, literally the universal church, for everyone would belong to it. Even the Teaching is lied about.

[. . .] Walter Benjamin's critique of *The Idiot* is truly fabulous and worthy of its object. I am so astounded I can't even experience it.

I would have faith in myself if I had written *one* properly *positive* sentence in my life that isn't full of lies. But I've never written such a thing.

November 25, 1917

Sunday evening. I've spent the day in unspeakable sloth because the storm outside (a proper fall storm) must have blocked the tempest in my soul. Shouldn't the spirit take revenge on us by forging a close relationship, a coalition, with the natural forces, with the aim of overcoming the disturbance we've created in the cosmos?

Walter Benjamin's critique of *The Idiot* is shattering.[46] What is the true reason for this? Because lurking in the background is the figure of his dead friend.[47] Benjamin has profoundly rediscovered in *The Idiot* the physiognomy of the youth movement's failure.[48]

What kind of inconceivable power his friend must have had that Benjamin can now write such mighty sentences on eternal *life*—and not the eternal soul but life, which is the center itself. What makes these sentences compelling is the responsibility with which he wrote them. It seems that a person needs to experience an eternal life in order to find it again, for how should the average critic find an idea in a book that no one has explained to him before? How should he praise Dostoyevsky in any other way than for his "psychology" if he knows nothing about the Teaching—if the Teaching has not been transmitted and taught to him, regardless by whom?

Walter seems to have had the Teaching transmitted to him from a teacher, namely, from his dead friend. He saw in him the essence of youth. He also saw in him how youth dies.

It is unimaginable, monumental, how Walter Benjamin has survived the death of his friend. I'm breathless that he was able to give up his own youth (and this is the first miracle) and yet continue living with the *idea* of youth. [. . .]

November 26, 1917

[. . .] What would happen if I went Palestine, perhaps as a teacher at a Hebrew high school, and were forced to leave again after six months, either because I demonstrate no talent in teaching, or because I am too honest and fight with the hotheaded chauvinists in Jaffa (a fight I would lose immediately, of course)? What would happen if I "failed" at my Zionist career? This is a serious problem that must be considered. I wouldn't want to return to Europe, and the university in Jerusalem—where I could save myself, and where I consider it my lofty aim in life to end up as a philosopher—still wouldn't exist. What could I do without becoming idle? I wouldn't have a dime, so I'd have to work. Yes, it would kill me to have to earn a living, and I'm sure I wouldn't even be able to. [. . .]

This is the legend of metaphysicians: There were no metaphysicians when God created men and distributed souls among them. Each man took the Order God gave him. But as the souls of men fell into chaos, God created an angel who, in each generation, had to travel through the lands to prevent despair. Out of piety he did so by being *deceitfully positive.* This is metaphysics.

It is not true that a person is born a metaphysician. He must decay into metaphysics, whereas decay is naturally not meant in a moral sense, as it's not an ethical decay. Yet it is somehow an ethical problem because only a sinner can be a metaphysician. *The* good person doesn't *know* metaphysics because *the* Good doesn't have any metaphysical system that could be *known.* This is important. Purity in metaphysics is *always* purity for repentance. Metaphysics knows everything, just not childhood, and all claims to the contrary are based on a deeply flawed point of view.

It may be that my only hope is that during the twenty years of my childhood and youth (which I'll complete in a few days) I've been living in chastity. I have not done anything irretrievable. Isn't it a miracle that my lips haven't yet been made impure! And who are they shouting at? Do they shout out at anyone? They shout out at Grete. [. . .]

I am fanatically determined to preserve my chastity.[49] [. . .]

November 27, 1917

I've begun working again after a long break, so I'm not idling my way through the day. I still intend on translating the lamentations, my farewell to Bible translation. [. . .]

December 1, 1917

Russia has made a peace offer, and the first humane voice during this war has sounded out from an official document. Is there anyone who isn't celebrating these Russians who will perhaps give humanity, with all its "overwrought dogmatism," something no "art of diplomacy" can: peace. With the English in Palestine and peace in sight, this war, along with all the events that go along with it, has managed to spark my interest.

Should the Jewish people be allowed to participate in the peace conference? In general, can European or Europeanized "humanity" recognize itself as a "tribunal," let alone as a *court of jurisdiction?* Without question, the Zionist organization will try to send its own representatives. Now, it's enough just to have peace in the world. The day after it arrives, the thick shroud that has covered us for three years will be lifted and we'll feel newborn. This vale has naturally surrounded us, too, even though we had nothing in common with it. The world's metaphysical power of evil—and the war's only *ethical* lesson is that evil exists—has often enough forced us into battle. [. . .]

Over the last three days I've been translating lamentations. I've done it with my entire soul, but it's the last thing I want to translate. I finished today. I'm not going to rework the translations: they are what they are. The power of Hebrew compels me to such a degree that I irresistibly experience Hebrew even in the German language. My total absence of the *German* spirit of language, which I experience only as a transplant, may rightly be used to question the legitimate validity of my translation. Still, for me this translation remains a great act: I have borne witness to my love and to my present stage in life. Obviously, there is nothing I long for more than to reach one day a different sphere in which Hebrew no longer communicates my own linguistic experiences through translation. But today I work from my own stage with an eye on the ultimate goal. There are also penultimate things which, when held in silence, immediately become revelations.

If I'm honest, I have to admit that my letters to Meta are a shade too warm and too loving. I really do like her, but at the same time I'm very well aware that I would write these same words to Grete with a lot more fire and truth than I do to this unhappy girl, with whom I'm inexorably heading toward some sort of bitter experience. I lack the strength to push her away (which is what it would require), to disappoint or desecrate her (she's still a pure soul who has placed her purity under my protection). [. . .]

December 3, 1917

[. . .] How have the heroes fallen / in war /Jonathan / you were slain at your height / . . . Saul and Jonathan / They loved each other . . . I grieve for you / My brother Jonathan, you were precious to me / Your love was more wonderful / than the love of women / Oh how the heroes have fallen / and are lost / Instruments of war.[50]

Yesterday I wrote the epilogue to the translation of lamentations. This translation has revealed to me the most fabulous things. [. . .] I have laid out things in the epilogue that come from the extreme depths of my heart. There is certainly no one on earth who can fully understand it. With this, I have really begun the continuation of the essay on language.[51] In it I have presupposed things that have never yet been uttered (for instance, on the four Orders of the symbolic).

Snow fell for the first time today. From my window I stare out at an incomparably lovely scene. Everything is so clear, so refreshing, so empowering. Maybe it would make spiritual sense to spend a summer in Jena as well. If I could only find something great here, something binding me, either in spirit, in the landscape, or God knows what else.

December 4, 1917

Werner Kraft suggested that we address each other as "Du," which completely surprised me, and I'm giving it serious consideration whether I have the right to enter into this kind of relationship with him. He sent me an essay he wrote in the past few days called "Gratitude." It's for my birthday, and in it he tries over and over again to rescue the German heart. Kraus, George, Borchardt. Perhaps it's good to finish up my twentieth year of life with such an act. Tomorrow I'll have completed two decades of life in poverty but not love, in mourning but not lamentation.

Only the pious are religious. Community with other people kills me. Each day I experience this afresh. It is only in letters that I enter into intercourse with people.

December 5, 1917

This afternoon, while I was sitting and thinking only about Walter and me (longing for him and asking myself why he hasn't written), a short letter from him arrived.[52] It put me in such a festive mood the likes of which I've possibly never before experienced.

He received my letter on his Dostoyevsky essay, and the absolute pinnacle of happiness is that he understood it. My letter moved him no less than his essay—and now his letter, which is evidence of just how moved he is—does me.

These ten lines bring healing to my life. Walter, O dearest Walter, I thank you from of the depths of my soul, and from such depths that I'll never be able to express to you. With what has happened today I have finally entered truly into a new phase of my life, because out of Walter's letter resounds friendship, renewed friendship. I can't put into words the vast emotions that are sounding out in my heart right now. Before me sits a silly letter I've been writing to Türkischer. Now I *cannot* continue writing it. My thoughts are elsewhere: they are with Werner Kraft, with Grete, and with Walter, the man who today has renewed my life.

Yes, God, I pledge to you that I want to be good. I know this because *he* has told me so through the voice of Revelation. I am good, O God, and you have not yet spurned my soul. (Thinking you had done so was an error I committed in my most difficult hours.) I am good. By Jove, God be my witness: I am good.

What kind of affliction can affect my heart now that *this* has occurred: now that God himself, speaking through the mouth of his truest servant, has awakened my *courage*. Yes, if I could only have him near me—and I want to have him very close—my healing would be complete.

Did I know earlier that I am good? No, this I didn't know. God told me I was good, but I didn't know it. Oh this endlessness that I cannot conceive of because I am in its midst! Joy will lead me once again onto the mountain peaks. Don't complain, O my heart. You are able to help someone, indeed to help many people, you or rather I can show them that life on this planet is still holy, and that all the sacrilege and the filth has not yet reached my young heart—nor will it ever reach me. If I once doubted God's existence—*that God exists*—I no longer can. I have known God. I have you to thank, my friend, for I have met God, who has lavished his majesty on us. The majesty of God is itself reverence.

I want to go before God in the lands of the living. I can offer no better vow on this holy day, nor can I express it better, than with the holy words of tradition, "I will go before the Lord in the land of the living." This is my religion.

I've written to Meta, confessing *everything* with utter honesty, out of the depths of my soul. I've copied out the letter, written in the wake of massive convulsions and with trembling hands, because I want to be able to interpret her reply properly.

Dear Meta,

I have to tell you that this day has been a grand and holy holiday for me. You won't be angry—you're too good for this—when I tell you it was not your words or those of many others who are (if very differently) close to my heart that is responsible for the enormity that has visited me this day, but rather a few short lines from my friend, Walter Benjamin.

I cannot recount to you what he wrote, as silence prevents this, but I must tell you, and no one else, that these words have made me *great*. No one on this earth could be a prophet of God besides him; he has purified and refined my spirit as only a prophet can purify and refine. After these few words, I know that God is there, even if I've doubted his existence till now. Your loving words have put me to great shame, but I must admit that if my friend had kept quiet, I would have remained sad the entire day.

I had been ruminating the entire afternoon about all sorts of things, such as how this day is really not a holiday for my soul. And then his words lifted me up. Now I am well. You see, Meta, while I am very fond of you, my soul follows a different star. I must tell you this so I won't drive you mad: you are not alone in my heart, because my friend and a different girl—who would possess his soul if it were female—still dwell there, and always will.

I've been liberated from the crushing doubts my evil nature plagues me with over and over, because this life of mine, which I live before the face of God, has been blessed with the enormous favor and grace of having you, her, and him. I am now in such a festive mood I could pray to God and thank him for my life, and praise him for making my life worthy.

You are very young and just at the beginning (for which you should be glad, as you don't have to overburden your youth with the worst sins that threaten your heart), and for this reason I can't allege before God to have helped you. I'd venture to say that it's easy to help someone who hasn't yet experienced despair. Since God has bestowed on me the task of helping people in despair—difficult labor I've not shied away from—I will allow myself the same: my friend will help me in my despair. You may not know how boundlessly despondent Gershom Scholem, this most "self-certain" person of all mankind, has been, particularly in the past year, which has been enormously significant for me; how I have gone to pieces after seeing into the depths of my own lies; and how I've recently tortured myself because of you.

I've known that I was far, far worse than others because I appear to be so much better. The irony of my fate seemed to be heaven's ghastly punishment for having succumbed daily to the mocking laughter of my life's magnificence. A quiet sentence, encompassing the silence of the world, has now given me immortality, and set me back on my feet. This man, elected by God, has never told a lie; the immensely healing power his being exercises on mine is the true incarnation of the truth. The foundation for my life has now been laid, and it can no longer be shaken. This is the gift this day, this hour, has given me.

Dearest Meta, you now have my soul, and being pure yourself, you will protect it. I do not believe that these words will cause you pain, but *if* they do and if you had imagined this soul to be different, you must say so, because I don't want there to be any dishonesty between us. If my life's infinity is of a sort you cannot endure, then you shouldn't be seduced. After all, wouldn't it be seduction to rob the soul of a maiden who can succumb only to the *power* of infinity and not its form and structure?

What more can I say? Either you understand everything, or even a hundred pages wouldn't help you. But you understand. I wouldn't have said these things if I didn't love you immensely. And now, when you come to me, I want you to do so with open eyes, open like mine, open to knowledge. God has sent me your youth as the other face of my generation (to which in truth I don't belong) to show me whether there's a way to reconcile me with my generation (which I spurn).

Gerhard

December 11, 1917

I wrote to Grete, whose soul skips carefully along in the recesses of silence.[53] On this, my birthday, I have delivered my youth back into the hands of God so it can come back to me as eternal.

Knowledge and religion have an integrated relationship: a person mustn't juxtapose them but must see them as integrated, *one with the other.* ("Faith" and "knowledge": what a grotesque confusion of undignified thinking!) My religion and philosophy are not the same. My philosophy should take me through knowledge to a place out of which my religion emerges, like beams of holiness from the black of night. Knowledge on the one hand, and knowledge of the divine on the other, do not go their separate ways but are intertwined. What we should strive for is a life lived on the very limits of the realms of religion and philosophy. The edge is the unity of the two.

Shall it be the task of philosophy to define God?

Religion is not given the task of knowing an already existing Order; rather, religion is the solution of this task in consciousness. The solution encompasses this task the way the life of women encompasses the coming generation.

Walter and Dora's pictures stand permanently before me on my desk. I can speak with them at will. Dora looks so endlessly lovely, and Walter so serious! This is their most beautiful birthday gift.

December 12, 1917

Today, Werner gets released from the prison where he has spent nearly all of 1917 in "contemplative rest."[54] I am quite excited to see him again—and to see if he'll behave like an arrogant martyr. [. . .]

December 19, 1917

[. . .] I love Meta[55] dearly, and yet I find myself in the same abyss as before. I kissed her and cuddled with her. Was I allowed to do this? She has blossomed like a flower in springtime.

While there can be no doubt whatsoever that Meta is far more worthy than Erna, it's a veritable disaster that she's spent the best years of her youth working in an office. She possesses an exceptionally deep and natural feeling for greatness and dignity, and the fact that she loves me could really be a support in many things. Maybe it's true that one of these days she'll have what Grete already possesses in such great measure; as tragic as this may sound, however, I have my doubts if I really love her with my entire heart as I do Grete: if I would go through fire for her, if I love her *entire being* and not just some nice things about her.

In the moments I had her in my arms, I may have had this feeling, and really meant it, though I normally don't. For her, though, she faces me with utter exclusivity, loving me with the eternal passion she is so capable of. With my kiss I wanted to make her lips—defiled by someone unworthy of them—pure again. (It was the first time I kissed a girl, and before I did it I shivered as never before in my life, and I was completely incapable of speaking.) But have I done so? Am I worthy? As far as she is concerned I am, which is a lot; but do I think I am? Oh the doubts! One evening, at 2 A.M., I permitted her a very deep glimpse into my soul by showing her my most sacred relic, the letter Walter wrote me for my birthday. It made a visible impression on her, and never did I kiss her more ardently than at that moment. [. . .]

I received a tormented letter from Wally. At the depths of my heart I know she loves me, and she's unhappy because I cannot requite her love, as she dwells in the outer courtyard of my soul and not in that holy place of the five shining stars: Walter, Dora, Aharon, Grete, and Meta. [. . .] I believe she is a forlorn maiden, but I can't do anything about this. I've bestowed my mouth on another. [. . .]

Yesterday and today I've written two letters to Benjamin. [. . .]

Living without coal is so terrible I've decided to leave tomorrow for Berlin for ten days. What's going to happen? How will I look my friends in the face? [. . .]

There is one thought that is simply peerless in its baseness, and may the God of goodness protect me from thinking it. It is the sneaking arrogance of thinking what would happen if I were dead in a month. God considers it extremely vile to be constantly trying not to disappoint people in their high expectations (and "people" "expect" from me "something"!). For four years now I've been grappling with my life, and I've tried to give it some structure. And everyone thinks I've succeeded, everyone except me!!! Is *this* not tragic? Is not my present misfortune in love not a logical result of this condition of my inner life? *Yet* I am exalted, exalted because of Walter, who never could be deceived by this. If harm should come to Walter, my life would be destroyed.

I am inaccessible. Oh God, it is so! I'm inaccessible in my deepest soul. Shall I perhaps allow people a peek into all the horror of this field of ruins, which is what my soul must look like to them? I can't. Only God can see all the way into my heart, and God reveals himself in it in his own way. I know that *my* life, of all lives, rests only and exclusively on God's goodness. But this I confess only to myself. Gershom Shalom[56] says: "Thank God, for he is good. His mercy endureth forever."

NOTEBOOK 4

February 22–April 18, 1918

I mustn't write Walter till it's certain; otherwise the subsequent disappointment will be measureless. No, it'll be a much more beautiful surprise when I ring the bell, Dora answers, and I say, "Good day, madam, my dear lady!" Oh, how I'd like to sleep till this moment arrives.

—Diary entry from April 18, 1918

February 22, 1918

Since the end of December I have once again grown silent. How my development has taken on a clear contour since then, how much groundwork for the future has been laid! [. . .] Yesterday morning I was once again at Buber's, and I've had more than enough of him for a long time to come. It's impossible to speak at a serious level with him; he simply *doesn't get it*. I challenged him over the Buberians, and we discussed the issue at length. Naturally, he denied any responsibility. He obviously had no idea what I really wanted from him. He liked the lamentations. [. . .]

The difference between "not," "nothingness," and "none" is of great importance for philosophy. The Kabbalah contains the fundamental notion (which reappears in Hermann Cohen) that God is nothingness. This lends itself easily to an entire treatise, which has probably already been written. Creation from *nothing* is a philosophical notion. Rabinkow once explored it at length, and has aptly explained it.[57] But the Kabbalah abandoned this path. Idols are called "nothing," while God is called "nothingness" (which is entirely un-Christian).

Werner Kraft is doing terribly, and my hopes are sinking by the day. His last letter was enough to bring a person to tears. One will just have to respond with silence. The divine judgment sitting over him has now been summoned. The awful thing about his inner state is that he has stepped into a sphere where *imperatives* can no longer reach him. Hence, he's lost. His life spins down in a racing spiral whose direction is within. Everything now depends on whether his life can survive the singular point and can then retreat back into the opposing direction. The tempo has taken on such a racing pace that he has lost all courage.

I understand Wally[58] and the others quite well, only Grete I still can't figure out. She's the only one who really sits deep in my soul. And yet isn't this also an error? I have not received a single line from her in three months.[59] She avoided speaking to me in Berlin (because she would have had to use "Du"). In Berlin I will behave very, very differently to everyone. What moves me is so profound, and still so obscure, that it cannot be confided even to this page. The only relationship that always and unconditionally holds firm is to Walter. I love Walter. [. . .]

What's needed is a different tack with people. My current approach doesn't work because it rests on a massive misunderstanding. The truth is that I need others and force myself on them, and yet they think I'm unapproachable. I should be (utterly) unapproachable, and then people will probably think we get along famously! I have to withdraw, only in a very different fashion. Either I'll discuss things frankly with Grete and offer her the "Du" again, or I'll avoid her altogether, and by doing so I'll finally prove that I also have some sense of shame left. My inner order of life must be altered. I'm not worthy of Walter.

February 24, 1918

Work on the songs of lamentation still has a way to go, not only the entire exposition—which is at least hinted at—but also in the most fundamental things. What's mostly lacking is the definition of silence from the perspective of the theory of language. Silence is the source of all language (and source and development should be distinguished here), and it is to non-speaking what nothingness is to nothing. For *us*—whose lives are grounded above all in Revelation—the kingdom of silence can be achieved only through the most extreme difficulty. What is needed here is a monumental sense of sight and of discernment. Music offers a particular possibility to speak out lamentations. I've been told that the viola is basically an instrument of lamentation. Music can lament in the acoustical sphere, though only without words. This is the basis for a very deep relationship (which the essay doesn't address) between *all* lamentation and music. Human lamentation is by its very nature musical. Even the elimination of words in music points to this, which is the metaphysical reason why one sings lamentations without ever having learned to do so. In nature, lamentation is *visible* (though not audible) in an entirely different fashion. Look at aspects of Walter's work. Dogs often have a fabulously mournful expression. [. . .] One single tree in a landscape could, for example, contain an important and very powerful lamentation.

I enjoy reading songs of lamentation aloud. As a person who otherwise doesn't have a good voice and doesn't read well aloud, I feel so swept up into their inner essence that I sometimes metamorphose and turn into a lamentation. [. . .]

Yesterday I wrote to Walter. I need to get a letter from him every day.

I have no doubt that someone who reads my remarks in these notebooks could point out my most obvious inner contradictions. Isn't it dreadful that I *can't* be different? And yet I have a center, this I am certain of.

February 26, 1918

[. . .] Erich Brauer wrote that he's getting a pass to go to Switzerland. It made me absolutely miserable again, even if it's wonderful that at least he can get out of this godforsaken country, where the worst kind of orgies are celebrated. Till now I simply haven't conjured up the courage to go to the precinct office because they'd certainly turn me away. But I must do it now, without any hopes. It makes me so impotent, so despondent, to think I won't succeed in getting a pass. Being mentally ill, I have no chance to get one: Switzerland won't let me in. On top of this comes Father's permission.

Sometimes I think I could tell people that I need to go because the only person who could help me lives there. Couldn't this make an impression on a humane physician? The fact is I *must* go to Switzerland; *only* there can I recover, and I'm in bitter need of recovery. And if I could be together with Walter and Brauer in Bern, I would have more than enough. I can't express how broken I feel, entirely inwardly broken. [. . .] Rarely in my life have I felt so wretched, even though I have everything: a girl who loves me the way only a girl can; a friend who longs for me just as I long for him; people who treasure me, who love me and respect me; orderly domestic conditions—yet now *of all times* my inner condition shows me how my life has yet to be directed at its true foundations. I'm a lot more lost than Kraft, who everyone knows is lost. What about me? Me!!!

March 1, 1918

Today's a sad anniversary for Harry Heymann: two years ago he was inducted into the military. Two years . . .

I've been in Erfurt for two days now. On the 27th I gave a lecture on the development of the Talmud using the concept of Tradition, which I did in a philosophical spirit. [. . .]

I really *have* to extract myself from the kind of relationships I now have. They are relationships that aren't relationships, being based purely on the law of inertia, or something worse. The only relationship that could go beyond this is with Grete, and this one is apparently dead. I naturally don't include Walter in any of this. He stands entirely outside of "relationships." He and he alone stands in the center of my life.

Who could imagine Walter as a political person? I for one can't. [. . .]

Walter has written an extraordinary letter, which I answered immediately. For some time now, the truly preestablished harmony mutually ordering our two lives has been the anchor regulating my life. This is astounding. Sometimes I fall into the most dialectical situations, but never has that which really determines my life ever been touched in the least. Walter alone sees directly into the structure of my soul, and can rightly feel bound to it.

There was supposed to be Friday dinner at Katie Holländer's, but no one could make it. I'm glad because I can remain alone with this expansive mood aroused by Walter's letter. My life's foundation must have more going for it than I'm aware of. Baumgardt[60] says that Walter was politically engaged in 1914. I can safely assume that Baumgardt sees this only superficially and not deeply. Walter Benjamin's life has profound parallels to both Lao-tzu's and Hölderlin's.

I can only declare, but not describe, how thoughts about my friendship with this prophet of God overwhelm me with measureless feeling. When Katie Holländer told her mother my name means "peace" in German, she replied, "Why doesn't he call himself 'Peace,' then?" Isn't this marvelous: May Gerhard Peace rest in peace.

March 4, 1918

I visited Werner yesterday. The sad fact must be faced that there is a *gigantic* and everlasting chasm separating us that cannot be overcome. He lives in a sphere I reject. I reject it. I reject it. If he weren't my brother, I would never associate with him. Such are the people who are always behind the failure of the revolution (or, more accurately, they make it a priori *impossible*). For Werner it's enough to be a famous demagogue. He is political in the worst sense of the word. It's sad to live with a stranger.

March 5, 1918

[. . .] The form of lamentation can perhaps be understood as the proportions of its limitations, its silence. No babbling verse can ever be a lamentation, for such a verse destroys its own proportions. [. . .]

The expression of lament is metaphysically conditioned by the elimination of an object's identity. All lamentation grieves that it loses its object: that the object loses its metaphysical constancy and thus becomes expressionless. It is precisely the *countenance* of this process that makes up the expression of lament. Screaming operates in similar ways. [. . .]

Recently—and I feel this clearly—I've been improving. I'm fine when I'm alone; it is only with others that I slip into danger. When alone, I take part in the deepest community of things. Only by leaving the state of solitude can I leave the community of things. The basic truth about today's world is that the deepest community and the final loneliness are identical. For this reason I'm a Zionist. I trust myself to expand my loneliness out to Zion.

Rarely has there been someone as religious as I. Alone and gazing into myself, I often gain an indescribably clear insight into the Order of my life, and this Order is one of those things that make possible the entire remainder of my life. But I have to keep this to myself. The language I'm now speaking is surely an individual speech no one else comprehends. That which is individual disappears in translation. There are moments when I think I understand the lesson of the Tao.

There are exceedingly important things I still don't know, nor will I anytime soon. To these belong Goethe and Spinoza. I don't read them and don't speak about them. I have yet to reach a juncture at which they (along with others as well) are fruitful for my life and advance me. Goethe has never spoken to me, which must mean something very important, perhaps that the Jewish genius in me demarcates itself somehow from the German world. Perhaps this is the reason I've grown up so completely and entirely outside the real German cultural network. I often feel myself as if on virgin territory.

March 7, 1918

[. . .] The essay on the songs of lamentation must be seen as a description of my inner state. *With this in mind,* God will have nothing to do with anyone who doesn't understand this. And the essay is *also* just such a description. This is what gives it meaning—namely, that I have managed to use the quiet language of theory to express that which is most glowing. For this reason, the essay is eternal truth.

March 14, 1918

I'm young and still have everything to learn. All my knowledge only reproduces my metaphysical existence. I am, as it were, a metaphysical psychologist. I can know only what I have seen, what I have beheld. This will (perhaps!!) be very clear in the essay I'll be writing over the next few days for *Jerubbaal*.[61] [. . .]

Today a *miracle* happened. For the first time in my life I longed to read Goethe. This too is a consequence of Grete's letters. Now I want to read Goethe's letters.

March 15, 1918

The Torah knows neither before nor after: *Ayn mukdam v-me-uchar ba-to-rah,* which is to say that the Talmud knows the *mediating* role of the Teaching. To Walter: "Sometimes I think with astonishment what I've been doing during the six years in which an entire episode of your life has concluded."[62] I have studied—though of course not in the German sense of the word, but with its untranslatable and immensely deep Hebrew and Yiddish meaning in which learning always involves the Teaching. It is a pure miracle that Walter is now also there.

"Tevye the Milkman" is unapproachably deep and lovely.[63] It was written from the center of the Torah and from the heart of the Talmudic jest.

March 16, 1918

Over this winter I've learned a simple yet horrible truth I didn't know previously in the way I do now: that most people are miserable. If you look deep below the surface, you'll see that all truly valuable people are in one way or another sunk into the inescapable abyss of misery. They live among others, cut off from the Teaching and Tradition. To change this would be the first and most essential task to be accomplished among men. In its deepest strata, Zionism shall bring *Tikkun*[64] to our lives. [. . .]

The notion of the Teaching as the center of Zionism hasn't yet been discovered. (Generally speaking, people see it as retrogressive!) Zionists have yet to recognize seriously the continuity of the great Jewish intellectual movements as the *central* truth of their lives. They have yet to succeed in connecting with the (properly understood) Torah. Our task is to recognize Zionism as essentially a matter of "translation." Yet when it comes to *seeing,* there's always a metaphysical blindness ready to create disruption.

How do things stand with Hebrew? A student of Hebrew learns from his teacher that the most important things are within the language, etc., etc., but no one tells him that in Hebrew he can discover divine truth. People lack a center to their lives, and *I* can't grant them one! I know I have one, and out of this center grow the stages of my Zionism. I have to confess, however, that in *my* condition I despair at the possibility of *giving instruction.* I can give to very few people—to those who have already progressed far enough. Only through my work can I raise the banner against everything that is softly lacerating in us. [. . .]

I must keep my silence for a long time before the public. I must work. The only reason I hold out any hopes for *Jerubbaal* is that, with the declaration of my basic principles, I can bid farewell to "youth." I want to turn the question "why" into the methodological principle of my life. Zionists cannot help me here; they themselves are in need of help. [. . .]

March 17, 1918

In Walter's first library (which has only works of ultimate greatness and importance, such as Lao-tzu, the Bible, and *Lesabendio*) there is nothing by Schiller, besides the Insel volume *Conversations with Schiller.* Benjamin once told me this book is extraordinary, and the only way to gain access to Schiller. This occurred to me today when I was in the Zeihsisch public library looking at books and I stumbled across the volume. [. . .] I think Walter's right.

I'm reading a lot in Brentano's letters to Sophie.[65] Last night I read for a long time. These days I'm feeling a deep desire to read such letters, which is the reason I picked up Goethe's letters to Frau von Stein a few days ago. I want to know about the endless variety of people's love. Every love is different, and when I reflect on my great love for Grete, I know how an entirely new and unhappy factor came into my life.

I need to write to Walter very, very much. I have an indescribable longing for him. [. . .]

I'm going to become invisible for a long time because I've noticed how I've become far too visible—and I'm not entirely blameless in this. What to do? I mustn't seek out intercourse with others. I must no longer tell them my views of truth, which I myself have not yet figured out. I must be for them a complete nothing. Walter's life is a model for me.

March 18, 1918

The previous lines were in actuality written this morning at three A.M., and now it is 6:30. This entire time I have sat here at my desk in the bitter cold. Most of the time has been spent reading Nietzsche's letters to Overbeck.[66] The brightness at this hour is very important. I'm astonished that I'm not tired in the least. I can't go to bed. What is there to do there anyway? [. . .]

March 21, 1918

[. . .] I expect and hope to get a letter from Walter. He must have received my songs of lamentation long ago. [. . .]

It often occurs to me that I can't even entrust very many ultimate things to these pages. In my own life, I understand with utter clarity the reasons for the prohibition against writing out the Oral Torah. [. . .]

Yesterday spring arrived with wondrous weather, but today it's once again dark, rainy, and foggy. Mostly we sat at home, studied Hebrew, and talked about one thing or another.[67] I couldn't help noticing clearly, indeed conspicuously, how we don't fit together in any way. Everything I said on the themes of lamentation and painting he countered with a rebuttal, albeit hidden and perhaps only half conscious (who can say if it was conscious or not!). He said impossible things against Walter, though he should have choked on his words. I believe our souls go in entirely different directions. With the exception of Walter, I am incapable of speaking to my friends about the things that most deeply move me. It's awful! I know I would just encounter boundless incomprehension.

This morning we were together with Gentz[68] and Harry Heymann. The weather was glorious the entire day. This afternoon we were in Weimar, where we spent a long time saying our good-byes. Today we also spoke about a range of things, and I'm once again reminded that he hasn't even begun *studying* seriously. I'm expecting a letter from Walter. I don't think Erich Brauer would understand Walter no matter how much he tried. And yet he's finally on his way to a deeper and more courageous Zionism, his only problem being that, to some extent, he knows it only by name, not content.

Over the coming days I'll have to write some letters that won't be easy for me. I'll do so with as much silence as possible. I'll have to be quiet. I'll be quiet.

Yes, I am often an agitator, and there's no contradicting me because I do it so apodictically.

Over the last eight days spring has arrived in glory. Certainly over Passover everything will be green. From my window there will be an unspeakably beautiful and glorious view. Spring can do a lot to lift me up and strengthen me, and when I gaze out the window I believe myself to be the lord of a castle within his lonesome park. The wonderfully ordered landscape shelters me with immediacy. No one should *thus* say, "I shelter it." This is purely reactionary.

I am constantly thinking about Zionism and the work I have to do. For me the time has come to carry out renewal by way of work in all its details. If all this were written down it would make a very beautiful book. I'll have to sit down and write it if I want to impact the new fraternal order of the Sons of Moses[69] that I'm convinced will arise in our lifetime.

In truth, the most essential ingredient of my work is the *oral teaching:* the personal (!!!) relationship to people from within the Teaching. And in this nothing can really be written down besides the *method*. Like all textual traditions, everything else that is written contains a paradox. I can put down on paper only what I reject in the contemporary world, while the core of this kind of writing can be gleaned only immanently; like the rays of light emanating out from it, it just can't be written down. The Zionist life must be very silent. It has to be guided by a power that, metaphysically speaking, gives the Zionist a quiet language; and only in this life's double points is the scream (Ze-aka, or as Walter calls it, "the howl") audible. The renunciation we call for must be the renunciation of the periphery and of the hybrid. This is a terrifying issue, as the hybrid is our most dangerous foe. It can be overcome only through justice. God takes the form of justice in the world.

The spiritual essence of man is language, but language *must* encompass silence, otherwise it is untrue. The highest task of the metaphysics of language is to recognize two polarities as identical: silence as a source of language, and Revelation as the source of language.

You should lament and not complain about the past. All truly profound talk about the past is lamentation. In a word, lamentation is language at the point of disappearance.

[. . .] I wrote a few letters, and read a bit of *Conversations with Schiller*. When I write letters, no matter to whom, even Walter, the same thing happens to me every time. Of the five sentences I'd like to write, I write only one. This is the reason it takes me so long to write even short letters. I think a lot about things I then choose to leave out. This is perhaps the source of the tight and concentrated rhythm that, according to Walter, my letters supposedly have.[70] The same thing occurs in *everything* I write. I am able to make absolutely visible only the smallest part of my written work's *substance*. There is *very* much contained in all of my essays, more than in any other writings of similar proportions that I know of. But perhaps I'm the only one who understands them. Or at least, the only one who understands them completely. [. . .]

It may be that the premier task of Judaism is to turn life in its absolute totality—in all its arenas without the slightest exception—into an ethical phenomenon. Myth, which rules life, has given up only a small province till now (which has been the most seminal event in world history). We call this province the ethical world. Hitherto, this region has been just as little captive to the consciously striving spirit of man as the movements of men who cling to myth. It's therefore hardly absurd to conquer new worlds for ethics by taking up the renewed struggle against myth.

Justice cannot rule in the world as long as people still relate their life and most of its manifestations to a mythic foundation. To strive after justice is the only *effective* way leading out of the realm of myth. Tradition also mustn't be mythical, and herein lies an unending task that Judaism, renewed in its innermost spiritual center, would have to perform. What seems likely to me is that the Jewish spirit is capable of adequately expressing itself only in the fulfillment of this task. Zionism is a movement within the Torah. Zionism can only be grounded within the world of the Teaching. Zion is the collective loneliness of all people, and hence the source for the messianic community of men and of "mankind." Zionism makes just one claim: that the final center of man's loneliness is the place where all men can meet together, and there can be no *other* such gathering place.

All of us can succeed in restoring a connection to the Teaching through this loneliness, a connection we lost after we sold ourselves to Europe. The community of men requires everyone to be given an identical foundation. This foundation has two names: Silence and Revelation. Babblers who lack silence also have no community. This is a profound accusation against the contemporary German people. Dostoyevsky said he could never imagine a godless Jew. This is the greatest truth a non-Jew has ever said about us. In this truth he recognized the basis of the Jewish community and of our national identity. *I cannot live in community with anyone whose very being does not radiate the same rays as mine. I can be in community only with people whose being is directed at the same basis as mine.* This is the holy *Volkstum.* [. . .]

Tradition is the only absolute object of mysticism.

It's typically aesthetic humbug, and shoddy mysticism to boot, to regard Essence as something individualistic. This is shoddy mysticism.

After I eat I'm going to write Walter. [. . .]

Alice Heymann must be very attached to Walter. Every time I go to her bedroom, there's a page from a letter in a very particular place, on the back of the couch. Even though turned on its face, it can only be from Walter because of the handwriting visible through it. She has a number of letters from him, and she obviously cherishes them dearly. She basically deems sacred everything connected to him (which has to be the only reason she trusts me so much). She once told me that she had never yet shown anyone else the essay on Hölderlin. She speaks his name in the same way Enoch[71] uttered names on that evening in Heidelberg—with a mournful affectation. If she weren't so terribly ill (I don't think she'll ever recover), one could never spend any time with her without demanding that she make a decision. Now she has the right to have respite and sympathy. She belongs among those people for whom God alone *fathoms* the meaning of their being. This meaning is renunciation.

To work out the duties of youth is the task of Young Judah. It is Old-New Land[72] in the sense that the old and the young coincide metaphysically. True youth is old youth, and this is *no* paradox.

This evening I tried to read Eckermann's *Conversations with Goethe* but found it impossible going.[73] It is one of those books for which I'm lacking in everything, and I don't know if I'll ever be able to read it. [. . .] Goethe plays no role in my life, and not in the way that, according to Goethe, Kant influenced Eckermann without the latter ever having read him. I believe my life is a pure example of an *absolutely* independent Order. [. . .]

I've been here in Koesen since early on Good Friday. Today's Easter, and in the morning I'll go with Mother to Jena. These three days with my parents (who brought with them the other chieftains of the Berlin pay office) have been for me yet another difficult trial. I'm able to win some very probing and valuable insights into the souls of the harmless petty bourgeoisie, but after 24 hours I always come back to the same point: that my parents' way of life is *unbearable* to me, and there can be no return to living in their house. [. . .]

I am very hopeful that in Jena I'll finally have a letter from Walter waiting for me. I've been waiting so much.

April 1, 1918

[. . .] The only organization Zionism has—which is identical with the truth—is the unification of all those who possess the truth. What is commonly called the "Zionist organization" has nothing in common with Zionism as a spiritual entity.

Youth worthy of the name must always and unflinchingly keep in mind that every sort of association not rooted in our lives is despicable because it's insufficient and carries no meaning for our Zionist center. Youth can attain eternal life only through anonymity. Youth whose language is the *Name* is lost. For only the quiet continuity of the Teaching, which is not a name, shall guide the life of this youth. Hebrew must be the superlative of the Teaching's silence. The person able to be silent in Hebrew surely partakes in the quiet life of youth. There is *no one* among us who can do this. *We* cannot use our existence as an argument precisely because silence, or more accurately stillness, is the step in which a life can become an argument. [. . .]

April 4, 1918

Today Mother left again, and I'm again alone. [. . .] This evening I was still with her. I brought her a nice Easter egg made of marzipan. We talked a bit, but I was very reserved and allowed her to choose the subject, though I took the opportunity in the course of the conversation to tell her very frankly what I thought about her situation. The thing she would like to do most, she said, would be to make the small paper boats she once made for me, which prompted my comment that such a life is *helpless*—and in every active and passive sense of the word. I made some comments that she said weren't true. My retort: it's a deeply symbolic truth that only children should be allowed to make miniature boats. [. . .]

It makes me very anxious that Walter hasn't been in touch. I so await his letter. I really wait longingly for the mail to arrive, but nothing comes (the day before yesterday Joel wrote me a letter in Hebrew). I don't know what to do with myself. Always just to hope and hope! [. . .]

April 5, 1918

[. . .] I wrote to Walter that Cohen and Jentzsch are dead.[74] [. . .]

April 6, 1918

Today a letter from Walter arrived. He writes with a restless tone, and I very much wish I could give him rest from afar. He also writes about the songs of lamentation, much of which is correct, but in other points he's mistaken. He's certainly wrong in what pertains to the translation, as this translation is *entirely* different from the Song of Songs.[75]

I find it *very* odd that he asks about Jentzsch in the letter because I wrote to him yesterday that Jentzsch died in battle. This really astonished me.

April 8, 1918

An example of Walter's boundless trust in me is that he has handed over to me his papers. They arrived today in two packages.

I've been in an extraordinarily elevated mood over the last few days. I can't understand it myself. While in this mood I wrote to Escha[76] (very mysterious, I think) and to Werner Kraft. [. . .] If I could only *once* write Walter a letter capturing what is in my heart, a never-ending letter in which I could pour out all those parts of my life no one grasps! It's my misfortune to live around people who make believe to themselves to have meaning. I would live more spiritually among carpenters and laborers. I always think to myself, "You *must* tell this to Walter; with the purest perfection, it'll show him what you're made of." Each time I try, however, I'm overcome with such boundless shame that I say nothing.

In the deepest sense, few people are as reticent as I. Perhaps Walter is the *only* one who knows me, not because I've shared myself with him but because he has, out of his own soul, opened me up. Walter has probably loved many people; the table of contents of the box of his manuscripts tells me this. I knew about Grete Radt, whom he still wanted to marry when I first met him. I've heard next to nothing about Carla.[77] [. . .]

A comical life (taken seriously) is something I can't even imagine. Humor has to adulterate love, which is something lamentations don't do. And it is only in love that what is creative in human existence can express itself. [. . .]

April 9, 1918

I never knew till today how it's possible to have an enjoyable day just writing letters. Till deep into the night I wrote letters (the last one to Walter was about many things, though by far not everything burdening my heart). I am unapproachable to everyone besides Walter. I made a bitter mistake when I showed up on this earth. [. . .]

In the middle of writing I went to a concert, the first orchestral concert of my life. It was colossally impressive. The music swelled up within me, and occasionally I was transformed by it. It was Brahms's great symphony in C major. The conclusion is a complete revolution.

April 10, 1918

In the local art club this morning I saw a few pictures. Nothing caught my eye except Franz Marc's *Resting Animals.* There is an infinite amount of swindle and perversion in the business of so-called modern artists.

I define Zionism as the object of my life. More I can't say. Everyone has only a symbolic relationship to Zionism as long as it hasn't become the object of his life. To take up Zionism into a false sphere is a metaphysical sin that necessarily leads to the innermost perversions. [. . .]

Later I went on a four-hour walk with Lene Czapski back in the woods. It was really quite lovely. We talked about everything—theater and the like. At my prodding she's now reading Creuzer's *Symbolism and Mythology of the Ancient Peoples.*[78] Her philosophical interests are truly astonishing, especially for anything related to mythology. We were late of course, and I showed up at Fräulein Heymann's[79] half an hour late. I stayed for three hours. We discussed a few things, very slowly and silently. [. . .]

I asked Fräulein Heymann if she has been to balls. She told me she had, during the last winter before the war. I said a few things about this that really made an impact on her. Never in my life have I been to a party. No one has ever recognized the ethics of a youthful life. Walter, too, has participated in all these things. Clearly, none of these people has ever noticed the monstrosity of this. It's abundantly clear why people in society tell lies about all higher things. The riddle I'll never understand is how people lie about having *fun.* This is the nature of a ball. The terrifying symbolism of a ball is unimaginable.

"He who studies a lot turns into a dreamer," writes Sebastian Brant in *The Ship of Fools.*[80] A wonderful epigram.

April 11, 1918

"He gave us the Teaching in signs and explicated it through tradition." Tanhuma 9b, cited in Hirschfeld's *Hagaddic Exegesis,* p. 211.[81] [. . .]

The moral gain from Dostoyevsky's *The Idiot* is not as a model, and not as an injunction, but only as the Teaching. [. . .]

To me, the words people use have something ghostly about them. I exist *before* language.

Passionate and silent—this is the secret of my (and everyone's) deepest love. Oh what a heavenly slipup, as I had wanted to write "life"! I submit myself to life!

April 12, 1918

I've experienced clearly over the last few days how I live within rare and costly borders. Everything strives to fit within these borders. One can say that the border is the main agent of my being. I magnify my own powers. This is dangerous business. [. . .]

Nowhere is a person's metaphysical unity (or lack thereof) expressed more clearly than in his letters. A person's letters are Revelations, and the greatest Revelations are involuntary. A person's degree of inner responsibility, his humanity, is manifested in letters. The thing that is forbidden to reveal in a letter must shine out from the unity of the letter's whole. This is what distinguishes the greatest, most beautiful letters. [. . .]

April 13, 1918

Oh, happiness! Lying on the couch and doing nothing this afternoon, which is to say my mind was on Switzerland and the possibilities created by Mother's letter,[82] the express post woman showed up with a letter from Walter. I opened it—and they have a son! The day before yesterday, on Thursday morning, Dora bore a son!

To me, everything turned into a celebration. I wasn't able to respond immediately; I first had to go out into the spring weather. How I love Walter and Dora! In this union everything deep and beautiful is joined into a living miracle. Often over the past year I've asked myself if they would have a child. Now it's here without my thinking about it, which explains the restlessness in his last letter, written before the birth. Lugarno must have been really good for her and the child. I wrote to [the child's] parents. One cannot really congratulate the parents for the child (for compared to the reality, how lame would such a congratulation be) but rather the child for the parents. I wrote to them, "Your marriage is the most beautiful miracle that's ever-occurring in front of my own eyes."

I donned my finest clothes so I could spend the evening in silent celebration. I'm no poet! In the meanwhile, Fräulein Heymann came over to
relax a bit. I had already asked myself how I would tell her. I gave her the
letter. At first she looked at me with uncertainty (she didn't know what I
wanted from her with a letter from Benjamin). I told her that it was permissible for her to read. She read it for a long time and was silent. She
gave it back to me. Later she said, "I would never have thought about
something like this, *here.*" She told me she would also celebrate quietly.

How fresh and lovely the word "mother" sounds at the end of his letter, as if God created it for Dora! I'm praying for her. [. . .]

April 14, 1918

[. . .] If I ever make it to Switzerland, a lot of things here in Germany will
also be resolved. Recently I've given very little direct thought to Grete
because all of my thoughts are with Walter. In Switzerland I would have
a very free relationship with her, because being together with both
friends would heal me. From there I would be able to write to her again,
free of embarrassment. [. . .]

April 15, 1918

[. . .] This evening I read with the greatest suspense *The Onion-Man
Named Kzradock and the Spring Chicken Called Methusalem.*[83] This im-
mensely great book speaks with a powerful language. "You must doubt.
You have to doubt in your soul." The book unfurls the metaphysics of
doubt. The terrifying law behind the soul's germination—if one *trusts*
the soul—is developed explicitly in this detective story. Its beginning and
end both rest in man's inexpressibly demonic regions, which only doubt
can overcome.

This book's knowledge is legitimate and its artistic unity morally shattering, for its unity arises out of the law of the demonic. Indeed, doubt
alone can make the madness in art bearable. Decisive for its idea is the
book's (metaphysical) anonymity. Madness is trust.

April 16, 1918

I'm spending the day virtuously. In the morning I read Kant, after lunch
it was a chapter from Cohen (in this way I hope to get through it gradually).[84] This evening I'll continue with some other fine book. [. . .] Thus
I await word from Switzerland. [. . .]

It's been a long time since I've read such a lovely and profound book as *The People from Seldwyla*.[85] It gives me the most lively and beautiful understanding of Keller himself. I want to buy it. It has an inexpressibly quiet language that, without losing itself, is projected into the narrative. [. . .] Stillness within the passions is achieved here. Keller has perfected something that we Jews lack (this is something I realized nearly three years ago when I first read *Der grüne Heinrich*). The Germanic spirit's treasures are gloriously spread out here—treasures that we Jews are better able to understand because of our desires. We lack this state of Being. But do we need it at all? Is this our task? I would now be inclined to deny it.

Life is an idea (in Kant's sense), which could well be the most valid statement a person can make on the subject. [. . .] The speechlessness of life leads one to the deepest strata of the metaphysics of life. Life receives a language when it is elevated into the Teaching, when it is directed toward the Teaching. It is in this sense that one may say that the language of life is immortality (i.e., death.) This is the only thing expressed with purity each time life achieves its pure form in movement.

The presence of death is the center of human life in its pure Order. This means that death is the metaphysical medium of life. The power of existence is none other than the power with which death shows itself to be the hypothesis of this existence. Death is the hypothesis of our life, just as birth (in a deep sense) is its *Telos*. The definition of *responsibility* is to direct one's life toward death.

In this war, the entire problem with war is summed up by death.

April 17, 1918

Finally, Mother's letter arrived today with news about sending the certificate. Early this morning I'll go to the doctor. I'm feverish because I have no idea whether or not the certificate will get me a pass. I'm reading Kant, Cohen, and Frege.[86] [. . .]

There is such a thing as *the* Jewish life. Is there *the* Jewish death? No. The distinction between "this" and "the next" world is shameful for us; it's a concession. The "next world" is nothing other than the foundation for "this" one. This is the reason why one says that he who commits some bad act of a particular sort loses his part in the "next" world. Henceforth, his life is without any foundation, which is to say, it has been destroyed from the inside.

Jewish death means to endure death as the Teaching. Surely only Christ has died a Jewish death, a death that has *nothing* in common with martyrdom. Christ's death was his Teaching; it was the quintessence of what he had to pass on. His *death* separates him from Judaism in its purest form. In his death, Jewish Teaching meets pagan myth, the one permeating the other. Redemption occurs. Only the *absolute* balance of elements could have preserved the purity of the idea of redemption, but it was quickly lost. Death as redemption (in an ultimate sense) became the new mythic center of Christianity and dictated its ethics, for good and for ill. The medium of death is love: this is the pinnacle of Christian confusion. *Existence* is, in this medium, not knowable; *faith* is needed to endure it. *Belief is the central category of Christian life,* the spiritual Order on which it stands. This Order perverts history.

This Christian fallacy is the largest and most terrifying mankind has ever fallen for. One can live a life through the medium of the Teaching, but a life lived through the medium of Christ is possible only surreptitiously. *Surreptitiousness is faith.* The mythical consequences in the development of Christianity are remarkable. Religions relate to one another the way languages do. Are they not languages? Judaism is certainly *no* language.

April 18, 1918

Last night I nearly couldn't sleep due to excitement. I was aroused to the bones by the anticipation of today. I got up early and went to the district doctor. And I got the certificate, as I could have only imagined in my wildest dreams! During the following hour I saw the heavens open; all of my inner desires seemed fulfilled. But I still have to wait. The assistant said the travel documents would take perhaps four weeks to arrive. Will something now happen to interfere? I won't celebrate till I have it in these hands of mine.

Still, I'm happy, immeasurably so. I transcribed the certificate for Freund.[87] None of the others should know about my plans to go there. Naturally I couldn't do a bit of scholarly work today. First I had to calm back down. I mustn't write Walter till it's certain; otherwise the subsequent disappointment will be measureless. No, it'll be a much more beautiful surprise when I ring the bell, Dora answers, and I say, "Good day, madam, my dear lady!" Oh, how I'd like to sleep till this moment arrives. I read *The Heretic from Soana.*[88] [. . .]

PART IV

JOB'S LAMENTATION: MAY 1918–AUGUST 1919

The statement "I exist" is always a lamentation.

—Diary entry from June 23, 1918

GERHARD EAGERLY TOOK up his friend's invitation to visit him and Dora in the village of Muri in Switzerland, where Benjamin was working on a dissertation on German Romantic criticism. After getting permission from the German military authorities, Scholem made his plans, ostensibly to visit a sanitarium. He did in fact travel to Switzerland to find healing, though it was through Benjamin that he expected to find it. He especially needed it after Grete responded to his love letters first with avoidance and then with the time-honored words, "Let's just be friends."[1] That he was at the snapping point can be felt in a four-page essay he wrote on Rainer Maria Rilke's *Notebooks of Malte Laurids Brigge.*[2]

Benjamin appeared to Scholem as a savior, a healer, and a redeemer, someone who had thrown him a much-needed line after he had been failed by God, his parents, Orthodoxy, Buber, Zionism, and the Zionist youth movement. Scholem looked to Benjamin as a "tremendous prophetic," "moral," and "spiritual" figure, and spoke of an experience of "positive redemption." To his future wife Escha he writes, "Other than my friend, I know of no one else who, not only through the ingeniousness of what he knows, but also through the perfect purity of his being, can become such a Teacher to me."[3] To illustrate Benjamin's "purity and absoluteness," Scholem likened him to a traditional rabbinical scholar who, finding himself in a secular world, seeks out his Scripture.[4]

Just as important for Scholem, he had finally discovered his own messianic calling, which was to revolutionize contemporary Jewish life through his own Teaching. He settled accounts with Herzl's political Zionism when he lashed out at *Jiskor,* a book Martin Buber and his circle put together to commemorate the memory of Jews killed during an Arab attack on an isolated agricultural settlement in northern Palestine. "In Palestine people are dying for phrases,"[5] he stated bluntly.

Gerhard arrived in Muri on May 4, 1918, and moved next door to Benjamin into a large attic in a postman's house overlooking a cornfield. In the thrall of Benjamin's hypnotic influence, the first few days were among the finest of his life.

While hundreds of thousands of corpses still littered European battlefields, the two friends confronted each other, and themselves. As they had done during his visit to Oberstdorf, the two met in the evenings to discuss literature and philosophy and to play board games. They read Karl Kraus's journal *Die Fackel* together and the literature of the German Romantic period. Given his dissertation topic, Benjamin was now entirely immersed in the literary world formed by Johann Hamann, Hölderlin, Friedrich Schlegel, and Novalis. Gerhard sat in rapt attention one evening as Benjamin discussed Goethe's "autobiographical life."[6] Benjamin gave Scholem yet another clue into his inner life, telling him that his own experiences with Dora had taught him the truth of Goethe and Goethe's marriage. "Renunciation and bounty: autobiography and the autobiographical life," commented Scholem in his diary after returning to his garret, "are rooted in concealment."[7] With Grete and his own lamentations fresh on his mind, he again was astounded at the spiritual affinity between him and his friend. Deep emotional forces are at work in criticism, and the more invisible they are to the superficial reader, the greater potency they pack for those privy to them. They become, as Scholem would say, Revelation.

Sometimes the two friends shifted over to philosophy and discussed Kant and Hermann Cohen. One evening Scholem read aloud Agnon's *Torah Scribe.* When Benjamin read from the sonnets he had written for Fritz Heinle, and talked about his plans for fifty such poems, Scholem spoke of the "fifty gates of insight, which according to the Talmud were opened to Moses."[8]

After Benjamin showed him "The Diary," another of his essays secretly commemorating the dead poet, Scholem went back to his garret and wrote out his reflections:

> You live alone in the diary of my life
> Leading an immortal existence page by page
> In death you have been given to me by Time
> Lest in you I lose myself to things too great.

Everything he read of Benjamin's reminded him of the emotional source behind his friend's maniacal devotion to his work:

> When all is said and done, his entire life is nothing more than one massive apology for his dead friend. Everything he does is nothing more than methodically taking the dark central point created by their friendship and lifting it up into *absolute* clarity. Every word he says about this genius proves this and also reveals his final intention: to make an accounting of himself to someone who is dead. I don't believe that since the prophets there has ever lived a man who has brought such a massive responsibility to completion. All of this occurs in utter invisibility. Instead of communicating himself, Walter insists that everyone sees him, even though he hides himself. His method is completely unique. I can't put it any other way than the method of Revelation.[9]

In the summer of 1918, the high-water mark of his hopes with Benjamin, the two friends jestingly discussed founding a University of Muri, with Walter as rector and Gerhard as the head of the philosophy of religion faculty. Scholem, happy as never before, wrote a number of sonnets as a birthday gift to Benjamin, all with a staccato-style cadence. In "The Ball" he writes of "messengers of silence"; in "WB" that "The world is built / on your silence"; and "For July 15," "Even silence is too hollow / Or too filled with righteous awe."[10]

�֎

Scholem's diary entries during his eighteen months in Switzerland invoke images from Thomas Mann's *Magic Mountain:* a brilliant young man nursing his sanity, staring out on the wind-blown trees in the forest as the wider world below is going to the dogs. It is also hard to escape the impression of Gerhard as a man adrift in a bohemian world he admired and openly worshipped and yet was unable to enter fully, with Walter and Dora smirking at what they mocked as his "outrageous wholesomeness."[11]

Gerhard failed to find his healing. In July his childhood friend Harry Heymann died of battle wounds. Not mentioned in the diary itself, his death makes an appearance in one of Gerhard's attacks on the Jewish youth movement.[12]

With Benjamin, on whom he had pinned so many hopes, he suffered a different kind of loss. Given his expectations, disillusionment was as quick as it was inevitable. Walter, older, married, and busy with his dissertation, did not share Gerhard's emotional needs. He was tentative, hesitant, and puzzled by Scholem's overwrought expectations of intimacy. Benjamin never wrote sonnets to Scholem.

Moreover, Gerhard had hoped to belong to a secret Jewish society, with him and Walter at its center. The problem with this was that Benjamin's most important influences were the Romantic writers, Wyneken, Heinle, and Max Noeggerath—all Christians. When Benjamin described to him Noeggerath's influence on his thought, he used the loaded Goethean expression *Verwandschaft,* or "affinity."[13]

Benjamin's "affinity" with a non-Jew put a spoke in the wheel of Scholem's belief in their unique Jewish bond. It didn't help matters when Benjamin and Dora made noisy love while Gerhard—to judge by his diaries at this point still very much a frustrated virgin—waited nervously downstairs for their evening discussion of Kantian metaphysics.

There were also violent arguments between him and Walter, and him and Dora. When Scholem wrote an open letter of protest to Siegfried Bernfeld, a friend of Benjamin's during his days in Wyneken's youth movement who had become a Zionist, Benjamin vehemently objected. Scholem, incensed at Bernfeld's lack of radicalism, spelled out his complaints openly, which ran counter to Benjamin's ethos of silence.[14] "In such things it is a matter of having the metaphysical laughs on your side," he instructed Scholem. In so many words, he told him to button his lip.[15]

Other clashes were more personal. The bohemian Benjamin was supremely unsuited to the role Scholem cast for him. The man Gerhard looked up to as a prophet was capable of being intellectually bullying and opportunistic. Even worse, he shocked his younger friend with an "element of decadence," an "amorality" and "nihilism" that worked against his intellectual purity.[16] Gerhard was appalled at Walter's insouciant attitude toward Judaism, along with his offhand remarks about matters of supreme importance to his younger friend. Gerhard discovered, for instance, that the same man from whom he had sought salvation denied the inviolability of the Ten Commandments. "Those like us are answerable only to ourselves," the saturnine philosopher declared, to Gerhard's shock.[17]

The clashes with Dora were even more catastrophic. Scholem's retrospective account half a century later sugarcoats their tumultuous relationship by mentioning her "loving intercession" that kept him and Benjamin from throttling each other.[18] In fact, it was Walter who stopped Dora from pitching Gerhard out of their home once and for all.

He, Walter, and Dora managed to survive their quarrels. Gerhard would arrive at the Benjamin home at prescribed times, discuss philosophy with Walter, and head back to his garret. Occasionally there were longer conversations over dinner, but the frosty formality of the "Sie" still didn't disappear.

In the fall Scholem moved to Bern and would see Benjamin only occasionally. For two tumultuous months he lived with Erich Brauer. He resumed his translations of lamentations (one, "Question, Burned in Fire," is an elegiac prayer chanted in honor of the dead); invited old friends from Berlin to visit; and despite an occasional bout of misogyny inspired by Dora and his unrequited love for Grete ("There is no female Torah," he muses), wrote long letters to Escha Burchhardt.[19] Her qualities as an "uncommonly quiet person with firm convictions" were precisely what he needed at the time.

But his failed intimacy with Benjamin continued to torment him, and suicidal thoughts, now deemed a "legitimate religious category,"[20] reemerged with frightful vigor. He was reaching a dangerous tipping point, and according to his own words the only thing keeping him from killing himself was cowardice.[21]

Paradoxically, just as he was coming to terms with the denouement of his earlier hopes, he was maturing into a scholar with an indefatigable drive and indomitable inner fortitude, or so it seemed. He had scarcely a good word to say for other "infertile" scholars. For good reason, he preferred Agnon's fiction with its biblical, Talmudic, and midrashic allusions woven into his narratives.

During these months Scholem made his first serious efforts at literary criticism. Philology was a "secret science," he surmises,[22] and a literary review is the place where the Messianic Order makes its appearance.[23] A raft of essays he wrote in these months—"Agnon," "And the Crooked Shall Be Made Straight," "On Hasidism," "On Jonah and the Concept of Justice," "Job's Lamentation," "Metaphysical Memorandum on the Progress of Zionism," and "A Medieval Lamentation"—show the first hints of a future master at work reconstructing Jewish tradition.

All the ideas he had learned from Benjamin—on the Teaching, Tradition, and so on—survived more or less intact. Given his state of mind at the time, lamentation lost its anticipation of immediate redemption and turned into an existential condition, with no end in sight. "Misery operates within Judaism as a historical category," he wrote.[24] An isolated scholar hunched over a pile of manuscripts became the locus of Jewish renewal; through his work, he was changing fundamental patterns of thought. The only power left him was longing, sadness, and lamentation. "We will not get our youth back: it has disappeared into God's lap—the abyss of sadness."[25]

These essays attest to a young man who expunged personal feelings and emotions to achieve "objectivity" in history, while his lonely self, longing for love and revolution, hid out in the past. In perhaps the saddest confession in the entire diary, he says of himself, "I am a composer of symbolic literature comprehensible only to myself."[26]

Death becomes a central motif—death of the body, the passing of time, the smashing of youthful illusions. Real historical time is tragic, death-filled, and illusory; immortality and hence redemption come to us alone through the timeless acts of canonical transmission.

It was in this state of mind that Gerhard experienced several of the most extraordinary moments of the modern era. For some the revolutions and upheavals that followed the defeat of the Central Powers at the end of 1918 and in 1919 heralded a new age of democracy and freedom; for others it only provoked anger and resentment. Soldiers, their erstwhile idealism badly mangled by the lost war, followed leaders who promised to bury the old order. Some leaders were genuine visionaries, others dangerous charlatans.

Gerhard responded to the political upheaval in Europe with a few laconic observations. The end of the war did not merit a single word, while the revolutions that swept away the mighty German and Austrian empires drew a bit more attention: "I take this revolution into my field of vision," he said with supreme aplomb.[27] At first he expressed sympathy for the terrorist practices of the Bolsheviks, in particular the destruction of middle-class illusions of eternal progress as practiced by his father, Arthur. Gradually he sobered up. Brooding alone on his Swiss perch gave him astonishing insights into the dangers of a mystical worship of violence, blood, and death. His comments on the murderous logic of scientific socialism are eerily prescient. Henceforth, the self-declared anarchist never swayed from staunchly liberal views on state and society.

After the war ended and chaos descended on most of central Europe, the sporadic fights between Gerhard, Walter, and Dora ceased, and for the first time the intimate "Du" brings a hint of deep warmth to their conversations. Walter and Dora were often sick with Spanish influenza, which reached pandemic proportions in central Europe and at one point almost killed Dora. When they were all healthy, they would sing songs, with Dora at the piano playing "Through Fields and Halls of Beeches" and "I Shall Drift along to My Cold Grave."

Scholem became acquainted with some of the other intellectuals Benjamin allowed into his circle. They were all eccentric, and most were somehow disabled emotionally or otherwise. Fritz Heinle's brother Wolfgang stayed with Walter and Dora for a month. The profoundly melancholy poet—a severe illness had rendered him indigent—read his enigmatic expressionistic-esoteric works. He would commit suicide in 1922. Another of Benjamin's acquaintances Scholem met was Hyne Caro, a twenty-year-old who had been nicknamed "Hyne," or "Giant," because he was so small. Then there was Hans Heyse, a severely handicapped philosopher and study partner to Benjamin. He later became a notorious Nazi philosopher. The one friend with a relatively sound mind and body was Ernst Bloch, who had just published his book *Spirit of Utopia*. Benjamin was impressed with what he called Bloch's system of theoretical messianism, and arranged for Scholem to meet him.[28]

With the war over and his parents no longer willing to support him in expensive Switzerland, Gerhard left for Munich, where Escha was studying, to continue his studies in philosophy, mysticism, and philology. Once there he began delving into the Kabbalistic manuscripts in the city, the largest collection in Germany. His focus was Abraham Abulafia, a thirteenth-century Kabbalist who was a good candidate on whose writings to try out his philological skills. With conscious reference to Benjamin and his "system," he writes: "My talent lies in the interpretation of those who can be interpreted."[29] Abulafia was in this sense imminently "interpretable."

The affinity between researcher and subject is hard to miss. Inspired by illusory visions, the young Abulafia embarked on a life of constant wandering. He ended up in Palestine in search of the Ten Lost Tribes of Israel. The mythic tribes were nowhere to be found; what he confronted instead was the carnage left by the Crusades. Back in Europe his messianism took a linguistic turn when he stumbled across a system of prophetic mysticism based on the commentaries and mystical system of the German Jewish mystic Eleazar of Worms (1165–1230). What he learned from this mystic was to discover truth esoterically through the analysis of the names of God and through encrypting the Hebrew language. Numerology was his preferred method: he gave a word's letters a numeric value, just the system Benjamin had discovered in Alexandre Dumas's novel *The Count of Monte Cristo.*

NOTEBOOK 1

Observations

May 4–June 16, 1918

You live alone in the diary of my life
Leading an immortal existence page by page
In death you have been given to me by Time
Lest in you I lose myself to things too great.

The Landscape turns into a shroud.
The enemy will rise against me in a rage.
And you, Beloved, also must take your place
Beside him lest he swear out loud.

—A poem from May 12, 1918, inspired by Benjamin's *Metaphysics of Youth*

May 4, 1918

Walter picked me up. "I am pleased with you," he said. I arrived about 9 P.M. and was with him till 12 o'clock. We discussed Werner Kraft's inability to stand up to the military or to anything else, and everything about him from the perspective of his innermost self. Kraft misses in me the speed of my comebacks, which is the "something" he had written me about. "It's a real pity he spoke this out to you," said Walter. Our convergence of opinion already shows itself in a most astounding way.

May 5, 1918

From 10:30 till one o'clock in the afternoon I spent with Walter. At first we went for a walk. We talked about smoking. As he lit up a cigarette, I said that one of my friends told me one mustn't smoke. Walter disputed this passionately and fundamentally. From there we discussed ethics (sin and responsibility). He's writing about ethics, something my letter on Strauss and metaphysics inspired him to do. His two important attempts are: "The Program for a Coming Philosophy" and "On Intuition."[1]

Later in the afternoon, from 4:30 till 8:00, we began with a ten-minute visit to Loni Ortenstein.[2] Then we discussed our life together, our work, and an academy where we are for ourselves. For a few days we'll gaze in wonder at ourselves. Dora is the most beautiful thing in the world. We discussed the practical and technical issues of my sojourn, which aren't so simple. His paroxysm occurred on January 13, the evening before my military examination.

May 6, 1918

Between ten and eleven I heard a lecture by Herbertz,[3] who's a philistine par excellence and speaks like a market peddler. Then we went for a walk and discussed Kant. Walter has trimmed his sails and is going full speed ahead of me into Kant. "Kant has argued in support of an inferior experience." He's opposed to Kantian ethics.

In the evening I heard Maync lecture on Romanticism.[4] "He discovers falsehood through kitsch." Later, after Dora's mother finally left, we celebrated my arrival with a festive meal. We discussed Stifter[5] a bit, and with *Rilke*[6] we went into detail by seeking out the spheres of his poetry. They gave me Tieck's *Fairy Tales*.[7] It was wonderful. Dora will be my mother. She calmed Stefan down herself.[8] Walter is going to study Hebrew after his doctorate.

May 8, 1918

I was at Walter's from five o'clock till midnight. First we discussed Balmer's detective novels[9] (the psychological method) and some philosophical objections to them. They are a mishmash of confession and circumstantial evidence: incest against the juridical person. Everyone has his sacred right of *denial*. After a light meal, Walter read to me a letter from Kosegarten and two from Samuel Collenbusch to Kant: measureless and magnificent letters, in particular the last two.[10] Next came three letters from the Goethe-Zelter correspondence.[11] We discussed Goethe at length. I should have written everything down because I *feel* that everything was true. I told him that what constitutes my relationship to him is the necessity of freedom. He also discussed for the first time his first engagement, to Grete Radt. This was in parallel to Goethe; he told me how it was through his own experience that he had learned the truth of Goethe and Goethe's marriage. Renunciation and bounty: autobiography and the autobiographical life are rooted in concealment. We ate dinner. Dora and Walter exchanged anecdotes about their birthdays and showed me their gifts. Walter read three poems from the Books of Maxims. "The demons must spare the Jews." Both were so happy in telling stories. Their love is a miracle to which I can only serve as a witness. [. . .]

May 9, 1918

Ascension Day. This morning from ten to twelve we were in Muri because of the apartment. It was wonderful, only a bit muggy. All three of us (or four!) want to live outdoors. We started to discuss Strauss's *Ethics,* which just arrived. We talked about a storm, essences, and today's philosophical style.

I was with them from five P.M. to 12:30. He read August Wilhelm Schlegel aloud. Among Germans, the ode is the subjugation of fire. But he feels himself related to Plato. Then came two sonnets from Dante, in Schlegel's translation. We spoke about Schiller, for whom morality is demonic. I connected these things to history. Jean Paul is the *only* writer who could stomach staying in Germany *without* its being held against him, because he lived within an extraordinary historical sphere. It can be held against Schiller, however, and there's no greater sham than his historic innocence. He never suffered from his suffering. Schiller's failure with Hölderlin derives from this.

Walter spoke about Philipp Keller and described how he met Fritz Heinle.[12] [. . .]

May 10, 1918

This morning at Häberlin's lecture we occupied ourselves by identifying the names of famous people starting with "M." Walter came up with 64 to my 51. We would have otherwise died of boredom.

From four in the afternoon till midnight I was at Walter's. Until dinner I spoke alone with Dora for the first time. I told her about my recent life. She also told me some things, and after dinner she talked about her and Walter. She spoke about Guttmann.[13] She urged me in the most loving manner to relax. She knows how much I love her. After the meal we played the mental guessing game "Concrete or Abstract." (Walter had to guess "priesthood.") Next we discussed Alice Heymann, after which Dora left and Walter read a few poems aloud. I read David's dirge, and we discussed the songs of lamentation. He also read from his remarks to Stifter. He gave me the "Conversation" and the "Diary."[14]

We never knew how well we mesh.

May 11, 1918

From 10:30 to 11:30 A.M. we did all sorts of nonsense, then, sowing destruction, we read through the first pages of Strauss's ethics. We left nothing standing.

Socratic men: Fichte, Kierkegaard, Freud, Hamann. On Romanticism: "The good man Scholem, that pious brute (is, we're sorry to say, still en route)." This is my nickname! Franz Delitzsch *very correctly* compares Johann G. Hamann with the Talmud.[15] [. . .]

Psalm 39. A Psalm of David[16]

I said, I will take heed to my ways, that I sin not with my tongue: I will keep a curb on my mouth, while the wicked man is before me. I was dumb with silence, I held my peace, had no comfort, and my pain was stirred up. My heart was hot within me; while I was musing, the fire burned: then I spoke with my tongue, LORD, make me to know my end, and the measure of my days, what it is; I will know how frail I am. [. . .]

May 12[, 1918]

Upon first reading "The Metaphysics of Youth":[17]

Paraphrase of the Prose of "The Diary"[18]
You live alone in the diary of my life

Leading an immortal existence page by page
In death you have been given to me by Time
Lest in you I lose myself to things too great.

The Landscape turns into a shroud.
The enemy will rise against me in a rage.
And you, Beloved, also must take your place
Beside him lest he swear out loud.

Even as you die, Youth, you establish History
From your love Time shoots forth like rays
And immortality blazes from your life.

The future was. The past shall be
The present will disunite us before God
In this estrangement we shall be free.

May 15[, 1918]

For July 15[19]

Friend. Expect no symbol
Portending your greatness.
Even silence is too hollow
Or too filled with righteous awe
A Revelation would be needed
At which I've never quite succeeded.
I have always gazed upon your years
Amazed how they appeared
To grow within a melody
Purely improvised out of the midst
Of God as a promise
Of the Teaching we held dear.

Friend. Accept this as evidence
I had no deceit in mind
Take Dora by the hand
Let the ban on presents be deleted

Look around and understand
You've finally been defeated.

The Ball

I am Youth you are Joy
Yet both of us are lies
Too enthralled by the ball
To be ourselves at all.

We reject what is common
Yet have now forgotten
That finer, purer home:
The joy of being alone.

Youth. Laughter is hard
When all silence is barred
Yet revulsion is not an escape
Blessed are those who seek change.

Our words achieved only eloquence
As messengers of silence
We two were only in rhyme
Having forestalled time.

Genius of Youth, climb free
Of the noisy ball, cease to speak
And let your silence bear proof
I am not this youth.

Farewell to a Young Girl
To Grete

Misfortune. The lament merely silenced at its source
In your life misfortune comes to be revealed
The heart of youth in me is now congealed.

The Teaching you transmitted, a question I endorse.
Your face of Being, averted, contains the days
That place us at risk—Ruins. As my defense
The deep knowledge that should your presence
Dazzle me, I might stare straight into its rays.

Your misfortune—Girl—lies in knowing the truth
That no one on earth has suffered as you do.
And Zion is misfortune's most holy site.

Toward which you now move, alone, leaving me behind.
You, my midmost self, we must lose ourselves before
Our paths lead that way, together once more.

Undated. Beginning of June 1918

O God, I cannot stand this! Today I wrote Meta an intimation of the horrific, bitter truth. My life converges on suicide. This is the naked truth that's been circulating in my brain like a millstone for four weeks now. Never have I considered death—death by my own hand—with such intense immediacy as in these four weeks. I do so day in and day out, night after night. And Walter and Dora, instead of helping me, only make it worse. Through some sort of dreadful imponderable they are literally driving me to my grave. There are moments—may God and the two of them forgive me for this—in which I consider them to be perfectly ignoble, especially in their behavior and in their daily lives. This kills me. [. . .]

In three days I worked methodically through all of the Psalms between 30 and 150—because I *must* find something to hold me together. I see Walter and Dora only occasionally, just three times a week. The rest of the time I have to be alone with my own death and with my abandoned life. (Oh, the monstrous double meaning of "task"!!)[20] And the landscape surrounding me is vicious in its joyfulness. Its restfulness makes me groan. Yet I love it.

Saturday, June 8, 1918

Last night I had the Friday meal with Walter and Dora. We discussed that catalog of Borchardt's works that has appeared in *Poetry.*[21] Walter and Dora were very tired. At the end (I wanted to leave) Walter read a poem, and so did I. They both laughed at the last lines, for reasons unknown to me, but neither does it matter to me. I *saw* this laughter and said to Dora something to the effect of, "What are you turning me into?" If I had not followed my principle never to reflect on such things but had continued delving into this laughter, I would have gone crazy. Half jokingly, yet with terrifying truth, I said that their behavior toward me is slowly but surely pushing me into death and madness. Walter was terribly agitated by this (just as he was two weeks ago by the story of the "Hebrew" factor), and thus began a melancholy two-hour discussion that Dora, only at the end, steered onto the right path through her goodness. She and Walter accused me of being naïve and of allowing myself to be ruled by my gestures, and that I produce pain through a health I don't possess but that possesses me. Everything they said was entirely true, and for me it was genuinely redeeming. Everything came out. Now I can take up my other life, be it life or be it death, with the conviction of responsibility. At the end, both of them had a nearly heavenly goodness about them. As Walter accompanied me out the door, I could have kissed Dora's hand. He held my hand for an instant and stared at me with an intensity I'd never experienced from anyone else. There was a terrifying tempest, but now things have cleared up. They are entirely correct: half of everything I say is purest gibberish, and there would *have* to be some sort of catastrophe if anyone ever took me seriously. This already occurred in Jena (only that there the catastrophe took the opposite course because the girls didn't have enough insight to know what was ultimately at stake), and it could happen again with double force. I have been swallowed by nothingness (it was there yesterday when I shamelessly hinted at the truth—though only once—that is to be forever kept silent. Walter was so right when he said he could never understand this: that he *eidetically* could not understand it). Nevertheless, it was during this evening that my death seemed avoidable for the first time in ages. If only I could write poetry, I would write a long string of sonnets about last night. [. . .]

This afternoon Walter came up to my place and we played a game of chess. There was the typical outcome. In the afternoon we read Cohen's highly dubious chapter on Locke and Hume. We discussed what the rationalists had to say about interpretation. The rationalist considers everything that is an object to be *absolute,* which means that not only the Bible (also Hölderlin, says Walter) *may* and should be legitimately commented on with violence, but also Aristotle, Descartes, Kant, and everyone else. This is also the critical point with rationalistic positivism, as it is with Hume and the phenomenologists. Kant asks: "What is behind causality?" Hume asks: "What do we *mean* by causality?" The phenomenologists are therefore right to go back to Hume. He wants absolute experience. Walter has recently spoken a lot about Nietzsche. He said he had to let out a scream when he realized that Nietzsche had been the only person in the nineteenth century—a time when people only "experienced" nature—to understand historical experience. [. . .]

June 9, 1918

Walter's dreams are among the most fabulous things about him. Since childhood he has had so many dreams; he's already told me many completely fantastic things. After a jokingly bitter conversation over our game (the encyclopedia of babble), he recounted last night's dream. There were twenty people who, after being given a theme, had to stand in pairs and depict a situation corresponding to the theme. Magically, the costumes corresponded to the theme. Whoever finished first set the tone for the others, and the one who best presented the theme won the prize. He should have won the prize with the theme of "rejection." He was a small, shriveled-up Chinese man with blue robes, and a pushy fellow who wanted something from him had crawled up onto his back. But two other people did their act just as well, and they were the ones who won the prize. Another topic was "jealousy." "I was a woman who lay stretched out on the ground. A man embraced me, and I looked at him from below with jealousy, and stuck my tongue far out of my mouth." Such things happen in Walter's dreams.

Anton Reiser's mother is astonished when he calls his father "the best father," for he has only one father. *Anton Reiser,* of which I've read about half, is monumental.[22] It really grabs me with full force. On nearly every page I stumble across some shattering anecdote or remark. This man must have been a Teacher, and in some ways he's reminiscent of Stendhal. But what surely sets the book apart is the massive and overpowering sadness permeating it and determining its metaphysical Order. The experience of a messianic future already in the living present—as portrayed in this book and in this man—must be disastrous because it is a claim that *cannot* be satisfied. Hence, the book turns into an accusation against the messianic realm itself—for the sake of the one who has suffered from it, who has been forever deceived. A greater catechism of true religious irony about salvation will never be written. And yet a lamentation, which is the higher redemption, towers with double force above all the lies of redemption which, in this book, die a far from glorious death. Anton Reiser mourns the loss of his youth. Never has there been a fiercer lamentation, for this lamentation isn't redeemed from within. Anton Reiser dies; he has been dying since birth because he leads a life devoid of youth. History itself is on the dock, and its laws have cruelly turned against themselves. Through his despair, Anton Reiser exercises immortal revenge on history—by describing it. He describes a life of naked hallucination, a life led mythically like no other. Myth here, however, is seen for what it is—and *this* is the real reason for Reiser's despair. This and nothing else is the definition of decadence: mythic life seeing itself for what it is.

Metaphysically, the end of this life (and its *continuation*) is *always* suicide, regardless of whether the person dies at a ripe old age. The greatness of *Anton Reiser* is that the Teaching, which it knows nothing about, beams out from within it. Yes! The only guarantee of a pure childhood and an inalienable youth is the Teaching as the *developed* foundation for all human relationships. Only in the Teaching are childhood and youth means, and not instruments to be toyed with. [. . .]

June 10, 1918

Taking an honest look at me, I basically lead the same kind of life as Reiser, at least in many points. I live within my own kingdom, and I fall to pieces when, with mathematical certainty, it's pointed out where my life's unreality manifests itself. I have waking dreams of a fabulous future that's not my own. I even imagine to myself (what depravity!) what the world (*ha-Olam*,[23] that cursed foundational concept of demonology) would say about my death. I thus rob my own death of redemption by allowing my loneliness to babble about it, which is nothing but vanity. When I'm at my best, I shiver in horror of myself, for I see how I've transformed reality into a hallucination. I'm falling apart *through* my own nihilism. [. . .]

June 11–12, 1918

I wrote a—basically shameless—open letter to Bernfeld.[24] [. . .] In essence, I say only this: "Take a look at what a gem you have in this Gerhard Scholem, and how he's been irrevocably lost to you." Walter says that silence itself mustn't appear in the method of silence unless it is required to. He may be completely correct, yet I'll have to send the letter anyway. [. . .]

It's evening. I see one thing with the most perfect clarity and certainty: my relationship with Walter is heading for a terrifying crisis. There are moments when I feel the urge to get up and leave. I'd rather be alone or return to Germany than continue in his dreadful sphere, whose mendacity at times rages all the way into my heart. One must sadly confess that Walter is not a righteous man. Regardless of the outcome or whether I give in or not, if he doesn't want an open letter forcing a decision on our relationship, which is very likely, it means that our relationship is over and done with. It is possible that my death is closer than I think. He asked me what makes my letter so urgent. Yes, an open letter to him is admittedly the *ultima ratio,* and I can only shudder to think about it. I suspect that this is what will happen. The entire purpose of my being here was revealed in the first three days, and after that I should have turned around and left. I cannot live with Walter and Dora. *Oh God, I can't.* Walter may be whoever he is, but he has boundaries over which he won't step, which I experience daily. Metaphysics turns him into a lunatic. His sense of perception is no longer human: it's that of a madman delivered into the hands of God.

June 16, 1918

Sometimes there are the most annoying scenes with Dora. If she rightly feels insulted by either Walter or me, she'll often leave the room. But what happened today was too much. Around five o'clock she sent the maid to me and asked me to come by. Fine, I went over and we had a delightful conversation. Then Walter arrived and we played a game of chess according to the new rules we set. [. . .] Suddenly she sprang up, and in less than a second she dashed out of the room. I didn't see her again. We'll never play this game again. Only with the greatest effort can I contain my disappointment in this person. If there was any woman I had considered free of hysteria it was her, and in six weeks she has systematically destroyed this illusion. Though I tremble in writing this, she is sometimes like Sophie Scholem back in 1915 during her terrible hysterical fit against me. I don't understand such things: or to be more precise, I understand them too well. At these times Dora reverts to her bourgeois nature. She wants to conceal her greatest lie by pretending (at least to me) to possess something eternal that she doesn't have, or only very occasionally. I am helpless. In three months these two people have turned me into an old man, a "man of experience" who has seen more than he desires to. Even their truths are only accidental. They tell too many fibs. Of all people, they can be a case study in the horrifying effects of mendacity on an honest way of life. They tell lies out of aesthetic pleasure, out of egotism, out of the need for leisure. Only gradually am I realizing how deceitful their lives are—also in their relationship to me. His honesty is in his poetry and philosophy, but beyond this point I have to say that, as a human being, Heller[25] probably stands head and shoulders above him. I often think that Heller wouldn't endure being together with him for an hour. [. . .]

NOTEBOOK 2

Journal for Murish[26] Art: The only edition. And annals of the local seminar in religious philosophy and its director.

June 17–August 1, 1918

I'm far sicker than I admit to the people close to me. They think I'm the picture of health. No one suspects that every afternoon I shiver as if in a fever. I'm totally sick. Nothing can help me. My first love *will* have to be my fate. [. . .] There's an awful truth to the Kabbalistic doctrine of the Breaking of Vessels.

—Diary entry from June 19, 1918

June 17, 1918

[. . .] I just have to face the fact that Walter and Dora aren't helping me *here.* They can't. [. . .]

Some Remarks on Judaism and Time

As a religious category, Time becomes the eternal present. This can be explicated using some related examples. The notion of God correlates to the idea of the messianic realm. God is 'ehje asher 'ehje—"I will be who I will be." What does this mean? In Hebrew *'ehje* means both the present ("I am") and the future. For God, Time is always in the future. Hebrew has no other means to express the concept of the eternal present than by making the future permanent. Cohen writes, "In the future when the meaning of the present is given, the difference between present and future will also be reduced. Existence will not be fixed in the present but will float above it. Present and future will be bound together in God's being." (*Religion in the System of Philosophy,* p. 22.)[27] God's true name is thus the Self of Time. His name means: "The Divine, which is the eternal present (the foundation, and at the same time the expansion) of all em-

pirical time, for through all generations God *was* what he will become."
The contemporary moment expresses this central point better than the
future because the true unreality of the present—because the present
only has existence as a *source* [. . .] whose nothingness gives birth to the
eternal Time as the empirical future—makes it suitable to express what
we intend to say here. This notion of Time corresponds to the messianic
realm (Cohen has an inkling of the true meaning of this on page 34).[28]
The messianic realm is history in the present. The prophets could speak
about this idea only hypothetically by using the image of the future.
What does "And in those days" mean? If one thinks it through to the
end, "those days" refers to these days. The kingdom of God is the *present*,
for the present moment is the beginning and the end. The kingdom of
God (not the present) has no metaphysical future. The God who "will
be" demands from Time that it "will be." But just as God *is*, so *is* Time.
All other type of time, the racing, constantly shifting time, is only distor-
tion; it is the unharmonious unrolling of this one historic Time.

God has no Existence; he has only Being.[29] Being represents itself.
Why does Rambam deny that God has life? Because by saying he's alive
contradicts the thought of the eternal present. Time in religion is always
a decision, i.e., the present.[30] [. . .]

All of this is intimately tied to the metaphysics of Hebrew, whose des-
ignation of Time is able to offer us the deepest possible clues. This is to
be developed in three areas: one, in the general presentation of the present through the future. The future is a *command*, just as is the command
in the present, *to be*, for instance: *Kedoshim thuju*, "you should be holy,"
that is to say, you should be, meaning both that you will be and that you
are. You *are* holy because I am holy. *Only* this is the meaning of the command to spread holiness into the present moment. The second area is the
Waw ha-Hippuch[31] of a narrative. What happens here? *Time is transformed
through fusion:* the past is in the future and the future is in the past.
How does this happen? Through the vehicle of the present. The conception of Time as the Waw ha-Hippuch is the messianic Time. Only the
name of God guarantees the metaphysical possibilities of this grammatical construction. Only what can happen again has happened. "Why *wa-
halach?*"—"Why did he leave?" Because one must add to this (and this
addition makes it profound) that he will go. The *Essence* inherent in this
construction (as Husserl says) enables the construction. This essence is
God's Time, which is the present. The past and the future can be trans-

formed through the present because they are equivalent. The third point is that a command in Wav ha-Hippuch may be spoken out in the *past*, as an obligatory past. *"Ve 'ahavta"*—You shall love, which is a command that can only be made because you have already loved. The most overpowering thing of all is when the messianic realm makes an appearance in language because messianic beams of light elevate the past. Only a *Jewish* language is capable of such construction. [. . .]

To judge by what Walter says, Kant's *Critique of Practical Reason,* which he is now reading, must really be dreadful. [. . .] I'll soon have to make a decision about the plan I've been walking around with: whether to publish my open letter under a pseudonym. Do I want to say one last thing using my own name? One possibility is the name Ben-bli-shem, "Someone-With-No-Name." Anonymous. Or *"The Zionist."* [. . .]

This evening Walter said unbelievable things about cosmology. He said he'd finally like to begin doing something with this. He started by reading aloud "Notes on Dreams and Clairvoyance." Sleep is a self-enclosed condition. The dream state and waking state are extremes along a spectral medium in the middle of which stands life and death. "In sleep, the body is dark." Walter explained the laws of interpreting dreams. "Notes on Clairvoyance" contains the rules governing ghosts: if some entity (who is always androgynous) dies, there appears in a parallel process the double of his female self. This double [. . .] characterizes ghostliness. We talked about this. The world has three historical periods: the ghostly, the demonic, and the messianic (as I suggested we call it). The real content of myth, which fills the demonic period, is the massive revolution that ended the epoch of ghosts. Myth is a *polemic* against ghosts: the creation of Eve from Adam's rib is polemical. Walter hopes to make something out of this notion of ghostliness. He recounted a dream he had in Seeshaupt three days before his aunt died, and for an hour afterward he tried to come up with an interpretation. In the dream he lay in bed, along with him on the bed was someone with his aunt, but no one interfered with them. People came by and looked through the window. What is the meaning of a window in a dream? Commonly, seeing takes place both as something that gives off a reflection and also as something through which one looks. In a ghostly state, these two can be interchanged. A window reflects, but through it a person sees not his own image but the truth. Seeing yourself is the *absolute* symbol of death. This has to have something to do with the seer. The seer is blind (Teiresias)[32] because he is a pure mirror. Pythagoras' table of categories has to be explained from this perspective. There are three processes: the animal, the vegetable (that of growth), and the ambivalent. Of the last Walter has discovered only one example: hair growth. He then explained the key role hair growth has played in mythology. We discussed sex. [. . .]

If creating a foundational science of mythology is successful—without which we cannot understand myth—Judaism can then continue with its work of overcoming myth through insight into the mythical.

Walter wrote to Ernst Schoen that Stifter's style is visual.[33] He doesn't know Revelation, for Revelation must be heard (in the metaphysical, acoustical sphere). Walter said the most illuminating things about this. Stifter wasn't supposed to be an artist. He somehow was given the task of becoming a *doctor*. And because of a lack of courage, he fled into art. He bought his repose, just as his artistry is a lie. I started learning colossal things during the evening. A few more evenings like this and I'll have an entirely new perspective.

Anton Reiser is entirely historical in style. It has the metaphysical appearance of a *chronicle*. Sadness is developed here as a historical phenomenon. It is sadness that cannot be dissolved into lamentation. It is not lamentation that is redemptive in this book of youth, but it's Revelation (that it is spoken out). [. . .]

June 19, 1918

Walter's statement that perception is reading requires the widest basis possible. [. . .] From this point, we returned once again to the theme of cosmology. During the epoch of ghosts there were no Zodiac signs, because reading began with the Zodiac, the script. The Zodiac performed for mythic heathens what later became the function of *Revelation*. In the epoch of ghosts, which was ruled by vegetative processes, there was also no death. There was clairvoyance, which was banned during the age of myth. In the age of myths there were dreams. The things that I learned would truly be enough to dumbfound anyone. But it often seems to me that everyone knows such things but only hides them out of a vaguely felt fear. What is fantastic about Walter's thoughts is that they seem obvious once you think about them deeply enough. They suddenly then become clearer than the rules of geometry. [. . .]

While I hoodwink myself in all sorts of ways, the truth is that I am doing miserably, also physically. I fear the afternoons. I'm glad I don't dream at night; it helps me get past the morning. At that point things are still bearable, and I'm able to forget about the strange pressures that break out in the afternoon. I fear these long afternoons, which I can't flee. My condition is simply wretched. I try to eat chocolate, but there's no sense in this; it only worsens my condition, producing in me a terrifying fever. I'm totally passive about everything. Even Rilke could almost put one over on me. I'm afraid of the Bible sitting on my desk because I have to vindicate myself before it. And I'm not able to. Thank God I can't write poetry, otherwise I'd come out with volumes of decadent verse. Something in my head, just behind the forehead, makes me contract indescribably, giving me these pseudo-headaches. My left arm has an abysmally painful feeling of exhaustion. My entire body is a void, and during these hours not a trace of spirit is to be found in me. I'm wretched. I see no way out. People who commit suicide are accused of weakness, which is nonsense. What is the purpose of life if it doesn't have afternoons? Am I mentally ill? No; and yet the more I know that I'm not, the more certain is death. This year I've been on the best of terms with death. If tomorrow morning I don't wake, it'll be the most blissful thing that could happen. I would be able to account for my death. I know my task. I'm far sicker than I admit to the people close to me. They think I'm the picture of health. No one suspects that every afternoon I shiver as if in a fever. I'm totally sick. Nothing can help me. My first love *will* have to be my fate. One could deduce this.

There's an awful truth to the Kabbalistic doctrine of the Breaking of Vessels.[34]

June 20, 1918

Using Walter's rules, I've tried my hand at a critique of *Malte Laurids Brigge*.[35] Perhaps there will be more to say. Most certainly. [. . .]

Walter came by this afternoon for an hour. When I stepped outside for a moment, he took the opportunity to place a letter to me from Dora inside *The Jew.* The letter states something horrifying: that I don't know Walter at all. This killed me, for by saying this she negated the letter Walter wrote to me for my birthday.[36] I still don't know what I'll do. If I reply, the answer will have to be extraordinary. I want to write a sonnet to Stefan. I did so (an hour later)!!! Maybe I'll send it to them.

June 22, 1918

I'm weeping over the letters I'm writing. If this isn't terrible, I don't know what is. This must astonish Meta, Escha, Leni Czapski, and everyone else.[37] Thank God I'll never have to reread them. Brentano acts as if he were the devil's uncle, which is in fact true: he's the son of Michael the archangel and of the devil's grandmother.

 I read the letter from the court preacher Sack to Schleiermacher (III, p. 227), but the one from Collenbusch to Kant is greater.[38] Schleiermacher's letters, the entire lot of them, are *extremely* tiresome.

June 23, 1918

Along with an anarchistic lustfulness, one of the common things I do during moments of total misery is to read famous people's letters. This happened back in March as well. I'm now reading Waitzen's *Caroline,* Schleiermacher's *Life in Letters,* and Novalis's *Letters.* Naturally, the only thing I'm looking for in these letters is the despair in the lives of these people. Nevertheless, I have no right to complain because it is my own demon that puts me in such danger and turns all of my laws into mockery. I could keep my silence. Who is forcing me to speak?

 On Friday I read aloud Agnon's *Torah Scribe*[39] to Walter and Dora. It was perhaps the tenth time I'd read it, and each time it grips me deeper, as I knew it would. At the first word I fell into such excitement that only with the utmost effort could I steady my voice, and I shivered as if being forced to kiss a girl. Maybe this is the reason I read it so well. The story's conclusion is in fact bad: Agnon has no right to employ a vision as the "climax," which is incapable of outdoing the reality of what came before. Walter and I discussed it for a long time afterwards. He considers the first two-thirds of the book among the greatest things he's ever heard. He said very correctly that if this story, *with* the conclusion, is so perfect, he doesn't understand why there's a Bible. We don't need the Bible. I told him about Agnon, and how unhappy he is, and how he really lives his pure life only within his books. I'm planning soon to write a short essay on him.

 Since yesterday the extremely beautiful weather is back. My gabled room is like a watchtower hovering over the world, and the world mirrors itself (but isn't reflected back) in my room. The wheat field below my windows shows me, every time afresh, what kind of richness and greatness there is in such a small and simple speck of nature. Now I know how profound and beautiful is the similarity between the sea and a wheat field blowing in the wind. The waves really do swell up onto one another, and there are moments when sound and a movement completely deceive me. I can stand at the window and look out for ages. Walter says in jest that I sit up here like a magician, producing weather with my strange brews. In a certain sense there is a kind of deep truth to what he says. I live up here above the grand life of a landscape. I cannot fathom what this landscape means to me. It is completely closed and unfolds itself—from a center point and source of a solid Order. The landscape is not lofty; it elevates. Houses sit only on the edges, pleasantly concealed or in the distance, like those in Gumlingen. Before me there are only fields, with the forest and mountains behind. The world ends there. There is no need for any other world. And yet I am in pain because I know that I will never be in the middle of this landscape, which is the real reason I never go out from here. I have yet to take a proper walk through the landscape, but I take it all in from up here. I fear for myself, or for the landscape. I know that once I go out in it, I will *have to* enter into its core, and I know that I *cannot* penetrate it. This would not heal me. The landscape would turn into something demonic for me. Its certainty, which is its greatness (everything is ordered in it, all the way to the smallest detail, to which one can only say "Amen"), would get lost in the wretchedness of my heart. My heart, which is an abyss, can swallow a lot. But I don't want the landscape to sink into it. I exist from the fact that the landscape is *outside* of me. Oh you mighty swindle of pantheism: how could I stand it being inside me? My life is first created through *distance;* distance is the only source of the laws; it is the law itself. Intermingling with the landscape is modernity's biggest and most horrid magical trick. It is aestheticism— the deep fear and murderous horror of distance, because distance could make demands. If I'm fused with it, the landscape makes no demands; it can be enjoyed. If nature and man become babble, it becomes possible to fabricate a sphere (an Experience) in which man and nature no longer co-relate but rather become one. The correlation is in fact the proper way. If I am in the landscape *(and I am ordered!!),* I am in its midst; I am the eternally near point where the landscape converges. We are in the relationship of existence. At the core of a landscape is the same as in all relationships: it is *genius.* I am the genius in a landscape. Does anyone understand what this means? It means that the desire to go into a landscape involves a colossal responsibility. It demands *dignity*.

Landscape belongs to the incalculably vital things that philosophers have given over into the hands of poets. (Writing a monograph on the landscape is among the ideas that Walter is always coming back to, as he wanted to do in Seeshaupt in 1916.) Before I can think about saying anything other than myths about nature and landscape, I'll first have to achieve clarity on the foundations of these Orders where distance takes place. And this is precisely what I want to see: a *Jew* going out into a landscape the same way the author of Psalms 104 did. My heart is overwhelmed each time I read it. Granted, genius is only the mythical counterpart to a demon. Still, even in a genius one must succeed in demonstrating, and with absolutely deep perception, how the messianic Time, or whatever one calls it, prepares itself through the genius. Something messianic must resound out from a lamentation of the landscape. The landscape's sense of Time must find a correlation in the Time of lamentation, and I haven't any doubts that the lamentation's Time is the highest of all orders of Time—it is where the messianic realm develops out of myth. *The statement "I exist" is always a lamentation.* The landscape also exists visually, and this is the reason for its lamentation. The landscape converges upon the genius, and its visage lets out a lament. Why? I don't know yet, but possibly because the genius is not yet in the landscape, or maybe because he rejects it. At some later point I'll know.

All sorts of things, many of them terrible, make me more certain than ever that I cannot have any friends. To take an honest look at my circumstances, none of these people with whom I have close ties is a friend. Heller is too good for me. Somehow, each time I look at him I feel something standing between us, preventing us from developing devotion and trust. And Walter? This is the real question. I think that only from afar can a person have an absolute relationship with him. Only in Jena did we have one, but now I'm full of doubts. With him I have to keep silent about almost everything that gives me fulfillment. One of the biggest blunders of my life was the letter in which I wrote about a preestablished harmony joining our two lives.[40] I can only say that I don't know where Walter is, he's just not where I am (this much I see); it only seems that he is. Are we going to commit some horrifying fraud one of these days by shockingly deceiving each other? [. . .] I came up with the idea for a "Ninety-five Theses on Judaism and Zionism" as a birthday present to Walter. It'll have to be reread in 25 years. I'm thrilled by the idea.

The following long letter to Heller is the first honest document from my present sojourn:

Dear Friend,

I can tell you openly the reasons for my reticence, if you haven't already guessed. I didn't want to write to you, of all people, until I could be fully open. Silence is better than writing a letter that would have inevitably given you a false impression of me. I should tell you directly why I was unable to speak frankly. Never before have I been in such desperate shape, inwardly, as in the period following my arrival here—or rather, in the first days after I began to come to grips with myself. Agreeable external circumstances allowed me to endure this all alone (which is the reason I haven't tried to establish contact with Erich Brauer, beyond a failed attempt during my first days here—I didn't want to irk him with all my misery). I see no one other than Walter Benjamin and his wife. I sit completely withdrawn in my attic room above the fields—like Agnon's Torah scribe, minus his peace of mind. For weeks I have feared the worst, and I feel crushed by a tormenting uncertainty about whether my recovery, obtained through Herculean efforts and at the most exacting price, will prove permanent. Here, of course, I can do whatever I want: I can work, think, take walks, or cry. And I can assure you that I have made particularly intense and despairing use of the first two. I also know quite well that I would be defenseless if my genius (I cannot use a lesser word for it) were to let me down. I now live as I did last summer, which is all the more terrifying since I must now fend off real, not feigned, madness. The only thing that keeps me going, in a grand and masterful way, is the indescribably magnificent landscape around me here. To show it my gratitude, I have invested my best efforts in philosophically coming to grips with the essence of a landscape, an undertaking that for me seems to have enormous value. If all goes well, I'll end it with a commentary on Psalm 104 you will find astounding. [. . .]

Sometimes I start to think that Friedrich Nietzsche is the only one in modern times who has said anything substantial about ethics. Until now I've read very little of his, and no doubt the worst thing he ever wrote *(Zarathustra)*. [. . .]

I've been thinking a lot about the metaphysics of time in Judaism, and in a related manner to lamentations. As before, a treatment of lamentations is something I'm really eager to pursue. One day perhaps an essay on lamentations will be one of my first large works. There's no end to the things that can be said about this topic, things of the greatest imaginable importance, and it may be that no one until now has bothered with it. Hebrew grammar, Jewish history, the prophets, and encompassing them all, the Torah: these are my quarries. And in them I'm working hard.

I argue the following theses (there are not yet 95 of them):[41]

(1) The time of Wav ha-Hippuch is the messianic Time.
(2) The conception of time in Judaism is the eternal present.
(3) Evil has no history (yes! Evil belongs in the here and now!!).
(4) The time of lamentations is the highest of all temporal orders.

O my friend, I have a ton of stuff like this, but I haven't pulled them out of thin air. There is no need for you to consider me crazy, and I thought such thoughts already at a time when I wasn't yet so miserable. If you only give it some thought, you'll understand all of this. [. . .]

June 24, 1918

I'm starting to intuit and understand that accompanying any final philosophy must be a very decisive insight into the art of poetry. In reading the letters of the Romantics, I often don't know if one should first write an apology or a polemic. At any rate, both are necessary. [. . .]

The greatest of all poems ever directed at man is surely Hölderlin's "To Landauer."[42] Landauer can live forever because he has become Revelation through this poem. No poem can ever be quieter, greater, and holier. Nor does it contain one single word that isn't *absolute*.

Observed from the totality of its idea, Novalis's "fragment" on "Europe or Christianity" is entirely repellent, for it somehow contains the typically Buberian *false teaching*. [. . .] Novalis was in fact *modern,* though like all the Romantics he was purer. While modern, his false teaching is not immoral. This afternoon, after writing this, I spoke about it with Walter, who liked it a lot and added a few good points. He said that the

Romantics did not fall into what affects us so much: namely, the opposition between the chimerical and the ordered, but within it is still pure chaos. Romanticism is the chaos that we must first bring to creation. One should not be surprised that the Romantics didn't understand one another. The personal relationships in their lives were completely disorderly. They only had letters, but failed in conversation. Their literary public was not the basically dubious thing that it's turned into today, but was absolute. Their lives were essentially lived out in *this public:* they are to be found in what they published. This is the reason they misunderstood one another. Friedrich Schlegel and Novalis had absolutely nothing to do with each other. Schlegel was basically a philosopher with an inkling of method, whereas Novalis had nothing comparable to offer. [. . .]

June 25, 1918

Today the Jüdischer Verlag sent me a free copy of Agnon.[43] I'm elated. If it were rebound I could possibly give it to Walter as a birthday gift. It would make a very lovely gift.

I'm reading a few poems by Hölderlin.

Many people are ingenious but there is only one genius. I'm noticing with great irritation that I express many things on Wally's[44] level of kitsch. The way I articulate genuinely deep things takes the life out of them. One could easily confuse me with Buber. This still clings tightly to me, and only the strictest self-discipline can defend me against it. Walter could be for me the most luminous example: nothing of the like ever comes out of him. His view of things can't lead him astray because he always and mercilessly goes directly to their core, *forcing* them into order. Language is his only great seductress, though I'm far too unclear about this to put it into words rationally. It is a seduction of a very special sort and has nothing in common with the run-of-the-mill seduction.

So what's Walter really up to now? What kind of picture does his existence offer to the person who can see it? From the outside, he's a man fanatically closed off, a man who works fanatically in creating the foundation for a fanatical system. Basically, he's *entirely* invisible, though he has opened himself up to me more than to anyone else who knows him. When all is said and done, his entire life is nothing more than one massive apology for his dead friend. Everything he does is nothing more than methodically taking the dark central point created by their friendship and lifting it up into *absolute* clarity. Every word he says about this genius proves this and also reveals his final intention: to make an accounting of himself to someone who is dead. I don't believe that since the prophets there has ever lived a man who has brought such a massive responsibility to completion. All of this occurs in utter invisibility. Instead of communicating himself, Walter insists that everyone sees him, even though he hides himself. His method is completely unique. I can't put it any other way than the method of Revelation. With him this method does not merely appear at small stretches of time, but *absolutely* rules the sphere of his existence. Surely no one since Lao-tzu has lived this way. He works as few people ever have. But it is precisely his labor that must be understood in the most profound context. There is something in Walter that is borderless, transcending all order, and that, by employing every effort, tries to order his work. Indeed, this "something" is the completely anonymous quality legitimizing Walter's work. For me, all of this is revealed in his marriage with Dora, which is the deducible permanence of this anonymity. Strictly speaking, I can't call this love because in this relationship, properly understood, love is totally secondary. Marriage enables him to bear up under this life of responsibility by turning anonymity into his betrothed. Thus is his marriage; this is what makes it into the miracle that—as an absolute—gives his life content. Compared to this man, one of these days Goethe and Plato will entirely fade into the background. People will understand his life to be a miracle in need of research (*if* they ever begin to understand him, which is something he'll quite possibly never experience himself); and to research his life means to grow silent. Walter's biography will only be able to be passed down; recording it would forge chains that would make people's life so impossible that, in a ferocious revolution, they might destroy his work and everything associated with it. [. . .]

June 26, 1918

[. . .] Kleist's *Michael Kohlhaas*[45] is without question one of the greatest pieces of prose German literature possesses. One could never meet a more complete purity of language, enormous linguistic constancy, chastity, and restfulness—even during the most stupendous occurrences where heaven and hell are called into play. What is it about Kleist's style that makes it so great? I find the metaphysical center of his style in the purity of *interpretation*. Language as absolute essence has developed itself in pure objectivity so it could fulfill its innermost laws. In language, the concurrence of "action" *must* be necessary. What radiantly stirs wonderment in the reader of this story is the *total legitimacy* of every circumstance and word. The story's language transcends time; it is *Kairos*.[46] Only in the linguistic Orders can there be silence. This story isn't beautiful, for *only* evil is beautiful—only evil is somehow incomplete and has not become a totality. But this story is absolutely *legitimate*. Silence may be necessary in something beautiful, while it is such an integral part of that which is legitimate that it cannot be sought out in any one point. The words—because they keep their *source* chaste—no longer have any limits: they do not border on silence because silence is built into the continuity. The *supremely* great text—the Bible, Dostoyevsky, or in this case von Kleist—is never beautiful. The law, however, *is*. Language and action meet in laws. The *law* is the mother's womb that gives birth to greatness.

Something great, something unconditionally legitimate in language, *has to be* historical. That Kleist fully measures up to this final standard means that no one will ever overtake him. The goal of prose is to make history operate from within language. Kleist and Agnon are in certain ways fabulously related.

June 28, 1918

The future hovers over my nights like the womb of birth. Perhaps only poetry, of which I am unworthy, can describe what the nights are for me. I don't have dreams. And yet in the inexpressible night I lead a life of my own reality. I'm beginning to understand what the night means to those who dream. But this is the gaping abyss, for night's category of time is not messianic. We are demons during the night. Messianic night is the center of the Time we are longing for. The darkness of night transforms us; and if the demonic forces knew something about Revelation, they would perfect it at night. But God reveals himself during the day, and therefore we are nocturnal demons: only the rays of Revelation renew the day. Who has never been defenseless at night? Landscape refuses to provide protection. He who knows love only out of desire is at the mercy of the demons, which turn us into demons during the night. Night is the Time of demons, just as the pale dusk is that of ghosts. The silence of night is an ambiguous tongue. The deepest source of power that the demonic has over us is the fact that we all must be renewed during the *night*. Only blind people renew themselves during the day, just as they alone see the messianic Time. Why does Hebrew call messianic Time "the days of the Messiah"? This is the reason the prophets speak of the light of the moon and the sun, light that has been brought together because it is demonic.

The new heaven is a heaven without night. As Walter says, the new creation is the Time that emerges at the end of all times.

Among the most profound tasks of cosmology is surely the metaphysical interpretation of *clouds*. What do clouds mean? I don't have a clue.

Diaries are written at night, making them demonic. What is needed with a diary is to rush quickly past the night, to fight it, to keep silent. At night, do we want to learn to see history and to describe our own history? The Jew overcomes the night in two ways: he transforms it into a time of lamentation and of learning Torah, just as during the day. Psalm 134.[47] [. . .]

Recently Walter and I have gotten along quite well. The reason for this is no doubt that I've found a place from which I can be against him, silently with my inner concerns. He doesn't suspect a thing, and everything's okay. Those scenes were essentially nothing more than moments in which he saw aspects of my inner condition that weren't destined for him. He himself divulges things that are not against me. Our partnership consists in that each one *tacitly* understands and honors the other's silence. [. . .]

I've written the Ninety-five Theses. I'm not happy with them.[48]

This afternoon I was with Dora, and I wasn't happy with her in the least. I find that she makes common cause with the domestics in her house, and in a very repulsive way and from a very rude point of view. Besides this, her tone of voice is purest hypocrisy. It's sad for me to have to witness this. They have such a fear of daily life that they're more philistine than the philistines. They think the worst about everything— and then they pretend that it's a philistine who thinks this way, and one must take "care." This is all a fraud. Philistines would never come up with all the nonsense that Walter and Dora fantasize about them. Their life is a lie. This is a bitter truth, and regrettably I can't find a single word I would take back from this statement. *Yes,* their lives are even more mendacious than mine.

[. . .] It's midnight on an unspeakably lovely night of stars. The entire Milky Way stretches out before me. I just got back from Walter's. It was an enormous day for us. The evening finally proved to me how, after two months, he still *sees* me. I am the first person who has gotten to know the sonnets to Heinle. This evening he read twelve of the fifteen, and some are overwhelming. Of course, one can't say much after the first hearing, but when it comes to the essential points—being something entirely original—maybe I'll always be at a loss for words. I absolutely understand what Walter said afterwards: that this work, which he has labored on for three years, was and remains the reason for his complete loneliness, also toward me. He said he could have a connection only with people with whom he can discuss this. I'm the first person to learn about it. The sonnets are Revelations. Afterwards Walter spoke a bit about Heinle and his brother, and about his literary estate. I will get to know a lot about all this. As he explained, he had waited so long to present the sonnets to me because one would have to speak for days to give me a foundation for understanding the things that followed after Heinle's death. I *see* him *void of images.*

[. . .] If I'm already a total madman, I might as well translate my own sonnets into Hebrew. Today I made at least a kind of fragment of it.

I've started to read a few essays in Freud's *Yearbooks,*[49] but I'll stop soon, otherwise I'll immediately slip into a whirlpool of identification, and in the deepest sense. Psychoanalysis is a dreadful thing; it's pointless to contradict theoretically because its results are correct, and then you'll have to look for a better foundation. [. . .] My dealings with psychoanalysis will, I hope, be short-lived. [. . .]

While in Bern this morning, Walter and I stumbled across the first volume of Bertuch's unbelievably beautiful picture book for children—for ten franks.[50] Walter was totally enraptured.

      Silly Verse (Or a Philosophical Alphabet . . .)

          On the pasture lives a man that you
          See yonder with his wife

> Walter Benjamin arrives
> And you tip your hat [. . .]
> A few people play Go [. . .]
> And blow lightly like the snow.
> The continuity of his system
> Seems for him all that is clever.

Maybe an entire alphabet will grow out of this, a culture of silliness. After two and a half years of promises, I finally got Walter and Dora to teach me to play Go. It's in fact a delightful game.

July 7, 1918

With a clear and precise purpose in mind, I wrote detailed letters to Werner Kraft, Toni Halle, and Werner, mainly because of Borchardt and above all Kraus.[51] Two of these letters bear stigmata from a man who has purchased his peace of mind with the certainty of suicide. I now know unimaginable things since death has become my bedfellow. I am restful, but dead. Just a nudge and *I'll also* become a ghost, and Walter will turn away from me in horror. This will be the signal for my death (not my death but my dying!).

July 14, 1918

[. . .] *Metaphysics is theory in its legitimate conjunctive voice.* This is the best definition I've been able to come up with. It says it all.

Over the last few days, particularly in Gstaad, I've read a lot of Cahan's poetry, and I couldn't help but detect a total negation and absence of any meaning.[52] It's absolute emptiness. One will have to conjure up a Hebrew critic who will banish all of this trashy literature springing up these days. To do so requires being able to write a proper, rigorous, and objective Hebrew prose. This and not lyric poetry is what you, Gerhard Scholem, have to learn.

July 15, 1918

Today is Walter's birthday. I presented him with Agnon and *Der grüne Heinrich,* and then I gave him the sonnet "Mournful One, Near Me Yet Always in Hiding."[53] Dora told me he was delighted with it. I had the "alphabet" with me when I came at 5 o'clock.[54] To be brutally frank, I feel that birthday parties like this are decadent. Oh Lord, being someone who strives to create a new and austere life of self-denial, I am forced to witness with my own eyes how *the only life* around me lived metaphysically—and this life is great, in every sense of the word—carries within it an element of decadence, and in terrifying proportions. However difficult it is to determine, there is a certain boundary in one's conduct of life that decadence oversteps. Regrettably, Walter obviously oversteps it. *His* way of seeing books as binding and paper is something I'll never learn till my dying day: I deny there are legitimate metaphysical insights to be had here. Walter has also a heap of illegitimate knowledge. And one can't change him; on the contrary, I only have to be on guard that in personal interaction *this* region of his does not rub off on me. For me, self-denial has not yet become a decadent aesthete's slogan for the education of higher forms of lust, but instead continues being God's demand to erect a true Jewish life. Walter's life, which also seeks to be a life of the Teaching—of Torah for its own sake—is in grave danger because of his insufficient self-denial. Buber too sits in a well-furnished room and babbles. I don't mean that Walter is to be confused with Buber—yet this is precisely the danger. [. . .]

W.B.

Mournful one, near to me yet always in hiding
Only your vocation holds you close to life
But you do not speak and the world is built
On your silence. Mourning is the eternal days

You greet. And that you have not yet died
Is a miracle that lies beyond my reach.
You simply are. And from your deep quiet
Arises the question that binds us, each to each.

You who stood by me during my difficult days
Are far from me who took you as his estate.
I must carry what I feel within me in silence.
For what you are going through is so great
That any words I find to cast it in
Would prove impure. Speech is thus a sin.[55]

July 21, 1918

I am so completely paralyzed I still don't know what to do. By no means can I be around them as long as Dora doesn't retract what she did. In the most unheard-of manner, she refused to shake my hand, and she treated me shamelessly. Why? I arrived at 5 o'clock to read Cohen with Walter. They were indisposed (at five o'clock!!!) and told me to go into the garden. I said I had work to do and didn't want to go into the garden. Thereupon she became agitated. Being innocent in this case—which is certainly a rarity!—I must insist on speaking about it. As never before, I feel myself totally altered. I had never thought Dora capable of such an affront against me. Now it has happened, and I can't but behave as clearly and precisely as the matter requires.

July 22, 1918

Yesterday evening I went to them, and over the course of a long conversation we traced the problem back to its roots. The Hasidic expression for a mystical act is really unusually profound: one approaches a thing *"mamtik be-shorosho"*—one brings sweetness to its roots. This is exactly what we did.

In my present philological studies of Isaiah in Gesenius and Duhm,[56] I'm gradually starting to understand the meaning of philology in a deep and historical sense. I've asked myself again and again what has happened to the philological work of entire centuries, which today goes entirely unmentioned. [. . .] Now I understand: philology is among the most precise examples of the proper conception of *Tradition*. The labor of an entire generation is condensed into a handful of sentences, which then form the basis for the next generation of work. Seemingly forgotten, previous labors vanish into this new foundation, where they remain vital. In Duhm, for instance, Vitringa[57] doesn't show up at all, and yet there is a clear, mystical line—in a good and deep sense—between them. This is extraordinarily profound. Just as Friedrich Schlegel once realized, in this way philology legitimizes itself in the highest possible degree as a secret science. Now I realize that the metaphysically diverse role of Tradition is a central criterion for the mathematical and historical sciences: precisely considered, Jewish Tradition is the unity of both. Jewish tradition is historical and yet maintains itself as if it were mathematical. [. . .]

July 23, 1918

[. . .] I wrote a long letter to Escha.[58] I can't deny that the uniqueness of my language, once absorbed into ordinary minds, runs the danger of making a person miserable, and in the worst sense of the word. The tradition of a way of life is a very difficult subject—and if nothing else, this is basically the meaning of Zionism. My first attempts at formulating this way of life run the risk of being not Revelations but translations, and in this case the disaster would indeed occur. If then someone gets it into his head to be my friend, and I'm not responsible enough to either turn him away or give him the proper transmission (which is spoken out in Revelations: or, as I like to say, as a legitimate commentary), he would torment himself through an infinite and unfruitful attempt at drawing near me (which *always* creates misunderstanding because it's impossible). He will try to approach me on a false plane, whereas this can only be done elsewhere. This is basically how Orthodoxy and dogmatism develop. Above all, it is here that my notion of renunciation comes into play. I don't expect an answer from most of the letters I write, and I hardly ever get one. With Escha it's different, for my intention with these letters is not to get a reply but to be swept up into her wordless silence, into her *love*. Her life, which I don't see, is her answer to my letters. A person has to love me in order to write a perfect letter, and he must at least be in love with me (in a good sense) to give me a reply. This is just the way it is. The only perfect letter I've ever received (I am still young) was the ten-liner from Walter.[59] My own letters are ruled absolutely by high mystical laws. In a precise sense, they are either love letters or letters that a priori can have no reply. I could come up with a theory for this. In sum, the metaphysics of letters is a subject unto itself. (Only to a very limited degree did I discuss this with Escha.)

It's been a month since I wrote to Heller and he hasn't written *me* even a single line in response. In a month I'll know *how* to interpret this silence. [. . .]

July 25, 1918

Isaiah says most clearly how one should relate to the World War: "You will get help only through repentance and silence" (Isaiah 30:15).

I have to reflect back on the past because I'm incapable of doing away with my own days of remembrance. Big or small, they come to me involuntarily; they are simply there. A year ago today I concluded my military career when I ended up in the military hospital's "psychopathic" ward. I left there as a human being, literally a *victor*. For once in my life, I tasted some victory. [. . .]

Since the end of the semester we've been reading Cohen for two hours daily. Cohen comes out with sentences containing real insight, just two hundred lines too late or in places where they don't belong. They come as side remarks, never with the sense that he has at last hit on something essential. [. . .]

Critique is mysticism: this is the most basic axiom behind Cohen's lack of scruples. To this enlightened generation, you can only deliver the truth (which is mysticism) wrapped in enlightened garb. This is also the way I do it. But in this case Cohen would have to profess himself to be a mystic, which is the *only* way the axiom is legitimate and profound. *His* critique is a mystification, not mysticism. In what has become a long letter, I've written to Wally some notes on the Talmudic style.[60]

July 26, 1918

[. . .] It's a petty-bourgeois fallacy that knowledge is there to disprove other people. Naturally the atheist may have a right to ask me about God, but I have an infinitely greater right not to answer him. A discussion lacking in resonance is a priori forbidden. [. . .]

July 30, 1918

[. . .] Ludwig Strauss sent me a copy of the George festschrift he put together with Schaeffer in the form of parodies.[61] This has put me in an uncomfortable position. Though I'm still laughing at every line in the book (not that it's good, but because its monumental historical blindness ends up mocking itself where it believes to be aiming at George), the book is among the most repulsive out there. I have to ask myself if I'll be able to have any more contact with this man. I'll have to bring all of this out in a letter, which greatly distresses me. The level at which both authors perform their parodies is the way someone could parody Gustav Falke.[62] It's utterly illegitimate. Besides, parody is an extremely dangerous undertaking with a double-edged sword. To be historical, jokes require an extraordinary freedom along with a high degree of historical, that is, messianic, insight—something Strauss cannot reveal because he flatly lacks it. The possibility of parodying a style (in its all-encompassing sense) requires overcoming it historically, and not being completely ignorant of it. That Strauss and Schaeffer don't do this is demonstrated most strikingly in their silence on the subject of George's madness. The silent omission of the most dangerous parts of the *Seventh Ring*, the *Star of Fraternity*, and *War*—even as elements in their satirical poetry—proves that it was never their intention (which alone could have given it legitimacy) to articulate or reject, even as a parody, the deeper Order behind George's insanity. Instead of this, they take flight into the arena that is occupied by every hack parodist and every schoolteacher who wishes to pour scorn on some poet: they try to empower George's most inalienable possessions. But they fail miserably. The point of view taken by a high school teacher (who looks at history as the history of literature and who regards himself to be modern because of the date of his birth) shows its entire repulsiveness in these poems. It is immoral drivel for Strauss to draw out the poison and yet not to reach insanity—because insanity still awaits him.

July 31, 1918

Today I finished Isaiah (I'm already familiar with Deutero-Isaiah), and at the conclusion I was thrown into a sweat by "The Song of Hezekiah."[63] Today, I don't think anyone can exactly pinpoint where serious research into this book should begin. This book is a completely locked-up palace. Marti[64] and Duhm have the wrong keys and unlock an entirely different hall from the one we legitimately desire. The simple truth is that the tradition of prophecy, which is nowhere to be found, will have to be discovered, even if we have to rediscover it from within ourselves. Somehow (and with full historical legitimacy) the prophetic tradition, *along* with its own historical tradition, were fully dissolved into the rabbinic order; that is to say, they have been transformed within this Order, just as the philological tradition of a problem turns up in the history of science. To be passed down, tradition must be rediscovered because it has been kept silent. It has been forgotten by a generation not able to keep quiet. The disaster and misery of Jewish history is that the silent tradition was lost the moment men forgot how to be still. It's lost not in language but in that abyss of forgetfulness where it awaits us—who are the ones who shall retrieve it. [. . .]

Jiskor[65] is immoral chiefly because it is translated (be it into German or English) and propagated as a political tool. It may be that the dead in this book were true Zionists; they kept silent. But now someone takes them and presents them to Europe, along with the bill. Worst of all is that the book was published with their pictures, which is the most shameless violation of the book's anonymity. [. . .] An assassination is taking place here. Literature on colonization can be ethical, even when dealing with death,

but no picture of *any* kind must appear. An image, understood compre-
hensively, is the metaphysical Order one implies (or rather excludes)
when speaking of anonymity. The dead, who are neither metaphors nor
symbols, also have no image. Legitimately, only one thing is possible for
them: a notice, an announcement, a report. An image is idol worship, and
here it takes on the form of the animistic treatment of the deceased. In
the larger scheme of things, the Zionist who dies enters into our tradition; for us, his image is forbidden because it belongs to the sphere that
permits no propaganda. What is transmitted is the report. This book is
impure in every sphere because it can't maintain itself in any way. It isn't
symbolic, despite the efforts of Alexander and others; nor is it realistic.
Instead, it is an attempt to invoke a magical force we are duty bound to
turn away from. This book wants to enable political magic, and in the
same way it has arisen, in its German form, out of a conspiracy of political mysticism. It may be that the lives of the deceased can justify the violence they employed. A book about these lives, however, written in a foreign language and for people who haven't lifted a finger themselves,
discredits it and publicly disgraces something that, if transmitted secretly,
might have revolutionary power. Zionism undermines itself by turning something that cannot be literature—because it was and is an oral
Teaching—into literature, and by withholding from literature what belongs to it: the truth of the idea. More than other books, *Jiskor* will un-
leash false enthusiasm; among the youth it will ignite a Jewish spirit of
the Wild West. [. . .]

August 1, 1918

The letters of Caroline expose the absolute difference between the Romantics' conception of the Order of life and what's going on today.[66]
[. . .] This woman's life was without tradition, even where it is gifted
with genius. In the aristocracy of the Romantics there was (namely, in
their lives) something of the upward mobility of the ennobled bourgeoisie. Their work ennobled them; they were the parvenus of their own
work. Their work was not the tradition they left behind but the tradition
they attached themselves to. It had to be the medium of their lives, but it
also hindered them from ultimate historical insight. When the Romantics began their struggle, they reduced to a minimum their regime of
daily life because this was the only way a maximum of public influence

could be historically established and attained. The same goes for Kant. Establishing a new foundation for experience required an experience with zero value. To elevate daily life—"sweetening it at its roots"[67]—required the Romantics to find and lead a life free of any independent content. This life had only literature. Dorothy seems to be the only one here with a new position. It is as if she, in stark contrast to Caroline, was aware of the existence of a *central* sphere of a personal life as the source of tradition (and not only a sphere with mistresses, though one didn't speak of such things). Somehow, the Judaism at work in Dorothy had an unbelievable strength. This "somehow" doubtless needs more precise definition. [. . .]

I wrote Ludwig Strauss an open letter on parody. It was merciless— and I didn't send it. (The letter I sent was silent about the entire affair.)[68] I feel greatly relieved at having settled matters with this unsent letter. Today it's been four years, though every word said on the subject is wasted. I am an apocalyptic man, and I live in peace. [. . .]

NOTEBOOK 3

The Zenith and Its Surroundings: Materials from the Region of Historical Astronomy

October 7–December 1918

My memories are the deep foundations from which I dispense prophecies on my future life.

—Diary entry from December 16, 1918

October 7, 1918

I no longer need to leap into loneliness; it has recently become obvious that I'm already there. All my few relationships here are now what they were fated to become, and I live outside of them. The seven weeks I lived with Erich Brauer in Adelboden began with enormous convulsions, followed by a dreadfully tragic drama that was largely played out in silence. We are so far apart that no one can say when and if anything fruitful will ever develop. For myself, I am not in a position to squander relationships in this way. [. . .] In the inner region of my life, I must draw the curtains shut around my loneliness, so I can overcome the convulsions that are soon to come (and that are probably my lot in life). I'm now passionately longing for what Agnon once described to Strauss as a "living word." If only Escha were here, or some other complete human being.

For me, the days in Böningen with Walter and Dora were far, far more torturous than all the weeks in Adelboden. I'm tortured by the entire relationship. Have Walter and Dora found out something about me? Or do I only see things differently now? Certainly it can't continue being so dreadful. I'll know this coming month what will have to happen. They have changed a lot in their behavior, very much to their disadvantage. The hours we spent together were for me horrific. On a long walk along the lake, to which they went out of their way to invite me, they bickered the entire time over where to live after Walter finishes his doctorate. It didn't occur to them how agonizing it was for me to be a part of this. Sometimes they treat me like a butler. And the love scenes that always follow only multiply this torment exponentially. Worst of all, there is the lurking danger that I'll completely lose my faith in Walter's purity in everyday life. He frequently seems to lack what one calls honesty. The dishonesty of his "practical" advice *enrages* me, and this must have deep roots. Above all, Dora stands between us. I *must,* and will, force a discussion with her. I simply can't interact with her without bringing up things we should talk about. She says I don't love her. But here I must say that I have loved her unendingly, boundlessly. But now the sun has set. Why? Because I didn't expect daily life with them to be like this. If she could prove to me that this isn't so, I'd always love her. Dora's a cynic. I shock myself by uttering this truth. I had believed I could tell her everything— but I said nothing, and I will say nothing. They don't know, but I do, that over the past three years I've always done the opposite of what they've advised me, especially with the most vital things. *Only* thus have I managed to do well. They are not Zionists, not yet. (It's forbidden to put down in writing anything more that this.) I'm alone, and in this loneliness I will be able to do ultimate work. Everyone can shun me as long as I have no cause to shun myself. [. . .]

October 9, 1918

[. . .] Today I went to Marzili[69] for the first time with Dora. It was cordial enough, perhaps because it was carefully harmless. She has become *even more* guarded than I.

On instruction from Agnon, Wally suggested in a letter today that I publish the sonnets.[70] To this suggestion, I have the following to say:

I can't. I am not mature enough to write in Hebrew, a language that I believe myself to be in the most legitimate stage of understanding and grasping. When I write poems in German (this happens only when I'm in absolute misery, overcome by the power of lamentation that rises up above the death—and therefore immortality—of the rays of light illuminating my youth), I do so in the Hebrew spirit. I don't want to be a part of German literature, except as a translator of the Bible. I could go on forever about Agnon's book; it continues nearly to defeat me, and I've spoken so little about it because I'm afraid of saying too much. The center of Torah—the place from which this book shines forth—is something I can only pass down in silence. These sonnets of mine are the froth left over from a time of lamentation, and their language can only be shared and made accessible to friends. I may not know him, but Agnon is my friend (even if I won't be his), and I don't dare offer him my thoughts on the book. His style, which I sense is fabulously related to mine (if it's not completely silly to say so), is proof of this. The foundation enabling his language (by which I mean his Hebrew) is visible to me, even if I still don't grasp it because of my youth and because I'm also carrying in me the abysmal chaos from the lost years of my childhood. I'd like to tell Agnon that I *know* how right he is when he says no one here really and truly understands him. Agnon's work, which is Order, looms over the chaos of German Jewry in infinite absence and rejection. Even the best among us have only begun the journey. All hail Agnon! But who will do the cheering? And from what sort of idiotic sphere? Agnon can't be happy with this Reichert[71] and [Jakob] Lubmann, and especially not with the aesthetes whose reverential distance—which is required from us even if we're standing in the center of a book—has become a pallid intermixture and violation of boundaries. As for Buber, I have nothing more to add. Jewish though he may be, he is nevertheless modern. This is a brute fact. Maybe one of these days I'll be in Agnon's camp. At least I know what I'm lacking. [. . .]

October 12, 1918

In the deepest, most literal sense, youth is a *dor tahpukhot*, a generation full of absurdities and perversions. This is the meaning of *tahpukha*. I've composed a poem today, which if someone were to read it someday he'd consider the work of a complete lunatic. Yet it's the profoundest thing I've ever written: it's absolutely clear.

October 13, 1918

The people next door just hit a child, a small ten-year-old. It's horrible to have to hear this. I notice for the first time how foreign this type of human being is to me. How can anyone be so beastly? It bothers me. I wouldn't hit a child. I've begun to read Wassermann's *The Little Goose-Man*.[72]

I've learned silence over the past six months. An enormous abyss hides away in the austerity of form. Sometimes things become so difficult that I think longingly about death. I live an unworldly life, though I often ask myself if I'm still too worldly. I've noticed this summer how I live in music. No one understands me; least of all do I understand myself. Out from me the darkness beams a great law, and I know I'm a conduit. I thank Grete for everything. If I were to die tonight, I'd die thinking about her. I think about her day and night. Thoughts like these have made me good. I've rejected greatness. This is the only thing I can say to God in my favor. I'm tormented by the symbolism of names in *The Little Goose-Man*. [. . .].

October 14, 1918

Reigning over me is an ineffable power. I'm once again morose around other people. I know some sort of decision has been made within me. I don't know what the decision is, and yet from the start I've sworn allegiance to it. I couldn't keep the Wassermann book in the house even a second after finishing it: an indescribable force compelled me to return it to Loni. I was glad she wasn't home. From the moment I saw her after my return I haven't been able to socialize with her. She's too pretty and too groundless. We would only sit together and cry our eyes out, recounting tales of woe. I avoid her. I keep away from everybody. I also haven't looked up Walter, though I know he's here. [. . .]

[. . .] I hope I've come back together with Walter. Too much time has passed since we've *talked* things out. For two evenings now we've been together till late, and it's been *very* beautiful. As I left yesterday evening, he shook my hand with greater warmth than at any time in the recent past. We must—and we can—discuss more serious concerns. Through his speech I am caught up ever more deeply in our silence. Last night we began by discussing *The Little Goose-Man* before moving on to his dissertation. [. . .]

I was with Loni again last night. She's begun thawing out. Together with Brauer, this evening I was invited to Hemerdinger's. Everyone was most friendly. They talked about the day's breaking news: Ludendorff's resignation.[73] Throughout the world people are wondering if the Kaiser will abdicate. [. . .] The fall now is unspeakably beautiful. In only three minutes I'm in the most beautiful fall woods.

Walter and Dora were at my house yesterday. It was quite nice. In the evening, I went with them to Marzili. There we had a long discussion of the Ten Commandments and the meaning of laws in the Torah. I read aloud my "Notes on Justice."[74] Walter was very pleased. Dora asked whether one is allowed to transgress the laws, which is a very important point, and I managed to offer them a lot of answers and to elaborate Jewish concepts. Afterwards we talked about his dissertation, its introduction and conclusion.[75]

Last night Brauer and I went over to Walter and Dora's, and the gruesome debacle that ensued—which I had never imagined possible—showed just how dimwitted Brauer is. Walter failed miserably in his desperate efforts to engage Brauer in conversation. Sitting silently and stupidly on his corner sofa, Brauer was the picture of desolation. I can only blame myself for always building him up far too much, which has only compromised my good judgment. The planetary chasm separating him from Grete's natural elegance is horrifying. In the end, Walter ignored him altogether (which is something he otherwise never does, in fact, he thinks it's wrong to do so), and spoke to me about our common interests. As the final sign of our failed visit and somewhat to cover up the guest's insipidity, Walter started clowning around. The evening was purest torment for me, and I'll never again initiate or support another like it. [. . .] The only impression Brauer made (which is unfortunately the way he is) was of emptiness. A tacit agreement kept us from mentioning his name during the five hours I was with Walter. [. . .]

Out of shame, I didn't say a word the entire time on the way home with Brauer. He must have known what I was thinking. This evening Dora came down with the flu. It was heartrending to see Walter before the doctor arrived. He asked me to stay for dinner till the doctor arrived. She's not yet in any danger; she only has a high fever, though both of us are quite frightened and worried. It was obvious—I heard it in everything he said—that Walter thought only about death and dying. That misfortune could befall Dora during the spring of her life is simply unimaginable. [. . .]

November 5, 1918

Around five o'clock in the afternoon I went to Walter's to play chess. Dora was much better, and we talked through the open door. Walter was very nice. Following his self-inflicted defeat, he read aloud from a few fabulous sonnets, and all was well. I was supposed to eat dinner with him. At eight o'clock he went into Dora's bedroom, and a short time later a terrible row broke out—I have no idea over what, which unfortunately is often the case. But this evening it was particularly torturous. At first I continued to sit in the next room, then I felt ashamed to be a witness to this. I went downstairs. Normally, everything's fine after a short time, and Walter comes after me. Not this evening. I sat for forty-five minutes in the dining room. I didn't want to eat alone while they argued upstairs, and so after Walter didn't respond to the maid's knocking, I left without dinner. It grieves me that such scenes are so frequent in a marriage like theirs. I am the only witness, which is absolute torture for me. What do they have together? Why the spasmodic running around? The screaming? The mood in the house is awful when they fight. The maid doesn't dare venture out of the kitchen; the soup gets cold; and you just hear Walter's excited steps upstairs. Finally, you're overcome with shame. Somehow they have no consideration at all for me, but neither do I demand it. I'd never say a word about it. It just tortures me that they pay no attention to me. After all, I'm no eunuch they can strip naked in front of, nor would they do so in front of anyone else. So I sat senselessly for two hours, as I really wanted to leave after the chess game. If it hadn't been for the stirring sonnet ringing out in me, I would have despaired. [. . .]

November 9, 1918

There is a general strike throughout Switzerland,[76] and Bern has taken on a strange appearance. Revolution has arrived in Germany; everything is happening with lightning speed. The armistice will be signed the day after tomorrow. [. . .]

Both yesterday and today I was at Walter's. It was beautiful. After six months of life together this relationship, the most decisive of my life (at least with another man), has been revealed to me in its purest light. I've written a lot of nonsense about this relationship, none of which is basically true—because one can only be silent about it. The sonnet I wrote for his birthday is the only time I've ventured into language. I'm again beginning to have an inexpressible love for Dora. I'm glad I'll spend my birthday with them. [. . .]

November 10, 1918

[. . .] It's now been a year since my final release from the military, and in the meantime I haven't become more demented, despite my "incurable" condition. It's nearly immoral to waste superfluous thoughts on this. Given the current situation, it is entirely uncertain when I'll be heading back to Germany: maybe soon, maybe in six months. I want to go to Göttingen—but will Escha be able to go? Who knows if anyone will be able to study at all? One will have to consider being one of the first immigrants to Palestine.

Four years ago we insisted on being revolutionary. Maybe something more is in play here: perhaps the hour has come when the German nation (of which I'm not a part) may and must let out a *scream*. Yet the revolutionary life I ascribe to and lead has an altogether different basis. The deepest spiritual foundations of the German revolution—which has just begun, but surely won't end on a messianic note—are still hidden and unknown. An endless intermingling prevents the pure tones of this revolution from ringing forth. I can only begin in silence. For years, Karl Liebknecht was just this kind of truly historical and invisible force. But we have an infinitely difficult path to follow. At the time when I joined the opposition circle in Neuköln I still lacked the central concept—that of judgment—now ordering my life. Now I am prosecutor, witness, and verdict. (This is also the life of the Russian revolutionary, and it is also *our* task to execute justice.) The execution of the Zionist idea through the revolutionary life must include these three; it has to be their unity. The magic of our lives must be established in penetration, transformation, and unity. To do all this and *yet* be righteous is the *enormously* difficult task set before us. Only *entirely* pure people can develop this unity. Only this unity can guarantee the purity of theory we so deeply need. Only where life has become a divine judgment can knowledge enter the pure sphere of theory. Justice is the knowledge of God's judgment. For Jews, the sole aims of the revolutionary life are the reestablishment of the eternal building (to quote Bialik's song) and the Orders of Jewish life.

This afternoon I was with Walter. I went to Loni's afterwards. [. . .]

November 13, 1918

[. . .] The difference between my attitude toward the war and the revolution is this: while participating in neither, with the war I turned away, and with the revolution I'm looking on. This needs to be understood in every nuance. I take this revolution into my field of vision. The basic difference between socialism and anarchism (which is the first step on the road to theocracy) is now clear.

November 18, 1918

Every day last week I was at Walter's, who has also come down with the flu. He's not doing well. The nervous exhaustion and excitement brought on by the revolution are being discharged through an ongoing reaction that will last for a while. We are now like *one* family: I am beyond all doubts. [. . .]

November 21, 1918

Yesterday for the first time I heard Fräulein Tumarkin, the local professor of philosophy, pretend to give a treatment of "idealism."[77] It was the most miserable event I've witnessed in ages. What came out most sinisterly was the total abomination and demonic overheating of a woman perverted by "science." She lectured with banal newspaper babble, which was incessant and basically employed as *argumentatio ad hominem*. A common slut is a purer manifestation of femininity. I don't fathom how girls can go to such a lecture, where they must feel ashamed to see the demon of their future, of their entire perverted lives, on display before them. Enough is enough. [. . .]

Evenings. I've known Escha for nine months now. While I was really with her for just three weeks in Heidelberg, and afterwards one day before my trip to Jena, she's my only hope. After returning from Walter's, I got my first reply from her with a "Du." I was just as excited as my first kiss. I calmed down with the restful certainty that I'll be good with Escha. I want her to come to me in Switzerland, even if with the difficulties now there's not much of a prospect for this. We will probably meet sooner in Germany. [. . .]

November 23, 1918

As the Hasidim famously say, all journeys have an esoteric meaning. What about the letters one writes? Isn't every line I've written Grete, Meta, and Escha esoteric?

There is no doubt that when I arrived at Walter's this afternoon I had the best of intentions and feelings. But I'm speechless at an entirely unprovoked explosion over some books he had lent Loni. I cannot tolerate this hysteria. In a tone of voice that was hurtful in the extreme, he said: "Once and for all, I want you to return the books immediately." A dreadful abyss opened up inside me. I will hold my silence and say nothing. I quietly lament the nonsense of a true friendship that takes on concrete form only through such things. I protest against a world whose most noble emissaries use hysteria as their instrument of despotism. [. . .]

November 25, 1918

I was at Hemerdinger's yesterday evening. I didn't go to Walter's, an inner resistance having prevented me. In the evening I reread Escha's letters from the past several months. They are irrefutable: they are directed at the one thing looming ahead of us. One letter is more puzzling than the next, and yet they contain no riddles. She has to love me if she writes this way. [. . .]

November 26, 1918

Grete arrived this evening. Erich asked me to go with him to pick her up, but I naturally declined by saying she would want to be with him alone, as they hadn't seen each other in nine months, which was of course just an excuse. I don't think it makes any sense to get mixed up in an insipid conversation on this first evening, and without her prior knowledge, like an invasion. This sort of welcoming hubbub isn't for me. I told Erich I'll be done at the university at nine A.M., and if she wants to greet me she can do it there. Nevertheless, in the evening I was so restless and unable to study that I went over to Loni's, where I had the best of luck: the seamstress was there, so I could sit for ninety minutes without saying a word. It was simply impossible for me to have gone to Walter and Dora's. Now I am once again alone and relaxed. [. . .]

December 1, 1918

Since Wednesday—today is Sunday—I've been with Grete, both alone and together with Erich. Basically, it's over. We had our first rendezvous on Thursday. I held my tongue about important things; I only challenged her absolutely wrongheaded notions on how I've changed my thinking about her. Of course, the details of our discussions can't be written down—I only mention this here as the foundation of my silence—for the simple reason that I lack the standpoint to do so. [. . .] Now I know that everything was correct, and that what I saw in her was final. But I failed in my efforts to make her reflect on this because of my imperfection. I couldn't do it. She nevertheless leaves in her wake a big question: that of Walter Benjamin's life. She has cast a radical doubt on his life—not through her arguments but the most silent thing of all: the question itself.

December 2, 1918

What attracts me to Grete is the pure power of her freedom. When we're together (which is often, yesterday it was the entire day), I can't stop staring. My only worry is that I would betray something. Everyone who *speaks* with her will be wrong, must be wrong. The task here is to eliminate speech. (Her brother solves the problem through copious babble, and if it weren't for Grete I would neither listen to nor tolerate it. There is no longer any way out of it. Once she leaves, I see no possibility of maintaining contact with him.)

December 5, 1918

Yesterday I was at Walter and Dora's, whose birthday is today. [. . .]

Just as Walter said today, it's no accident that Plato assumed music to be the pinnacle of art, while for Aristotle it was poetry. The latter view is a sign of decay.

Today is a horrible symbol for terrifying, penetrating nothingness.

The unmentionably empty hours I spent with the two of them will remain indelibly stamped on my memory.

With undiminished force, everything in me that hasn't found support and anchor in Escha belongs to Grete. In comparison to Grete, I'm left speechless at the complete and full negligibility of all of the relationships in my life, with the exception of my relationship to Escha. I still love her, and I know that this love will remain my deepest treasure. [. . .] Everyone I meet educates me, because there was a time when no one educated me, and now I have some catching up to do! When I am with her, however, I realize how no one has influenced me with such direct, pure, and visible power. She sits before me as the Teaching itself, whereas Walter and Dora are but intimations of a coming sun. [. . .]

It's Sunday, and for seven hours we were outdoors near Zollingen. It was really quite nice, in complete contrast to last Sunday in Hurmschwanden. We later went to my place. I could really be with Grete if I could only conceal from her what I know about her; everything's fine to the degree I succeed. What's become obvious to me is how these fourteen days with her have been, and will remain, the highlight of my Swiss sojourn. I'm once again building up a great deal of substance; her luminous existence has stirred me to life. Walter can't do this. This is the difference between them: his *writings* do this; with Grete, it's her being. She has no true relationship to writing. [. . .]

[. . .] It was a strangely warm evening. Both had left earlier, and I went with them. Later I walked for an hour with Grete all the way to her hotel. I can't do a thing about it: Grete's stillness and greatness wield total power over me. I'm happy to walk with her through the evening, quiet and alone. She keeps me in her grasp through her mere presence. I don't say a thing. I'm now quietly friendly. She too has surely become friendlier and more open over the past week. I was deranged to believe that someone here could make me love Grete less. I now see with total clarity that I could easily exchange Walter and Dora for Grete, who has more greatness in her little finger than the two of them (who are obviously great people) put together. She towers infinitely above Dora through an

Order I still can't pinpoint with final certainty. Eternally separating them is Dora's cynicism and Grete's sadness. I can only wish to see one thing: Grete and Escha together. [. . .]

[. . .] I went to Walter's this evening. I knew what to expect, and I would have been astounded if Dora had *not* been hostile. Naturally Walter exercised more self-control than she. But the atmosphere was icy. I didn't say a word to Dora; I only looked at her frequently, and she assiduously took no notice of it. No one can blame her in light of her private calamities (in Germany someone stole her suitcase with her entire wardrobe worth 20,000 marks). I won't be studying Greek with her, and I took my books back. Walter read aloud from "Notes on Cynicism."[78] There are many good things in it, yet something must be missing. The subject really astonished me (when I think about cynicism, my mind often turns to Dora). I didn't say a thing. Is there really no possibility to be together with them now that Grete has entered into the picture? Do I have to choose?

It's only after the radical point of no return in your life that loneliness is ever truly achieved. A community based on the possibility of going back is useless—and is precisely the sort of community I have to liberate myself from. Surrounding me are numerous tornadoes, and even double twisters (like Erich Brauer). I know that the movement of my life, its sense, has reached a single point. (In mathematics, *sense* signifies direction!! It is the direction in which something occurs!) All my tangents must disappear.

[. . .] Hebel writes in his diary: "If not everything is possible, the illusion of everything being possible is."[79] This is one of the greatest truths ever uttered.

William Sacher, formally the leader and co-founder of Young Judah, was killed shortly before the end of the war on the Western Front. He was an enthusiastic war volunteer, and since 1914 I had nothing more to do with him. Only indirectly did one hear unpleasant reports about him. Now, after six years (the group began in November 1912), Young Judah has finally disbanded. It has collapsed organically, each member having embarked on the path that must come. There is no longer any fraternity, no friendship. Girls are the ones who must renew Zionism. This is their task, but one mustn't tell them until one of them realizes it. Isn't the messianic realm as configured in Grete entirely different from what I saw in Dora? Though paradoxical, it's true that Grete's virginity makes her nobler than Dora. Grete would be a virgin even if she weren't one. Through her I can understand the concept of the Immaculate Conception.

December 15, 1918

Zionism is the limit-phenomenon of the Teaching within human existence—a definition certainly every bit as accurate as it is unintelligible to people who haven't stumbled across it on their own. I'm writing a few notes on the fundamentals of "becoming" a Zionist: namely, what these fundamentals would be if it were at all possible to describe how a person becomes a Zionist. But it doesn't work that way, which is a truth that can be refined with as much clarity as needed.

In the evening I was at Walter's for two hours. Dora was basically the same as yesterday. Next time I'm going to wait before I say anything. The atmosphere gets really stifling when people don't speak openly to one another. I'm noticing this quite strongly again.

"If one could say how we became Zionists."[80]
In our childhood we were lost because only an illusory light shone in the great palace where we lived. Our deepest guilt was that nothing broke apart around us; the walls never came crashing down. We didn't know we were a whirlwind because we never made distinctions. Poverty never elevated us. [. . .] We all lived in a reflected light. The secret joy of our youth was always theft—theft not of property (which we never recognized) but of the dreadful continuum of illusion. We wanted to steal our own selves, and all the sweets our parents—rarely—offered us were nothing compared to the rapture we felt at successful theft. We lived *on the other side* of Time, and we never understood that something could uncover our theft. Yes, we had stolen Time. Back then we didn't know we had the right to steal. [. . .] We never wanted to redeem anything except ourselves, and yet we ended up redeeming whatever we stole.

We never spoke; we knew that there was nothing to say. We envied silent nature. We loved the naked houses in our city because they were gray and said nothing at all. We loved everything unknown, and were pious because God always kept silent. Our parents' answers shattered us. Our language died when they forced us to question.

Our childhood was empty, impure, and beautiful. For eons we'll pay penance for this beauty.

Then came the year we became crafty. What was our craftiness composed of? We devised the index to the dark things. We contrived the everlasting powers of the reflection. We became vain because we had discovered the mirror in which things transform and are emptied into symmetry. We saved ourselves because death already lay behind us, and we didn't believe in multiple deaths or in the deceitfulness of the material. Then we discovered the shifting path that always leads from words to lust. We stole only whatever had inherent power. We robbed books of their language, for we had no other way to force words into silence. This was the secret meaning of our voracious reading. It was *murder*. We slew the mirror of things, and the mirror of its mirrors. But we redeemed these things. They reflected themselves forever, and our task was that of irony. Back then we were ironical because our existence was irony. Back then we forgot about dreams, and a dreamless existence was our greatest form of irony. We ourselves sat on the throne of our own kingdom. Words were our servants; and we used words in the great war we undertook against our moral enemy's kingdom: with words we sought to battle things; with words we sought to keep silent. We were politicians. Things insulted our majesty, and politics was the process we used against things. Yet the court, where this trial was played out, turned into our crisis.

II

We did not divine our calling from the stars. And though the judgment—whose deferment is our daily life—is heavenly, it is not written in heaven. We refused to give fate a hearing. Thus began our deepest fatalism.

But before judgment overpowered us and turned against us—for we saw ourselves as plaintiffs against what we demanded to be destroyed—a victorious plaintiff (oh, a man of lamentation!) grew up unexpectedly out of the womb of history. Previously, we had been inextricably engaged in years of growing up. In the years that ensued—without volition or even noticing it—we were embraced by the close spherical mirror that reflects us, and our ego was given up to arrogance, as if the ego were the automatic focus of all reflections, and nothing else existed. This reflection is called friendship. Because we had become political, we had lost all the friendships we had built in silence during our childhood years.

From this point onward we recognized only comrades in the struggle for a relationship, and our friendship, because it was substance, was taken from us (we don't know who took it: maybe we did so ourselves). Our friend was the center of the things we fought against. Never was our friend our comrade. We tried to strike things up with girls. This was the meaning of those agitations, which is another word for fleeing from an intimate knowledge of our whirl of passion. The illusion of our relationship to girls—who, like us, wished to take flight—was our weapon against our friend. And yet before we became unchaste, the eternal court threw us back into the long severity of our late youth, where chastity remained preserved as our central delineating power. We had to practice renunciation because we lived on the border.

III

Time repeats itself in the life of every Jew. Our nation being the only life we have, as soon as we were set adrift, we assumed that Time lay *behind* us. We may have forgotten the nation, but Time continued its cyclical work.

Then on that predestined day, we recognized Time. An unimaginable passion for purity overcame us and changed our life. The purity of objects could wait, though the purity of language had been sinned against. Thus we abandoned the language of our childhood and we began learning the language of our youth with unending resonance. At that time, we knew Hebrew to be the only way. The flow of words failed where the venerable stuttering of the old vocabulary set in, renewing us. [. . .] Our existence, which is founded and festooned upon *the Teaching,* is the primordial unity in which work and knowledge beam out from their common center. Since our being is no longer an example but a Teaching, the demand for justification has been lifted, and we've been elevated into the greater unity of the canonical Order, which is called Revelation. [. . .]

December 16, 1918

What a person must do after making a decision is always the same, and it's among the most remarkable criteria out there. I can literally no longer do anything "extraordinary." The pictures able to mirror changeability have disappeared. But it would be a grievous error to believe that my life has therefore been *vindicated.* The memories of Grete are to me like flowers in a fall meadow. "Living historically" has a dual meaning: either to live in the past or to live facing the past. The critical function of our lives rests on this minute transformation of relations. Love, too, only elevates us before the face of history. My memories are the deep foundations out of which I dispense prophecies on my future life. The power of constancy has always triumphed over me. Inconstancy is truly evil. My life has been changed (that is, it changes itself) through the invisible forces of constancy, be they in language (because the metamorphosing language is the constant one) or wherever else they are called. Grete first came into my consciousness as everything else had already happened; during those months of silent work, I had retreated into myself. [. . .]

December 19, 1918

[. . .] The profession of librarian surely suits me best, and is the one I'll have. [. . .]

How quiet it has become around me! Often it seems as if the people I correspond with have fallen asleep: I hear nothing at all, or something only every few months, from Kraft, Meta, Wally, or even those who stand in my center. Walter and Dora have somehow become obscure to me, while other secondary relationships have disappeared altogether. My life faces the need to be entirely rebuilt.

Dora's birthday fills me with enormous anxiety. I'm suffocating. I don't relate to birthdays the way she does. However critical our situation, I can't see what I could do that wouldn't just arouse her suspicion. First and foremost, we *have* to establish clarity. Maybe tomorrow or the next time I see her. I cannot endure or approve of this method of not speaking one's mind.

December 21, 1918

Since yesterday evening there *is* clarity; there is no room for misinterpretation. What I have seen coming for six months has now arrived. After Loni was with me in the afternoon, I went to them. It was seven o'clock. Walter read Pindar's odes in Greek followed by Hölderin's translation (we never made it to Borchardt's).[81] We began eating. Dora was unchanged: cold and alien. After dinner I told Walter I wanted to speak to Dora alone, adding, "What's with Dora? The way she treats me has changed completely." He only retorted, "You've already realized quite correctly that you need to speak with my wife." I went to her and asked. Gradually everything came out that has been building up: Brauer's visit (after which I had completely kept silent), Hanukkah, the way I "mystify" my personal relationships (Grete, oh if she had known this!!), and so on and so forth. Some of what she said was totally twisted, some was dead on.

For my part I didn't explain a thing, in particular concerning Hanukkah. I knew I'd have the opportunity over the course of the evening. She said last month I'd been simply impossible: in the way I had treated her, I swept them—that is, their existence—entirely *beneath* the threshold of my consciousness. I knew this was coming. I actually said very little. Then for once I finally directed the conversation back to the fundamentals by telling her that we lead different types of lives: namely, Zionism and the youth movement. I said that I live with Heller (without of course mentioning his name) in anarchic community, even though we don't socialize and, in the realms of knowledge, have taken wholly different paths. Nevertheless, I *see* and affirm his life, which isn't the case with them.

We had a very reasonable and lengthy discussion. We came close to the point of more or less unraveling the problem. I said that my life with Walter is not a totally unchanging anarchistic community, but one that is still governed by historical laws: only through revolutions can our relationship be actualized. The good moments are when I leave her and Walter feeling liberated, as if after a revolution. The best times of all go beyond this, achieving (Zionistic) constancy. I said that something entirely positive had brought me together with them, and consistently keeps me trying to find trust with them, but that this has not always been established or actualized.

I talked a lot, though essentially only in symbols because I could not address Zionism directly. Besides, they have an inkling of what is at stake. I then added that there are times when I'm crushed by the fact that our relationship has not been actualized. These are the worst times for me. When asked for examples, I finally brought up the ghastly tale of the winter coat. Then I came out with it (with *total* awareness and after months of thinking about it): that there is dishonesty in Dora's expressions (I could have used the word "violence"). We began to discuss this, and in the thick of it she sprang up, called me loutish and [. . .] dished out other insults and marched out of the room. She said she wanted nothing more to do with me.

There began long negotiations, according to which I should write everything out. In truth, I wasn't decisive enough because I didn't tell the *whole* truth. At any rate, when I left around midnight, Dora let me know that she didn't have the slightest thing against me, but because I saw violence rather than goodwill and concern in her expression—which she said had *perhaps* contained a bit of jocular violence—it was impossible for her to alter her behavior toward me ("till further notice"). She terminated communication with me; she will make no further appearances. This is immeasurably sad—*but* it doesn't demoralize me. Maybe our entire relationship will soon come to an end [. . .]—that is, if I cannot bear entering into their home as a "scholarly guest," where the woman of the house avoids interacting with me. Or she will have to change. At least the crisis has finally and fearfully (and, for me, fruitfully) arrived. My return to Germany has now moved closely into the realm of the possible. Everything depends on Escha.

This morning I met Walter in the library. He was very cold, but maybe it doesn't mean anything. We didn't say anything to each other. Yesterday evening he was completely present, and even more receptive than I had thought he would be. Dora said I don't know her in the slightest, that for me she's a piece of dirt. Is this true? No, it's not; but separating us is something fundamental and elementary. Her life (and nothing less than life, and life *alone,* is at stake here) is no longer illuminated for me through its magical powers. In every sense of the word, Grete played the leading role in this entire crisis. Her question provoked my demand to revise our relationship. Grete, whose total purity and integrity I *see* in the supreme sense, compelled me finally to discuss with Dora everything I'd been bottling up. We direct our lives at different aims. The youth movement, whose picture I silently hold within, is among those things I must eliminate from my life, even if I maintain my respect for it, as I should. Ultimately, the contradictions within our relationship are maintained, and periodically renewed, by a different conception of renunciation. My notion of renunciation leaves *nothing* outside of it, whereas for Walter and Dora there are things they have a right not to renounce.

I engage all the people with whom I have inner relationships (even if misunderstandings and the like arise), and yet in an entirely different manner. Walter and Dora's notion of propriety is catastrophic. An outsider who comes along (Brauer, for instance) can't breach this wall of propriety. I told them so. "Yes, yes," they retorted. "It was up to you to help him break through the wall." I *am* (or was, for right now I'm somehow on the outside) openly opposed to this decorum. Grete could take hold of me in a few days because there is no such wall separating us. Only the Law stands between us. Dora no longer has this power over me (which I believe she once possessed).

What was so terribly irksome for me this summer was when this became increasingly clear. I have only to consider the kind of life we had together. I can lament Walter forever; I can't lament Dora, or not any longer. Something is gone. It's possible that we missed some opportunities, or that it's my fault. I'm not free of guilt, but I have to admit that the problem was already built into our relationship (which I've known for a long time but made all sorts of excuses to myself). *I erred* when I wrote (to Grete, I believe) that my relationship to Walter was utterly positive. I must recant this, even if at the cost of my present cramps. Three years of an attempted and unrealized fellowship with him have taught me, educated me, spurred me on, and hemmed me in. Either this fellowship will become something of the past (whereby it will never become nothing), or the future—namely, that the crisis will engender a greater purity. This is what I'd like to hope for. What I want to avoid is a general confusion of relations. One way or the other, I need *order.* [. . .]

Was a dead relationship buried yesterday? Aren't such burials immoral and forbidden? That's it: relationships are not living organisms! To bury a relationship means multiplying it by zero. Maybe Walter was right when he said he had grudgingly permitted the conversation, and that he should have prevented it. Dora speaks for herself, he said. Yes, but how can I look at her independence without seeing violence?

December 22, 1918

[. . .] I wrote to Kraft.[82] There's a line at the end which came out entirely unmediated and which was the reason for writing the letter: "Revolution is an ambiguous act." There is "the" symbolic revolution, which is mine, his, and *Walter's*. Then there is the other one. [. . .]

December 23, 1918

Yesterday Erich recounted a dream he had at night (and he's the one who once said, after Grete had told me about her *very* revealing dreams, that one shouldn't talk about dreams, which isn't such a dumb thing to say).

He stood with Heller and me on the intersection of the Berlin railroad bridge and the Bellevue railroad bridge. We were waiting for Heymann, who wasn't dead in the dream but was supposed to return from the war.[83] "He's coming," I said. But when we looked, he wasn't there. The dream ended at that point. Heymann never showed up. There's a lot to read into the dream, even at a superficial level. He stood with Heller and me at a crossroads between Young Judah (we always traveled home by way of the Bellevue station because Young Judah was on the Turmstrasse) and that which he was opposed to, which was represented by the new world of Bern. Heymann, who has been much on his mind since he died, was supposed to decide. I'm the illusion Heller destroys. Everything has a double meaning, however. He doesn't know what to do.

I rented an apartment with French speakers. I was with Walter in the evening to give him something he had asked for. This afternoon I wrote him for the first time, but in the evening I couldn't say a thing (it's always the same story!). We really need to talk about the structure of our lives. There can be no conditional deferment here, whereas an unconditional deferment—that is, if it coincided with the end of my dealings with Dora—would mean the dissolution of our relationship. Dora also means a great deal to me; but doesn't everything in the coming three months depend on the development of her relationship to Grete and Escha? At the moment, though not fundamentally, Dora is for me a function of both Grete and Escha, who can just as easily make her disappear as turn her into something forever-becoming.

What does "Talmudic" mean? In the perverted modern usage it means the splicing of words in a judgment in order to bring out the contradictory elements. Practiced as a *capricious* method, it's a mechanical way to produce an infinite number of jokes by means of a mathematical progression of analysis. And in every mathematical progression there is an endless series of prime numbers; similarly, every Talmudic analysis contains an infinite number of jokes. Systematic disputation is the rule governing the series. The Jewish joke, when it is turned ironically against itself, also uses this form of Talmudic process, admittedly in a very different fashion than is commonly applied. Could it be that the Jewish joke developed through the systematic mix-up between the canon and the transmission of tradition? In which case the Jewish joke would conceal within itself an unmistakable symbolic reference to the deepest danger of what is Jewish, namely, the deep strata of self-accusation. Ultimately, every joke would be a warning against what is ultimately Christian. What is certain, however, is that everyone who makes a joke puts himself in the dock. But the joke is *only* an accusation, and nothing follows from it. Or better, by laughing the jokester forces his adjournment; he prevents judgment by way of self-accusation. For there is an ancient Jewish legal precept according to which no one can condemn someone who accuses himself. Laughter is the unending acoustical resonance of adjournment: the joke is the absolute means of creating—which means forcing—*distance.*

December 24, 1918

[. . .] I think I've gradually gained some clarity into the reasons why I have such a hard time writing. I can't manage to do what writers do: to write about everything that is obvious, and to throw words at things that anyone who's insightful passes over.

I feel ashamed when I read topics belabored uselessly, long after the essential points have been made. For myself, I can't do this. Consequently, only with greatest difficulty will I be able to write a dissertation. The swindle of bulk strikes terror in me. I always prefer writing too little rather than too much. It's from this angle that I enter into what I consider legitimate Talmudic realms with such lightning speed. I think not in thoughts but in systems. I'm young and in my most decisive years. Isn't the most important metaphysical task first to map out the terrain? I'll possibly have another life to learn to write (very possibly, but this isn't as important as the foundations and foundational account I'm now producing). Today I still can't write. I am a composer of symbolic literature comprehensible only to myself. If I could write like the philologists— and if I were truly *permitted* to write thus (granted, there are frontiers where this seems to be the case)—I could create a forbidden library out of the few things I hope to know someday. But I would transmit the system of philosophy (which is certainly paradoxical) only as an eminently Jewish paradox.

With the best of intentions, Erich Brauer's landlady put up a Christmas tree in his room. It was the first Christmas tree of his life. The good lady didn't know he's Jewish. We studied Hebrew under, or rather next to, this little tree decorated with all sorts of colorful trappings. We of all people! In the next room people played old Christmas carols on a gramophone. [. . .]

December 25, 1918

A letter to Baer:[84]

The clearer it becomes to me that theocracy is the only organized social and state form for human beings, the sharper are its criteria, as well as the criteria of the value of revolutions. I'm considered to be an avid sympathizer with the Bolsheviks. However utterly ludicrous this opinion may be, there's something to it. Or to be more precise, when it comes to contemporary history, it is only in the idea of Bolshevism that I find a thoroughly consistent revolutionary intensity—mainly in the idea that only the absolute dictatorship of poverty can lead to the establishment of the messianic kingdom. While I reject our present world, the moment I affirm it at all, Bolshevism seems to me to be the unavoidable consequence. As theocracy has yet to take hold, however, I've opted for the anarchistic method rather than the Bolshevik one (people very wrongly confuse the two). Anarchism, not socialism, is as it were the only conceivable ideal steppingstone to the Divine State. This doesn't mean that anarchism is a condition to be strived for. Anarchism is the theocratic state of mind opposing every contemporary period of time that's not an eternal present. I am, so to speak, too far to the left for today's revolution, which has only a faint and indecisive understanding of its mission. I am *entirely* beyond this revolution.

For me, "socialism" is a dubious and highly ambiguous concept. I cannot call myself a socialist with a clean conscience for the simple reason that justice—and it's justice that's at stake here—cannot be developed in a socialist society. Justice is *not* "social" (and it's a disastrous error to think that Judaism is a "social" religion). From the perspective of anarchism, it scarcely needs to be said either that *political* socialism must be rejected in every respect or that theocracy is really worth fighting for. The messianic realm cannot be confirmed through elections. Community, which is the highest thing we strive for, is not a political idea. [. . .]

I must be doing well because I don't think I've written a poem in six weeks. This is a sign. I don't write poetry when I'm doing well. When I'm in a state of pure enthusiasm, I write prose; if I'm miserable, poetry; when indignant, a letter; and in the state of *Tikkun,* I keep silent. At the moment I'm writing to Escha.

[. . .] I'm going to speak with Walter this afternoon, even if I firmly believe it will once again lead nowhere. I just finished reading the Book of Numbers with Erich Brauer, and afterwards we continued on to the synagogue. Then I went to Walter's. There we discussed the letter—the short letter I had written him.[85] As before, I saw he had no clue *what's* driving me to all this. It was clear to me that I could no longer speak against him. In our relationship, we now find ourselves at such a plainly demarcated penultimate sphere that a clear outcome is the most one can hope for from the crisis. To speak with him means discussing Grete, Escha, Heller, and perhaps others, which is something I can't bring myself to do. I'm in debt to him, not he to me, because I have concealed things from him he should have known long ago. Admittedly, I didn't do so for subjective reasons. I'm noticing how the word "objective" often sends him into a rage, which is no accident. But for such things I put a lot of importance on objectivity. If this continues, our interaction will soon become ironical—if only to avoid its becoming catastrophic!

Shall it once again come to the point that in translating lamentations I can weep over each and every word? The law to which I submit myself cannot be overturned, and the crisis of all my relationships must be solved from the center. What's the good of all the peripheral regions of the world if clarity, but also the Symbol, is unattainable? I have no hope for myself, but I certainly still have tasks. I've rediscovered the reverence for my own death, though in the present situation this of course doesn't mean much. Death is *manifestly* not at stake here, but rather the boundaries of life. There is an absolute difference between them. It comes down to the boundaries of Life and the boundaries of lives. Walter and Dora are not the only ones dwelling in this region; almost everyone does. The greatest exertion is needed for me to avoid being caught up in a whirlwind. Four years ago it was hard enough to escape the one thing that threatened me. Today I have but one thing left: work.

What I'll become one day is a matter of complete indifference to me. In the most decisive sense, I will always be a teacher of untaught subjects, regardless of whether I'm formally a teacher, an academic, or a worker. All three are entirely possible. I find myself permanently in a place where everything has the same physiognomy of correctness. One of these days someone, a person I've not yet met, will once again exercise enormous influence over me. I am certain of this. [. . .]

Why do I say that Grete's influence on me has been immeasurably more powerful than Walter's (even if I'm fully aware of the weightiness of his influence)? In brief, it's because of her *moral* influence. I've seen in Walter, and I still do, this moral power, but it had no effect; something else that is enormously deep has rendered it ineffective. With Grete, nothing has stood in the way of a pure influence. She has never uttered a sentence that seemed subversive, and has never spoken flippantly but always with the highest nobility. And then there is the absolute consistency through which she has reached the center of all things and has transformed all things. She is anonymous, the way the female nature has always been in Judaism. If there is anything that can be learned from her, it is the meaning of peace. She embodies it: peace as the loftiest expression and the central idea of all constancy. Walter is a revolutionary, which is the quintessence of everything that stands between us—that is, between us along the decisive journey to Zionism. An ongoing volcanic eruption is necessary to eliminate the revolutionary impulse. This is paradoxical. [. . .]

December 29, 1918

The Destruction (as Grete placed a question mark behind her).

> The sin you don't forgive
> Is only rarely committed
> Yet your difficult question
> Gives me my only bearings
>
> No more will I go with a smile
> Into a foreign home
> I evict myself
> Till you are not poor, till you are good
>
> When you despair I cannot
> Turn away in forgetfulness
> A judge now sits on high
> He calls me as a witness
>
> The seer has long ago left
> But my testimony is true [. . .]

Today is Werner's birthday, but I didn't even bother to write him. A mountain of estrangement separates us (anyway, what is there left in him to climb over?). Recently, terrible, demonic forces have ruled over him from deep inside. We will both die without having spoken to each other. I don't know him; I don't know his wife; I don't know what gave him the right to have her. With him I have what I term well-wishing neutrality. [. . .]

I thought a lot about Blum this evening. The crisis—the Zionistic crisis—that must come had already been overcome in our friendship. When he died there was nothing more to explain. One was able to trust him, and one did.

Today the goyish lady in our pension (her name is something like Guyer) asked me if I could recite to her something in Hebrew. She told me afterwards that she thought I was a Catholic! She's basically a woman one could learn a lot from, which is the reason I talk to her a lot. For someone like myself who has never really had anything to do with them socially (Briese, who died in the war, was the only one!), the goyim are absolute strangers to me.[86] I stand before them and they before me as something entirely different. Regrettably, I have to say that I see through them quickly. And I know heaps about their latent anti-Semitism. This Fräulein, however, is a very pious Christian and always someone you can think about. Jews are absolutely mysterious in her eyes. She has had hardly any experience with the Zionists, and she's now astonished because it seems that I'm confirming all of her splendid suspicions about us. [. . .]

December 30, 1918

My request to heaven two days ago must have been the right one. Though I hadn't given the songs of lamentation any more thought, spontaneously I've begun working on them again. This is deeply revealing: I must be doing poorly. I began with a sonnet, and then went on to a lamentation from the third chapter of Job. I've put a lot of work into it. Songs of lamentation are what I believe I've conquered the best until now.

Today I took my books to my new apartment. At least it's a good place for them. Loni did the packing, and Erich Brauer found a boy who will take the things over with me tomorrow.

I'm noticing very clearly that I have absolutely no longing, or only very little, to spend time with Walter. I'm not going to him today. I could, but I feel it would be a lie. Nor can I stand to go to Brauer's for more than ten minutes, either because of the cold apartment or for some other reason. [. . .]

This evening I was once again with Horodezky.[87] We talked about all sorts of things; though he wanted to stick to politics, eventually we ended up in more pleasant realms. He talked about some literary things: Levertoff (I'm the one who told him about his newfound Christian Hasidism).[88] [. . .]

There are people who compromise the entire mystical guild. To be more exact, they are the historians, and among them certainly belongs Horodetzky. If I'm wrong about this, then it would be a mystical—a highly mystical—error. For this could be possible only through a massive act of concealment on his part.

December 31, 1918

The Swiss have a genuinely refreshing honesty about them. Today during the busiest time, around midday, I left my beautiful schoolbag at the central post office. I just wasn't thinking. Only later after lunch, as I was already heading back, did it suddenly occur to me. I raced back and indeed: someone had turned in the schoolbag at the counter. This hardly would have happened in Berlin. One has to give the Swiss their due: they have an incomparably high level of what one so humorously characterizes as "public morality." No one should ever have to lock his home in Palestine. [. . .]

Three years separate the *Blue-White Spectacles* from "Farewell"[89]—or perhaps more accurately, three girls do (if one could only express truths about girls in this way). All three have been described in these pages. When I think about Escha, it's comforting to know that I didn't compare her to Grete, but neither am I looking for comparisons. She is somehow just as solid, and in all the nuances implied by this word (I can't yet translate this into Hebrew). [. . .] If she were to come here, the entire crisis with Benjamin would be over in a couple of days because I could discuss everything with her, and I'd know what to do. She would radicalize me, which I have to say is what I desperately need. I'm not radical enough, which is a bitter judgment. If a person's radicalism isn't *entire*, then it's reprehensible, root and branch. I know this all too well now. I am *very* fainthearted.

NOTEBOOK 4

How a Person Errs So Long As He Doesn't Know the Truth:
The Dark Mirror

April–June 29, 1919

The way I study philosophy resembles a chimneysweeper scaling a house. My philo-
sophical talent has nothing to do with the ability to figure out how other people
think, which on the contrary I can't do at all. Instead, it's a matter of chiseling all
ideas out of a very stubborn granite mountain that's inside me. Hence my talent for
interpreting people who are interpretable in my sense of the word.

—Diary entry from July 15, 1919

Undated 1919

Kabbalistic literature has more or less without exception been entirely
falsified. The idea of falsification belongs to one of the biggest problems
of history. Walter says that falsification is a legitimate historical idea.

April 23, 1919

This morning I went to Walter's, but they hadn't yet returned from their
Easter trip. Just as I turned to leave, Heinle came down the stairs and we
walked together.[90] It was the first time we had spoken alone together;
until now I had seen him only very fleetingly. We took a walk for an
hour, had a bite to eat, and discussed Goldstein, whom he got to know
very well over a period of a few weeks in Frankfurt, and could really
judge him. He said that he belongs with people pieced together like
Goldstein.[91] I also pointed out what distinguishes me from Goldstein and
Frau Lissauer (Heinle knows her only by sight), and why I regard her as
calamitous.[92] If it's possible, I'd really like to have a proper conversation
with him. It could only be a good thing, as we have little to hide from
each other, and maybe we'd have a myriad of things to discuss. He's open
and has a very pleasant style when he speaks. He counseled me against
going to Göttingen. The city is so awful, he said, that it forces you to
confront nature absolutely, which either makes big demands on a person
or ends in a catastrophe. [. . .] One look at Heinle and you realize he
must have gone through a rough time recently. He spoke of his poetry
only by mentioning Goldstein's assessment of it. It may be that he assumes I know more than I actually do. I'll tell him.

Yesterday and today I translated the dirge "Question, Burned in

Fire."[93] I was completely drawn into its clutches. I don't think I've sinned against rhythm by not keeping to the syllable metrics, which basically don't mean a thing. I may read it to Walter. With or without a couple of lines, I'd also like to send it to Buber for inclusion in *The Jew.* Generally speaking, it looks like the long three-month rest did me some good, as I'm getting back into the swing of working and thinking. In my discussions with Escha, and more recently with Berlowitz,[94] a number of things that had been previously floating in midair have become clear. Moreover, my personal relationships have become purer and more transparent—or are on the way to becoming so, and not only with Walter and Dora (with them I'm now hoping for community beyond the familiar chasm) but with everyone else, too. Escha really was the catalyst here. [. . .]

In the last few days I've read Flaubert's *Bouvard and Pécuchet,* Else Lasker-Schüler's *Faces*[95] (only rarely did her prose help me overcome the book's gloomy atmosphere), and Sinaida Hippius's *The Devil's Puppet.* Tomorrow the university begins!

There's a revolution in Munich and Hamburg. In Hamburg, Escha sits in a house that, after all those awful tales from last February, I can only imagine with horror. She's waiting for my letters. [. . .]

After getting to know Caro in Zurich,[96] I'm convinced I'll see him again. The second conversation we had was incestuous. Was it his appearance that excited me? Or his philosophy? The conclusion of the conversation went well. I said, "I'm leaving tomorrow evening," to which he replied, "So, that means you'll travel on the Sabbath." He thought I was an Orthodox Jew. I'm a skeptic, I retorted: I doubt everything—really everything. He then said he would take back what he had said to me, to which I retorted, "Excuse me, but my skepticism doesn't apply to the Torah, only to everything related to the Torah's concretization." (I only forgot to add the word "today's.") He said he understood. I don't believe in this sort of Judaism. I'm no longer a believer. As for mystical matters, if they are legitimate, then error is law. In other words, if Caro really lives in this center, then it's mystical and hidden, in which case I've got it right when I am mistaken about him.

April 24, 1919

[. . .] Around evening I went to Walter's. He was studying philosophy with Herr Heyse[97] in preparation for the oral exams. Something awful had happened there. It's not only that Heinle is suddenly traveling to

Germany the day after tomorrow; other factors could be playing a role. (According to Dora, he won't be returning right away.) But there was something else going on. I spent two hours alone with Dora, who looked extremely disturbed. She told me she might be able to talk about it later. They're doing horribly. They are completely restless again, living in a constant whirlwind—which they probably don't even notice. It's all so sad.

April 26, 1919

Today in a long letter to my parents I openly and naturally presented my intentions and plans for study! I wrote how I want to combine philosophy, mathematics, and Oriental philology. In the evening at Walter and Dora's I read aloud the dirge[98] "Question, Burned in Fire." I'm definitely going to send it to Buber. It made a great impression on Walter (he objected only to the word "henceforward").

May 1, 1919

I read the corrections for *The Jew*. [. . .] The counter-title to *Jiskor*: "If I don't forget thee . . ." Forgetfulness is the Zionist's virtue against memory. What's needed is to eliminate the public sphere from revolutionary action, and the Messiah needs to be anonymous. [. . .]

May 7, 1919

My enthusiasm for translating Horodetzky has hit rock bottom. I push the work off from one day to the next, and then suddenly I'm going to have to do the entire thing in three days. But it still goes against my grain to do it. There is nothing fertile in this work. [. . .]

It would be possible to understand the theory of Judaism, which today continues to be a complete enigma, in conjunction with the Talmudic concept of the "law of the messianic Time." In principle, a theory of Judaism would require developing Jewish phenomena from the standpoint of the "law of the messianic Time," which would also account for the riddle of the Torah's concretization. What is hence to be postulated or established is the applicability of the Torah as a *messianic* idea, a historical applicability that is to be understood solely in connection with the idea of messianism as the *present moment*. The Torah can be applied from within the present moment *only* insofar as the present is messianic—and to this extent it is messianic. According to this principle, every Jewish law is a "law of messianic Times," which is to be understood as one of the most constitutive and profound ideas of the Talmud. The idea of there being a direct relationship of theory to messianism can only be compared (that is, not compared!) to the Platonic theory of ideas. The relationship between theory and messianism leads to an additional consequence: The Talmud is not a work of legal judgments. As for the connection between the present moment in time and the Torah, what will become increasingly clear, and in an *all-encompassing sense,* is that the Torah cannot be taught before it is realized—in other words, the Torah cannot be taught before the days of the Messiah. [. . .]

May 10, 1919

I've been busy translating Horodetzky's scribblings on Jacob Josef of Poland.[99] It's an awful bit of work, and I don't want to translate this sort of stuff anymore. Objections include: (1) inexpressible superficiality and shallowness of perspective; he doesn't even make the attempt to come up with his own idea of what could be behind or within this Hasidism. (2) There's an unjustifiable claim to be scientific. As an article in the feuilleton section of a newspaper, it might work well enough, but just throwing together a couple of citations doesn't make a work scholarly. It's a mere patchwork. (3) Then comes the insolence of repeating the same things, often even the same sentences, over and over again and tirelessly in new essays, with only the order being changed. There is absolutely no justification for it. This fellow is a sort of Hasidic citation juggler. I will end my dealings with this man. [. . .]

May 12, 1919

According to the Zohar, there are heavenly palaces that only music can unlock (Levertoff, p. 68). [. . .]

Salomon bin Gabirol supposedly died at the age of twenty-nine, the same age as Novalis,[100] which is astounding given the abundance of his work.

May 15, 1919

I'm worn out and can't say why. I've been overcome by a sudden and unfathomable inability to work. Instead of taking walks during the glorious spring morning, I sit at home silent and immobile, and I ask myself pointedly why I'm not writing to Kalischer and Meta Flanter,[101] and whether there is some deep reason at work behind it. I'm often thinking about the coming year, with the goal being no longer mathematics but to become, or to be, a Judaic teacher, occupying myself entirely with Judaism. No doubt a number of things could justify the effort. As soon as I get back to Germany, perhaps I'll study philology more systematically (I'll stop pretending that mathematics is my first priority, a status it doesn't deserve). My relationship to mathematics, however good and deep, exists no doubt on a completely different plane from what I could reach through long, continuing studies on my own. I neither want nor will achieve "positive" results in this field; my passions are with philosophy and Judaism. And I can sorely use some philology. [. . .]

May 19, 1919

We were rained in on Sunday. In the afternoon I went with Ernst Bloch to Interlaken, and we talked about Judaism for nine hours or more straight, from 6 P.M. to 3:45 A.M. I also read aloud from Agnon. It was a relatively good conversation, even if in the end I don't have much in common with his views. Sometimes I run into a real iron wall. Benjamin calls him an analyst of forms. I don't know if I'll see him again. As serious and probing as our conversation was, my initial impression was that this won't be an ongoing affair. At seven in the morning I returned to Bern.

After the lecture this evening, around seven, I went to pick up Walter for the Münster concert, where Verdi's Requiem was to be played and sung. I talked about Ernst Bloch.[102] Dora took on a polemical (though friendly-polemical) tone of voice that didn't bother me in the least, but Walter was once again very upset. He realized that she had said things she could not seriously back up. There was a bit of a storm, but I thought we were still according to plan. We said our good-byes and I was already out of the room waiting for Walter, who remained inside for a minute. Then he came outside and told me he was not going to the concert and asked me to go alone. As always, I was simply flabbergasted. I agreed, said good evening, and left the house. These pointless and unpleasant scenes—and they continue even now, in my presence or not—are appalling. They are among the things one cannot discuss with the two of them. I was mightily impressed by the Requiem.

May 22, 1919

Last night I went to hear *Die Meistersinger von Nürnberg*. The performance was awful, a third-rate comedy.

Walter, inspired by Poe's "The Gold Bug," thought out the following excellent principles for writing a secret code: first you randomly assign each of the 24 letters of the alphabet a two-digit number (for example, "a" is 24). Then, likewise randomly, you assign the numbers 0–9 to one or more of the 24 letters, so that they all make an appearance (for instance, "4" is "e" or "f" and 6 is "g," and hence "e" multiplied by "g" is "a"). A marvelous opaqueness is achieved through the double coordination with the business of the *double* digits. [. . .]

Walter distinguishes between the following two sorts of historical writing. (1) Writing in which (doctoral) students try to demonstrate scholarly acumen with as much noise as possible. (2) Then the professors who try to deliver scholarship with as much subtlety as they can, and to do so they think out the most desperate and artful arrangements.

May 29, 1919

Regulating the soundless occurrence are the three cosmological ur-phenomena: mourning, community, and dissolution.

The senselessness, humor, and outrageous stupidity of Weber's *Theology of the Talmud* lay in its idiotic method,[103] which is characteristic of a kind of research done in other religious-historical fields where better insight is not as easy to uncover as in Judaism. The method, systematically carried out, makes it possible not to find a single insight in the entire work; Weber has made this a priori impossible. But the Haggadah *is* something with an extraordinarily deep and systematic structure, though on an *entirely* different plane from the structure referred to here. This book serves as a warning about where archival research can lead once the good spirit of insight has abandoned the researcher. Imagine what happens with savage religions and all the other unknown religions! Judaism can only be deduced. This esoteric statement is, I think, the best research principle for Jewish topics. [. . .]

I'm beginning to question whether it wouldn't be better not to join Walter and Dora on vacation. I'll have to think about it carefully. I don't want to be at fault for turning our last weeks together into an irresponsible torment for me. [. . .]

June 1, 1919

Both yesterday and today I've walked with Walter from Biel to Neuchâtel, where we've been for a day. I don't want to write much about

it. It was partly immensely beautiful, partly so massively awful that it's become obvious I shouldn't undertake or do anything to be together with
him in August. Walter is terribly mistaken in thinking that his way of life
and mine are the same and that when I deny this I'm just being coquett-
ish. This says everything. In the end we had a major clash.

We discussed politics, about which he has a particular theory. He
made a lot of jokes. [. . .]

At present, my unwritten essays (and those I could write) include: (1)
The language of medieval Hebrew poetry and the problem of translation. (2) The recent representations of Hasidism (a critique of Levertoff's
book). (3) Journalism and the Musiv style. (4) Contra *Jiskor* book.[104]

Walter's definition of intuition: The object of intuition is purely articulated content in the emotions that is demanding to be perceived. The
perception of this need is called intuition.

June 7, 1919

Isn't it remarkable inner progress to be more cheerful than ever, at a time
when I'm obviously not doing well at all, in fact, when I'm in a very critical position because I'm confronted by—or am already in the midst
of—a new beginning in my life? I'm writing witty letters to everyone,
yet with absolute lucidity (I'm not torn within myself) I am completely
somewhere else. The truth is that I'm delighted to have this period of my
life end in a month. I'm not accompanying Walter on the hiking trip, but
will remain alone. I see too clearly that in the near future the only way to
maintain contact with him is through written correspondence. Life together with young men and women this coming winter will be evidence
either for or against me: whether it'll be easier than this relationship, in
which I'm always walking on eggshells.

Recently I've given Escha very little thought, which doesn't mean a
thing. Everything shall begin anew and shall change. [. . .]

June 12, 1919

Seen in its entirety, the visage of Germany's Jewish youth is distorted by a
lack of chastity (oh, the irony of this!). The entire misery of our youth
could perhaps be traced back to this terrifying inner destruction of chastity, that is, of the reverence for women. This not only occurs among
males (and who has ever experienced the Baucus drinking bouts among

"Zionist" fraternity members and how they talk at 2 A.M. without having to burst into tears—or being rendered incapable of tears?), but has even nestled itself deep among many girls. Politics has spread its devastation here, with the corpses of girls stacked up high, lined up along the path forged by Martin Buber, a path that has only liberated girls' inner licentiousness. This is a politics of decadence ideally suited to them. That's it. It's not as if Buber's writings were written with a political bias: they *work in tandem* with such a bias. It's a feminine perception that causes the entire female Order to come crashing down, and hence begins a massive, licentious overstepping of borders which, in the end, leads to despair (first comes euphoria, then babble). The life of Jewish youth has been undermined by promiscuity on all levels and wherever promiscuity can exhibit itself. From the ideology of sex as mere pleasure all the way to the sublimated feminine attitude of fornication vis-à-vis the natural landscape (and the latter is even more horrifying than the former), a terrible chain of reciprocally reflected promiscuity is forged. Everyone who has not yet lost his innocence, regardless of how confused he is, is a possible candidate for the real youth movement: namely, Jewish anarchism. Silence, too, can be promiscuous. The healing of our souls and the purity of our lives are not necessarily the same thing. The first of the two (at least for now!) is a pseudo-idea and counts for nothing. By contrast, everything depends on the purity of our lives. To be miserable in one's purity is surely nothing to strive for, though it's the last step that—no longer in need of ethical transformation—directly leads to redemption. [. . .]

I don't like getting the sort of letters I just received from Ludwig Strauss:[105] there's a bit too much flippancy and too many false notes, which can't be otherwise in a single page. He wants my permission for his Weltverlag to publish my translation of the songs of lamentation. I don't think this is going to happen, at least not anytime soon. I'll reply cautiously, without saying a word about my return or anything of a personal nature. It's not that I look at Strauss as impure; he's just abysmally confused when it comes to the Center. It's this confusion that pushes him into the neighborhood of decadence. Poetry, Ha-poel Ha-Zair,[106] ethics, and philosophy are all thrown together in a dangerous brew. Maybe Strauss is simply too feminine.

I've been successfully avoiding meeting up with Horodetzky. Now that our business together has come to an end, there is also no reason for it, nor is any demon forcing me into wasteful discussions. [. . .]

June 13, 1919

I'm starting to understand how the expression "Nothing comes from nothing" acquires in politics an extraordinarily surprising meaning. To the extent that socialism has or acquires power, it feeds off of it. [. . .] Out of nothing comes something: this is the historical idea, the idea of direct action. Out of nothing comes nothing: this is the political idea, the idea of mediated action.

June 14, 1919

Once I'm back in Germany, I'll give a long series of battle speeches in which I'll wrangle with the idea of creating (and preparing for) the band of fanatics I have in mind. As large a number of young men and women as possible (or what one considers a large number, for as things stand with us, two people are already an enormous magnification of the potential of one) would be needed to live together in the same spot, and to see if it's possible to forge together a radical communist association, which is what it'll take if one wants to go beyond pure politics and do something human. [. . .]

I'm still very skeptical about the aims of the Volksheim.[107] It's hard to fly when something is loaded down with such inertia. The Volksheim is sadly not an airplane; and, given its need for aesthetic gratification, if it were a weapon it could only be defined as a stink bomb. [. . .]

June 15, 1919

In a long aperçu on language there is the following sentence in Lange-wiesche's Ruskin anthology (page 97):[108] "It is impossible for a language to have any nobility if its words include a call to action, like blasts from a trumpet." As formulated, the statement is very good and perceptive. The prophetic element in the practical application of language is to be uttered with great chastity. [. . .]

June 16, 1919

The German revolution is making rapid progress.[109] By the time I get home either a communist regime will already be erected . . . or the most embittered uprising will spread. In many ways, the trial going on in Munich against the leaders is worth noting (it's become clear that the city's entire intelligentsia took part in the Council Revolution).[110] Unprecedented juristic outrages are taking place. Cronauer, leader of the Revolutionary Tribunal, received the minimum prison sentence even though the court had to thank him for the salutary work he had performed in the court. Despite this he wasn't acquitted! Benjamin says that Noeggerath will also get time.

Rabbi Akiba wanted to do away *entirely* with the death penalty (Makkot I.10).[111]

June 17, 1919

Theodor Lessing's definition of morality is, "Morality is to be sick" (in the dual meaning of the word).[112]

June 18, 1919

I read Theodor Lessing's *Philosophy as Action*. This man would be the best model imaginable for a monumental book on the convergence between Judaism, greatness, and decline. For this convergence, which is historically certainly remarkable, rarely exists with such clarity—one prefers avoiding the term "purity"—among other paradigmatic Jews. (Lessing discusses nearly all of them, in particular the philosophers.) Lessing must be a really miserable human being. He's so miserable that his intellect prevents him from being political, which is his only "emergency exit," as he puts it. In my opinion, this highly cultivated man (who unfortunately suffers from the hideous flaw of, maybe unwittingly, showing off his superb education at the wrong moment) lives within the transitional epoch of German Jewry's smashed illusions. He even has fantastic insights, though he's not always the easiest to read, even if on the surface it seems that he is (he's a sort of inverted Lotze,[113] and in many other respects besides his style). To put it radically, his style has the wild irony of a desperado; armed with metaphysical claws, he delivers his punches invisibly, but with all the more sensitivity. He puts the reader of his book on trial. His insights range all the way to Zionism—yet he doesn't see Zionism at all! He doesn't cross the border of regions where Zionism is to be found. Probably the man can think, but what's certain is that he just can't renounce anything. There are places in which his manner of seeing is absolutely horrific. If philosophy is an action, then introjections are perspectives and Martin Buber's mysticism has value. This I deny.

Yesterday afternoon Reserve Lieutenant Hoppe, that obscene monster, came by again to play chess. Tomorrow he's off to Germany. I'm glad to have made his acquaintance—he's a prime example of the species that will need to be exterminated. I've had some good experiences:

he embodies the Kraut principle in its purest, highest, and therefore all the more harmless blossom. What more can one hope for after November 9? [. . .]

Today in Switzerland is the so-called day of mourning for the victims of pogroms. I went to the lecture hall to ask Martin to cancel Aramaic, and I then went to the synagogue. Messinger[114] gave an appalling speech that contained an excellent interpretation of the biblical "the voice is that of Jacob, but the hands are those of Esau." It was used in the context of spirit and power, but surely came from some wise man other than Messinger! For me, the blatant dishonesty practiced by Jews in reporting the pogrom grieves me just as much as the pogrom itself. It's terrible to say, but these people have to embellish reality because it's not yet bad enough for them. In this way they declared the pogroms in Polish cities to be far worse than the Armenian atrocities. They only hurt themselves with such gibberish. Besides, what good do *comparisons* do when it comes to death? What's the sense in prattling as a "warrior for truth" and spouting out disingenuous metaphors in speeches, magazines, and declarations? There are still people who can't sleep at night until they have proven that we are the greatest victims among the nations. The fact that this isn't true, that it is simply wrong, doesn't seem to bother anyone besides me. People live in a delirium. Now it's a delirium of protests. [. . .]

It has now been two years since being inducted into the army. It's almost unimaginable that so much time has already passed. My struggle against the German military has already become so foggy that nothing is left beyond the nice insight I gained into psychiatry.

June 19, 1919

"[. . .] One searches everywhere, just not behind the phenomena. The phenomena themselves are the Teaching," says Goethe. Excellent. But *science* they are *not*. The Teaching is a religious phenomenon. Science, however, is not directly the Teaching, and in this sense Goethe's statement is true mysticism. A mystical image is that of measureless, reflected temporality.

June 20, 1919

This afternoon I went to Heyse's doctoral exam.[115] It was very interesting, insofar as I now realize that one doesn't have to lose a minute's sleep over the oral exam. It's a farce played out in front of the dean. I'll never go to another one, and I wouldn't have gone today had Benjamin not asked me to. Walter's attitude vis-à-vis his exam is simply unbearable: he lives in a dissolute and indecent angst, and in the true etymological sense of the word. The only good that'll come out of my going is that he may calm down a bit. Only rarely do I have any desire to visit him and Dora, despite the fact that they are now very friendly to me. I think that they've also dropped the idea of spending our vacation together in August. I don't want to vacation with them. [. . .]

June 21, 1919

[. . .] All the friendships I've made over the last few months in Bern—and there weren't many to begin with—have fallen by the wayside. Once again, I can't see other people. I'm still lacking the proper discipline; and there are few things that shame me as much as the realization that I've rushed too quickly in making positive judgments about people. Not many Jews are what they should be. Almost without fail, each time a particular empirical case leads me to deviate from my maxim—namely, that one mustn't get to know the Jewish people before having deduced it—the ensuing disappointment reminds me once again how right my maxim was in the first place. [. . .]

Memories of Escha: Escha is very pretty and very large, with eyes like those of a very young girl. I don't recall what color they are. When she looks at me, she always has the purest expression of a child. She is entirely direct, and when she reflects on something, it is only a preventive action. When she came to me, she didn't love me yet, but this took only a few days. Now she wants everything she can get: to be my lover, my wife, but all she really wants is to have children. Escha is the type of mother God intended. Is it necessary for this eternal picture of motherhood to languish without children? She is really languishing. Only because she's now certain of her claims on me is she less miserable than before. I kissed her many times, and this is something I have to run through my mind a lot. But I told her I couldn't have a lover. It's certain that one should love her deeply; she has such a feminine movement to her. Movement is the medium by which the world has order, and women live more exclusively within this movement than we do—and with such responsible devotion that it's astonishing. Basically, Escha knows everything, that is, everything necessary for her to be a decent person.

This evening I went to the cinema to see a film made by the Society

for the Struggle against White Slavery. It wasn't bad. A huge stream of
people naturally went by because of the announcement on the cinema:
"Hyena of Lust: The Greatest Sensation of the Year" (!!!), and it drew a
large public not otherwise in the market for morality. Practically speaking, the only impression it left was an impressive exhortation (and an exhortation done with pictures always leaves a much deeper impression
than the printed word) not to put a girl out on the street because of one
bad night. I really believe that films like this can have a big impact. Later I
thought a lot about the issue. The white slavers are almost all Jews (in the
East they are often pious Jews, they even have their own synagogue in
the city in eastern Galicia where Türkischer's father comes from). There
is *no* justification for this, not even an economic one. Working-class Jewish girls being shipped off to Argentina as whores is the most terrible sign
of our inner decay, the most sacrilegious Judaism imaginable. [. . .]

June 22, 1919

I'm working on two songs of lamentation. There's an absolutely hard
kernel and an unearthed treasure lurking in this thin volume of poems.
At present I'm translating *"I said: leave me in peace, bitterly do I want to
weep."*[116] It's very hard going, less because of the language than its total
structure. For many dirges I can't manage, or haven't yet succeeded, at
capturing in German the literary character of lamentation. In this case,
however, I'm well on my way to success.

Today the German national assembly voted with a majority of 100
(237 to 138) to accept the peace accords. No one can say that therefore a
new epoch has begun. The vote doesn't even bring the old epoch to an
end. [. . .]

June 27, 1919

I read Plato's *Phaedra* and the *Symposium* again, now I want to go on to
Parmenides because it's really essential that nothing can be proved. The
best thing Plato can teach a man of science (he can certainly teach a philosopher *even* more, though this insight has enough reach) is that philosophy can't prove anything because the correct system of coordinates rests
within philosophy itself and not in relation to the object of proof. Philosophy is comprehensible only in the way it creates its own foundation
(which is always a mystical *circulus vitiosus*). [. . .]

The idea of a messianic movement growing out of a gang of swindlers is reason enough to go out into the masses and to live in purity among thieves, pimps, and sluts. Through a revolutionary process, it is here that the influence of Judaism (which is massively negative) can be given a positive foundation. God's chosen people as swindlers—this would be quite a movement. [. . .]

It's evening. This afternoon Walter was awarded a summa cum laude, and he's finally free from the university—until he goes back to it on a different path! We were together this evening. Dora, letting her guard down, was as happy as a child. We all told silly stories. Walter passed all three—the dissertation, written exam, and oral exam—glowingly. He said that they all behaved extremely affably, and were even enthusiastic. No one can say what's going to happen now. Walter and Dora haven't yet discussed with me their plans for the winter; perhaps they haven't yet made any decisions. Their attitude toward the present is entirely split: they go back and forth between earning a living at all costs and becoming a private scholar. [. . .]

June 29, 1919

A socialist's logical fallacy: pure community is redemptive; socialism wants to create a pure community; therefore, socialism brings redemption. This is what I call the journalistic non sequitur, or the chimera of the will, the point being that pure community cannot be willed into existence. (If this were possible, liberalism would have been right.) Such a will would be chimerical. The pure community exists beyond the will; if it's not chimerical, goodwill is pure mysticism. Only mystics can want to *call forth* the Messiah (whereby out of principle he never arrives). If, however, socialism were to be established on any empirical basis whatsoever, it would be a hopeless form of mysticism. One can approach evil only because it doesn't exist, while things that do exist, the Good among them, cannot be approached. There is really only *one* hope of ever putting economic socialism into practice, which is a radical, iron-willed determination to kill off all intellectuals (there can be ideologies for this): to murder at once and without mercy people and their ilk who think for the sake of thinking. For every intellectual subverts the entirety of economic socialism because he recognizes no limits, absolutely none, and the more finely tuned his mechanism (such as Hölderlin's), the less he'll fit in. The Greeks, who had such intellectuals and were able to give them a place, were the polar opposites of socialists. There is no such thing as spiritual socialism. The poor in spirit are right (there is a double meaning here). In a socialist system, intellectuals would consequently be regarded as lunatics; to ensure the survival of the system, no madmen would be admitted. (The fear would be of revolts.) [. . .]

NOTEBOOK 5

A New Row of Pictures from a Dark Mirror

July 7–August 13, 1919

July 7, 1919

[. . .] In Tieck's *Runenberg,* which is an extraordinarily lovely tale, the old man says to Christian, "You are still young and cannot yet bear the rigors of loneliness."[117] Silent and pure in its formulation, this is an argument against the youth movement, as we are forced to see it today. It is a German argument. For lacking the rigors of loneliness, youth are without calling. He who transmits his calling into society—into the imperfect society—only ends up corrupting it. Human society continues to be rooted solely in lamentation. It is profoundly true, and this applies especially to Jews, that what keeps us humans together is divine judgment and not empirical forces. He who maintains that persecution alone has preserved us really has a point. Only during times of *Tikkun* can a community be held together through song. We, however, are weak.

It dawned on me yesterday that the phrase "Death is the task of life"[118] has a massive double meaning. [. . .]

A letter to Kraft: What makes Karl Kraus incomprehensible (and I believe he is) requires a very different explanation than his relationship to his generation.[119] On the contrary, his incomprehensibility has an inner and imminent relationship to the word "incomprehensibility" itself. To put it radically, the *Neue Freie Presse* would be right if one could understand an essay by Kraus in the same way one understands, say, Kleist. That is to say, Kraus wages a war on incomprehensibility, yet the person who understands him actually misinterprets him, and in two ways. Kraus has a feeling for the canonical even though he knows nothing about it. Perhaps it's best to express his struggle by saying that he wants to discover the canonical by using a language that no longer has a canon; and he applies his Jewish pathos to an object that is great, but that is nevertheless despairingly hopeless. Kraus doesn't know a thing about Mendele or Agnon, and he's certainly ignorant of Hebrew. Indeed, he has taken on himself an endless task either always solved through its endlessness (namely, through the play on words, jokes, each comment, every citation), or it has no solution. He's forever approaching a goal that doesn't exist (and you can approach an object eternally only if it doesn't exist), which is the canonical quality of the German language. This Jew has therefore uncovered unexpected Jewish regions within German. His style bears an undeniably *legitimate* likeness to the Musaf.[120] Journalism and Kraus are both progeny of the Jewish Middle Ages, though Kraus is its worthy and therefore miserable child. In general, it's quite wrong-headed and nearly insane to think there is any Jew who has overcome the Middle Ages. No such Jew exists. While we are no longer Jews from the Land of Israel, all of us have been formed—to the extent that we have anything (and dissolving into nothingness hardly constitutes being modern)—by the same forces that produced the Kabbalah, legal and philosophical rationalism, and the books of the Musaf. Nothing has changed: our instincts, feelings, and inclinations all remain medieval. [. . .]

July 8, 1919

Agnon doesn't want to marry Wally because she lacks ultimate virginal propriety. Yet this marriage would be really compatible and good for him (all the more so because with Wally he'd be with someone who loves him). There could be no better help for Wally to see through the evil spirits of ecstatic and worthless devotion and readiness, even through the dear God in heaven, than marriage to this man, who could be her teacher. It could perhaps be questioned whether marriage is the sort of institution in which perfection can be achieved *while in it* rather than entering it with all the requisite knowledge. In terms of what is needed to repair here, it seems to me that such an education is permissible *in* marriage (and is even impossible outside of it). For there can be no doubt in her mind how she'll live with her husband, which is the critical knowledge and a priori of marriage. This is the only piece of knowledge not to be discovered first in the marriage. Decent and upstanding people don't play around with marriage. If Escha does as I've asked and presents Agnon with a different picture of Wally's uselessness (her taint), success is assured. Helping to bring about this marriage would really be a good deed.

Yesterday I came across a copy of Büchner's *Hessischem Landboten* from the fin-de-siècle socialist period,[121] along with two of Weitling's writings[122] (all for the truly non-communist price of 5 franks). In these books the socialist *movement* still seems to have something pure and undiluted about it. Even if Weitling can't hold a candle to Marx or Lassalle, these writings can. It's crazy to accuse such books of not having penetrated the "knowledge of the laws" of the social structures, and of having observed and battled, in a one-sided manner, what they see from an entirely simplistic, unproblematic standpoint. In truth, this way of seeing things is every bit as legitimate as the scientific or sociological one. For political agitation, in the best sense of the word, cannot be stirred up without moral pathos, without a justified pathos (and how else do Lassalle's famous speeches operate?).[123] There is not an iota of deceit in these writings (and the jury's still out as to whether religion is used ironically or as a means to an end). [. . .] To be sure, the *Hessische Landbote* didn't have the slightest effect on the generation of the peasant wars, and it may be that the peasants, his audience, didn't know how else to respond than to hand it over to the police (David writes about this).[124] This book was ill suited to have the influence he had intended—precisely because it was *pure*. This is just the way it is: to have some influence one must reach and seize a region's border markers; the transitional spheres must be reached and captured. [. . .] The Good has always suffered from the fact that it's good: it has only a historical influence, without affecting the contexts of life that can be experienced. It was in this way that the prophets had their inexhaustible influence on the realms of history, world history, and the history of Judaism (or rather, of the Jewish people: I still don't know if Judaism has a history). Yet the actual people they addressed [. . .] were never touched by them. *Politically*, the prophets realized their aims *ironically* by not having accomplished them. The *prophet* has always been a historical phenomenon, in contrast to the *righteous* man who influences men, who speaks to them. It should therefore come as no surprise that after the Second Temple, when Jews no longer wanted to influence history, the righteous man stepped onto center stage in the Jewish imagination. Until Hasidism, he fulfilled the task the nation required of its individual members (with some word twisting this could be called "political"). There is in fact precisely an inverse relationship between the historical influence of the prophets and the righteous man's total lack of it; and in this sense it wouldn't be stretching terminology to call Moses Hess a prophet (which is what I do).[125]

Hasidic holy men were not prophets, absolutely not. The renewal of prophecy would be a sign of a world-historical rebirth with incalculable consequences. The fact that Büchner's *Hessischem Landboten* speak to people they weren't written for—namely, the educated sons of capitalists—is a more vexing problem than it first appears. These writings fulfill a deep inner paradox in language. Marx's *Capital,* which is an obscure, thick, and scholarly tome, whips the workers into action even though they surely have no more understanding of it than they once had of Christianity (it's hard to put a finger on what exactly the common man understands of such things).

By contrast, Büchner's manifesto hits us, the bourgeoisie, foursquare. This is mysticism of the first order. The materialist conception of history doesn't help in the least when it tries to solve the mystery by simply employing a prosaic language, which only ends up transforming it (the way a transformation of coordinates doesn't solve a problem but only reformulates it, and whether the reformulation is better or worse depends entirely on the method of transformation). The most elaborate sociological study of the means of production can't explain the most meager phenomenon and riddle of language. In each text lurks countless linguistic armies, lined up and half asleep, and the most curious operations are at work in language and in its relationship to the outside—what is commonly called its *influence.*

Within us, words are silent or speak in an inexplicable succession. They speak to me, and to you they are silent. The psychologist would say it all hinges on the person because a word is nothing in itself. This just isn't so, because it also depends in part on the word (finally, it depends on neither me nor the word but on the religious relationship between us, which we call *reading* and which has *absolutely* nothing to do with the person). The person who could read and the literature he reads would be equally bad if they were satanically intertwined. *The canonical word is lusterless;* it holds back the abundance of its bright rays. [. . .]

The question is this: who are political writers? One could say that the only candidates here are the great agitators such as Thomas Münzer,[126] the men of the French Revolution, Tolstoy, the 1848ers, and many others like them. [. . .] To judge by the introduction to *Hessischem Landboten* [. . .], it's obvious that the religious part of the pamphlet doesn't stem from Büchner at all, but underwent a major editing job by one of his older fellow revolutionaries, a *pastor*. It is precisely here where it becomes clear that the meaning of something is entirely different from its intention. The pamphlet's physiognomy, and hence its greatness, is a product of just this "disjointed" mishmash of biblical citations and the stomach. Büchner had focused only on the stomach, and was outraged at the editorial job.

The most fantastic things grow out of the greatest imaginable errors. Maybe the Bible—and all other literature—developed this way. But seen objectively and dispassionately, it doesn't matter in the slightest. The first rule in literature is that revelation is not an intention. With the possible exception of mythology, revelation cannot be recognized at its "source." As commonly understood, a phenomenon's genealogy doesn't say a thing about the heavenly revelations that may or may not occur within it. If Deuteronomy is, as biblical scholars maintain, a product of priestly deception (which for the sake of honesty we have to admit), it would say nothing about the transcendental issue, even if the deception had been done absolutely *consciously* ten times over, making out of it a forgery. [. . .]

Undated, 1919

Friedrich Hölderlin lived a Zionist life from within the German people. Hölderlin's existence is the canon of every historical life. [. . .] The canonical is here to be defined as pure interpretability.

July 10, 1919

[. . .] This evening, after Loni stopped by and as I was reading aloud from a Midrash on the creation of a child, a telegraph from Mother arrived announcing her arrival early tomorrow morning. Some interesting days now lie ahead. I gave Loni back the copy of Büchner's *Leonce und Lena* I had borrowed from her. It's a lovely piece of writing with a good style.

The mythological interpretation and systematic-theoretical deciphering of the Talmudic and late Jewish texts is a task that, till now, has barely been tackled (at most, theosophists have ventured into the field). Formal scholarship has been satisfied with sticking to a philology that doesn't even exist! In our abysmal state, we're more or less in the dark when it comes to the meaning of the convoluted signs and figures residing in such abundance in these Jewish texts. Essentially, this is one of my life's task, if not my true task. The system would also find its traditional rebirth *in this kind* of interpretation, in a truly new sort of commentary. Through immanent dependence on the jurisdiction of its subjects, the system would enjoy the freedom of not being forced into any unnatural opinions through a falsely conceived notion of context and development. The Midrash on the creation of a child [. . .] merits a detailed study—if one only had the *knowledge,* which is the condition of possibility for such a study. [. . .] Jewish scholarship is in an especially paradoxical and indeed extremely enviable position. It is not as if it invokes spirits that refuse to come. Quite the opposite: Jewish scholarship expends its full efforts at turning away the invoked spirits, just as it denies that they're there. But the spirits come *anyway.* They are always there. Always. And they want to be redeemed through the work of insightful scholars. Just look at Ernst Bloch.

July 11, 1919

I can hardly string two thoughts together because the last few days with Mother have really worn me out. I also notice in my dealings with her how much I've changed over the past year. Now I can sit (relatively) peacefully and listen to a lot of things that would have irritated me last year. It's only terribly wearying. She talks a lot about Berlin. She's the same old person in the way she talks. [. . .]

Mother gave me as an "arrival gift" the gorgeous three-volume edition of Immanuel Kant's letters published by Georg-Müller Verlag. I'm really intrigued by the volumes, which have become classics because of a few particular passages. Only rarely do I think there's ever been such a fantastic letter as Collenbusch, the rural doctor's, to Kant (on Kant's ethics "without hope," a letter from a "zealot").[127] How else is one to penetrate this impenetrable jungle with which Kant encircles knowledge than through his letters. I consider them to be true *letters.* (I don't yet know them, but I have to assume it, given the entire character of the man.) [. . .] I'll put the letters aside until I'm again in such bad shape that I need to read letters.

July 13, 1919

[. . .] I had an idea for a detective story in which for the first time the detective is *ugly!* (Why are Herr Lecoq, Sherlock Holmes, and the detectives in all the movies always the paragon of male or female beauty, according to the taste of the authors and the public?) I don't know why a detective shouldn't also be ugly. Or is there an ideology here that goes beyond the desire of the masses?

July 14, 1919

In his letters Ludwig Strauss showers me with all sorts of—unfortunately baseless—compliments about my knowledge in areas in which I'm still an absolute novice. I'm well aware of this. Everyone else also massively overestimates my knowledge. Because people know nothing about, say, medieval poetry, they consider someone to be a great expert who has just started to delve into it, and who has perhaps picked up some basic knowledge (which doesn't suffice for anything besides promoting the central part of a productive work). One day I'd very much like to be a scholar who can say something sensible about Jewish learning, on all its various linguistic levels. But now, after a couple of years of studying like a dilettante, I'm hardly there. I have some ideas, though I lack the comprehensive factual knowledge necessary to put a productive stamp on scholarly ideas. I am through and through a student, a *Talmid*,[128] a beginner. [. . .]

July 15, 1919

Thinking about it correctly, we Zionists live in a state of silent renunciation incapable of articulation, which is so difficult for us only because of our lack of language. People become impure from living outside of this renunciation and not wanting to live within it. Our hearts are being ripped apart by our shameless epoch in which people throng around us, screaming out their mindless freedoms. We are victims, and a person is sadly misguided if he thinks he's not. The seduction of things has passed; hence begins the greater seduction of love. These days a life of justice is attainable only by means of renunciation. Perhaps one is permitted to say something, but it doesn't occur to anyone to speak. *What* is in need of renunciation is nothing other than language itself. [. . .]

The way I study philosophy resembles a chimneysweeper scaling a house. My philosophical talent has nothing to do with the ability to figure out how other people think, which on the contrary I can't do at all. Instead, it's a matter of chiseling all ideas out of a very stubborn granite

mountain that's inside me. Hence my talent for interpreting people who
are interpretable in my sense of the word. [. . .]

July 17, 1919

With people of real depth, an astounding number of things remain completely unsaid. This is a claim that should be easy to prove whenever one
is able to observe people in their personal expressions outside of their
work. It is as if some things have a silent but highly effective resistance
against certain forms of transformation in language or in the system of
literature in general. It's nearly impossible to overestimate the esoteric
side of human thinking. [. . .]

July 20, 1919

I actually read a novella by Hugo Salus,[129] and the entire time I asked myself why he wrote it in the first place. The only real thought that came to
me was that life as a doctor in Prague must be really good. What is certain is that I really didn't get anything out of it. I'm generally not very
"gifted" when it comes to making observations, first of all because I
don't think much of them, and second because I don't even know what
they are. My incomprehension extends far beyond this to include all such
conceptual constructs that lack a context. Basically, my sense of understanding never goes beyond language. For me, whatever is ineffable is a
priori incomprehensible; *if* at all, it is accessible to me only as the basis for
a symbol. It's a really hopeless exercise to use intuition to explain a rose.
This is particularly true when one picks out an example as poor as this
one, for if one could intuit anything at all, it would be nonexistent.

An intuitive testament to this would be this diary, where everything
possible comes to the fore except daily happenings, which are not re-
peatable and, at least for now (I'm still very young), aren't even fit for
commentary. This journal is an ongoing and highly justified act of "step-
ping over into a different realm."[130] Just as Satan has played no major role
in my life (my temptations are of a different, though no less dangerous,
Order), in these pages there is no elimination, not even of evil. This diary
is, as it were, a boundless homage to Time; and in this diary, Time's only
priceless garment (the "garment of Time," to cite the magnificent passage from the Zohar that appeared in the most recent edition of *The
Jew*)[131] is regarded with wonder. Preserving the reverence of this act of
wonder is the true labor of my youth. [. . .]

[. . .] Along with buying Loni a copy of the *Italian Journey*,[132] I also picked up for myself Pantheon's anthology of Rückert, edited by Loerke.[133] I did so because I've become really quite interested in this poet, in particular after I learned about his funeral dirges for children (I believe it was in the *Jewish Encyclopedia*). The anthology includes a few such poems, some of which are really lovely. Among the most beautiful elegiac work I know is the short poem "You are a shadow in the daytime, at night you are a light." There's really a hint of what lamentation is all about here. Rückert, the great Orientalist, may have gleaned from his Semitic studies—and without even having a conceptual grasp of what he was doing—a conception of our sense of lamentation, especially in this poem's unbelievably dense cycle, which completely disappears in itself. (He may have even translated Arabic or Hebrew lamentations. It'll have to be looked into.) In a true act of magic, the poem ends by elevating itself. I'll really have to get a hold of the entire book.

I wrote to Escha, Toni, and Werner Kraft[134] about the question of the semester in Freiburg. To the last two the tone was very enigmatic. Escha's was half in Hebrew, with some Talmudic linguistic jests thrown in. I also had a few serious things to say about hell, the upshot being that no one wants to go to heaven after Anatole France described the place (in *La Révolte des Anges*), whereas hell has turned into a luxury resort for all upstanding people after Stefan Zweig attacked Samuel and applied the verse "And thy nation, they are all just,"[135] to all the members of this nation of pimps. [. . .] A great holy man said long ago that he would gladly go to hell under the condition that everyone else went to heaven. [. . .]

[. . .] In my letter to Ludwig Strauss I inferred, though really very clearly, that the question of sects is really what's at stake. I admit simply, directly, and honestly (not "openly," because the adjective doesn't fit the subject) to belonging to a sect. It's my opinion that we have to do what people from time immemorial have always done when they really wished to actualize something true—people who are not seeking a realm of babble but who seek through their actions to uncover new messianic dimensions in their respective generation. It's nonsense to call this Christological, as some people have. [. . .]

July 25, 1919

In the evening I went to Waldhorn. [. . .] Having sat the entire day in the library (which is real work) in search of the biblical source of the lamentation "I said: leave me in peace" I asked Schklar[136] if he knew perhaps where to find the verse "You have fallen as one has fallen before the sons of the spiteful,"[137] which I hadn't managed to locate. In fact, he knew by heart that it's from the lamentations of Abner[138] (which I really should have known, but it's always this way: one overlooks the most remarkable things). I have been seeking in vain the sources for the lamentations in Rilke's novel.[139] In Iseltwald I spoke to Benjamin about it and told him I'd love to know. While thumbing through the volume of dirges today, I noticed one beginning with the words "And my harp music turned into lamentation." (I noticed it because by chance it was right after the dirge "I said: leave me in peace, bitterly do I want to weep.") This immediately reminded me of the final words in the Rilke quotation. I looked it up in the concordance under "harp" and discovered in the simplest way what I should have been able to deduce: that it comes from Chapter 30 of Job in Luther's translation (Luther's language in Job is especially powerful, which may be due to the text's difficulty which leaves a lot of free play for interpretation and one's own opinions). The riddle has thus been solved after more than a year! [. . .]

July 28, 1919

Harry Heymann died one year ago today. For me, knowledge of him is concentrated in his name: in other words, when I think about him, nothing else comes to mind other than his name. I have to conjure up forcibly every other memory of this man who was so terribly betrayed. What touches me in his name is its anonymity, which seems to me to be the most desirable thing in death (and in life) for people who have died in a hopeless struggle, such as the struggle pitting Germany's might against the Jewish people's claim to the inalienable rights of youth.

These youth, often with their eyes wide open, allowed Germany to betray them. Harry Heymann was aware of the kinds of forces that, in Germany's name, were driving the war; but he was too weak to resist this evil actively. In the end, he was fooled by this pseudo-ideology of attack and defense. In the final months of his life, I was outwardly estranged from him. Inwardly I had figured him out, and for this reason I knew we had nothing in common. I had hoped from our friendship that at some later point we would, in mutual effort, return to the ideals of truth—which he was prepared to trade for power, even in Zionism. He loved Judaism, though not the invisible streams that it so powerfully manifests, but rather its violent and secularizing tendencies [. . .].

I'm seriously considering the possibility of doing my dissertation in an area of the Jewish theory of language. If I could only devote myself to the study of the Zohar for a given time (and if this book only had an index!), it would be rather easy for me. [. . .]

August 2, 1919

There's really still some hope out there! In the most recent edition of *Schweizer Isrälitisches Morgenblatt,* someone has *issued the appeal to compose songs of lamentation.*[140] Rabbis and others should compose them, basing them on the older model of dirges (the author gave a few examples), and they would then be edited and absorbed into the liturgy for all eternity. There's something remarkable about the call, "Sound out with lamentation." The author thinks that, for the mechanics of the thing, it's more or less irrelevant whether I invoke lamentations as pure politics or as a prophetic call. If strangely wrongheaded, this is nevertheless proof of a return to life of lamentations. [. . .]

August 5, 1919

Bramson[141] came by this afternoon and told me that Weizmann[142] would probably give a speech later in the evening, and that at 6:30 I could get more details. I went to the train station with Brachmann and Bramson and looked for the room with the "lecture." I thought that this man would perhaps have something worthwhile to say to a small circle, and since no club was sponsoring it, it was worthwhile to go. [. . .] Fine, so around nine o'clock (it was really supposed to *begin* at nine) I went with Bramson. Frau Locker, who was there, greeted me with a few sweet words. Fine, so I waited and waited, sitting there and wasting time. I was a bit surprised by it all. I hardly recognized anyone. Around 9:30 Weizmann shows up along with what looked like bodyguards: a couple of people from Basel and Feiwel.[143] Then *Nothing.* A bit later Buchmann stands up to greet Weizmann—a not very sympathetic looking character with a black goatee—with a couple of lines in Hebrew and says that he's supposed to tell us about the possibilities of going to Palestine and working there. [. . .]

More time passes. By this point I'm beginning to feel ashamed of my-self. It's getting muggy. Up at the front the "gentlemen" are whispering to one another. One sits around a table, does nothing, at most a bit of small talk. A few people like Schaichel give some kind of speech. The blood is rushing to my head. It's ten o'clock! I've been sitting for an hour. It keeps going this way, and it doesn't occur to anyone in the room to *explain* the reason for this desolate silence. Not even a word, such as Weizmann is tired or hoarse, or whatever. People are looking around, as Jews do. I get a note signed by several people with the jest, *"What now?"* Of course no one passes the note to the front. I ask the guy next to me what's happening. Bramson and Schaichel want to pretend to be restless.

At 10:45 I tell Reiner I'm leaving, and he should tell me when he wants to come to me. Reiner, twisting and turning in his chair, says I should wait "thirty seconds." Which passes and he doesn't say a word. I'm thinking whether I should say a couple of lines in Hebrew about this *disgrace*. After a minute, Schaichel (who has been looking at me with a restless expression, telling me with a wink that I should sit tight) asks if we should leave. "Great," I say, "let's go." I stand up. Horrified, he wants to drag me back to my seat. He's afraid of creating a scandal. I tear myself free, rage overcomes me, and I march straight out of the room. No one follows me. I don't know if anyone noticed. And who cares anyway? *I'm ashamed of myself,* ashamed at having sat there senselessly for an hour, ashamed at all those people sitting around.

Berger told me that Feiwel's a great guy. *No, he's not.* He sat there with-out moving. It can't even be *put down on paper* what a disgrace this nation is, full of people who speak about work, redemption, and Lord only knows what else. On the way home I was so irritated I wanted to let out a scream. I had received a bad Teaching. And the way these people sat around the table like good peasants (one person ate ice cream, another drank tea, et cetera)! And this was supposed to be the hour of *redemp-tion!!!* What a mockery!!! I don't need to seek out a culprit, for the guilt lies with the *insanely duplicitous Jewish spirit in our midst,* a spirit damning us to Exile. And none of these speeches and nice goings-on can exorcise this spirit. The Original Sin is that in large part these people don't even *realize* what stands in the way of redemption: to wit, *themselves,* their way of life, and their never-ending blasphemy. We are really in sad shape. [. . .]

[. . .] In the evening I took a walk with Loni all the way to Bramson's apartment. I asked him about the previous evening. Weizmann kept silent till the end. Bramson said that afterwards Weizmann let it be known through friends that he had expected to be invited to a student drinking party!!! Indeed, that's what we are. Why did this gentleman keep his mouth shut after he saw that this is really what we are? This is the way a Zionist leader behaves among reveling students! [. . .]

I wrote to Werner the following regarding the *Volksstimme:*[144]

> I read your newspaper with an open mind. I looked for something that could produce a *pure* spirit—upright, uncommon (in the moral sense of non-vulgar), and forward-looking—but in the last four weeks I have found *nothing* of the kind. To the contrary, I have come across the most pitiable and depressing evidence of deceit (vis-à-vis the outside world, but even more so an *immanent* deceit directed *inwardly* and full of self-contradictions, and whose *only* rule seems to be not to state the truth, but only those things that can harm Noske[145] and the other conservative socialists in the eyes of party members). I discovered a *lack of purity* and, in a simple and direct sense, a shortage of humanity. I'll have a lot to say to you that won't be nice. I don't know if you'll consider me bourgeois if I tell you that, other than the cover, nothing sets your paper apart from the nastiest of the bourgeois rags, be it the *Frankfurter Zeitung*[146] or even worse. The *shocking* baseness of your language in all of your political articles—which must corrupt your readers and their language—teaches me that nothing can be expected from the communism of a party that speaks *in this way.* [. . .]

> [. . .] My hope in your party was an illusion. If one of these days you ever gain power (which is a good possibility), then the entire lack of purity, demagoguery, and all the evil you have gratuitously injected into workers (who trust you) through your rapid-fire clichés will present a terrible obstacle *against* any serious work. Nothing is more pernicious for a community than demagoguery. Because you have fed people an impure language, rotten ideology,

and self-righteousness *à tout prix,* instead of preparing them in a high and decent sense, your regime—lacking a foundation—will unavoidably drown itself in a sea of blood. [. . .]

August 12, 1919

[. . .] Berger[147] asked me if Jews think in *objects* rather than concepts. He says this would be a great advantage for Jews. "No," I replied. "Jews don't think in objects," which isn't even possible. [. . .] No, while the Jew doesn't think in concepts (he surely doesn't do this), he does so in *words.* The Jew thinks linguistically. This is a double-edged sword. In the religious sphere, this thinking contains the loftiest things; it gives legitimacy to revelation within our nation; it bears witness to the highest purity, reverence, and true national greatness. At the same time, this way of thinking can be perverted, as it is all too frequently today to our great shame. The redemption of the word and the positive renewal of language is the seal of success of the Jewish people's rebirth. The big question is whether we will avoid the abandonment of linguistic thinking but can lead it back once again to its roots—to "sweeten it at its roots." The cheap accusation of "word fetishism" doesn't faze us in the least.

To put it somewhat differently, everything hinges on whether we succeed in eliminating Yiddish, this monstrously demonic purgatory of words. We are all still stuck in Yiddish—and I'm the most guilty of all, being someone who says he thinks entirely in Yiddish, and whose structure of language is still Yiddish. We have yet to integrate the entirely simple and lofty cadences of Hebrew *purely* into our language. We have a gigantic task ahead of us.

August 13, 1919

[. . .] Erich Brauer asks if there are objective reasons or proofs why someone should be a Zionist. *No.* These are all demands that are rooted in a system and can by no means be proven. It cannot be demonstrated through proofs that a person should lead his life—even in its most hidden strata—in a special sense before the face of history. In the end, the requirement not to *steal* is just as devoid of proofs. If you could *prove* the Good, the Good would not exist. After all, what would be the unquestioned foundation of such a proof? A mathematical proof (which is the only sort of proof that *exists*) has foundations, *none of which* can be denied unless a person is a lunatic. [. . .]

CONCLUSION:

MELANCHOLY REDEMPTION,

1919-1981

Recollection is the only paradise from which we cannot be turned out.

—JEAN PAUL

SCHOLEM'S JOURNALS largely conclude with his return to Germany at the end of 1919. The few pages he did write between then and his emigration to Palestine in 1923 give the impression of a man who had battened down the hatches to prepare himself for the lonely journey ahead. They can be likened to his remarks about the neglected, despised books of the Kabbalah: "Betrayed a couple of generations back, their bright rays are projected back within themselves and into an invisible magical life that awaits demystification."[1]

Scholem's few diary entries from this period never mention Benjamin, though his occasional visits to Berlin, where Benjamin was living, were enough to confirm in his mind his friend's status as a "new Rashi" whose "speculative talent no longer aimed at devising something new, but at penetrating something existent, interpreting and transforming it."[2] (During one of these visits Benjamin introduced him to a new young acquaintance named Leo Strauss.) Their relationship, kept afloat through physical distance, produced numerous ideas for common projects, none of which came to anything.[3]

Back at the University of Munich, Gerhard was a scholar ascetically devoted to ancient Hebrew and Aramaic texts, and the three essays he wrote on the Kabbalah there were products of a mature thinker.[4] Eventually he settled on a dissertation topic. His study of Abulafia would have to wait until *Major Trends* to see the light of day. For his dissertation he decided to produce a translation and critical edition of the Sefer ha-Bahir.[5] He called his undertaking "a vast foundational philological-philosophical monograph on an early kabbalistic text from around the year 1230. [. . .] Nothing worthwhile that's any longer than four pages has been written about it."[6]

Reactions to his various productions ran the gamut from enthusiastic applause to utter incomprehension. ("Your study shows an inverse relationship between the amount of knowledge pumped into it and the clarity of its expression," quipped Arthur after reading an essay titled "Lyric of Kabbalah.")[7] His professors awarded him a summa cum laude for his spadework on the Sefer ha-Bahir. They failed to notice something the German hermeneutical philosopher Hans Gadamer picked up on years later: that its author approached his subject not with the "skeptical-critical distance" of the academic professional but with a "shocking identification." The Kabbalah had seized the "researcher's fantasy and sharp reasoning with an unrelenting grasp."[8]

The wide range of tumultuous emotions he had earlier poured into his diary was now being diverted into his scholarship. The philological perfectionism that dazzled his professors was part of the concealment process that hid his idiosyncratic view of Judaism, history, Germany, his family, Benjamin, and himself. His mental and spiritual condition was concealed carefully in his various essays, but not in his diary.

Ambivalence toward his petty-bourgeois parents, which had only increased after his return to Germany, now shows up in one of his writings as an attack on the "demonic powers" manifest "in the most frightening manner in mothers, who pay for their lifestyle with demonology . . . and the banality of language."[9] He reserved even more venom for old-fashioned scholars, such as his *Doktorvater* and others at the University of Munich, whom he lampooned for their "astoundingly thoughtless, utterly inadequate, and all-too-often murderous style" of scholarship that exorcises youthful magic from tradition, thereby creating a "future without passion."[10] One translator's incomprehension of "mystical eroticism" hinders deep insight into the "true, erotic elements" of medieval Jewish poetry.[11] A careful reader of Stefan George's *Star of the Covenant* is better equipped at grasping this poetry, he writes.[12] To attract the "enthusiasm of the insightful ones," he concludes, modern Judaism is in need of a "deeper-seeing philology" able to restore "total splendor" to "dusty" texts. He speaks of a "journey of discovery through the *terra incognita* of our literature."[13]

The same essay praises the "adventurer" and "impetuous zealot" who dares to venture into "our dangerous" and "antibourgeois" heritage, made up of "iniquity, vice, and perfection." A "genius," equipped "with a rare and luminous urgency," can conjure up the spirits of the past and give back the "youth's language as the people's most precious possession."[14]

But Scholem knew this was going to be a lonely task without the backing of the *Geheimbund* he had once longed to lead, and also without his friend. Only History, and not the sheer act of will, could bring forth followers who would join him in penetrating the mysteries of the esoteric "double meaning" and "rebellion" beneath Judaism's "official exoteric" surface. And until that moment arrived, he was prepared to go it alone.[15]

His essays "Observations on the Meaning and Appearance of the Kabbalah" and "On Kabbalah" describe serious philological study of Kabbalah as a necessary "illusion" in "non-messianic times." Alluding to the metaphor of Plato's cave, he writes, "The philology of the Kabbalah is but a projection upon a surface." Most people mistake the flickering image on the cave wall for the truth. But what they see is merely the "great illusion" of orderly historical progress and linear historical development. Only the masters of "transmission and language," who are the "bearers and defenders of the secrets," are able to interpret what they see.[16] The like-minded must pass through the veil of critical history to gain real insight into the deeper meaning of Jewish mysticism.

> There is a secret realm of connections [. . .] that meets also our human experiences. We are not lacking in a key to these things. What we lack is only courage, courage to venture into an abyss that, to our surprise, can only end in ourselves: courage to pass through a plane, a wall—that is, History. The mountain, the corpus of things, does not require a key; history's veil of fog must only be passed through.

Privy to the esoteric mysteries, he "who manages to go through the projection and to stand in the middle [. . .], where the living sources can speak to him as a simultaneous phenomenon, experiences salvation, and is himself a savior."[17]

Scholem left Germany in 1923, just in time to miss Hitler's Munich Putsch in November 1923 and the nasty outburst of anti-Semitism that followed. General Erich Ludendorff, the hero of the battle of Tannenberg in 1914, supported Hitler's failed coup and denounced Jews and their "deadly superstition of Jehovah."[18]

In Palestine Gerhard now went by the name Gershom. His secret codes were complete, his inner self fixed, the main structures of personality in place. The philosophy of Tradition and language he developed during World War I remained so firmly cemented in his thinking that decades later it would crop up unchanged in letters and essays.[19]

Some of his friends had preceded him. In 1922 Meta Jahr moved into the still wild countryside, where she helped found the kibbutz Beit-Sara. More important, Escha was now living in Jerusalem, where she helped Gershom land a job at the nascent Jewish National Library run by Hugo Bergmann. Their relationship, with the exception of the round of kisses he gave her during her visit in Switzerland, had previously evolved in a series of glacier-like moves, mostly carried out through letters. Within three months of his arrival they were married, without fanfare or enthusiasm.

The extraordinary strides the Zionist movement was making in Palestine had nothing to do with his decision to move from Berlin to Jerusalem. Before setting foot on its soil, he had judged Palestine and found it wanting—because he was certain that none of the local Zionists shared his passion for metaphysical renewal. "To be free of illusions," he writes about the Zionist project, "is an art."

> Zionist despair comes from the skepticism as to whether or not empirical Zionism can be achieved. [. . .] This is a terrifying and constant form of despair, and some Zionists have already plunged over the edge into it. It is not as if they lack illusions; rather, their disillusions are prophylactic. [. . .] To live this sort of Zionist life requires ethical genius (in a total sense). It is a life of sacrifice. [. . .] Only the genius can bring redemption to Zionist despair.[20]

Shortly before his departure, in a page of notes titled "The Truth," he heaped scorn on the colonization effort and all its romantic sound and fury. Political Zionism was for him a pernicious diversion deflecting attention away from "lamentation," an existential state for someone who had concluded that—in this non-messianic world—love is impossible, intimacy out of reach, community an illusion. By 1923 Scholem had become, to quote George Steiner, a "master of disenchantment."[21] And he would remain so, as attested to by "Melancholy Redemption," a poem written years after he had become a professor at the Hebrew University in Jerusalem:

Melancholy Redemption

The light of Zion is seen no more,
The real now has won the day.
Will its still untarnished ray
Attain the world's inmost core?

We have been mired far too long
In what makes our heart most race,
And, staring annihilation in the face,
We hate those who seek our love.

Soul, you believe you are alone
And stand condemned in God's sight
For some failure on your part.

Wrong! God never comes closer
Than when despair bursts into shards:
In Zion's self-engulfing light.[22]

The poem ended up in the same place as his diaries, deep inside his desk drawer, far from public view.

Scholem lived a reclusive life of scholarship during a never-ending series of crises that uprooted everything that once had defined his life. A succession of disasters battered Germany. Inflation wiped out the savings of the middle class, and a decade after Scholem's emigration, Hitler came to power. In Jerusalem, Scholem's marriage to Escha ended after their next-door neighbor, the Kantian philosopher Hugo Bergmann, snatched her away. He quickly married a relative of Sigmund Freud, his young student Fanya Freud.

On the run from the Gestapo, Walter Benjamin committed suicide in 1940. Scholem's brother Werner was murdered in a Nazi concentration camp. His mother, Betty, broken, died in far-off Australia, where Scholem's surviving brothers had emigrated and were running a five-and-dime store. (His father, Arthur, had already died of a heart attack in 1925.)

Gershom's social circle largely included fellow German Jews. During the war, a discussion circle grew up around him called "Pilegesch," or "Concubine," an all-male lineup of Jerusalem's scholarly elite, mostly native German speakers such as Hans Jonas and George Lichtheim.[23]

Arab-Jewish violence swept the country in the immediate postwar period, and in 1948 the state of Israel was established. The Zionist dream had been fulfilled, though for Scholem the Jewish state had little in common with his private Zionism, which only became more esoteric as death continued to whittle down the ranks of those capable of understanding it. His close friends or pupils George Lichtheim, Peter Szondi, and Jacob Weiss all committed suicide. The one close friend who did not was Werner Kraft, and the two of them met weekly at the home of Ernst Simon to talk about Benjamin. "Both of them cursed him, week after week, year after year. I think it was only because they never felt loved by him," remarked Simon's widow. "Walter was like a deity who let them down. Or maybe they thought they had failed him."[24]

Work—not friendship, politics, Israel, or Fanya—dominated Scholem's life. Most of his labors were ponderous studies adhering to the strictest codes of philological research, but he also wrote for a wider audience. Most of these non-scholarly books returned him to his past and to the memory of Benjamin. To write his two autobiographical works (*Walter Benjamin: The Story of a Friendship* and *From Berlin to Jerusalem*) he consulted his diaries, reliving the joys and sorrows of his youth. Together with Theodor Adorno, he edited Benjamin's collected works, along with two volumes of general correspondence. His *Correspondence of Walter Benjamin and Gershom Scholem* was published in 1980, three years before Scholem's death. In these final years of his life he did what disciples have often performed for holy sages: in one essay he gave a "Kabbalistic" reading of the name Benjamin, and in another he compiled his friend-cum-mentor's genealogy, proving an old hunch that Benjamin was related to Heinrich Heine. The very last essay of his life was devoted to Max Noeggerath, Benjamin's "genius."

※

Although the memory of his dead friend continued to have a near ubiquitous presence in Scholem's life—Fanya said after his death that Benjamin was the only person he had ever truly loved—it only rumbled silently beneath the surface of his scholarship. Never does he give full credit to his dead friend's influence; often he seems to go out of his way to efface every obvious trace of it. One of the greatest philologists of our age, he quotes regularly from tattered diaries and letters of obscure rabbis or merchants, figures who had otherwise vanished into the immensity of history, or he draws his sources from modern philosophers, historians, and thinkers. The nineteenth-century Catholic scholar Franz Joseph Molitor earns numerous footnotes. But when it comes to giving credit to the man whom Scholem trumpeted as the greatest Jewish theologian of the century, he remains eerily silent. (In one case he removed a reference to him in galley proofs.)[25] It was as if all the deeper feelings aroused by the friendship had been expunged from his life, deleted as mere youthful illusions.

It was only at Scholem's annual postwar appearance at Carl Jung's ERANOS seminars in Switzerland that he publicly inhabited the world of his youth. Here, where he was away from his duties as a professor in Jerusalem, speaking in his native language, and in the Swiss village of Ascona so reminiscent of Muri, his lectures show how the "esoteric philology" he had picked up from Benjamin—namely, the belief that true Words and Teaching never vanish without a trace but live on as a hidden power until resurfacing—continued to determine his life and thought. Much of what he said sounded as if he had lifted it straight from his diaries.[26] "The sum of religious phenomena known as mysticism," he said in one lecture, "consists in the attempts of mystics to communicate their experiences to others."[27] In "The Name of God," another of his lectures, he stated: "What the value and worth of language will be—the language from which God will have withdrawn—is the question which must be posed by those who still believe that they can hear the echo of the vanished Word of the creation in the immanence of the world."[28]

In "Revelation and Tradition," Scholem said of words, facts, and the entire past that they are "meaning that is itself meaningless," an "indefinable something" with an infinity of possible meanings and interpretations; they are "meaningless" and hence purely interpretable. They gain meaning only through "Revelation," which is the "absolute giver of meaning," by bringing "words" into a "continual relationship . . . with the present."[29]

This is the task of the Teacher who is also the mystic—not in the sense of a person gleaning magic incantations from a secret book but as a commentator exercising hidden influence on Tradition by "forcing truth onto texts."[30] Teachers remain anonymous, concealed within the Tradition they help form. Revelation, which is variously called "Teaching" or "interpretation," is defined as the "spontaneous element of human productivity."[31] The Teacher works spontaneously to transform the past into something living for the present, and produces the material for future generations to relate to the past.[32] He puts his stamp on history without anyone's noticing. "Every generation's accomplishments and contributions to Tradition are projected backwards into the eternal present of Sinai."[33]

✳

Just as Benjamin did not mention his friend Heinle by name in his essays and books, Scholem's stubborn refusal openly to acknowledge Benjamin's massive influence on his development as a thinker had nothing to do with ingratitude or intellectual plagiarism. Quite to the contrary, his silence was systematic: it was a part of the very "Teaching" he devoted much of his career to passing down. To borrow from Josef Weiss, his friend's silent voice can be detected in certain expressions or adjectives, or even in the manner in which Scholem created his characters and situated them on the stage he set for them. The nihilistic Jakob Frank, the addled Sabbatai Sevi, his clever sidekick Nathan of Gaza, and Abulafula all responded to catastrophe through an extraordinary creative expansion of tradition, enriching culture dialectically by using their inner and outer lives as an interpretive compass.

In this way Scholem was very much like the characters he created. Like them he transformed tradition during a time of overwhelming catastrophe. Silently passing on the Tradition he had learned from his friend, Scholem introduced his own passions, memories, messianic desires, love, and torment into forgotten and despised texts, and thus presented them to the world as a living, thriving, and vital tradition. It was this personal dimension of his work on the Kabbalah that helped Scholem contribute to the extraordinary revival of Jewish culture after the Holocaust, and it can also be seen as the most enduring monument to his friend Walter Benjamin.

NOTES

INTRODUCTION

1. Gershom Scholem, *Walter Benjamin: The Story of a Friendship,* trans. Harry Zohn (Philadelphia: Jewish Publication Society of America, 1981), p. 63.

2. Gershom Scholem, *On the Possibility of Jewish Mysticism in Our Time and Other Essays* (Philadelphia: Jewish Book Society, 1997), p. 171.

3. Gershom Scholem, *Briefe,* vol. 1, ed. Itta Shedletzky (Munich: Beck Verlag, 1994), p. 444.

4. Ibid., p. 449.

5. Scholem to George Lichtheim, January 4, 1968, in *Gershom Scholem, A Life in Letters,* ed. Anthony David Skinner (Cambridge, Mass.: Harvard University Press, 2002), p. 427.

6. Scholem writes this in a letter to Siegmund Hurwitz on October 24, 1947, in *Briefe,* 1:330.

7. "He does his best to appear as one of those scholars who devotes himself in impersonal anonymity to his area of research, and who has no spiritual potency behind his scholarly efforts." Josef Weiss, "Gershom Scholem: Fünzig Jahre," *Yedioth Ha-Yom,* December 5, 1947.

8. Ibid. See also Scholem, *Briefe,* 1:459.

9. A writer may write like a harmless pedant far from the "holy war of mankind," says Strauss. "Only when he reached the core of the argument would he write three or four sentences in that terse and lively style which is apt to arrest the attention of young men who love to think. … His reasonable young reader would for the first time catch a glimpse of the forbidden fruit." Leo Strauss, *Persecution and the Art of Writing* (New York: Free Press, 1952), p. 55.

10. This comes from a letter reprinted in Peter Schaefer, "'Die Philologie der Kabbala ist nur eine Projektion auf eine Fläche': Gershom Scholem über die wahren Absichten seines Kabbalastudiums," *Jewish Studies Quarterly* 5 (1998): 22.

11. Quoted in Ilan Stavans, "Why Jorge Luis Borges Wished He Was an 'Israelite,'" *Forward,* August 6, 1999.

12. Cynthia Ozick, "The Fourth Sparrow: The Magisterial Reach of Gershom Scholem," in *Art and Ardor: Essays* (New York: Knopf, 1983), p. 145.

13. See Gershom Scholem, *Tagebücher,* vol. 2 (Frankfurt: Suhrkamp Verlag, 1999), pp. 219–220.

14. July 24, 1919, ibid., p. 493.

PART I: A ZARATHUSTRA FOR THE JEWS

1. Walter Benjamin, "Juden in der deutschen Kultur," *Gesammelte Schriften,* vol. 2, pt. 2 (Frankfurt: Suhrkamp Verlag, 1977), pp. 807–813. Benjamin refers primarily to Friedrich Gundolf, Ernst Kantorowicz, Karl Wolfskehl, and Margarete Susman.

2. Gustav Wyneken (1875–1964).

3. Quoted in Thomas Maasen, "Man-Boy Friendships on Trial: On the Shift in the Discourse on Boy Love in the Early Twentieth Century," *Journal of Homosexuality* 20, nos. 1–2 (1990): 57.

4. Ibid., p. 51.

5. Wyneken was convicted of pedophilia in 1921.

6. Gershom Scholem, *On Jews and Judaism in Crisis* (New York: Schocken Books, 1976), p. 6.

7. Scholem wrote this in a diary entry on December 19, 1918.

8. Gershom Scholem, *From Berlin to Jerusalem* (New York: Schocken Books, 1980), p. 63.

9. Scholem, *Tagebücher,* 2:366.

10. Ibid.

11. Frenssen died in 1945 and has been largely forgotten.

12. The clearest expression of the group's collective thinking appeared in 1913, when the avant-garde publishing house of Kurt Wolff brought out *Vom Judentum,* an anthology of articles written by a number of people influenced by Buber. Contributors included Gustav Landauer, Arnold Zweig, Hugo Bergmann, and Max Brod.

13. Martin Buber, "Die Lösung," *Der Jude* (April 1916): 1–3. *Der Jude,* a journal of contemporary Jewish literature, thought, and scholarship, was founded by Buber in 1915.

14. See Hugo Bergmann, "Jüdischer Nationalismus nach dem Krieg," *Der Jude* (April 1916): 7–13.

15. Scholem wrote this in a diary entry on November 15, 1914.

16. Ibid.

17. Scholem, *From Berlin to Jerusalem,* p. 60.

18. Scholem, *Story of a Friendship,* p. 75.

19. Diary entry from May 8, 1915.

20. Diary entry from December 7, 1914.

21. See Benjamin to Ludwig Strauss, January 7, 1913, in Benjamin, *Gesammelte Schriften,* vol. 2, pt. 3, p. 842.

22. Theodor Adorno, writing in the 1960s, claims that Wyneken had the "strongest influence of anyone" on Benjamin. See Benjamin, *Gesammelte Schriften,* vol. 2, pt. 3, p. 824. See also *Gesammelte Schriften,* 1:70.

23. Benjamin to Carla Seligson, June 5, 1913, in Benjamin, *Gesammelte Schriften,* vol. 2, pt. 3, p. 884.

24. Ibid., p. 910.

25. Benjamin to Carla Seligson, September 15, 1913, in Walter Benjamin, *Briefe,* vol. 1 (Frankfurt: Suhrkamp, 1966), pp. 92–93.

26. Quoted in Benjamin's essay "Die Freie Schulgemeinschaft Wickersdorf," in *Gesammelte Schriften* vol. 2, pt. 3, p. 829.

27. Ibid., pp. 855–856.

28. Ibid.

29. Ibid., p. 871.

30. See Werner Kraft's essay on Heinle in *Herz und Geist* (Vienna: Bölau, 1989), p. 410.

31. Benjamin, *Gesammelte Schriften,* vol. 2, pt. 3, p. 933.

32. Ibid., p. 864.

33. Quoted in a letter from Benjamin to Ernst Schoen on June 23, 1913; see Benjamin, *Gesammelte Schriften* 1:237.

34. Bernd Witte, *Walter Benjamin: An Intellectual Biography* (Detroit: Wayne State University Press, 1991), p. 26.

35. Ibid., p. 887. For an excellent look at the role Heinle's death played in Benjamin's life, see Martin Jay, "Walter Benjamin, Remembrance, and the First World War," in *Benjamin Studies,* vol. 1, *Perception and Experience in Modernity,* ed. Helga Geyer-Ryan (Amsterdam: Rodopi, 2002).

36. Benjamin, *Gesammelte Schriften,* vol. 2, pt. 3, p. 840.

37. Benjamin to Scholem, April 25, 1930, in Benjamin, *Briefe,* 1:513.

38. See Benjamin to Scholem, February 1, 1918, ibid., p. 174.

39. Kurt Hiller to Theodor Adorno, February 6, 1965, quoted in Benjamin, *Gesammelte Schriften,* vol. 2, pt. 3, p. 916.

40. Gershom Scholem, *Walter Benjamin: Geschichte einer Freundschaft* (Frankfurt: Suhrkamp, 1975), p. 36.

41. Scholem, *Story of a Friendship,* p. 6. See Jeremy Adler, "There Stood My Mr. Benjamin," *Times Literary Supplement,* July 7, 1996, pp. 10–11.

42. Scholem, *Story of a Friendship,* p. 29.

43. Ibid., p. 23.

PART I NOTEBOOKS

1. Koeben is a small town not far from Glogau on the river Oder.

2. This is the location of the Jewish cemetery at Weissensee, the largest in Berlin.

3. His mother—who nicknamed him "Philadelphia"—dressed him as a girl for family plays she wrote.

4. The Reform synagogue attended by the Scholem family was on the Lindenstrasse.

5. This was the location of the Orthodox synagogue.

6. A report on the twentieth annual meeting of the Farmers' Association appeared in the *Berliner Tageblatt* on February 17, 1913.

7. Werner Scholem (1895–1940), Scholem's brother, was a socialist and was therefore in constant conflict with Arthur Scholem.

8. This is a reference to the beginnings of emancipation in Prussia in the 1840s.

9. Leopold Zunz, one of the founders of the Wissenschaft des Judentums, or Science of Judaism, wrote "Nekrolog Krochmals" in 1844. See Lunz, *Gesammelte Schriften,* vol. 2 (Berlin: Curatorium der Zunzstiftung, 1876), pp. 150–159. Nachman Krochmal (1785–1840), a pioneer of modern Jewish scholarship, applied modern Enlightenment ideas to the writing and teaching of Jewish history. He wrote his most important work in Hebrew, *Guide to the Perplexed of Our Age.*

10. Scholem is referring to Heinrich Graetz's *Kritischer Kommentar zu den Psalmen, nebst Text und Übersetzung* (Breslau, 1882–83), and Samson Raphael Hirsch's translation and commentary on the Psalms, *Die Psalmen* (Frankfurt, 1882). Heinrich Graetz (1817–1891) and Samson Raphael Hirsch (1808–1888) were leaders in the effort to revive Jewish learning and practice. Unlike those associated with the Wissenschaft des Judentums, the two men sought to awaken Jewish spirituality within modernized Judaism. Graetz was Hirsch's pupil but eventually fell out of favor with him. Graetz is considered the father of Conservative Judaism. His teacher Hirsch is widely recognized as the founder of neo-Orthodoxy.

11. Moses Hoffmann (1873–1958) was a rabbi in Emden, a port city in northern Germany. Werner Sombart, a leading German sociologist and close colleague of Max Weber, wrote a book on the Jewish role in the economy, *Die Juden und das Wirtschaftsleben* (Berlin, 1912). At the time Sombart was touring Germany, delivering lectures on the theme. Hoffmann's article was "Judentum und Kapitalismus: Eine kritische Würdigung von Werner Sombarts *Die Juden und das Wirtschaftsleben*" (Steglitz: Hobbing, 1913). Many of his comments—such as "There is nothing so foreign to Romanticism as the purely Jewish discursive way of conceiving and understanding the world"—gave legitimacy to what "vulgar" anti-Semites had been saying all along. Surprisingly, Buber's group of followers in Prague actually supported him. See Michael Loewy, *Redemption and Utopia* (London: Athlone Press, 1992), p. 51.

12. Richard Horowitz was a fellow member of Scholem's Zionist youth group, Young Judah.

13. A member of Young Judah. Young Judah was hardly free from either the strengths or the limitations of German youth culture. A songbook members used during trekking adventures includes a verse about returning to Zion and having there "a new, marvelous, free life," but also about the singers' "overflowing feeling for

God's free nature, their joy and suffering from love, their happy wanderlust and delight in wine and beer."

14. Ludwig Werner (1855–1929) was a member of the Prussian parliament between 1899 and 1908. He was also the editor of the anti-Semitic weekly *Reichsgeldmonopol*.

15. Houston Stuart Chamberlain was a rabidly pro-German Englishman who settled in Germany (he also married Richard Wagner's daughter). He wrote the anti-Semitic book *Foundations of the Nineteenth Century* (London: J. Lane, 1911). The first German edition appeared in Munich in 1899. Chamberlain had the highest praise for the noble German "race-soul," poetry and music. Jews were by contrast materialistic and legalistic.

16. George Scholem (1868–1928) was Arthur Scholem's brother. Scholem was particularly incensed at the mockery of tradition. See Gershom Scholem, *On Jews and Judaism in Crisis* (New York: Schocken Books, 1976), p. 6.

17. A separatist Orthodox synagogue located on the Artilleriestrasse in Berlin.

18. Gustav Frenssen (1863–1945), *Klaus Hinrich Baas* (Berlin: G. Grote, 1909). Scholem may be referring to Theodor Herzl's *Unser Käthchen: Ein Lustspiel* (Vienna: Buchdruckerei Industrie, 1899). Herzl wrote a number of plays both before and after he wrote *The Jewish State.* His favorite genre was comedy, or *Lustspiel*. He predicted that the "first great literary form of neo-Jewish culture will probably be the comedy" (Herzl's diary entry from April 25, 1897).

19. Gustav Frenssen, *Der Untergang der Anna Hollmann* (Berlin: G. Grote, 1911).

20. Oskar Cassel (1849–1923) was a Jewish lawyer and member of the progressive party, Volkspartei. Cassel served in the Prussian parliament between 1903 and 1918. He was also chairman of the Union of German Jews organization.

21. This was reported in the *Berliner Tageblatt* on February 22, 1919. Adolph Hoffmann (1858–1930) was an editor, book dealer, writer, and member of the Prussian parliament from 1908 to 1919.

22. Max Nordau (1849–1923) was a popular writer long before he joined Herzl's Zionist movement. He was best known for his critique of "effete" civilization and its degenerate art, by which he meant realism. After his conversion to Herzl's cause he continued to write books, pamphlets, and plays. The play *Doktor Kohn,* which appeared in 1898, treats the subjects of assimilation, mixed marriage, baptism, and anti-Semitism.

23. Samson Raphael Hirsch, *Über die Beziehungen des Talmud zum Judentum und zu der sozialen Stellung seiner Bekenner* (Frankfurt, 1884); Alexander Berg, *Judentum und Sozialdemokratie* (Berlin, 1891).

24. An international philanthropic organization founded in Paris in 1860.

25. Edouard Adolphe Drumont, *La France juive* (Paris: Flammarion, 1883). According to Drumont's tract, simple, hardworking French shopkeepers and peasants were no match for the greedy, mercantile Jew. The book went through 114 editions in one year.

26. August Wünsche, *Der Talmud* (Zurich, 1879). Emanuel Oskar Menachem Deutsch, *The Talmud* (Berlin: F. Dümmler, 1869).

27. Raphael Hirsch, *Chover: oder Versuche über Jissroëls Pflichten in der Zerstreuung* (Altona, 1837).

28. Heinrich Süssigruth's bookstore was founded in 1885.

29. Wilhelm Marr, *Sieg des Judentums über das Germanentum* (Berlin: Georg Frobeen and Co., 1873). Marr, a German anarchist and anti-Semite, coined the term "anti-Semitism" and founded an "Anti-Semitic League."

30. The *Berliner Tageblatt* was a Berlin newspaper founded in 1872 by the liberal Jewish publisher Rudolf Mosse.

31. Friedrich Ernst Freiherr von Langen, *Das jüdische Geheimgesetz und die deutschen Landesvertretungen* (Munich, 1892).

32. The *Choschen ha-mishpat* is the breast shield of the high priest. It is discussed in part four of Joseph Caro's *Shulhan Arukh.*

33. Caesar Seligmann (1860–1950), leader of Reform Judaism in Germany and chief rabbi of Frankfurt.

34. Theodor Herzl, *Altneuland* (Vienna: B. Harz, 1919). Herzl envisions the future Jewish state as a socialist utopia, more Viennese and central European than traditionally Jewish. According to Amos Elon, Herzl's biographer, the book's "pursuit of Arcadian bliss within a mystic community and its haunted preoccupation with dreams recall Gustav Mahler's music." Cited in Theodor Herzl, *Old-New Land,* trans. Lotta Levensohn, intro. Jacques Kornberg (Princeton: Marcus Weiner, 1960), p. 1.

35. Agudah Yisrael was an Orthodox organization.

36. Jacob Segall (1883–1959).

37. Harry Heymann (1897–1918).

38. Jakob Jahr, a fellow Zionist and brother of Scholem's friend Meta Jahr.

39. Martin Buber, *Die Geschichten des Rabbi Nachman* (Frankfurt: Rütten und Loening, 1906). Comparing Buber's tales to the Brothers Grimm, the Jewish writer Arnold Zweig said, "Only such legends are capable of bringing back an alienated youth to the spiritual essence of Judaism." Arnold Zweig, "Über jüdische Legenden," *Mitteilungen des Verbandes der jüdischen Jugendvereine Deutschlands* (1914): 65. The concluding words to Rabbi Nachman illustrate the power Buber's book had over young Zionists. Buber writes of Rabbi Nachman's trip to the Holy Land: "Here in the land of Israel, the purification of the imagination takes place. It is not for nothing that the sounds of the words *adama*—soil—and *medame*—imagination—resemble each other: the fullness of the elements comes to the imagination from the earth. But the purification of the imagination by faith can take place no other way than through the consecrated earth, and the consecrated earth is here in the land of Israel."

40. Strauss, who studied under Schleiermacher and Hegel in Berlin, wrote his principal theological work, *Life of Jesus,* in 1835. Strauss stirred a sensation by stripping the Bible of miracles. In *Life of Jesus* he explains the miracles in the New Testament as purely mythic and devised by the early church to promote its cause.

41. The Baedeker volumes were popular tour books at the time.

42. Sabbatai Sevi (1626–1676), the son of a fish merchant from Smyrna, real-

ized his messianic calling as a young man, and over time managed to get Jewish masses from the Balkans to western Europe to follow him. Sevi's later apostasy to Islam confronted the Jewish world with the preposterous case of a renegade messiah addled by self-delusion. And it was precisely his madness that appealed to young writers. In 1925 Josef Kastein, a disciple of Buber's, would write a best-seller based upon Sabbatai's life. It reads like an expressionist novel, with a gripping narrative and catchy chapter titles such as "The Prophet and the Whore," "Tumult," "Echo," "Catastrophe," and "Death Tremors."

43. See 1 Kings 5:13.

44. Gerhard Hauptmann, *Der Narr in Christo Emanuel Quint* (Berlin: Fischer, 1910), p. 27.

45. Søren Kierkegaard (1813–1855), Danish philosopher considered to be a founder of existentialism.

46. Georg Brandes, *Søren Kierkegaard,* vol. 3 of *Gesammelte Schriften* (Munich, 1902), pp. 258–445. What attracted Scholem, as it did many people at the time and since, was Kierkegaard's break with rationalism, be it in the prevailing Hegelian philosophy or in religious orthodoxy or its liberal counterpart. Instead of reason, Kierkegaard turns to the believer's anxiety, melancholy, and sense of paradox and the absurd. Rather than rational codes, the manner in which one lives one's life was for him the only real standard for living in the truth.

47. Paul Anton de Lagarde (1827–1891) was considered a prophet of German *Volkstum.* He was also a well-known anti-Semite. See Fritz Stern, *The Politics of Cultural Despair* (New York: Doubleday, 1965), pp. 27–70.

48. "I believe because it is absurd." The remark is attributed to the early Christian theologian Tertullian.

49. Latin for "if only!"

50. Jettka Stein.

51. Salomon Ludwig Steinheim (1789–1866) was a physician, poet, and philosopher of religion. He maintained that human reason, incapable of reaching truth, is dependent on divine revelation.

52. Reference to Kierkegaard's *Either/Or.* Kierkegaard published the book in 1843 using the pseudonym Victor Eremita, or "victorious hermit."

53. Franz Oppenheimer (1864–1943), "Zur Psychologie des Sozialismus," *Neue Rundschau* 2 (1913): 1193–1209. Oppenheimer was a physician, journalist, and professor of economics in Berlin.

54. Samuel Saenger, "Werturteile," *Die Neue Rundschau: XXIVter Jahrgang der Freien Bühne* (1913): 1329–30. Michel de Montaigne (1533–1592) was a French writer famous for his skepticism and dry wit. One of his famous statements in *Essays* was, "I have never seen a greater monster or miracle than myself."

55. Friedrich Nietzsche, *Also Sprach Zarathustra* (Leipzig, 1885). The book, mimicking Luther's biblical language, begins with the lines: "When Zarathustra was thirty years old, he left his home and the lake of his home, and went into the mountains. There he enjoyed his spirit and solitude, and for ten years did not weary of it.

But at last his heart changed, and rising one morning with the rosy dawn, he went before the sun, and spake thus unto it: Thou great star! What would be thy happiness if thou hadst not those for whom thou shinest!"

56. Jens Peter Jacobsen (1847–1885). Hermann Sudermann (1857–1928).

57. Anatole France (1844–1924), pseudonym of Anatole Thibault, French novelist and satirist.

58. Hans Blüher, *Wandervögel: Geschichte einer Jugendbewegung* (Berlin: Weise, 1912).

59. Rainer Maria Rilke (1875–1926), German poet.

60. This is the first verse in Rilke's *Das Stunden-Buch* (Leipzig: Insel Verlag, 1905), p. 36. Rilke wrote *The Book of Hours: The Book of Monastic Life* after a tour of Russia in 1899, when he visited Russian monasteries and met Leo Tolstoy.

61. Richard Dehmel, *Schöne wilde Welt: Neue Gedichte und Sprüche* (Berlin: Fischer Verlag, 1913).

62. The lines "Uns aber is gegeben / Nirgends zu ruhen" come from Hölderlin's *Hyperions Schicksalslied*.

63. The name of the legendary Wandering Jew. It is also the title of a novel by Fritz Mauthner, *Der neue Ahasver: Roman aus Jung-Berlin*.

64. Hölderlin and Nietzsche both went insane.

65. Stefan Zweig (1881–1942), *Erstes Erlebnis: Vier Geschichte aus Kinderland* (Frankfurt: Fischer Verlag, 1976). In his *World of Yesterday,* written after Hitler's seizure of power in Germany, Zweig describes central European Jewish life before World War I. He writes, "When I attempt to find a simple formula for the period in which I grew up, prior to the First World War, I hope that I convey its fullness by calling it the Golden Age of Security."

66. "Brennendes Geheimnis," in *Vier Geschichte aus Kinderland,* pp. 86–208.

67. Johann Wolfgang von Goethe, *Die Leiden des jungen Werther* (Leipzig: Insel Verlag, 1911).

68. The headlines in the *Berliner Tageblatt* on November 16, 1914, read, "A Great Victory in the East! 28,000 Russian Prisoners Taken. Russians Pushed Back Past Kutno."

69. Goethe's translations of Ossian's ballads occupy several pages of *The Sorrows of Young Werther.*

70. Friedrich Nietzsche, *Unzeitgemässige Betrachtungen* (Stuttgart: A. Kröner, 1964).

71. Gustav Frenssen, *Hilligenlei* (Berlin: G. Grote, 1905).

72. Fritz Mauthner, *Beiträge zu einer Kritik der Sprache* (Berlin, 1906–1913). Mauthner (1849–1923) was the editor of the cultural pages for the *Berliner Tageblatt.* His books on language appeared in three volumes in 1901–2. Mauthner wrote a history of atheism, *Der Atheismus und seine Geschichte im Abendland,* 4 vols. (1923).

73. George Philipp von Hardenberg (1772–1801), who wrote under the pseudonym Novalis, was a German Romantic poet.

74. Peter Hille (1854–1904), author of *Gestalten und Aphorismen,* in *Gesammelte*

Werke, vol. 2 (Berlin, 1904), p. 119; Karl Joel (1864–1934), author of *Der Ursprung der Naturphilosophie aus dem Geiste der Mystik* (Jena: Diederichs, 1905).

75. Isaak Bleichrode (1867–1954) was the rabbi at the Orthodox synagogue. See Scholem, *Story of a Friendship,* p. 15.

76. Hermann Leberecht Strack (1848–1922). Israel Hildesheimer (1864–1943). Hildesheimer was the rabbi at the Adass Israel synagogue.

77. Original written in Hebrew.

78. Friedrich Nietzsche, *Also Sprach Zarathustra: Werke VI* (Leipzig: Insel Verlag, 1885), pp. 63–65. Nietzsche writes in the chapter "Preachers of Death": "There are preachers of death: and the earth is full of those to whom desistance from life must be preached. . . . There are the spiritually consumptive ones: hardly are they born when they begin to die, and long for doctrines of lassitude and renunciation."

79. Semjon Juschkewitsch, *Ghetto* (Vienna, 1903).

80. Julius Wellhausen (1844–1918) was a professor of Old Testament in Göttingen. In his *History of Ancient Israel* (1878) Wellhausen argues that the first five books of Moses were most likely written many centuries after Moses. For Wellhausen's theory of ancient Israel, see his *Prolegomena to the History of Israel,* trans. J. Sutherland Black (Atlanta: Scholar's Press, 1994).

81. Berthold Auerbach (1812–1882), a German-Jewish writer, wrote a series of romantic tales of village life called *Black Forest Village Stories.*

82. August Strindberg (1849–1912) was one of the fathers of modern theater. He went through various periods and styles, and in his later period—after a disastrous divorce—he adopted Swedenborgian mysticism. He began to infuse his writings with symbolism combining realism with religious mysticism.

83. *Ha-Shem,* literally "the name," is the Hebrew expression for God.

84. These were words uttered by Herzl, urging his followers not to lose hope in the dream of creating a Jewish state. "If you desire it, it is not a fable," was Herzl's prophecy at the end of *Old-New Land.*

85. Max Brod (1884–1968), one of Buber's closest followers, won fame at the time for his book *Über die Schönheit hässlicher Bilder* (Vienna: Zsolnay, 1967).

86. Hugo von Hoffmansthal (1874–1929).

87. Arabic for "fate" or "destiny."

88. "With Scholem's heart, with his entire spirit."

89. In *Zarathustra,* Nietzsche writes in the chapter "OLD AND NEW TABLES": "O my brethren, not backward shall your nobility gaze, but OUTWARD! Exiles shall ye be from all fatherlands and forefather-lands! Your CHILDREN'S LAND shall ye love: let this love be your new nobility,—the undiscovered in the remotest seas! For it do I bid your sails search and search! Unto your children shall ye MAKE AMENDS for being the children of your fathers: all the past shall ye THUS redeem! This new table do I place over you!"

90. Hermann Cohen (1842–1918) founded the Neo-Kantian movement known as the Marburg School. He was the most famous and influential Jewish philosopher in Germany at the time, and as such was looked upon as a leader of Ger-

man Jewry. His *Religion der Vernunft aus den Quellen des Judentums, Deutschtum und Judentum* established him as a central figure in modern Jewish thought. Cohen regarded Judaism as the quintessential religion of reason and universal ethics.

91. Leo Tolstoy's *Confessions* (1882) deals with his conversion to Christianity. The book recounts the squandered years of his youth, years he could not "recall . . . without horror, loathing, and heart-rending pain," and how he had found the truth in "Christ's humanity."

92. Jesus says in Luke 10:38–42, "Martha, Martha, thou art careful and troubled about many things; but one thing is needful."

93. Erwin Briese was a member of Young Judah.

94. Karl Liebknecht (1871–1919) was the only member of parliament to vote against extending war credits to the government.

95. Emanuel Swedenborg (1688–1772), Swedish scientist, religious teacher, and mystic.

96. Arthur Bonus, *Zur religiösen Krise* (Jena, 1911). Arthur Bonus tried to rid Christianity of Jewish elements and to refine its "Aryan" Germanic powers. Bonus's books, in particular his Icelandic sagas, were popular reading among German prisoners of war.

97. Arthur Bonus, *Deutscher Glaube: Religiöse Bekenntnisse aus Vergangenheit und Gegenwart,* ed. Ernst Michel (Jena, 1914). Diederichs Verlag was a leading publisher of avant-garde literature.

98. The Sefer ha-Zohar (Book of Splendor) is the central text of the Kabbalah. In the Zohar, *Siwwug* is the longing for marriage to God.

99. *Zimzum* is the notion of divine contraction attributed to Isaak Luria (1534–1572), a founder of the school of Kabbalah that bears his name. See Gershom Scholem, *Sabbatai Sevi: The Mystical Messiah, 1626–1676* (Princeton, 1973), p. 28. Also Scholem, *Kabbalah* (New York: Meridian, 1978), pp. 129–135.

100. Friedrich Theodor Vischer (1807–87), *Auch Einer: Eine Reisebekanntschaft* (Stuttgart: Deutsche Verlagsanstalt, 1908). Vischer recounts in his books conversations with the philosopher Schopenhauer, who says that "a stupid devil, the so-called will, created the world."

101. Max Stirner (1806–1856) was a founder of anarchism. He wrote *Der Einzige und sein Eigentum* (Leipzig, 1845).

102. Traditional prayer said for the dead.

103. Henri Bergson (1859–1941), French philosopher best known for his book *Creative Evolution* (1907). Jakob Wassermann (1873–1934) was an editor of the avant-garde journal *Simplicissimus.*

104. Zionist critics described as *Mauscheln* the demeaning way Jews traditionally spoke with gentiles. According to Herzl's "Mauschel" (*Die Welt,* October 15, 1897), it is the "perversion of the human character, something unspeakably lowly and disgusting."

105. In Theodor Herzl's utopian novel *Altneuland* (1919), a future state for the Jews is a showcase for modern industry, labor laws, and rules of justice. Young Jews

such as Scholem were critical of the vision because Herzl shut religion out of this future state.

106. Young Judah planned a discussion evening on the writings of Martin Buber.

107. Ignaz Zollschan (1887–1948), like Buber in his own way, delved into the racial question from a Jewish angle. His main book is titled *The Racial Problem from the Particular Perspective of the Theoretical Foundation of the Jewish Racial Question (Das Rassenproblem unter besonderer Berücksichtigung der theoretischen Grundlagen der jüdischen Rassenfrage* [Vienna, 1910]).

108. Gershom Scholem, *The Fullness of Time,* trans. and ed. Richard Sieburth (Jerusalem: Ibis, 2003), pp. 47–48.

109. Karl Türkischer, Walter Czapski, Henry Klein, and Harry Levy were members of Young Judah.

110. Erich was serving in the military in Belgium.

111. Scholem ironically uses the expression "Praemissis praemittendis," an archaic form of address.

112. Martin Buber, *Drei Reden über das Judentum* (Frankfurt: Rüttem and Loening, 1911), pp. 81–88.

113. The English passenger ship was torpedoed on May 7, 1915. This led to the entry of the United States into the war.

114. Henri Bergson, Gustav Landauer, Georg Simmel. One of the most famous essays by Simmel (1858–1918) was "Essay about the Stranger" (in *Soziologie: Untersuchungen über die Formen der Vergesellschaftung* [Berlin: Duncker & Humblot Verlag, 1908], pp. 509–512).

115. Martin Buber, *Daniel* (Leipzig: Insel Verlag, 1913); *Ekstatische Konfessionen* (Jena: Diederichs, 1909).

116. Micha Josef bin Gorion, *Die Sagen der Juden* (Frankfurt: Rüttem and Loening, 1913).

117. The poem is found in *Das Zeit-Echo: Ein Kriegs-Tagebuch der Künstler* 13 (1914): 186.

118. Eduard Grisebach, *Schopenhauer* (Berlin: E. Hofmann, 1897).

119. Johann Georg Hamann (1730–1788), *Magi und Sokratische Denkwürdigkeiten* (Leipzig: Insel, 1915).

120. Søren Kierkegaard, *Concluding Scientific Postscript,* trans. David Swenson (Princeton: Princeton University Press, 1940); *The Present Age,* trans. Alexander Dru (London: Oxford University Press, 1940). In the latter, in the chapter "The Present Age and of the Difference between a Genius and an Apostle," he writes, "The present age is one of understanding, of reflection, devoid of passion, an age which flies into enthusiasm for a moment only to decline back into indolence."

121. Peter Chelezizky (1390–1460) was a leader of the Hussite movement, a religious movement eventually suppressed by the Roman Catholic Church.

122. Johann Georg Hamann.

123. Meister Eckhart (1260–1328), German mystic. At the time there was a

wide revival of interest in Eckhart's writings, largely thanks to the work of Gustav Landauer, who was a close friend of Martin Buber's and who published a three-volume translation into High German of Eckhart's mystical writings, *Meister Eckharts mystische Schriften* (1903).

124. Max Frischeisen-Köhler was a neo-Kantian philosopher. Scholem attended his lectures on the introduction to philosophy in the summer semester, 1915.

125. *Shalem* is Hebrew for "complete."

126. Edgar Blum (1897–1917) was Scholem's closest boyhood friend.

127. Theodor Herzl, *The Jewish State* (London: Pordes, 1967).

128. Scholem had read Henri Poincaré's *The Foundations of Science: Science and Hypothesis* (Lancaster: Science Press, 1946).

129. Hermann Bahr (1863–1934). Christian Morgenstern (1871–1914). Elsewhere in his diaries Scholem returns to Morgenstern's poem "Das gross Lalula," in *Galgenlieder* (Berlin: Cassirer, 1909).

130. Rudolf Steiner (1861–1925), German scientist, philosopher, and mystic. Steiner was the founder of anthroposophy.

131. Israel ben Eliezer (ca. 1700–1760), known as the Baal Shem Tov (master of the Name of God), was the founder of Hasidism, a renewal movement among eastern European Jews. Martin Buber popularized the teachings of the Baal Shem Tov with his bestselling *Die Legende des Baalschem* (1908).

132. Kurt Hiller (1885–1972). Hiller, who studied law, then turned to literature, was the author of *Die Weisheit der Langweile* (The Wisdom of Boredom), which Scholem had read. See Scholem, *From Berlin to Jerusalem,* pp. 76–77; and *Story of a Friendship,* p. 5.

133. James Stirling (1692–1770). The formula was developed in his book *Methodus Differentialis* (1770).

134. Erich Brauer (1895–1942).

135. A play on the title of Buber's essay on Herzl, "Er und Wir," *Die Welt,* May 20, 1900, pp. 445–446.

136. The site of a public library founded in 1905 by the Social Democratic politician Hugo Heimann. Ernst Mach, *Erkenntnis und Irrtum* (Leipzig: J. A. Barth, 1905).

137. *One and For All* is the subtitle of Nietzsche's *Zarathustra.* Laurence Sterne's *The Life and Opinions of Tristram Shandy, Gentleman* is a nine-volume experimental novel published between 1759 and 1767. The first volume begins with reflections on the ill effects of Tristram's father's actions on his "genius and the very cast of his mind."

138. See note 100.

139. In March 1915 Scholem was expelled from school because of an antiwar letter he had written.

140. *Die Internationale: Eine Zeitschrift für Praxis und Theorie des Marxismus,* a journal edited by Rosa Luxemburg and Franz Mehring (Berlin, 1915).

141. *Der Anfang* was a youth journal associated with Gustav Wyneken and the German youth movement. Benjamin published essays using the pseudonym "Ardor."

142. *Lichtstrahlen: Monatliches Bildungsorgan für denkende Arbeiter,* a journal edited by Julian Borchardt.

143. Friedrich Wilhelm Schelling (1775–1854), German Romantic philosopher.

144. This is the main street in the center of Berlin where the University of Berlin and the Berlin State Library are located.

145. Victor Klemperer, "Arthur Schnitzler," *Ost und West* (September 1906): 371–378. Arthur Schnitzler was the author of the novel *The Way into the Open.* See note 190.

146. Johann Paul Richter (1763–1825), who used the pseudonym Jean Paul, was a German novelist whose writings are noted for their idealism, humor, and warm portrayals of simple life. More pertinent to Scholem, he was also a religious thinker. One of his famous lines, for instance, is, "God is an unutterable sigh, planted in the depths of the soul."

147. Mauthner's critique of language takes aim at "word-superstition . . . the tyranny of language." Unlike for Benjamin, who looked for truth within language, for Mauthner the essence of philosophy lies beyond language, in the realms of silence. See Fritz Mauthner, *Beiträge zu einer Kritik der Sprache,* vol. 1 (Leipzig, 1922–23), pp. 1, 713.

148. Wilhelm Julius Foerster (1832–1921), an astronomer who gave a series of public lectures titled "Cosmic Knowledge and Ethics."

149. Epimenides (sixth century B.C.), a Cretan said to be a prophet. According to legend, he fell asleep in a cave and awoke fifty-seven years later. Goethe wrote his drama *Epimenidines Erwachen* in 1814.

150. Gustav Landauer (1870–1919). His article "Stelle Dich, Sozialist!" appeared in *Der Aufbruch: Monatsblättern aus der Jugendbewegung,* a journal edited by Ernst Joel (July 1915): 14–19. Gustav Landauer, a close collaborator of Buber's, broke from him in part over Buber's support for the war.

151. Karl Lamprecht (1856–1915), professor of history at Leipzig.

152. Baudelaire's *Les Fleurs du Mal* (1857), translated by Stefan George as *Die Blumen des Bösen* (Berlin, 1901).

153. Heinrich Wilhelm von Gesternberg, *Ugolino* (Berlin: E. Ebering, 1898).

154. Friedrich Gottlieb Klopstock (1724–1803).

155. Martin Buber, *Reden und Gleichnisse des Tschuang-Tse* (Leipzig: Insel Verlag, 1910).

156. A reference to articles in *Blue-White Spectacles (Blau-Weisse-Brille).*

157. Ismar Löwenthal, a friend from Young Judah.

158. Jean Paul, *Titan* (Berlin: R. Matzdorff, 1800–1803). *Titan* appeared in four volumes. Jean Paul's fiction was heavily influenced by the idealist philosophy of Johann Gottlieb Fichte, who was intrigued with the question of identity and the selfhood of the self. Jean Paul liked using images of doppelgangers and multiple selves.

159. Karl Türkischer, a friend from Young Judah. See Scholem, *From Berlin to Jerusalem,* pp. 71 and 146. Gotthold Kalischer; Henry Klein.

160. Moses Calvary (1876–1944) was one of the contributors to *Vom Judentum*. His article was "Das neue Judentum und die schöpferische Phantasie," in *Vom Judentum* (Leipzig: Kurt Wolff 1913), pp. 103–116.

161. The Kol Nidre is the prayer chanted on the eve of Yom Kippur, the Day of Atonement.

162. Leviticus 23:32.

163. The *Vorwärts* was the central publication for the German Social Democratic Party.

164. Fritz Mauthner, *Der letzte Tod des Gautama Buddha* (Munich: George Muller, 1921).

165. Herodotus, *Historians,* 5.105.

166. Ernst Haeckel (1834–1919), zoologist and defender of Darwin's theory of evolution.

167. *Lustigen Blätter: Schönstes buntes Witzblatt Deutschlands* (1885–1941).

168. Scholem is citing from Martin Buber's *Daniel,* p. 62.

169. Scholem is referring to the correspondence between Nietzsche and Brandes in Friedrich Nietzsche, *Gesammelte Briefe,* vol. 3 (Leipzig: Insel, 1905), pp. 282–284.

170. Nietzsche, *Also Sprach Zarathustra,* p. 86.

171. Harry Aharon Heller (1899–1967).

172. Alfred Rabau (1896–1958) was a law student in Berlin and a member of a Jewish university fraternity whose pro-German stance Scholem rejected.

173. Simchat Torah is a festival celebrating the completion of the annual reading of the Torah.

174. Jakob Wassermann, *Die Juden von Zirndorf* (Munich: Langen Müller, 1999).

175. Agathon Geyer, the main figure in the novel, has a vision of himself being anointed Messiah.

176. Hans Hirsch, Betty Scholem's brother.

177. Walter Benjamin, "Das Leben der Studenten," in *Gesammelte Schriften,* vol. 2, pt. 1, pp. 75–87.

178. Paul Scheerbart (1863–1915) was a novelist who combined fantasy, philosophy, and art (he illustrated his own books). His outlandish style in both writing and life influenced the expressionists and Dadaists.

179. Bonaventura, *Nachwachen* (Leipzig: Insel Verlag, 1909).

180. Hermann Amadus Schwarz (1843–1921) gave a course in the winter semester of 1915 on analytic geometry at the Friedrich-Wilhelms University in Berlin.

181. See Scholem, *Briefe,* 1:21–25.

182. Clemens Brentano, *Die Märchen* (Stuttgart, 1879).

183. "Das Märchen von dem Schulmeister Klopfstock und seinen fünf Söhnen."

184. Stefan George, *Der Siebente Ring* (Berlin: George Bondi, 1907).

185. In a letter to Scholem she complains about too much talk, too little action. Scholem, *Briefe,* 1:328.

186. This was a group of Arabic scholars in the tenth century in Basra.

187. Paul Scheerbart, *Tarub, Bagdads berümte Köchin* (Berlin: Verein für Deutsches Schrifttum, 1897).

188. Jakob Böhme, *The Way to Christ* (New York: Harper, 1947). Jakob Böhme (1575–1624) was a cobbler who had a religious awakening after light from a pewter dish sent him into an ecstatic trance. His writings on the "Abyss" and "Non-Being" subsequently influenced the German Romantic writers Franz von Baader and Friedrich Schelling.

189. Paul Deussen, *Jakob Böhme: Über sein Leben. Rede* (Kiel, 1897).

190. Gottfried Keller (1819–1890).

191. Arthur Schnitzler, *Der Weg ins Freie* (Berlin: Fischer Verlag, 1908). Schnitzler (1862–1931), a Viennese Jewish physician, describes in his book conflicts between Jewish and non-Jewish youth. The novel is largely concerned with the question of anti-Semitism, assimilation, and Zionism.

192. Schnitzler wrote a play by this title, *Der einsame Weg* (Berlin: Fischer Verlag, 1904).

193. Samuel Hirszenberg (1865–1908) was a painter who studied in Cracow, Munich, and Paris. He moved to Jerusalem in 1907. His painting *Golus,* along with his sketches, were published in the periodical *Ost und West* (1904): 553–562.

194. Buber, *Die Legende des Baalschem,* p. 93.

195. Hans Blüher, *Wandervogel: Geschichte einer Jugendbewegung.*

196. Bertha Freifrau von Suttner (1843–1914) was an Austrian novelist and ardent pacifist.

197. Gerstenberg, *Ugolino.*

198. Latin for "wisely" or "discreetly."

199. *Zaddik* is the Hebrew term for "holy man."

200. Landauer founded the periodical *Der Sozialist* (1891–1915).

201. *Die Sagen der Juden,* an anthology of Jewish tales.

202. During the war, Palestine was infested with a plague of locusts.

203. The legal part of the Torah is composed of 633 commandments.

204. Leonhard Frank, *Die Ursache* (Leipzig: Insel Verlag, 1915).

205. Josef Freiherr von Eichendorff (1788–1857), *Von Wald und Welt* (Düsseldorf: Bücher der Rose, 1909). Eichendorff was one of the last German Romantic poets. His *Good for Nothing* (trans. A. L. Wister [Philadelphia: J. B. Lippincott Company, 1906]) starts with a father lashing out at his son for being a "good-for-nothing," sitting in the sun instead of working. He throws him out of the house. "'Well,' said I, 'all right; if I am a good-for-nothing, I will go forth into the world and make my fortune.'"

206. The German title is *Taugenichts.*

207. E. T. A. Hoffmann (1776–1822), German Romantic writer.

208. These were Goethe's dying words.

209. Scholem read the German edition: Kierkegaard, *Gesammelte Werke: Stadien auf dem Lebenswege* (Jena, 1914). *Stages on Life's Way* was published under the pseud-

onym Hilarius Bookbinder. The full title is *Guilty or Not Guilty? A Story of Suffering: An Imaginary Psychological Construction.*

210. Kraus says this in his essay "Heine und die Folgen," *Die Fakel,* August 31, 1911, pp. 1–33.

211. Gustav Wyneken, *Schule und Jugendkultur* (Jena, 1913). Hans Levy (1886–1916) was a law student. He would soon be killed in the war.

212. Hedwig Scholem was the wife of George Scholem, Gerhard's uncle.

213. Kierkegaard, *Stadien auf dem Lebensweg,* p. 400.

214. Scholem read the German edition, *Der Augenblick,* in *Gesammelte Werke,* vol. 12 (Jena, 1909). For Kierkegaard, Christianity is the "single individual," whereas Christendom is the masses and the crowd, the state and society, with all their leveling tendencies. He writes about his contemporary Christendom: "The present age is essentially a sensible, reflecting age, devoid of passion, flaring up in superficial, short-lived enthusiasm and prudentially relaxing in indolence. . . . [W]hereas a passionate age accelerates, raises up, and overthrows, elevates and debases, a reflective apathetic age does the opposite, it stifles and impedes, it levels."

215. Jehudah Steinberg, *Writings* (Odessa, 1909).

216. Saul Tschernichowski (1875–1943), Hebrew poet, published his *Shirim* (Poems) in Odessa in 1910.

217. Haim Bialik was the leading Hebrew poet at the time.

218. Walter Hirschfeld (?–1918).

219. Jean Paul, *Titan,* p. 767.

PART II: BLUE-WHITE SPECTACLES

1. See Benjamin, *Gesammelte Schriften,* vol. 2, pt. 3, p. 916.

2. Benjamin wrote "Der Ursprung des deutschen Trauerspiels" between June and November 1916.

3. Benjamin, *Gesammelte Schriften* 1:319.

4. Ibid., p. 354.

5. Norbert Bolz and Willem van Reigen, *Walter Benjamin* (Frankfurt: Reinhe Campus, 1991), pp. 31, 32.

6. See Scholem, *From Berlin to Jerusalem,* pp. 74–75, 99–100.

7. Scholem, *Story of a Friendship,* p. 33.

8. Benjamin, *Gesammelte Schriften,* vol. 2, pt. 1, p. 239.

9. Benjamin to Scholem, December 3, 1917, in Benjamin, *Briefe,* 1:157.

10. Benjamin, *Gesammelte Schriften,* vol. 2, pt. 1, p. 239.

11. Walter Benjamin, "On Language as Such and on the Language of Man," in *Selected Writings,* vol. 1 (Cambridge, Mass.: Harvard University Press, 1996), p. 74.

12. Scholem, *Tagebücher,* 2:86.

13. Ibid., p. 430.

14. On Scholem's adoption of the terms *Lehre* and *Ordnung,* see *Story of a Friendship,* p. 56.

15. Diary entry from October 18, 1917.

16. Diary entry from August 16, 1916.

17. Diary entry from October 12, 1916.

PART II NOTEBOOKS

1. Martin Gumpert (1897–1955). In 1915 he published poems anonymously in the expressionist journal *Die Aktion*. He was also one of the founders of Wyneken's journal *Der Anfang*.

2. Scholem attended a seminar on differential equations held by Konrad Knopp (1882–1957) at the University of Berlin.

3. Jakob Lubmann came from Palestine and studied mathematics at the University of Berlin.

4. The Herzl Club was founded in Berlin in 1907 to give a Zionist education to young people working in the retail trade.

5. Hermann Schwarz (1843–1921) held public lectures at the University of Berlin.

6. See Scholem, *Berlin to Jerusalem*, p. 74.

7. Scholem was denounced by a fellow student for an antiwar letter he wrote to the *Jüdische Rundschau*, the official newspaper of the German Zionist movement.

8. Franz Goldschneider was Scholem's mathematics instructor at the *Gymnasium*.

9. Friedrich Bodenstedt (1819–1892) was a translator and author.

10. Jean Paul, *Hesperus oder 45 Hundsposttage* (Berlin: Reimer, 1819), and *Campanerthal* (Erfurt, 1797).

11. Erich Brauer.

12. Aurel Voss, *Über das Wesen der Mathematik* (Leipzig: Teubner, 1908).

13. Walter Benjamin, "Das Leben der Studenten," in *Gesammelte Schriften*, vol. 2, pt. 1, p. 75.

14. Thomas Mann, *Friedrich und die grosse Koalition* (Berlin: Fischer Verlag, 1915).

15. Arno Holz (1863–1929), German naturalist poet.

16. The Shemone Esre, or "Eighteen," is the central prayer of the morning, afternoon, and evening services.

17. *Der Jude,* a journal edited by Martin Buber.

18. Benjamin first mentions the essay in a letter to Scholem in November 1916. In this letter he tells Scholem that the essay would try to analyze language through the first chapter of Genesis. See Benjamin, *Gesammelte Schriften*, vol. 2, pt. 3, p. 931.

19. The article, "Der Krieg der Zurückbleibenden" (The War of Those Who Stay Behind), appeared on February 5, 1916.

20. Alfred Lemm, "Wir Deutsch-Juden," *Die Tat* (1916): 946–957.

21. The Hebrew word *shalem* means "complete," "entire."

22. Alfred Kerr, "Bleibt unverwirrt," *Das Zeit-Echo: Ein Kriegstagebuch der Künstler* 4 (1914–15): 41–42.

23. Jewish Publication Society translation.

24. Scholem published this in *Blau-Weissen-Brille*.

25. Werner Scholem (1895–1940), Gerhard's older brother.

26. Otto Weininger (1880–1903). Weininger's *Sex and Character* achieved cult status after his suicide in 1903.

27. Georg Simmel, *Sociology of Religion,* trans. Curt Rosenthal (New York: Philosophical Library, 1959).

28. Georg Simmel, *Hauptprobleme der Philosophie* (Leipzig: Göschen, 1910).

29. Hans Blüher (1888–1955) wrote *Die deutsche Wandervogelbewegung als erotisches Phänomen* (Berlin: B. Weise, 1912).

30. This is a reference to *Das Ziel,* a journal edited by Kurt Hiller in Munich in 1916. Ludwig Rubiner, "Die Änderung der Welt," *Das Ziel: Aufrufe zu tätigem Geist* (1916): 99–120.

31. The philosopher Immanuel Kant lived in Königsberg.

32. The French mathematician and philosopher Blaise Pascal lived in Port Royal.

33. Carl Friedrich Gauss (1777–1855) is considered one of the greatest mathematicians of all time. Edmund Husserl (1859–1938) was a founder of the school of phenomenology.

34. Martin Buber lived in Heppenheim.

35. Isaiah 40:9, 51:8.

36. Elias Auerbach, "Traditionelles und nationales Judentum: Ein Gespräch über Jüdische Erziehung," *Der Jude* (1916–17): 244–249.

37. On August 1, 1914, the German Kaiser signed the decree ordering general mobilization.

38. Hugo Haase (1863–1919) was a lawyer and a leader of the Social Democratic faction in the German parliament. Eduard Bernstein (1850–1932) was a founder of the reform wing of the German Socialist Party. Together with Haase, Bernstein wrote the antiwar article "Das Gebot der Stunde," calling for an end to the war.

39. Adolf von Harnack (1851–1930), a professor of Protestant theology at the University of Berlin, supported the war.

40. Jakob Wassermann (1873–1934).

41. Kaddish is the mourners' prayer.

42. This passage comes from Isaiah 2:3.

43. Not extant.

44. Werner was wounded in a battle on the Western Front.

45. Wilhelm von Humboldt, *Briefe an eine Freundin* (Leipzig: Insel Verlag, 1916).

46. Isaac ben Solomon Luria (1534–1572), nicknamed "ha-Ari," or "the Lion," gathered around him a group of mystics in Sefad.

47. The main Reform synagogue in Berlin was located on the Fasanenstrasse.

48. This passage comes from Deuteronomy 6:7.

49. *Das Reich* was edited in Munich by Baron von Bernus. The first edition was published in 1916.

50. Else Lasker-Schüler (1869–1945) was a German Jewish expressionist poet who belonged to the Blue Rider circle. Her article in memory of Franz Marc appeared in *Das Ziel* (1916): 253–254.

51. Alfred Henschke Klabund (1890–1928).

52. Algernon Charles Swinburne, "Ein Chor aus der Tragödie Atalanta," *Das Reich* (1916): 246–247.

53. Scholem took these expressions from Buber's "Mysterium Gottes" (*Das Reich* [1916]: 263), and "Der Geist des Orients und das Judentum," in *Vom Geist des Judentums* (Leipzig: Insel Verlag, 1916), p. 26.

54. *Ain-sof* is Hebrew for "without end."

55. This prayer is taken from Psalms 36:7.

56. According to the Kabbalistic teaching, the Shekhinah is God's spirit. See Gershom Scholem, *Major Trends in Jewish Mysticism* (New York: Schocken, 1954), p. 229. Also see Scholem in *Eranos-Jahrbuch* 21 (1952): 45–107.

57. Leo Deutschländer (1890–1935).

58. Samson Raphael Hirsch, *Neunzehn Briefe über das Judenthum* (Altona, 1836). The book was a basic text for modernized Orthodoxy in Germany.

59. Abaje and Rabba bar Josef bar Chama are teachers in the Babylonian Talmud. The reference here is to a reform introduced by Rabbi Hillel allowing creditors to demand payment of a debt even after the end of the Year of Jubilee, which, according to the original Mosaic law, wiped away all debts.

60. Arthur Aharon Rau (1895–1962). Harry Levy (1893–1978).

61. *Die Weissen Blätter* (1913–1920) was an avant-garde journal.

62. This is an ironic reference to the *Vossische Zeitung,* a Berlin daily.

63. The essay was Benjamin's "Das Leben der Studenten," which appeared in Kurt Hiller's journal *Das Ziel: Aufrufe zu tätigem Geist* (1916): 141–155. Scholem's letter to Benjamin is not extant.

64. *Offenbarungen der Schwester Mechthild von Magdeburg* (Regensburg, 1869).

65. Max Pulver (1889–1952), a historian and philosopher, published poetry and essays in *Das Reich.*

66. Dora Sophia Pollak (1890–1964). Leon Kellner (1859–1928) wrote for the Zionist newspaper *Die Welt.* He was a professor of English at the university in Czernowitz.

67. Friedrich Schlegel, *Philosophie der Geschichte* (Vienna, 1829), p. 82.

68. The essay "The Jewish Youth Movement" is Scholem's own reckoning with his earlier Zionism. See Scholem, *Tagebücher,* 1:511–517. The essay appeared in Buber's *Der Jude* in March 1917. In the essay Scholem accuses the youth movement of not being a movement at all. It lacked "completeness," "spirit," and "greatness." "Proof" of this was the way Jewish youth rushed to join the fighting. This was the

"final and highest triumph of confusion, and the deepest Original Sin we have yet witnessed."

69. Ahad Haam, pseudonym of Asher Ginzberg (1856–1927), author of *Am Scheideweg* (Berlin: Jüdischer Verlag, 1904).

70. Scholem is responding primarily to Buber's essay "Das Gleichzeitige," in *Das Zeit-Echo: Ein Kriegstagebuch der Künstler* (1914–15): 90–91.

71. Diotima is a figure in Plato's *Symposium.*

72. Georg Wilhelm Friedrich Hegel, *Phänomenologie des Geistes* (Berlin, 1832), p. 245.

73. Ernst Joel (1893–1929), a member of the German youth movement. He wrote the essay "Kameradschaft" in *Das Ziel* (1916): 156–166. See Scholem, *Story of a Friendship,* pp. 12–16.

74. Hermann Graf Keyserling, *Unsterblichkeit* (Munich, 1907); Franz von Baader, *Vorlesungen über eine künftige Theorie des Opfers* (Münster, 1836).

75. Hillel Zeitlin, "Aufgaben der polnischen Juden," *Der Jude* (1916–17): 89–93.

76. Siegfried Lehmann (1892–1958) founded the Jüdische Volksheim in 1916 to care for the children of Jewish refugees fleeing pogroms in eastern Europe. Writing under the pseudonym Salomon Lehnert, Lehmann described the principles behind his work in the article "Jüdische Volksarbeit," *Der Jude* (1916): 104–111. See Scholem, *Story of a Friendship,* pp. 104–105.

77. Max Hodann was a leader of the youth movement.

78. Jakob Lubmann had come from Palestine to study mathematics in Berlin.

79. Arthur Schragenheim (1893–1981) was a philosophy student and a member of Young Judah.

80. Walter Zadek (1910–?) was a member of the Wandervogel.

81. Toni Halle (1895–1964) studied in Berlin, Freiburg, and Heidelberg. Scholem met her in Heidelberg.

82. These terms appear in Martin Buber's *Legende des Baalschem*. The Hebrew word *avodah* means "service"; *kavanah,* "intentionality"; *shiflut,* "humility"; and *hitlahabut,* "ardency."

83. The subterranean dimension of Judaism is a major theme in Buber's *Die Legende des Baalschem.*

84. This is a reference to the youth home led by Ernst Joël. Johann Gottlieb Fichte (1762–1814) wrote *Speeches to the German Nation* in response to the French occupation of Berlin.

85. Bernhard Bolzano, *Paradoxien des Unendlichen* (Berlin: Mayer and Müller, 1889).

86. Ahron Markus, "Besprechung," *Monatsschrift für Geschichte und Wissenschaft des Judentums* 18 (Breslau 1910): 749–755.

87. *Der Pentateuch,* trans. and annotated by Samson Raphael Hirsch (Frankfurt: J. Kaufmann, 1908).

88. Ernst Lewy (1881–1969) was a philologist and professor of Finno-Ugric

languages at the University of Berlin. Benjamin had taken a course with him on Wilhelm von Humboldt's philosophy and language, and he liked Lewy because he was an outsider and an eccentric. He also admired his epistemological insights in his essay "Zur Sprache des alten Goethe," *Das Ziel* 4 (1913): 103–116.

89. Heinrich Graetz, *Geschichte der Juden vom Aufblühen der jüdisch-spanischen Kultur bis Maimunis Tod* (Leipzig: O. Leiner, 1891); *Geschichte der Juden von der Verbannung der Juden aus Spanien und Portugal bis zur dauernden Ansiedelung der Marranen in Holland* (Leipzig: O. Leiner, 1891). For Scholem's discussion of Graetz's views, see *On the Origins of the Kabbalah* (1962).

90. Rashi is the acronym for Rabbi Solomon ben Isaac (1040–1105), the medieval author of the authoritative Bible commentary.

91. Gematria unlocks the mystical meaning of words through numbers assigned to each letter.

92. The unpublished translation is in the Scholem archives at the National Library in Jerusalem.

93. This is a reference to Friedrich Nietzsche's *Unzeitgemässige Betrachtungen* (Leipzig: Insel Verlag, 1873). It is in this work that Nietzsche develops his theory of simultaneity, or *Gleichzeitigkeit*.

94. See note 57.

95. Through his close reading of the original, Hirsch denied that the Bible teaches that men have an "evil drive." See Samson Raphael Hirsch, *Pentateuch: Die Genesis* (Frankfurt 1893), pp. 167–181.

96. Ahron Marcus, *Hartmanns Philosophie im Chassidismus* (Vienna, 1888), p. 26.

97. Martin Heidegger, "Der Zeitbegriff in der Geschichtswissenschaft," *Zeitschrift für Philosophie und philosophische Kritik* (1916): 173–188.

98. Benjamin to Scholem, November 11, 1916, in Gershom Scholem, *A Life in Letters* (Cambridge, Mass.: Harvard University Press, 2002), pp. 38–39.

99. See "Notizen zu einer Arbeit über die Kategorie der Gerechtigkeit," in Scholem, *Diaries,* 1:401.

100. Franz Joseph Molitor, *Philosophie der Geschichte* (Frankfurt: Hermann, 1827), p. 63. On Scholem's relationship to Molitor, see Scholem, *From Berlin to Jerusalem,* p. 113.

101. Ernst Cassirer (1874–1945) was a professor of philosophy at the University of Berlin. Scholem attended his lecture on the history of philosophy.

102. Ernst Troeltsch (1865–1923) was a professor of philosophy at the University of Berlin.

103. This expression is taken from Deuteronomy 31:9.

104. This is in the Babylonian Talmud.

105. Scholem is referring to W. M. L. de Wette's "Beytrag zur Charakteristik des Hebraismus," in *Studien* (Heidelberg, 1807), pp. 241–312.

106. The suffix *-emo* appears in Moses' song, in Exodus 15:7 and 9.

107. This is a reference to his visit with Benjamin in the summer of 1916.

108. Harry Aharon Heller.

109. This is taken from Exodus 4:25–26, a passage that refers to Moses' circumcision.

110. An ironic allusion to Ahad Haam.

PART III: THE IDIOT

1. Scholem, *From Berlin to Jerusalem*, p. 66.

2. On Benjamin's secret letter, see Scholem's letter to Werner Kraft of July 14, 1917, in *Briefe*, 1:66, 67.

3. Scholem, *Story of a Friendship*, p. 41.

4. See Scholem's letter of July 7, 1917, in *Briefe*, 1:81.

5. Diary entry from September 2, 1917.

6. Scholem later described the book as "a detective story without any point, a hidden metaphysics of doubt" (*Story of a Friendship*, p. 46).

7. These translations are found in Scholem, *Tagebücher*, 2:112–127.

8. Diary entry from March 24, 1918.

9. Diary entry from December 1, 1917. Scholem, "Über Klage und Klagelied," in *Tagebücher* 2:128–133.

10. Diary entry from December 3, 1917.

11. In the words of one scholar, "In the place of the actual person of the dead man, his name, distilled into pure language, moves gradually to the center of Benjamin's remembering consciousness." Witte, *Walter Benjamin: An Intellectual Biography*, p. 26.

12. Diary entry from November 25, 1917.

13. Ibid.

14. Scholem, *From Berlin to Jerusalem*, p. 104.

15. Scholem writes in *Story of a Friendship*: "These lines, and my reaction to them in a lengthy diary entry, bear witness to a strongly emotional moment in our relationship, a relationship that presented itself to us in greatly heightened fashion. Owing, among other things, to his complete seclusion and the tenor of his utterances, Benjamin's figure had assumed a prophetic proportion in my eyes" (p. 49).

16. Diary entry from February 24, 1918.

17. Diary entry from March 24, 1918.

18. Benjamin may have gleaned the term from Goethe. See Scholem, *Tagebücher*, 2:456.

19. Gershom Scholem, "Offenbarung und Tradition als religiöse Kategorien im Judentum," in *Judaica*, vol. 4, ed. R. Tiedemann (Frankfurt: Suhrkamp, 1984), p. 93.

20. Scholem, *Tagebücher*, 2:359

21. Diary entry from October 18, 1917.

22. Scholem, *Tagebücher*, 2:358.

PART III NOTEBOOKS

1. Harry Heymann to Scholem, December 29, 1916, in Scholem, *Briefe,* 1:60–63.

2. Here Scholem refers to his brother Werner.

3. Franz Werfel, "Die Christliche Sendung," *Neue Rundschau* 1 (1917): 92–105.

4. The letter of November 11, 1916, was the basis for Benjamin's essay "Über Sprache überhaupt und über die Sprache des Menschen," in *Gesammelte Schriften,* vol. 2, pt. 2, pp. 140–157.

5. This was the Scholem family's address in Berlin. Gerhard was evicted from his home for his antiwar views.

6. Beit Wa'ad Ivri Merkasi be-Berlin, or the Central Hebrew Association of Berlin, offered Hebrew courses, lectures, and discussion evenings.

7. Max Strauss was Agnon's translator. He was also the brother of Ludwig Strauss.

8. After leaving home, Scholem lived in the Pension Struck.

9. Salman Rubaschoff (1889–1974) was a Russian who studied at the University of Berlin. He later became president of the state of Israel.

10. Zvi Kitain. See Gershom Scholem, *Von Berlin nach Jerusalem,* rev. ed. (Frankfurt: Suhrkamp, 1975), p. 94.

11. Sophia Scholem, the wife of Scholem's uncle.

12. Moritz Steinschneider (1816–1907) was one of Germany's leading scholars of Judaism. See Scholem, *From Berlin to Jerusalem,* p. 122.

13. Erich Cohn (1887–1962) was a member of a Jewish student fraternity and dueling society and editor of the journal *Der Jüdische Student.*

14. Gerda Goldberg (1898–1986) later married the Zionist leader Chaim Arlosoroff. In a letter to Scholem on July 24, 1917, she complained about his cryptic vocabulary and asked him to lay out his philosophy in plain terms. She said that she couldn't make any sense of the terms "Torah" and "the Teaching," and then went on to declare herself an atheist and "absolute skeptic." From the psychiatric ward he responded on August 6 and explained that he couldn't lay out his philosophy; to an outsider it would remain obscure: "I can be understood only by those who think like me, whereas to others I remain a closed book because they do not understand my language." See Scholem, *Life in Letters,* and *Briefe,* 1:77 and 361.

15. The exhibition included works by Braque, Chagall, Kandinsky, Kirchner, Kokoschka, Léger, Marc, and Picasso.

16. *Sturm* was an expressionist magazine founded by the poet Herwarth Walden (his real name was Georg Lewin) in 1910. Walden was married to the Jewish poet Elsa Lasker-Schüler.

17. Scholem was studying mathematics at the University of Jena.

18. Ahad Haam, *Am Scheidewege: Gesammelte Schriften,* vol. 4 (Berlin: Jüdischer Verlag, 1916), pp. 124–132.

19. Ahron Marcus, *Der Chassidismus* (Pleschen, 1901). Marcus (1842–1916) was a Hebrew scholar, philosopher, and linguist.

20. See Buber's *Vom Geist des Judentums,* pp. 49–74.

21. *Shalom* is the Hebrew word for "peace."

22. Meta Jahr (1900–1992), the sister of Jakob Jahr, belonged to Scholem's Zionist youth group.

23. Harry Aharon Heller.

24. "The genius" was Benjamin's nickname for Felix Noeggerath (1885–1960). Benjamin took his theory of experience partly from him.

25. This was a comment Benjamin made to Scholem. See *Tagebücher,* 2:201.

26. Scholem used the Hebrew-German expression "Hatschi-Zionist," or half-Zionist.

27. Käthe Höllander studied mathematics with Scholem.

28. Mawriki Kahn; see Scholem, *Briefe,* 1:190.

29. Modeled after the Wandervogel, Blau-Weiss was the largest Jewish youth group in Germany.

30. Werner Kraft (1896–1991) was a German writer, poet, and essayist. See Scholem, *Story of a Friendship,* pp. 39–41.

31. Rudolf Borchardt (1877–1945) was a lyric poet, essayist, and translator.

32. Shmuel Yosef Agnon [pseudonym of Samuel Josef Czaczkes] (1888–1970) was the greatest Hebrew novelist of his generation. He lived in Germany from 1913 to 1924.

33. See Scholem to Kraft, October 18, 1917, in Gershom Scholem, *Briefe an Werner Kraft* (Frankfurt: Suhrkamp, 1986), p. 40.

34. Valeria Grünwald.

35. Heinrich Rickert (1863–1936) was a neo-Kantian philosopher at the University of Heidelberg.

36. Martin Buber, *Ereignisse und Begegnungen* (Leipzig: Insel Verlag, 1917).

37. Scholem read Ernst Barthel's essay "Basic Geometrical Concepts" ("Die geometrischen Grundbegriffe") after Benjamin brought it to his attention in a letter of October 22, 1917. The letter is reprinted in Benjamin's *Briefe,* 1:152.

38. The writer Frank Wedekind's most popular play was *Spring Awakening,* about the joys, despair, and longing of youth. It was also, if between the lines, about sexuality.

39. In the Old Testament, Ophir was a region famous for its gold.

40. See Walter Benjamin, "Über Sprache Überhaupt," in *Gesammelte Schriften,* vol. 2, pt. 2, pp. 142–144.

41. See Scholem archive at the National Library in Jerusalem, file 1917, p. 33.

42. Werner Kraft (*Briefe an Werner Kraft*) writes to Scholem on November 3, 1917, that the "power out of which you live and suffer is a miracle in which I believe."

43. Bruno Bauch, neo-Kantian professor of philosophy. Scholem attended his course in logic. See Scholem, *Story of a Friendship,* pp. 48–49.

44. Kurt Goldstein (1878–1965), a psychiatrist and neurologist, taught at the University of Frankfurt.

45. Another term for the Bolsheviks in Russia, who published their peace offer two days after seizing power on November 7, 1917.

46. Walter Benjamin, "Der Idiot von Dostojewskij," in *Gesammelte Schriften*, 2:237–241. The essay was first published in 1921 in the journal *Die Argonauten*.

47. Fritz Heinle (1984–1914). For more on Heinle's life and work, see Werner Kraft, *Herz und Geist* (Vienna: Bohlau, 1989), pp. 410–420.

48. Benjamin writes, "Dostoyevsky's greatest lamentation in this book is the failure of the youth movement" ("Der Idiot," p. 240).

49. See Scholem archives, National Library, Jerusalem, file 1917, p. 41.

50. 2 Samuel 1:17–27.

51. The reference is to Benjamin's essay "Über Sprache überhaupt und über die Sprache des Menschen."

52. Benjamin to Scholem, December 3, 1917, in Benjamin, *Briefe*, 1:157.

53. See Scholem archives, National Library, Jerusalem, file 1917, p. 55.

54. Werner Scholem was in prison for nine months for participating in an antiwar demonstration.

55. Together with Erna Michaelis, Meta Jahr visited Scholem in Jena for a week.

56. "Peace" in Hebrew.

57. Salman Baruch Rabinkow (1882–1941) was a Russian Jew who taught Talmud in Heidelberg.

58. Valeria Grünwald was Scholem's first Hebrew pupil.

59. Scholem wrote love letters to Grete Brauer in Berlin, but she rarely wrote back. In one letter Scholem spoke of a "crisis," saying that she and Benjamin were "literally the only ones who have ever affected the essence" of his life, and that he had been able to resist madness while in the military only because the "power of your being . . . prevented me from going up in flames in the red-hot coals in which I lived and continue to live." He sent her his translations of lamentations as a testimony. His letter concludes, "My love, I count the hours until your reply arrives" (March 7, 1918, in Scholem's *Briefe*, p. 144). Four days later she told him: "I can't be the person to give you what you require and hope for. . . . I want to remain your friend, but more than this I cannot give you" (ibid., p. 375).

60. David Baumgardt (1890–1963) was born in Erfurt and studied philosophy, physics, and history at the University of Freiburg. He served in the military between 1914 and 1918.

61. *Jerubbaal: Eine Zeitschrift der jüdischen Jugend* was a publication for Jewish youth.

62. See Benjamin's letter to Scholem of February 23, 1918.

63. "Tevye the Milkman" is a story by Scholem Aleichem (1859–1916).

64. *Tikkun* is Hebrew for "healing" or "repair."

65. *Briefwechsel zwischen Clemens Brentano und Sophie Mereau*, ed. Heinz Amelung (Leipzig: Insel Verlag, 1908).

66. Franz Overbeck was Nietzsche's publisher. *Friedrich Nietzsches Briefwechsel mit Franz Overbeck*, ed. Richard Oehler and Carl Albrecht Bernoulli (Leipzig, 1916).

67. Scholem was with Erich Brauer.

68. Katharina Gentz was a student in Jena. See Scholem, *Berlin to Jerusalem,* pp. 100–101.

69. According to a tale in the Midrash, the "Bene Moshe," or "sons of Moses," was a group living beyond the legendary river of Sambatjon.

70. See Benjamin's letter to Scholem of February 23, 1918, in Benjamin's *Briefe,* 1:177.

71. Enoch was a friend from Scholem's time in Heidelberg in February 1918.

72. This is an allusion to Herzl's utopian novel *Alt-Neuland.*

73. Johann Peter Eckermann, *Gespräche mit Goethe in den letzten Jahren seines Lebens* (Jena: Diederichs, 1908).

74. Robert Jentzsch (1890–1918) was an expressionist poet and mathematician.

75. See Benjamin's criticism of Scholem's translation in a letter from March 30, 1918, in Benjamin, *Briefe,* 1:179–185.

76. Escha Burchhardt (1896–1978) became Scholem's first wife.

77. Scholem discusses Benjamin's relationship with Grete Radt in *Story of a Friendship,* p. 12. Benjamin met Carla Seligson (1892–1956) in Freiburg.

78. Georg Friedrich Creuzer, *Symbolik und Mythologie der alten Völker* (Leipzig, 1843).

79. Alice Heymann.

80. Sebastian Brant, *Das Narrenschiff* (Leipzig: F. A. Brockhaus, 1872), p. 8.

81. Hirsch S. Hirschfeld, *Der Geist der ersten Schriftauslegungen oder die hagadische Exegese* (Berlin: Athenaeum, 1847), p. 211.

82. Betty Scholem wrote on April 12 that his uncle George Scholem, a physician, agreed that Gerhard should go to Switzerland for his health.

83. Louis Levy, *Die Menschenzwiebel Kzradock und der frühlingsfrische Methusalem* (Berlin, 1912).

84. Hermann Cohen, *System der Philosophie* (Berlin: Cassirer, 1902).

85. Gottfried Keller, *Die Leute von Seldwyla* (Berlin: J. G. Cotta, 1916).

86. Gottlob Frege (1848–1925) was a professor of mathematics at the University of Jena. See Scholem, *Story of a Friendship,* pp. 48–49.

87. Benjamin Freund.

88. Gerhart Hauptmann, *Der Ketzer von Soana* (Berlin: Fischer, 1918).

PART IV: JOB'S LAMENTATION

1. In a letter from Grete to Scholem, March 5, 1918, in Scholem, *Briefe,* 1:375.

2. Gershom Scholem, "Über Rainer Maria Rilkes Aufzeichnungen des Malte Laurids Brigge," in *Tagebücher,* 2:292–296.

3. Scholem to Escha Burchhardt, October 26, 1918, *Briefe,* 1:177.

4. Scholem, *Story of a Friendship,* p. 53.

5. Scholem, *Tagebücher,* 2:304.

6. Scholem, *Story of a Friendship,* p. 63

7. Diary entry from May 8, 1918.

8. Scholem, *Story of a Friendship,* p. 15.

9. Diary entry from June 25, 1918.

10. Quoted from Scholem, *In the Fullness of Time,* trans. and ed. Richard Sieburth (Jerusalem: Ibis, 2003), pp. 20–21.

11. Scholem, *Story of a Friendship,* p. 54.

12. "The life of Harry Heymann was potential, his death judgment, but his being remains one of movement, a movement that must now be kept in silence." Scholem, *Tagebücher,* 2:350.

13. Noeggerath's notion of "experience" lay behind Benjamin's essay "On the Program of the Coming Philosophy." See Benjamin's letter to Scholem of October 22, 1917, in Benjamin, *Briefe,* 1:151.

14. The letters are printed in Gershom Scholem, *On Jews and Judaism in Crisis* (New York: Schocken Books, 1976), pp. 54–60.

15. Scholem, *Story of a Friendship,* p. 73.

16. Ibid., p. 54.

17. Ibid.

18. Ibid., p. 53.

19. The bulk of this correspondence remains under lock and key at the National Library in Jerusalem.

20. Scholem, *Tagebücher,* 2:321

21. Diary entry from June 28, 1918.

22. Diary entry from July 22, 1918.

23. Scholem, *Tagebücher,* 2:319.

24. Ibid., p. 318.

25. Quoted from "Die Wahrheit," ibid., p. 712.

26. Diary entry from December 24, 1918.

27. Diary entry from November 13, 1918.

28. Their nine-hour conversation did not go very well. Scholem wasn't certain what to think of Bloch, while Bloch later complained to Benjamin that his younger friend was an "ass." Scholem, *Story of a Friendship,* p. 80.

29. Scholem, Story of a Friendship, p. 85.

PART IV NOTEBOOKS

1. Benjamin, *Gesammelte Schriften,* vol. 2, pt. 1, pp. 157–171.

2. Leonie Ortenstein was Scholem's cousin. See Scholem, *Von Berlin nach Jerusalem,* pp. 27, 43, and 140–144.

3. Richard Herbertz (1878–1959) was a philosopher and historian at the University of Bern.

4. Harry Maync (1874–1951) was a professor of German language and literature at the University of Bern.

5. Adalbert Stifter (1805–1868).

6. Rainer Maria Rilke (1875–1926).

7. Ludwig Tieck (1773–1853), *Märchen und Geschichten,* ed. Paul Ernst (Berlin, 1916).

8. Stefan Raphael, the Benjamins' son.

9. Edwin Balmer, *A Wild-Goose Chase* (New York: Grosset and Dunlap, 1914).

10. Immanuel Kant, *Briefwechsel,* vol. 1 (Munich, 1912), pp. 58–60; and vol. 3 (Munich, 1912), pp. 60, 68. At the time Benjamin was gathering together letters written during the period of German Romanticism. Under the pseudonym Detlef Holz, in 1936 he would publish the letters in an anthology titled *Deutsche Menschen.*

11. *Der Briefwechsel zwischen Goethe und Zelter,* ed. Max Hecker (Leipzig: Insel Verlag, 1918).

12. Benjamin met Philipp Keller (1891–1973) in Freiburg. Keller was a friend of Heinle's.

13. Simon Guttmann (1891–1990) was one of Benjamin's friends from Berlin.

14. See Benjamin's "Stifter" in *Gesammelte Schriften,* 2:608. The essays "Conversation" and "Diary" are in "Metaphysik der Jugend," ibid., pp. 91–103.

15. Franz Delitzsch, *Zur Geschichte der jüdischen Poësie* (Leipzig: K. Tauchnitz, 1836), p. 31.

16. This translation is from the Jerusalem Bible.

17. Walter Benjamin, "The Metaphysics of Youth," in *Selected Writings,* vol. 1, trans. Rodney Livingstone (Cambridge, Mass.: Harvard University Press, 1996), pp. 6–18.

18. Translations found in Scholem, *Fullness of Time,* p. 53.

19. July 15 was Benjamin's birthday.

20. Scholem plays on the words *Aufgabe,* or "task," and *aufgegebenen,* or "given up."

21. *Die Dichtung,* edited by Wolf Przygode (1918–19): 1000. Rudolf Borchardt (1877–1945) was a poet and essayist.

22. Karl Philipp Moritz, *Anton Reiser: Ein psychologischer Roman* (Leipzig: Insel Verlag, 1911), p. 93.

23. Hebrew for "the world."

24. Scholem, "Abschied: Öffener Brief an Herrn Dr. Siegfried Bernfeld," *Jerubbaal* (1918–19): 125–130.

25. Harry Aharon Heller.

26. This refers to Muri, the village where Scholem and the Benjamins were living.

27. Hermann Cohen, *Der Begriff der Religion im System der Philosophie* (Giessen: A. Töpelmann, 1915).

28. Ibid.

29. Scholem writes that God has no "Dasein," only "Sein."

30. Scholem is paraphrasing Cohen on Maimonides. In his reading of Mai-

monides (Rambam), Cohen goes beyond interpreting him according to his medieval historical context. He reads him according to ideals of universal justice still to be realized in the future. See Cohen's *Ethics of Maimonides,* trans. with commentary by Almut Sh. Bruckstein (Madison: University of Wisconsin Press, 2002).

31. Wav, the sixth letter in the Hebrew alphabet, can give a verb either a past or present sense.

32. Teiresias was a prophet of Thebes.

33. See Benjamin to Ernst Schoen, June 17, 1918, in *Briefe,* 1:197.

34. *Shevirat ha-kelim,* or "breaking the vessels," is a concept attributed to Isaac Luria. He explained the existence of evil through the "breaking of the vessel" that once contained the light of creation.

35. See Scholem's "Über Rainer Maria Rilkes *Aufzeichnungen des Malte Laurids Brigge,*" in *Tagebücher,* 2:292.

36. See diary entry from December 3, 1919.

37. Scholem's letter to Escha from June 21, 1918, is in *Briefe,* 1:158.

38. Samuel Collenbusch to Kant, January 23, 1795, in Kant, *Briefwechsel,* 3:60, 68.

39. S. J. Agnon, *Und das Krumme wird gerade,* trans. Max Strauss (Berlin, 1918), pp. 253–264.

40. Scholem's letter, which is not extant, was a reply to Benjamin's letter to Scholem, February 23, 1918, in Benjamin, *Briefe,* 1:176. See also his diary entry from March 1, 1918.

41. Scholem's reference is to Luther's Ninety-five Theses. This was a birthday gift he planned to present to Benjamin. The text would eventually be called "Ninety-five Theses on Judaism and Zionism," as mentioned earlier in this entry.

42. Friedrich Hölderlin, "An Landauer," in *Werke,* vol. 4 (Leipzig: Insel Verlag, 1916), p. 52.

43. The volume he received was *Und das Krumme wird gerade.*

44. Valeria Grünwald.

45. Heinrich von Kleist, *Sämtliche Werke,* vol. 4 (Leipzig: Die Tempel-Klassiker, 1859), pp. 3–125. Kleist's book is about an honest horse trader who is wrongfully cheated and who gets no justice because his opponent enjoys the protection of those in power. The horse trader thus becomes a rebel and, in the eyes of the law, a criminal. Eventually he is condemned to the gallows.

46. Greek for "at the right moment."

47. Psalm 134: "Behold, bless the LORD, all you servants of the LORD, who stand by night in the house of the LORD. Lift up your hands in the sanctuary, and bless the LORD. May the LORD who made heaven and earth bless thee out of Zion."

48. Scholem, "95 Thesen über Judentum und Zionismus," in *Tagebücher,* 2:300. Scholem had hoped to present these theses to Benjamin for his twenty-sixth birthday, and finished them two weeks before the birthday on July 15, 1918. For some reason he never presented the gift. They first appeared in print as "Ninety-five Theses on Judaism and Zionism," in *Gershom Scholem: Zwischen den Disziplinen,* ed. Gary Smith and Peter Schäfer (Frankfurt: Suhrkamp, 1995), p. 290.

49. See Sabrina Spielrein, "Über den psychologischen Inhalt eines Falles von Schizophrenie (dementia praecox)," in *Jahrbuch für psychoanalytische und psychopathologische Forschung* 3 (1911): 329–400. Also Siegmund Freud's "Psychoanalytische Bemerkungen über einen autobiographisch beschriebenen Fall von Paranoia," ibid., pp. 9–68.

50. The book they came across was *Bilderbuch für Kinder* (Weimar, 1790) by Friedrich Bertuch, a member of Goethe's Weimar circle. Benjamin would later write an essay titled "Old Forgotten Children's Books."

51. Karl Kraus (1874–1936). Kraus's *Die Fakel* was one of the leading satirical publications at the time. See Scholem to Werner Kraft, December 28, 1917, in Scholem, *A Life in Letters,* p. 66.

52. Yaakov Cahan, *Sefer ha-shirim* (Warsaw: Tushiyah, 1914).

53. See Scholem's *Tagebücher,* 2:297.

54. In 1927 Scholem completed the "philosophical alphabet" and had his father's shop print up 250 copies. He called it the "Amtliches Lehrgedicht der Philosophischen Fakultät der Haupt- und Staats- Universität Muri." See *Tagebücher,* 2:307–310. See also Scholem, *Story of a Friendship,* p. 58.

55. Scholem, *Fullness of Time,* p. 63.

56. Wilhelm Gesenius, *Der Prophet Jesaia* (Leipzig: F. C. W. Vogel, 1821). Bernhard Duhm, *Das Buch Jesaia* (Göttingen: Vandenhoeck und Ruprecht, 1902).

57. Campegius Vitringa (1659–1722) wrote a commentary on Isaiah.

58. Scholem to Escha, July 23, 1918, in Scholem, *Life in Letters,* p. 77.

59. The reference is to the letter Benjamin sent Scholem upon reading Scholem's response to *The Idiot.*

60. Scholem, "Notiz über den talmudischen Stil," in *Tagebücher,* 2:311–312.

61. Albrecht Schaeffer and Ludwig Strauss, *Die Opfer des Kaisers* (Leipzig: Insel Verlag, 1918).

62. Gustav Falke (1853–1916) was a German writer.

63. Isaiah 38:9–20.

64. Karl Marti, *Das Buch Jesaia* (Tübingen: J. C. B Mohr, 1900).

65. *Jiskor: Ein Buch des Gedenkens an gefallene Wächter und Arbeiter im Lande Israel* (Berlin: Jüdischer Verlag, 1920).

66. *Caroline: Briefe an ihre Geschwester,* ed. G. Waitz (Leipzig: S. Hirzel, 1871).

67. The Hebrew expression is *le-hamtik otam be-shoroshim.*

68. Scholem to Strauss, August 1, 1918, in *Briefe,* 1:168. For the letter he did not send, see p. 170.

69. Marzili is a neighborhood of Bern.

70. Scholem wrote sonnets on the main figure in Agnon's *Und das Krumme wird Gerade.* Some were later published in *Judaica,* vol. 2 (Frankfurt: Suhrkamp Verlag, 1970), p. 128. See also his essay "Agnon: Und das Krumme wird Gerade," in *Tagebücher,* 2:319–322. Scholem later translated three short stories in the volume *In der Gemeinschaft der Frommen* (Berlin: Schocken Verlag, 1933).

71. Israel Reichert, one of the founders of the Zionist group Hapoël Hazair.

72. Jakob Wassermann, *Das Gänsemännchen* (Berlin: Fischer Verlag, 1915).

73. General Erich Friedrich Wilhelm Ludendorff (1865–1937). On November 9, 1918, large protest marches swept through Berlin. A revolution broke out as soldiers joined the movement. Philipp Scheidemann, the leader of the Social Democrats, proclaimed a republic. Two days later, on November 11, hostilities with the Allies were formally ended.

74. "On the Book of Jonah and Its Conception of Justice."

75. See Walter Benjamin, *Der Begriff der Kunstkritik in der deutschen Romantik,* in *Gesammelte Schriften,* vol. 1, pt. 1, pp. 7–122.

76. On November 9, 1918, the Swiss Federation broke off relations with the Soviet Union, leading the trade unions and communists to call for a general strike.

77. Anne Tumarkin (1875–1951), professor of philosophy at the University of Bern.

78. See Benjamin, *Gesammelte Schriften,* 4:56.

79. Johann Peter Hebel, *Tagebücher* (Berlin, 1903), p. 418.

80. See Scholem, *Tagebücher,* 2:552.

81. That is, Borchardt's translation of Pindar.

82. Scholem, *Briefe an Werner Kraft,* p. 99.

83. Harry Heymann died on July 28, 1918.

84. Albert Baer (1888–1975) was a Zionist, member of a Jewish fraternity, and belonged to Siegfried Lehmann's circle in Berlin.

85. Like most of the letters Scholem wrote to Benjamin at the time, this letter is not extant.

86. Erwin Briese. See Scholem, *Von Berlin nach Jerusalem,* p. 84.

87. Samuel Horodezky wrote *Rabbi Nachman von Brazlaw: Ein Beitrag zur Geschichte der jüdischen Mystik* (Berlin, 1910).

88. Paul Levertoff, *Die religiöse Denkweise der Chassidim* (Leipzig, 1918).

89. "Farewell" was Scholem's open letter to Siegfried Bernfeld. "Abschied: Offener Brief an Herrn Dr. Siegfried Bernfeld" appeared in Bernfeld's journal *Jerubbaal.*

90. Wolfgang Heinle was the younger brother of Fritz Heinle.

91. Kurt Goldstein (1878–1965) was a psychiatrist and neurologist.

92. Grete Lissauer introduced Scholem to Goldstein in 1917.

93. See Scholem, *Tagebücher,* 2:608.

94. Hirsch Berlowitz. See Scholem to Werner Kraft, April 10, 1919, in Scholem, *A Life in Letters,* p. 101.

95. Else Lasker-Schüler, *Gesichte: Essays und andere Geschichten* (Leipzig: Verlag der Weissen Bücher, 1914).

96. Scholem met Siegfried Caro in Berlin, where Caro was studying political science. See Scholem, *Story of a Friendship,* p. 108.

97. Hans Heyse (1891–1976).

98. The Hebrew literary form *kinah* (dirge) is an elegiac lamentation chanted in honor of the dead.

99. Samuel Aba Horodetzky (1871–1957), *Religiöse Strömungen* (Berlin: E. Bircher, 1920), pp. 68–144. Jacob Josef was one of the closest followers of the Baal Shem Tov.

100. Ibn Gabirol (1021–1058) was a Spanish Jewish poet, philosopher, and moralist. Heinrich Grätz called him "the Jewish Plato."

101. Gotthold Kalischer and Meta Flanter were friends from Berlin.

102. Ernst Bloch (1885–1977) lived in Switzerland during the war. Bloch's *Geist der Utopie* appeared in 1918.

103. Ferdinand Weber, *Jüdische Theologie auf Grund des Talmud* (Leipzig: Dörffling and Franke, 1897).

104. *Jiskor: Ein Buch des Gedenkens;* see diary entry from February 22, 1918.

105. Ludwig Strauss (1892–1953) was a poet, literary scholar, and Zionist. Strauss tried unsuccessfully to enlist Benjamin into the Zionist movement. He married Buber's daughter. Strauss's letter is in Scholem's *Briefe,* 1:392.

106. "Young Workers," the Zionist socialist party founded in Palestine. A chapter was founded in Berlin in 1917.

107. The Volksheim was founded by Siegfried Lehmann. See diary entry from December 21, 1915.

108. John Ruskin, *Menschen Untereinander,* trans. Maria Kühn (Leipzig: Langewiesche, 1904).

109. On April 7, 1919, a group of (largely Jewish) intellectuals established a revolutionary government in Munich. A month later it was violently crushed. Felix Noeggerath, who supported the revolution, was arrested. Benjamin feared he would be shot. Kurt Eisner, the leader of the revolution, was murdered.

110. The leaders of the Soviet Republic of Munich, who had been arrested after the paramilitary Freikorps stormed the city, were standing trial for high treason.

111. Rabbi Akiba, one of the authors of the Mishnah, discusses the death penalty in Makkot 1:10. Scholem writes more on Judaism and the death penalty in *Tagebücher,* 2:337.

112. Theodor Lessing, *Philosophie als Tat* (Göttingen: O. Hapke, 1914), p. 107.

113. Hermann Lotze (1817–1881) was a logician and philosopher. Scholem read his *Logik: Drei Bücher vom Denken* (Leipzig: S. Hirzel, 1874).

114. Messinger was a local Swiss rabbi.

115. Hans Heyse studied philosophy at the University of Bern.

116. This verse comes from a traditional book of dirges recalling Tishah-b'Av, the day memorializing the destruction of the Second Temple. This verse comes from R. Kalonymus ben Judah, in *Seder Kinot ha-Mevuarot* (Jerusalem, 1995), p. 161.

117. Ludwig Tieck, *Märchen und Zaubergeschichten* (Breslau: Bibliothek der deutschen Literatur, 1825), p. 116.

118. See note 20.

119. Scholem's letter to Kraft is from June 6, 1919, in *Briefe,* 1:207.

120. Musaf is traditional moral literature.

121. Georg Büchner (1813–37) wrote various revolutionary tracts collected in *Hessischem Landboten* (Frankfurt: Insel Verlag, 1965).

122. Wilhelm Weitling, *Das Evangelium eines armen Sünders* (Bern: Jenni, 1845).

123. Ferdinand Lassalle, *Reden und Schriften* (Berlin: Dietz, 1892–93).

124. Eduard David, "Des Verfassers Leben und politisches Wirken," cited in Büchner, *Hessischem Landboten*, p. 3.

125. Moses Hess (1812–1875) was a socialist and supporter of Marx. Hess eventually turned away from Marx's cosmopolitan socialism by stressing the importance of nationalism. His *Rome and Jerusalem* was published in 1862.

126. Thomas Münzer (1486–1525) was a leader of the peasant revolts in Saxony in the sixteenth century. Though an early supporter of Luther, he was later slaughtered by Protestant princes and landowners.

127. Collenbusch's letter would later be published in Benjamin's anthology *Deutsche Menschen* (Frankfurt: Suhrkamp, 1962).

128. "Student" in Hebrew.

129. Hugo Salus (1866–1929) was a Prague gynecologist and avant-garde writer.

130. Scholem uses Aristotle's expression "metabasis eis allo genos," from *Analytica priora*, 1.7, 75a30–b20.

131. Ernst Müller, "Übertragungen aus dem Buche Sohar," *Der Jude* (April 1919): 88–89.

132. Goethe, *Italienische Reise* (Stuttgart: Cottaischen Buchhandlung, 1819).

133. Friedrich Rückert, *Gedichte*, ed. Oskar Loerke (Berlin: Pantheon, 1911).

134. In a letter on July 9, 1919, Kraft asks Scholem whether he should move from Freiburg to Munich for his studies.

135. This passage is taken from Isaiah 60:21. Scholem refers to Zweig's polemics against the anti-Zionist writings of Rudolf Kayser and his notion of a "Jewish-European mission." Kayser, "Der neue Bund," *Der Jude* (1918): 523–529.

136. David Schklar, student of medicine at the University of Bern and Scholem's Talmud teacher.

137. 2 Samuel 3:34.

138. 2 Samuel 3:33.

139. Rainer Maria Rilke, *Die Aufzeichnungen des Malte Laurids Brigge* (Leipzig: Insel Verlag, 1918), p. 77. See Scholem's article "Über Rainer Maria Rilkes *Aufzeichnungen des Malte Laurids Brigge*," cited in note 35.

140. Felix Kanter, "Neue Klagelieder," *Israelitische Wochenblatt für die Schweiz*, August 1, 1919.

141. Leo Bramson; see Scholem, *Von Berlin nach Jerusalem*, p. 125.

142. Chaim Weizmann (1874–1952) became the president of the Zionist World Congress in 1920.

143. Berthold Feiwel (1875–1937) was a Zionist publicist who edited the Zionist newspaper *Die Welt*.

144. Werner Scholem was editor of the *Braunschweiger Volksstimme*.

145. Gustav Noske (1868–1946) was a conservative member of the Social Democratic Party. He earned the title "bloodhound" after he suppressed an uprising in Kiel in 1918.

146. *Frankfurter Zeitung* was a leading liberal newspaper in Germany.

147. Julius Berger (1883–1948) was a Zionist leader.

CONCLUSION

1. See Scholem's "Lyrik der Kabbalah," in *Tagebücher,* 2:657.

2. Scholem, *Story of a Friendship,* p. 113.

3. The two discussed collaborating on Benjamin's idea of a literary journal he wanted to call *Angelus Novus.* Benjamin and Heinle had first thought of it together, and now Benjamin wanted to enlist Scholem's help. The plan went nowhere. See ibid., p. 106.

4. The titles of the essays are "The Teaching of Zion," "The Lyric of the Kabbalah," and "Observations on the Meaning and Appearance of the Kabbalah."

5. The Sefer ha-Bahir (Book of Brightness), a twelfth-century commentary on the Old Testament, was written in Hebrew and Arabic and is based on ancient mystical ideas originating in Asia. Its emphasis on the mystical significance of the shapes and sounds of the Hebrew alphabet had great influence on the development of the Kabbalah.

6. Cynthia Ozick, "The Heretic: The Mythic Passions of Gershom Scholem," *New Yorker,* September 2, 2002.

7. Arthur Scholem to Gerhard Scholem, March 12, 1921. See Scholem, *A Life in Letters,* p. 119.

8. Gadamer is quoted in Scholem, *Briefe,* 1:xv.

9. Scholem, *Tagebücher,* 2:332.

10. Ibid., p. 658. Scholem worked with Dr. Fritz Hommel, professor of Semitic languages at the University of Munich.

11. Ibid., p. 664.

12. Ibid., p. 675.

13. Ibid., p. 660.

14. Ibid., p. 657.

15. Ibid., pp. 662–663.

16. Ibid., p. 688.

17. Ibid., p. 685.

18. For this quotation, see http://www.remember.org/guide/History.root .modern.html.

19. This can be seen in a 1937 birthday greeting to the department store tycoon and publisher Salman Schocken, a letter he cobbled together from two short essays he had written while finishing his dissertation in Munich. See Scholem's letter to Salman Schocken, cited in David Biale, *Gershom Scholem: Kabbalah and Counterhistory* (Cambridge, Mass.: Harvard University Press, 1979), p. 215.

20. "Zionist Despair" was written on June 16, 1920. See *Tagebücher,* 2:638.

21. George Steiner, "The Remembrancer: Rescuing Walter Benjamin from the Acolytes," *Times Literary Supplement,* October 8, 1993.

22. Quoted in Scholem, *In the Fullness of Time,* pp. 69, 95.

23. See Steven Wasserstrom, *Religion after Religion: Gershom Scholem, Mircea Eliade, and Henry Corbin at* ERANOS (Princeton: Princeton University Press, 1999), pp. 149–150, 152, 214, 226, 244.

24. This comment was made during an interview with the author in July 1998.

25. See letter from Benjamin to Scholem of November 27, 1921. In the original draft to his essay "The Lyric of the Kabbalah" in 1921, he alluded to Benjamin's essay "Task of a Translator" by remarking cryptically that the principles of translation had been laid out "often enough." In the final draft even these sparing remarks had disappeared.

26. His lectures at the ERANOS conferences included "Tradition and New Creation in the Rites of the Kabbalists" (1949); "Transmigration of Spirits and Sympathy of Souls in Jewish Mysticism" (1955); "Religious Authority and Mysticism" (1957); "Toward an Understanding of the Messianic Idea in the Kabbalah" (1959); "The Mythical Shape of the Godhead in the Kabbalah" (1960); "Tradition and Commentary as Religious Categories in Judaism" (1962); "The Crisis of Tradition in Jewish Messianism" (1968); "The Name of God in the Kabbalah's Theory of Language" (1970); "Nihilism as a Religious Phenomenon" (1974); and "Identification and Distance: A Retrospective Glance" (1979).

27. See Scholem, "On the Kabbalah and Its Symbolism." The title of the lecture was "The Meaning of the Torah in Jewish Mysticism."

28. "The Name of God and the Linguistic Theory of the Kabbalah," *Diogenes* 79 (Fall 1972): 59–80, and 80 (Winter 1972): 164–194.

29. Gershom Scholem, "Offenbarung und Tradition als religiöse Kategorien im Judentum," in *Judaica,* vol. 4 (Frankfurt: Suhrkamp, 1984), p. 110. The essay was originally delivered as a lecture at the ERANOS Seminar in Switzerland.

30. Scholem, *Offenbarung und Tradition* (Frankfurt: Suhrkamp Verlag, 1984), p. 197.

31. Ibid., p. 92.

32. Scholem's clearest discussion of this is ibid., pp. 90–120.

33. Ibid., p. 202.

INDEX